The Dragon's Journey

Also by James Knight

Lee²,: Lee to the Power of Two
Mark Waugh: the Biography

The Dragon's Journey

Duy Long Nguyen
and James Knight

HarperCollins*Publishers*

Front cover photo of Longy as a young child shows him wearing a shirt on which Teresa had embroidered stars on the lapel (like his father) and a dragon on the front. He wore it proudly.

HarperCollins*Publishers*

First published in Australia in 2004
This edition published in 2006
by HarperCollins*Publishers* Australia Pty Limited
ABN 36 009 913 517
www.harpercollins.com.au

Copyright © Duy Long Nguyen and James Knight 2004

The right of Duy Long Nguyen and James Knight to be identified as the authors of this work has been asserted by them under the *Copyright Amendment (Moral Rights) Act 2000*.

This work is copyright. Apart from any use as permitted under the *Copyright Act 1968*, no part may be reproduced, copied, scanned, stored in a retrieval system, recorded, or transmitted, in any form or by any means, without the prior written permission of the publisher.

HarperCollins*Publishers*
25 Ryde Road, Pymble, Sydney, NSW 2073, Australia
31 View Road, Glenfield, Auckland 10, New Zealand
77–85 Fulham Palace Road, London, W6 8JB, United Kingdom
2 Bloor Street East, 20th floor, Toronto, Ontario M4W 1A8, Canada
10 East 53rd Street, New York NY 10022, USA

National Library of Australia Cataloguing-in-Publication data:

Nguyen, Duy Long.
 The dragon's journey.
 Bibliography.
 Includes index.
 ISBN 0 7322 7924 0.
 1. Nguyen, Duy Long. 2. Refugees – Australia – Biography.
 3. Vietnamese – Australia – Biography. 4. Alternative medicine specialists
  – Australia – Biography. I. James Knight, 1967– . II. Title.
305.906914

Cover adapted from the original design by Louise McGeachie
Picture of James Knight: Anthony Gordon
Typeset in 10.5/13 Sabon by Kirby Jones
Printed and bound in Australia by Griffin Press on 79gsm Bulky Paperback White

6 5 4 3 2 1   06 07 08 09

To Mum, thank you for letting me be who I am.
To all my family, both in Vietnam and Australia,
I love you.
I wish special respect to all my 'uncles'.
To all the ARVN soldiers who fought and died, together
with their American and Australian friends.
God bless all the souls of the people who lost their lives at
sea trying to escape communist Vietnam.

An Lộc dịa sủ ghi chiến tích biệt kićk dù vi quôć vong thân
*'There is a place in history for the victorious battle at An
Loc town. Special Forces members had given their lives
for the fatherland.'*
ARVN SOLDIERS' SAYING

Longy

To Mum
Thank you.
I'm the luckiest son in the world.
I love you.

James

〜

CONTENTS

Authors' Note   ix
Foreword   xi

ONE	The Little Soldier	1
TWO	The Road of Flesh and Bone	10
THREE	The Mango Tree	20
FOUR	Goldfish and Silver Dollars	32
FIVE	At the End of the Track	52
SIX	Good Morning, Pleiku	63
SEVEN	Saigon	78
EIGHT	The Fall	98
NINE	One Month in a Lifetime	107
TEN	Uncles	115
ELEVEN	Hitting the Streets	130
TWELVE	Poultry Pugilism	141
THIRTEEN	Gone Today, Back Tomorrow	156
FOURTEEN	The Nicotine Gang	173
FIFTEEN	The Wrong Side of the Law	186
SIXTEEN	Doing Time	195
SEVENTEEN	The Camp	215
EIGHTEEN	When the Time Comes	226
NINETEEN	Fear and Freedom	242
TWENTY	Looking for a Home	256
TWENTY-ONE	Snow, Sumos and Sake	268
TWENTY-TWO	Welcome to Australia	289
TWENTY-THREE	To Educate and to Protect	302

TWENTY-FOUR	Mum	319
TWENTY-FIVE	Healing Travels	325
TWENTY-SIX	Coming Home	335
TWENTY-SEVEN	Agent Longy	341
TWENTY-EIGHT	Making the Grade	354
TWENTY-NINE	Pressing the Flesh	366
THIRTY	Memories	381

Acknowledgments — James Knight	*399*
Acknowledgments — Longy Nguyen	*401*
Bibliography	*403*
Index	*407*
About James Knight	*419*

AUTHORS' NOTE

Because of the sensitive nature of some of the information in this book, some names have been changed or removed altogether, primarily in the section describing Longy's involvement with the New South Wales Police, and his time as a 'protector' and debt collector in Chinatown and Sydney's western suburbs.

In the chapter concerning Longy's time in prison the names Nha, Tuan and Luong are fictitious.

Furthermore, the descriptions of Teresa's death and Hien's experience in a re-education camp have been kept to a minimum out of respect for the Nguyen family. As Thao Nguyen says: 'These are times I choose not to remember.'

FOREWORD

We have had the pleasure of meeting many inspiring people, but few are more remarkable than Longy Nguyen. His achievements are a lesson to us all — no matter what hardships we face, it is important to keep fighting, to keep believing.

Longy's life is a study of the times, indeed a journal of recent history. War, death, politics, violence, crime, refugees, integration, racism — all are themes that cut through society, regardless of culture or creed. Longy has dealt with each, and much more, in his own unique manner. And all throughout, he has managed to maintain a positive attitude when mental weakness would have undoubtedly destroyed many another individual.

When placed in a similar position, how many of us could have stared at the atrocities of war as Longy did? His childhood in Vietnam was unfathomable, yet he survived and even prospered because of his uniqueness and undeniable faith in his own abilities. Of course, he can be thankful that he had a wonderful, loving family that supported him. This is another strong theme in his life, particularly his relationship with his mother, Teresa. Much can be learnt from this by families the world over.

After fleeing Vietnam, he faced new challenges, but again, never gave up. He in fact thrived on adversity. A true fighter. A true opportunist always looking to make the best of any situation, good or bad.

That perseverance has now been rewarded with a fruitful, happy life in Australia. After all the horrors he was forced to endure as a child, Longy (and indeed all his family) deserves nothing but happiness. They are wonderful examples of successful immigration.

We are just two of hundreds, probably thousands, to say how grateful we are that Longy has succeeded ... because without his healing intervention we would not be as active as we are. Anyone who has had back problems will know how limiting they can be.

Longy is a remarkable human being. We both feel privileged to have met him. This book deserves to be kept on the top shelf of any collection.

RUPERT MURDOCH AND
FRANK LOWY, 2004

ONE

The Little Soldier

'I used to see Vietnam as a war, rather than a country.'
JOHN PILGER, AUSTRALIAN JOURNALIST

The church bells clanged in a heavy metal chorus that in another time and place would have shocked the morning, or at the very least given it an impolite tap on the shoulder. However, this abrupt 5.30 wake-up call was, in the circumstances, a most peaceful start to the day; any sunrise that wasn't accompanied by the spitting of gunfire, exploding bombs, whining planes, or the *whop whop* of the Huey helicopters was a reason to thank God.

The size of the congregation always depended on the state of the war. On this day, leaning into the hill's gentle slope, steady numbers of people walked quietly towards the Army Catholic Church, a brick building with a belfry and spire that reached high above the rusty, dusty, dilapidated buildings surrounding them. It could be seen from many parts of town, adding weight to the Catholics' belief that their God rose above one and all.

A few hundred metres away, a young barefoot soldier in army greens watched and waited. He had climbed the mango tree before dawn, clambering up the trunk then wedging himself in a fork; he was now hidden by thick, shadowy leaves and the half-darkness of the early light. He knew the strength of an attack lay in the element of surprise.

About ten people were approaching. There were no children, just old men and women — then again, nearly everyone seemed old to him. They would soon be within reach.

He counted their steps: ten, nine, eight, seven, six, five, four, three, two, one ... *Now!*

The soldier pulled the pin — *click* — then hurled the weapon with all his strength through a gap in the leaves, over the high wire fence, and onto the road. *Klink! Bang! Fssssst!* The thick blue smoke spread quickly, a blanket of billowing darkness that chased the panicking people into every possible place of refuge. Some ran towards the church or the nearest houses; others hid under frangipani trees or risked crouching where they were, folding their arms over their heads, frozen in fear. What was happening? An attack by the Viet Cong? Another Tet Offensive? *Please God, look after us.* In the mango tree, the soldier giggled softly to himself — it was a successful raid. So he climbed down and walked triumphantly along the few steps of the driveway back to his home. It was time for breakfast.

Later that day, Inspector General Hien Duy Nguyen, one of the highest-ranking officers in the Army of the Republic of Vietnam (ARVN), spoke sternly to the soldier in his office.

'I've been told there was another attack near the church this morning.'

'Yes, sir.'

The Inspector General sighed: it had happened all too many times before.

'Do you understand they are not toys?'

'Yes, sir.'

'I am grateful that you are sensible enough not to use a real weapon. But please don't take any more smoke grenades out of my Jeep!'

The soldier nodded, finding it hard to hold back a grin.

'Right,' said the Inspector General. 'Now go and do your homework.'

'Yes, Dad.'

As he watched his seven-year-old son walk away, Hien knew this wouldn't be the last time he scolded the child. When not making trouble, this cheeky boy was invariably finding it. He wasn't so much the black sheep of the family as the albino — black sheep were altogether too common for someone as unique as this free-spirited soul. Perhaps Hien and his wife, Teresa, had expected something unusual from the moment they named their boy Duy Long. In English it means 'There is only one dragon'.

The path to the dragon's existence began in 1951 when twenty-year-old Hien, a novice soldier, and Teresa, an eighteen-year-old member of the local Catholic Church choir, met at a Mass in Hue, the former imperial capital of Vietnam. Within a year they were married. While the two staunch Catholics began their lives together, Vietnam was in the midst of a violent division that would have an impact not only on Hien and his wife, but also the lives of their future children.

France, which had claimed control of some parts of Vietnam in the 1860s, was at war with the League for the Independence of Vietnam (Viet Minh), which was under the leadership of the communist Ho Chi Minh, whose power was strongest in the north. Ho Chi Minh was the soul of the communist push. A revered leader who refused to be beaten, he'd warned the French: 'You can kill ten of my men for every one I kill of yours, yet even at those odds you will lose and I will win.' In March 1954 the Viet Minh attacked a French military outpost at Dien Bien Phu, in the remote northwest. It began nearly two months of bloody fighting that ended when 10 000 demoralised and starving French soldiers surrendered. It was the decisive event in an eight-year conflict that had killed tens of thousands of men on both sides.

Within two and a half months, peace negotiations in Switzerland led to the signing of the Geneva Accords, which temporarily separated Vietnam into north and south at the 'seventeenth parallel'. Under the agreement, the French were to leave and all Viet Minh forces had to withdraw to the north. Vietnam would then be brought back together after an internationally supervised election in July 1956. However, the United States refused to acknowledge the accords, and supported the establishment of a non-communist government in the south. The proposed national elections were never held. Vietnam, a country that had endured French rule, Japanese military occupation during World War II, civil conflicts fuelled by dynastic rivalries and a millennium of Chinese domination, was yet again searching for its identity. Few of its people could have forecast what would happen in the following twenty years when Hien and Teresa were raising their children.

Both husband and wife had come from large middle-class families. Teresa, the only daughter in a family with five sons, had lived her entire life in Hue. Her father worked as a general office assistant for various businesses while her mother was employed full-time rearing the family. Both of her parents had many Chinese friends, shrewd people renowned for their sharp entrepreneurial skills and an ability to prosper regardless of any hardships they faced. During her childhood Teresa learnt much from these people that would help her in the years to come.

In contrast to his wife's city childhood, Hien came from a farming family in Quang Binh. He had three brothers and three sisters, all of whom were raised on hard work; long hours in the fields ensured an ample supply of both rice and blisters. Although Hien became hardened by his surrounds, nothing could prepare him for the most harrowing moment of his formative years: he was away at boarding school when he received the news that his mother had died. Tragically, the lack of efficient transport options prevented him from going home for the funeral. It was not until some months later that he tearfully visited her grave for the first time. It wouldn't be the last occasion such delayed grief would affect the family.

Moulded by his childhood, then regimented by the church and army, Hien matured into a man who displayed little emotion. Smiles were minimal; so were frowns. His highly disciplined manner was contrary to Teresa's warm and open character, which was reflected in a kind, round face framed by short hair that often followed the Western styles of the day. Teresa was broad-shouldered and, at five foot three, quite tall for a Vietnamese woman. In shoes with just a little heel she stood taller than her husband, whose lean frame, spectacles and immaculately parted hair, glossed with brilliantine, gave the impression of scholar rather than soldier.

However, a soldier he was. A thinking soldier. He entered the military in late 1951. By 1954, Hien had earned the rank of captain after graduating from the National Military Academy in Dalat. He shared a common bond with many of his officer colleagues: a majority were Catholics, a reflection of the nature of the power base in South Vietnamese politics.

After graduation, Hien was posted to Hoi An, south of Hue. The riverside town, site of the first Chinese settlement in South Vietnam, had been a thriving port for Eastern and Western traders, dating back hundreds of years. Its architecture was a fascinating mix of European and Asian influences that these days has merited a world heritage listing. However, the romance of the setting meant nothing at a time when the Viet Minh was trying to strengthen its position after the victory over the French at Dien Bien Phu.

A month after that battle, in April 1954, the reality of the period screamed into the Nguyens' lives when Hien, then twenty-three years old, was captured by the Viet Minh while on patrol outside of Hoi An. As he was taken away to a prison camp, the news reached his wife. Although Teresa had long prepared herself to be a widow, the timing of her husband's absence and uncertain future could barely have been worse — she was eight and a half months pregnant.

Teresa sought support from her mother, who rushed from Hue, but before the two established generations could welcome the first member of a third, they were the beneficiaries of an extraordinary act of humanity. Within days of Hien's capture, the Viet Minh had overrun the army base where Teresa was living. While supervising the lines of new prisoners, a Viet Minh officer noticed the mother-to-be buckling under the weight of her load, and her situation. 'This is no place to give birth. You must go,' he said.

Teresa and her mother were allowed to collect their belongings, leave the camp and travel to a part of Hoi An that was still to fall to the Viet Minh. From there, they hitched a ride in a truck to Hue, where Teresa went into labour and suffered excruciating pain in childbirth. With no epidural injection to numb her daughter's nerves, Teresa's mother turned to a family practice that had soothed her when she was in the same position so many years before. She rolled and lit Teresa a cigarette made from *Cam le* leaves that were so strong only a person with cast-iron lungs would dare draw back. Teresa braved a quick puff; the sharp sensation stung, then tickled her tongue. A strange feeling was spreading over her — she was still in pain, but at least she was beginning to relax.

By the time Teresa left the hospital, she not only had a healthy baby girl, Maria, but an addiction to *Cam le* that would last for life.

Six months later, Hien arrived unannounced at his mother-in law's door. He'd been one of the first soldiers to be released under an exchange program with the North. There were no obvious signs of his imprisonment — perhaps he was a little thinner, but he had no complaints; he had been treated well. And for once, he allowed his emotions to take over. He hugged Teresa, laughing with delight, and carefully stroked Maria's little head. He was a lucky man — God was looking after him.

With his wife and daughter, Hien settled in Hue and resumed military duties. Over the following years, as tensions continued rising in the country, the number of Nguyen children also climbed: two boys, James and Lam, and another girl, Van.

Then came the dragon, Duy Long, born 17 October 1964.

For Hien, the birth was a cause of emotional confusion. Just weeks earlier, his closest brother had been shot and killed while on patrol near Hoi An. How could he celebrate the arrival of his third son when he was mourning the loss of another family member?

In Vietnam, just as there was life and death, there was war. A brutal war. Raped women; decapitated heads displayed on the ends of bamboo stakes; bodies shredded by antipersonnel bombs; others melted beyond recognition by napalm; men thrown from helicopters; mothers and children murdered; villages razed. Endless atrocities. All sides were to blame. This was the 'dirty war' — and the framework for the Vietnam in which Duy Long would be raised.

By the end of 1964, Vietnam was in turmoil. Apart from the political differences between the North, South, and increasingly intrusive United States, the country was being torn apart by extreme civil unrest, corruption and religious anger. The Americans were yet to send combat troops, but already had thousands of military personnel on the ground.

ARVN forces had been relocated across the south, which had been divided into four tactical zones, called Corps.

Just before Christmas a serious Hien told his wife: 'We are moving.'

'To where?'

'Pleiku.'

Pleiku housed the headquarters of Corps II, the biggest geographical zone. The market town was nestled in the central highlands, a region dominated by rolling mountains and dense, sometimes impenetrable jungles. It was in a strategically crucial position at the junction of highways that ran to the north, and west to Laos and Cambodia. Camp Holloway, an American air base, had already been established there.

The Nguyen family arrived in January 1965. As an officer — he was now a major — Hien was allowed to live in town, about a 5-kilometre drive from ARVN headquarters. The roads were a mix of streets tarred by the Americans and dirt tracks that either kicked up choking red dust or became gluey strips during the wet season.

The early weeks were understandably an unsettled time for the Nguyens. House-assistants had to be found, the children needed to adjust to their surrounds, and Teresa was eager to establish business contacts — feeding and maintaining a growing family would be much easier with an additional wage to supplement Hien's relatively meagre income.

Even as the Nguyens began adapting to their new lives, though, trouble was stirring in the nearby jungles. Over the past decade, the Viet Minh had been reorganised into several branches, most notably the People's Army of Vietnam (PAVN). In the south, the fight for communism was led by the National Liberation Front (NLF), which established the People's Liberation Armed Forces (PLAF), nicknamed the 'Viet Cong' (Vietnamese Communists or VC) by the Americans.

Many of the Viet Cong, or 'Charlies' as the Americans also called them, were poorly educated, impoverished and ill-equipped. With little conventional artillery, they relied largely on mortars, rockets, and cunning. Their methods were primitive and, at times, barbaric. They dug pits and filled them with bamboo stakes, and used tripwires that triggered uncoiling branches to fling spears. Wearing rubber sandals made from car or truck tyres, they travelled along a vast network of tunnels, and a multitude of tracks known as the Ho Chi Minh trail that stretched along the Cambodian and Laotian borders. Their biggest ally was darkness, whether it was provided by vegetation or the night. After all, how could their enemies shoot at something they couldn't see?

In the early hours of 7 February 1965, with their cloaking friend in the midst of its work, about 300 VC sappers sneaked beneath the outer fence of Camp Holloway. They advanced one by one; step by step. At about 2 a.m., the calm was shattered by machine-gun fire and the whistling thumps of mortars. Some landed harmlessly; others slammed through huts into men groping for their weapons and clothes. The sappers continued to attack, sprinting across the airstrip, blowing up planes and helicopters as they advanced.

When the damage was assessed in daylight, it was discovered that eight Americans had been killed and more than 100 wounded, and ten aircraft had been destroyed. Few VC were captured, either dead or alive. The attack prompted US President Lyndon Johnson to increase his country's involvement in Vietnam's civil conflict, most notably with the launch of air raids. A month later, the first US combat troops landed.

All this, however, meant nothing to a baby boy oblivious to the world beyond his cot. But it would change soon enough. Duy Long Nguyen was destined for a childhood conditioned by war and, in turn, a life conditioned by his childhood.

TWO

The Road of Flesh and Bone

From his first breath, Duy Long was known by his family as either Long or Longy. He wasn't the only product of the era to have two names: his early life coincided with the first official period of the 'Vietnam War', as it was called by the Western world — or the 'American War', as it was recognised by the Vietnamese people. By mid-1965 there was an Australia subheading too, after Prime Minister Robert Menzies committed combat troops (Australia had already been providing military advisors to the South for three years).

Little Longy heard the sounds of war almost daily: sirens, explosions, gunfire, and the skies humming with aircraft. For a child who knew nothing else, though, this was simply the way life was. Nothing was unusual. Not the bunkers in and outside the family home, nor the bullets that were used as gambling chips in card games that his father played with other men dressed in green. Not his father's absences —

sometimes Hien would be away for weeks at a time, but sooner or later he always came home dressed in sharp green clothes and shining black shoes — nor his high-nosed Jeep. And not even the men with missing arms, legs and eyes, who worked on the pig farm near Camp Holloway that Teresa had established in partnership with a close friend. Longy's mother employed war veterans, she not only felt pity for them, but she also realised they made good guards; they held little or no fear. One worker had a scar that stretched across his torso, a memento of the day he fell into a Viet Cong bamboo spear-pit. He was forced to lie there with one spear skewering him behind the ribs and threatening to poke into a lung if he tried to move. It was several hours before he was found.

Such stories wouldn't be told to Longy until he was older. In the meantime, he followed a typical childhood route — look, listen, touch, learn, and cry when harassed by your older siblings. He was generally a cheerful boy who, after beginning to walk, was invariably on the move discovering new things.

Longy had a strong relationship with his mother. Without an obvious reason, Teresa seemed to devote more attention to her youngest son than to her other five children (Thao, the latest addition, was born just ten months after Longy's arrival). At dinner, which was always preceded by bowed heads and the murmurings of grace, mother and son sometimes seemed detached from the family by their own special bond, with Teresa loading her chopsticks with child-size bites of meat and rice, and Longy with mouth wide open and eyes fixed on his mother. He didn't wonder about the apparent favouritism; he was more fascinated by the sight of everyone sitting on chairs around a table. He thought this was unusual, because he had seen other families squatting by the roadside to eat their meals. He was too young to understand the economic disparities that existed.

The Nguyen home was the most striking example of Longy's relatively wealthy upbringing. Once a convent, it was a single-level white concrete building with a door, and a window behind a pair of shutters at the front. It remains the same today, much less conspicuous than forty years ago when the surrounding homes were primarily single-room wooden huts with iron roofs and shining red dirt floors that were marble-hard from the continuous traffic of feet.

Hien and Teresa slept in the front room. Behind this, a bunker built from sandbags dominated a large open area in which the family ate, and the children slept on fold-out aluminium beds. As he grew older Longy would treat his bed as a swag, asking a house-assistant to set it up wherever he felt like resting. Next to James. Near the bunker. Next to Maria. Next to Lam. Or sometimes in the driver's and house-assistants' quarters next door. The assistants varied in number from one to several, depending on demand. They were always busy cooking, cleaning, washing, running errands, walking children to school or going to the markets.

The house, nearly always bustling with activity during the day, was further crowded by the presence of several Korean soldiers who rented a building from Hien at the rear. Longy spent hours watching these disciplined men practising tae kwon do in a small garden near their dwelling. He was so fascinated by every movement that he began mimicking the soldiers, consequently displaying a refined sense of coordination, although there were times when his flurry of arms and legs led to a tangle of confusion — and a backside parked on the dirt.

Longy's favourite playground was in front of the house, where a much bigger garden bloomed with adventures. It was surrounded by a 2-metre-high wire fence knitted with meshing to stop hand grenades and bullets. The fence ended at an iron gate at the top of a 20-metre-long driveway that sloped down gently towards the house. There was a bunker, ferns, bougainvillea, a jackfruit tree, and a tap that exemplified the

Nguyens' privileged position — while most of Pleiku's residents were forced to use communal wells, Longy's family received regular supplies from a truck that pumped water into a reservoir at the back of the house.

There was one other important feature in the garden: a mango tree near the driveway. From all appearances, it was just another mango tree — long, dark green leaves and glowing fruit — but to Longy it was a second home. It offered protection, as its dense foliage was an umbrella in the relentless rain of the wet season, and a parasol in the heat of the dry months. For a curious boy not yet strong enough to climb, the main appeal lay in the mystery of the branches that stretched into the sky. One day Longy would reach them. One day, too, he would be taught a Ho Chi Minh saying: 'It takes ten years for a tree to grow, but one hundred years for a human being.'

The Nguyens wouldn't have enjoyed such a comfortable lifestyle if it hadn't been for Teresa's businesses. Hien's rank brought a sufficient rather than sizable wage, but once added to Teresa's returns, there were never concerns about how the family would be fed or clothed. Apart from farming pigs, Teresa part-owned a cinema in the middle of town. Her diverse interests revealed her sharp mind for opportunities: pork and chicken were staples of the Vietnamese diet, and entertainment was desperately needed by both civilians and soldiers wishing to escape the war for a few brief hours. For Teresa, pork plus celluloid equalled profit.

She was also the member of a band of businesses that privately offered, protected and exchanged money and the more favoured currency, gold. It was a word-of-mouth bank that was founded on one basic rule that Teresa upheld rigidly during all her dealings: 'Repay your debts.'

It's highly likely Teresa earned more money than her husband, and perhaps this prevented Hien from thinking about, or turning to, corruption. After General Nguyen Van

Thieu became South Vietnam's president in 1967, it was conservatively estimated that about 70 per cent of all South Vietnamese generals and colonels were corrupt.

Although he rarely showed his feelings, Hien found his riches in his family. He was a very proud father who took delight in seeing his children grow, and in particular hearing of his older ones' rates of progress at school. He considered a good Catholic education an essential precursor to responsible adulthood.

When circumstances allowed, Hien and Teresa took their children on picnics with the families of other officers. Sometimes they'd go to a coffee plantation on the edge of town, but the favourite destination was Bien Ho, a volcanic lake just outside Pleiku.

From Longy's view, the water that flowed into Bien Ho from the surrounding mountains seemed to stretch forever. How could he reach the other side when there seemed to be no other side? What would happen if he were caught way out there, a long way from anywhere? Would anyone be able to see or hear him? Would anyone be able to save him? Perhaps when he was older he would know the answers.

Longy loved his time at the lake. Although he enjoyed playing with his family, he spent much of the time exploring by himself. Up a track, behind a rock, under the Jeeps. He was energetic, inquisitive, and never afraid to be alone. These traits caused considerable worries for his parents, who knew if they took their eyes off their carefree boy for too long, the picnic would turn into a search-and-rescue operation. Teresa feared that Longy wouldn't be satisfied by merely dipping his toes in the water; if given the chance, he would surely challenge himself to go beyond his limits — and he was not yet able to swim.

Such concerns were swept away by Longy's one overwhelming reason to stay near his family: food. Fish, vegetables, meats, and the succulent fruits with juices that slid from the corners of his mouth and hung on his chin, teasing his tongue: golden mangoes; papayas; sweet, squishy lychees; custard apples; jackfruits; durians, and saboches — Longy's enormous appetite required fuel to keep pace with his rapidly growing physique. As a three year old he was not only tall for his age, but more thickset than many of his playmates. His legs were skinny, but he was strong through the chest, and he had inherited his mother's broad shoulders. If he could fill out his frame in the years to come, he would be an imposing sight — that is, if he wanted to look imposing, because at this age he wore a grin as often as his father donned a uniform. The major's son was cheeky and interminably chatty with anyone and everyone.

The picnics were wonderful times filled with banter, laughter and the enviable innocence of children. On other occasions the adults had their own parties, many of which Hien and Teresa hosted at home. These nights overflowed with food, beer, whisky, laughter and conversation, while the military police (MPs) patrolled the streets outside. Reality always touched the hungover mornings when beggars lined up outside the house for food. What couldn't be given away was used to feed Teresa's pigs.

One evening in early 1968 the Nguyens had a special reason to celebrate, as Hien had been promoted to lieutenant colonel. By this time he rarely saw a battlefield, as most of his day was spent behind the lines developing combat strategies — which was a relief for his family.

No sooner had the bottles been cleared after the party than it was time to prepare for the most important celebration on the Vietnamese calendar: Tet, the lunar New Year festival, which would begin at the end of January and traditionally last for a joyful week. As Tet eve approached, Longy, full of questions, flitted between his family, the house-assistants and even the Korean soldiers. Who would let off the firecrackers? What would be the best firecracker? Would everyone get new clothes? How would the house be decorated? The previous year, a watermelon had been brought fresh from the markets, then sliced open in the house, its rich red colour said to bring good luck. There were flowers, and endless bowls of food needed for all the friends who visited at any hour of the day. Some visitors gave money in envelopes to the Nguyen children — another symbol of good luck. Just as a Western child waits for his stocking to overflow on Christmas Day, Longy counted the seconds until Tet eve.

When it arrived, the Nguyen household bubbled with excitement soon after dawn as all the children received new clothes. Hien shone as the mature mirror image of his sons, and Teresa was a model of elegance in her *ao dai*, a flowing silk top over trousers that tickled the ground. To Longy's eyes, the material floated like angel's wings.

The Army Catholic Church was only a few hundred metres from home, an easy walk, but when trying to control six children in a festive mood, Hien knew it was simpler to drive his miniature troops rather than open the gate and see them scatter across the road on foot. Perhaps only one child would be difficult, but that was reason enough to use the Jeep. Longy sat in the front between his parents, as forcing him into the back usually prompted an outbreak of whinging or deliberate misbehaviour.

The trip would take just a minute or two. Left out the driveway. Up to the corner. Left again. Go forward a block, then take a ... *what!* Why was there a wire barrier stretched across the road opposite the church? And why were two MPs standing there?

Hien stopped the Jeep and stared at columns of smoke rising from the mountains on the outskirts of town; his expression gave nothing away. The MPs approached him and saluted — then came gunfire from the mountains. Hien frowned. There had always been a ceasefire during the Tet holiday period — so what was happening now? After listening to the MPs' reports, he swung the Jeep around and headed home. The celebrations were over.

Within minutes Hien had changed into full army uniform and was gone. The last reminder of his presence was the smell of brilliantine that trailed through the front door to the driveway. The rest of the family remained inside, aware of the growing rumbles of conflict.

By the end of the day Teresa had received word from her husband that PAVN and Viet Cong forces had mounted surprise attacks throughout the south. About 100 cities, towns and places of military importance were under fire. No-one in the Nguyen family was allowed to leave the house. The days passed, each filled with uncertainty, fear, and Longy's apprehension:

> There were skyraiders, American planes going boom boom boom with their guns to try to push the Viet Cong back. From day to day you'd hear ttttt-ttttt-ttttt. Then it would be quiet for a few minutes, sometimes a few hours, then it would start again: *ttttt-ttttt-ttttt*. For days and days and days — *ttttt-ttttt-ttttt, boom boom boom, ddddd-ddddd-ddddd.* Sirens too. Then it would be quiet again. Everything would be quiet. We'd freak out. We were inside the house for weeks. Dad came home only once. The rest of us couldn't go anywhere.

This was Longy's first real lesson in war. His mother told him that all those different sounds meant there were many ways a man in green, a soldier, could be hurt, or that something even worse would happen — the man would never return. And even if he did, he might be put in one of those boxes that would sometimes pass the Nguyen home on a cart pushed by hand, and be followed by rows of crying people on their way to church. That meant the man was 'on his way to God'.

Each night Teresa led her children in prayer, asking that Hien not suffer the same awful fate: 'Please, God, look after our father, and let him come home to us.'

And he did. Three weeks after he'd made the U-turn near the church, Hien eased the Jeep down the driveway in front of his home. He was safe. But before he could settle, there was something he needed to do.

'Come with me,' he said to Longy and Lam.

They needed no encouragement. After all, they'd just finished serving their first sentences as prisoners of war, trapped behind family walls until the master of the household returned.

Hien clunked the Jeep into gear, Longy bouncing excitedly in the front and his brother sitting quietly in the back. There was no right time for what they were about to experience, but Hien felt it would be wrong to shelter his children any longer. Sooner or later they would find out, so it was best they were exposed to the truth while they were with someone who could explain. Or try to. Then again, no words would really be needed.

The smell was first. A stench that grew stronger the further Hien drove along the quiet streets. Doors and windows were shut, and bikes leant lazily against walls. Longy felt sickness rising in his throat; he swallowed. Hien turned a few more corners, pushing the Jeep towards a higher part of town. He slowed. The smell was becoming unbearable. Lam tried to spit the taste out of his mouth. Longy copied him. Another corner, and suddenly they were there, the two brothers in disbelief, and their father, hands on the steering wheel, with eyes on the edge of what the Americans knew as the 'thousand-yard stare', the look of a soldier who'd seen his share of war.

Hien drove forward. Longy, without a door to hinder his view, peered over the side. So that was what the smell was: death. It was impossible to count how many Viet Cong bodies there were. Some sprawling, some scattered, some splintered, some open-mouthed in a silent scream — and all needing boxes. Apart from his mother's explanation of 'on his way to God', Longy hadn't been taught about death.

He'd heard his parents use the word, but what did it really mean? Dead people weren't like the glasses that the house-assistants refilled with water at every meal. Dead people were more like coconuts: once their milk was gone, they were thrown away. Dead people couldn't breathe or move. Dead people couldn't eat. Dead people couldn't talk. Dead people were ... yes, now he was beginning to understand.

At three and half years of age, Longy was serving his initiation as a child of war. About 45 000 Viet Cong and PAVN soldiers were killed during the Tet Offensive. It's estimated that the ARVN lost more than 2700 men, and the US forces, 1500. In a purely statistical sense, the North had suffered a horrendous defeat, and seemingly nothing was achieved, yet in the United States (and Australia) news of the attacks stirred doubts and negativity among the public and a growing number of politicians. Support was dwindling for a war that was becoming unwinnable.

In May 1968 peace negotiations in Paris broke down, and by the end of the year the US had voted in a new president, Richard Nixon, whose future campaigns would include a promise to seek 'peace with honour'. The following year Nixon was to introduce the 'Vietnamisation' policy which would phase out American troops and leave the responsibilities of war entirely to the Southern forces.

Longy, too, was heading in a different direction: 1969 was to be his first year at school. The nuns at St Paul's were about to meet a boy they would never forget.

THREE

The Mango Tree

*'The childhood shows the man,
As morning shows the day.'*
JOHN MILTON

On the first morning of his formal education, Longy travelled to St Paul's School on the back of Sen, the Nguyens' senior housekeeper. Her hunched figure holding a giggling boy riding high would become a familiar sight on the Pleiku streets in the months ahead. On other occasions they'd walk side by side, hand in hand for the twenty-minute journey. Sen would then wait at the gates for Longy to return after morning classes. They'd travel home for a siesta before going back for a further three hours of learning, and waiting.

Despite Longy's love of walking — he could control the pace — vehicles were the most common mode of transport to and from school. When Hien's Jeep was unavailable, the academic delivery was made in Teresa's Jeep, painted white to differentiate it from those in military use.

It took just days for the St Paul's nuns to discover that,

although the white vehicle may have been for civilians, its owner had the presence of a general. They first met Teresa's wrath over a simple matter of dexterity. Longy was a southpaw, but, as was standard classroom procedure, all pupils had to learn to write with their right hands. When Longy resisted, he was stung into submission by a series of blows across his knuckles from his ruler-wielding teacher. Forget words or numbers, his first lesson in repetition was pencil etiquette. Pick up left-handed — *whack!* Pick up left-handed — *whack!* Pick up right-handed ... no whack. Not surprisingly, he quickly learnt the accepted way to do it, but he was confused. Did this mean he had to change the way he used his chopsticks? And what about the stones he threw at the birds in the jackfruit tree at home? Could his left hand be used for anything? When in doubt, it was best to ask Mum.

Teresa's reaction was swift. She rushed out of the house, snapping at her driver: 'St Paul's!'

Minutes later, she was shouting at the nuns.

'That is not the right way to punish children — don't you do it again!'

From that moment, the appearance of the white Jeep at the school could cause considerable apprehension among the teaching staff.

The nuns weren't the only people to fear Teresa: Hien also knew when to keep his distance. He disagreed with his wife's reaction to the writing episode, but he dared not make an issue of it because he knew he would never have the last word. This was generally the way it was in the Nguyen household — mother would act, father would accept. This didn't mean Teresa always supported her children. When a firm hand was needed, she would apply it. That is, of course, to everyone but Longy, whose relationship with his mother continued to take its own irresistible path.

In something of a contradiction to his increasingly independent personality, Longy openly displayed his attachment to Teresa. He hugged her, held her hands, and sometimes tugged incessantly at her clothes until she bent down and offered him a cheek to kiss. His behaviour was the same no matter where he was: at home or the markets, in the Jeep, at church or school. He loved all his family, but no bond was as strong or as meaningful as that with his mother.

In his early days of school, Longy was grateful Teresa was just an angry Jeep ride away, because St Paul's unsettled him. He was used to doing his own thing and having his own way in a warm and loving environment, but now he was in a strange place being controlled by people he didn't know or care for.

The school's main building, a double-storey brick beehive of classrooms, was imposing. It towered above a sprinkling of huts, and a dirt quadrangle in which the children assembled each morning. The only feature that somewhat tempered Longy's angst was the barren red playground with a rise in one corner that was big enough to be called a hill by the students. Matted with weeds and dust, it was a favourite place for the children to sit and look out over the lower parts of Pleiku, or take siesta when the school closed in the middle of the day.

Slowly, the child became more comfortable in his surrounds. He began to make friends, and was often the centre of attention in the playground, where he devised simple yet captivating games. One of his favourites involved trailing his fingers along ferns with leaves so sensitive that they clamped shut if triggered by the slightest touch or movement. Once Longy discovered these plants could trap insects, he and his friends hunted for sacrificial ants that were dropped onto the leaves one at a time. Anyone whose ant escaped was crowned the winner.

Not all games were as harmless. A hospital that overlooked the school grounds was a lure for an inventive child looking for a toy. Anyone willing to sift through the rubbish bins at the back of the building was likely to find bloodied used syringes that became sought-after weapons. They could be filled with water and held discreetly behind backs or in pockets until the time was right for ambushes or direct combat. Not surprisingly, when Teresa found out about this her white Jeep was soon hurtling through the streets heading for St Paul's. Thankfully she was never told of the rumour that a man's arm had once been found among the rubbish.

The playground provided Longy with confidence for the classroom. At first he detested lessons, worrying he would receive further slices of the ruler for the slightest misbehaviour. A rap on the knuckles wasn't the worst punishment. More than anything, the children feared stints in the long wooden box under the blackboard. Poor conduct landed both boys and girls in the 'coffin', sometimes for hours at a time, peering through cracks at fragments of their peers arched over rickety desks, or their teacher standing on the lid while giving a lesson. Longy successfully avoided it.

The classroom was crammed with about fifty children. Few were younger than Longy, then four and a half. The oldest students were about ten. The children came from an array of backgrounds, from farming families whose income depended on the amount of vegetables they sold, to business families who counted carats of gold. Their clothes reflected their wealth: those less fortunate wore threadbare dresses, shorts, shirts, and nothing on their feet; others with substantial money dressed in brand-name jeans, shirts and leather shoes. Longy was undoubtedly a top-end child. Apart from the occasions he wore pink pyjamas to school because he didn't feel the need to change, he was usually kitted out in clean and crisply pressed shorts or jeans, and a shirt. He wore black shoes, the habit of protecting his feet having been firmly entrenched by Teresa, who'd seen too many barefooted people of all ages with soles torn up by streets always littered with glass and tins.

It was difficult to stand out among the hundreds of students at St Paul's, but Longy and the other children of army officers were an exception. They were the barometers of conflict who, ironically, were most conspicuous and valuable when absent. If they were suddenly taken out of school (apart from the times Longy feigned sickness) the nuns wanted to know why. And when no army child arrived at the beginning of a day, there was a strong reason to close the school and send everyone home. On other occasions, mere rumours of impending trouble were enough to shut the St Paul's gates.

There were, however, no interruptions when it came time for the school's showpiece, the annual concert. It was always likely that Longy would be chosen to play a lead role because he'd been recognised by the nuns as a most confident and capable child. Perhaps there was also his teacher's wish to repair any lingering ill feeling within Teresa.

Whatever the reason, Longy glowed when he told his mother, 'I am singing the first song of the concert.'

'Good boy. What are you singing?'

'"My Mother's Vegetable Garden".'

The evening before the grand performance, Longy, wide-eyed and eager, watched Sen iron his best shirt and pair of shorts. Every inch was meticulously pressed; each crease became sharp and defined. Later, just before going to bed, Longy cuddled into his mother's side in the family room.

'I'm very excited, Mum,' he told her.

'Tomorrow is going to be a very happy day for all of us,' she replied. 'You will do well. And if you're nervous, just look up at the ceiling, or the walls, or look at me.'

Look at his mother! Longy knew that would only make him more jittery. He was so desperate to make her proud of him that a mere glance in her direction would surely add to the pressure. He barely slept that night, tossing and turning, reciting his few lines, and recalling what the head nun had told his class hours before: 'Do not make fun of Longy. It is very important that the concert begins well.'

Longy beat the sun up in the morning. He was ready before breakfast: washed, dressed, black shoes shining, and his hair glistening with a handful of his father's brilliantine.

Time ticked by. Roll call. Early lessons. Final preparations in the hall — another row of seats here, put some flowers there. The closer the time came for the concert, the more the minutes dragged. A crowd was gathering; there were more Jeeps and soldiers than students — it seemed Hien had not only invited every off-duty colleague but officers from Camp Holloway as well.

The hall, filled with adults, children and expectations, was an intimidating arena for anyone, let alone a boy not yet five years old. Everyone settled, official welcomes were made; then, amid applause, Longy stepped onto the stage. All eyes were on him. If only he could reach the microphone that stood like a playground bully staring down at him. No-one came to his aid, so he took a breath and began, staring up at the ceiling, thinking of nothing but the next word.

'My mother's vegetable garden, vegetable garden, vegetable garden. Fresh and green. Fresh and green...'

It happened so quickly — in the space of just a few squeaky bars, Longy's moment in the spotlight passed. 'My Mother's Vegetable Garden' had suddenly become a memory, but one that was framed by a standing ovation.

That night Longy fell asleep hugged by his mother's words: 'We are very proud of you.'

It didn't surprise Longy's parents that their son had performed without missing a beat. They'd already recognised that he was a leader, and rarely a follower. This pleased Teresa, because she insisted that all her children think for themselves. It was a necessity of the times. Once she recognised that Longy was beginning to understand the impact of war — he had matured markedly since the Tet

Offensive — she encouraged his independence. She had to make all her children realise that they could be without parents in the snap of a finger. Death was an all too real possibility, especially for Hien. But Longy hated such talk; he continually told his mother there could be nothing worse in life. But he accepted what she said. He had no choice.

Longy's growing self-reliance was augmented by the absence of his oldest brother, James, and sisters Maria and Van. Sent away to schools, they returned only every few months. Longy adapted easily to being the second oldest child in the household behind Lam, who was two years his senior. But he looked forward to the times when all the family was together.

James's visits home from his school in Hue were most anxiously awaited. Longy idolised his brother. There were nearly eight years between them, an enormous gap for someone as young as Longy who considered James to be all grown up. So, as happens the world over, big brother became the person whose every step, every action, had to be followed by little brother — a rare example of Longy happily changing roles to be a follower.

Each visit would begin with a trip to the airport. Hien would usually be at work and Teresa preferred to stay home, leaving one of the drivers to make the pick-up. After arriving, Longy and Lam would squint at the sky, looking for the smallest dot that could be the commercial DC3 with precious cargo. They'd hear it before they saw it, the low drone of propellers churning the air. Once the plane landed, they stared at its door, and counted the passengers until a tall, lean youth dressed in jeans and a T-shirt strode onto the tarmac. Longy always thought James looked cool — the way older brothers should look.

James generally stayed home for just a few weeks, during which time Longy rarely left his side. The younger boy hung on the older's every word. It was as though James lived in a different world when he spoke about geography, science, maths and all he was being taught by his teachers, who were priests, no less.

Longy was infatuated with one subject above all others: judo. Sure, he'd already seen the Koreans practising tae kwon do, but watching and copying his brother do something similar was much better fun. Unlike the Koreans, James had a proper uniform: a stiff white jacket, trousers, and a yellow belt that Longy believed made his brother look very important, like a soldier.

'What does the yellow mean?'

'It shows how good you are. There are many different colours.'

'What is the best colour?'

'Black.'

'One day I want to wear a black belt.'

It was a statement flavoured by a boy's imagination, but simmering underneath was a sense of self-belief that few people would ever question.

While Longy dreamed, US President Nixon battled choices posed by reality. Adhering to an election promise, he announced the first withdrawal of American ground troops from the south in June 1969. Prior to this, he approved the launch of secret air raids along the Cambodian border, where the Ho Chi Minh trail continued to be the main passageway for the PAVN and Viet Cong. So the war wasn't moving towards peace — it was just changing direction.

So was Hien, who unexpectedly received a promotion as incredible as it was sudden. After spending eighteen months as a lieutenant colonel, he was stunned when told he'd been appointed as 'Tong Thanh Tra', the Inspector General of Corps II. It was a powerful and revered position: he was to oversee all military operations in the region, and would answer to just one man, the Commander of Corps II, who in turn needed only to answer to President Thieu. Hien received a certificate signed by Thieu, who had personally approved the appointment. Furthermore, he was given a medal, surely the brightest in his collection of decorations.

Widespread corruption tarnished the awards given to some, if not many, high-ranking officers at the time. They were political appointees, so chosen because they posed no threat to Thieu's leadership. In return for their subservience, they were financially rewarded. Hien was an exception. He had never met the President, nor would he receive, or be offered, any kickbacks. Whatever the reasons behind his new appointment, nothing could hide the fact that he had become a 'no-star' general, three stars behind the highest possible ranking in the ARVN.

By this time, 79-year-old Ho Chi Minh was in poor health. He was still President of the North, the Democratic Republic of Vietnam, but he was rarely involved in day-to-day decision-making. Before long, in early September, he died. To his sorrowful followers, his legacy befitted the rough translation of his name: 'Bringer of Light'.

For Longy, an understanding of Ho Chi Minh was still many classrooms away in the future. Instead, the rest of 1969 was filled with a fifth birthday, playground games, writing right-handed, practising side-kicks and blocks, and the undeniable lure of the mango tree.

The tree had the appeal of the forbidden. As its slippery trunk had no knots, nothing that could be used as footholes until the first branch some two metres from the ground, Hien warned his son against climbing it, claiming it was too dangerous.

Teresa worried too. She'd started checking her son's fingernails and clothes for bark when he returned home from school because he'd already learnt to scale other trees, primarily to pick flowers which he'd wrap in paper and give to the girls in his class — a fearless boy with a romantic streak.

What were his parents so worried about, though? With his legs clinging to the mango tree's trunk, Longy was strong enough to climb far enough until he could reach a branch and pull himself up. Easy! From there, he could weave his way further towards the top, or sit on the lowest branch and look out over the entire garden, the roof of the house and parts of the street. Longy was the self-appointed 'king of the mango tree'.

With royalty, however, comes treason. The traitor was an overconfidence that eventually goaded Longy into experimenting. Tired of taking the easy route up the bark, he grappled with the challenge of edging up a length of rope that he tied to the lowest branch. It was hard work: one handful at a time, fingers and toes burning, body twisting. Once that was achieved, what else could he do? Climb down again. And after that ... how about swinging? Then what? How about making a loop with the unattached end? Wrap the rope this way, tie a knot here, and it's done. Then? Why not put your head through the loop, hold your hands on the rope above, push your feet against the trunk, and try climbing again.

The first few steps went as planned, but with the mere slip of a foot, everything spiralled towards disaster. The sudden loss of traction sent Longy's feet spinning away from the tree, his hands lost grip on the rope, and the loop slipped and tightened around his fragile neck. Feet scratching the air, hands frantically moving, and a boy without breath, dancing with death.

His fingers reunited with the rope; his first reaction was to reach for the knot in the loop, but it was locked hard with tension. With all his remaining strength he held onto the rope, curled his legs, and thrust them above his body towards the branch. Slowly, painfully, he hauled himself to safety just in time.

The incident didn't deter him from climbing the tree, but it did give him a greater respect for it. There'd be no more playing with the rope — hands and feet were enough. The biggest remaining danger was being caught by his father, a fate Longy tried to avoid with the help of an unusual ally:

the siren on the side of Hien's Jeep. Its laboured wail was frequently used to cut a path through the traffic whenever Inspector General Nguyen was returning home from work. Longy could hear it from streets away, and if he was climbing at the time he knew to make a hasty retreat.

When the siren wasn't used, Longy relied on his sight, with one eye on his climbing, the other fixed on the street outside the house. Even from the most difficult positions he could be on the ground in about thirty seconds, which, all but once, was enough to avoid detection.

On the occasion he was caught short, his punishment was impromptu imprisonment: 'If you like being up there so much, you can stay there all night,' said Hien firmly.

It was late in the afternoon, still warm for a barefoot boy in shorts and a shirt, but within hours the night would be cold enough to raise goose bumps. Longy waited. The sun went down. More waiting. The aroma of dinner-time spices teased him. More and more waiting. The street became quieter; the lights from kerosene lamps dwindled. Curfew came: it was midnight ... and still Longy waited.

In the early hours of the morning, the child perched on the lowest branch of the mango tree, so temptingly close to the ground, heard the front door of the house creak open.

'Get out of the tree, Longy. I don't want to see you up there anymore,' whispered Teresa.

Had anyone won? Could Hien claim victory for imposing such a tough penalty? Or had Longy triumphed? After all, not many boys had such willpower. If he had come down earlier, Longy knew he would have escaped further discipline because Teresa would have prevented it. So why did he stay so long?

'Because I wanted to prove to my father I could do it,' he says now.

Their five-year-old son's stubborn determination both warmed and warned his parents. Yes, Longy was going to be able to look after himself. But how much trouble, and damage to himself, would he cause along the way?

Hien began taking his wayward son to the ARVN base, reasoning that if he couldn't be looked after by the military, he wouldn't be safe anywhere. The visits launched a new phase in Longy's life, as for the first time he was in regular contact with soldiers. Real soldiers. Not like the guards outside the Nguyen home or Hien's personal assistant. These were men who gambled with their lives nearly every day.

While Teresa and Hien had instilled the love of God in their children, Longy was soon to decide that there were others deserving of his worship.

FOUR

Goldfish and Silver Dollars

*'While we're fighting in the jungles they were
marching in the street.
While we're dying in the rice fields they were
helping our defeat.
While we're facing VC bullets they were
sounding our retreat.
As we go marching on.'*
THE BATTLE HYMN OF LT WILLIAM CALLEY

It was impossible not to notice Longy when he visited the ARVN base. Although there were other officers' sons who occasionally marked time there, only one boy brought along his pet goldfish in a plastic bag.

There was actually a succession of goldfish, because few lasted any significant length of time. Try as he might, Longy just didn't have the preserving touch. If he thought his companion was looking ill, he'd hurry to the infirmary to steal a squirt or two of oxygen from the cylinders near the operating tables. The new breaths in the bag could be enough to keep the fish alive for hours. But there was also the problem of bag maintenance, a challenging assignment when Longy was clambering over turrets or crawling through bunkers. If the fragile receptacle sprang a leak, emergency accommodation could easily be found in a combat helmet.

Longy felt at home at the base. He was very proud of his father whenever they travelled through the main gate, side by side in the Jeep, acknowledged by the guards springing to attention and saluting. It was always a stirring arrival.

From there, they'd drive past more Jeeps, tents, tanks, trucks and more starched salutes, until they arrived at Hien's office. Longy was then given an extraordinary amount of freedom. Apart from returning regularly to prove to his father that he still had all his fingers and toes — and hadn't cost anyone theirs — he wandered the length and breadth of the base, swept away by his imagination. There were real tanks to be loaded with invisible shells that were so heavy they caused a buckling at the knees when lifted. He sat behind the wheels of lorries pretending they were bumping and grinding into the jungle. There were buildings to hide under when helicopters flew overhead. There was the hospital to struggle to with the wounds of a make-believe bullet fired into the heart. And there was the parade ground on which to address a whole invented army.

Not everything, though, was as cheerful as childhood. When he wasn't playing, Longy sat and listened to the soldiers who fought the real war. These were men, often as young as eighteen, who were shaped by every precious day they survived. Some became harder; others were maimed both physically and mentally.

Because of this, Longy was never sheltered from reality. If he was old enough to walk around an army base, he was old enough to hear and see the truth. That was the view of nearly every soldier he met, and certainly the view taken by his father. The child was indeed becoming a little soldier.

There were the cheeky moments when he saluted the Inspector General, and in return received a 'kick up the backside'. There were also times of savage behaviour and disturbing sights, none more grotesque than that of returning commandos wearing as necklaces the torn-off ears of the Viet Cong stuffed into grenade rings.

The commandos were Longy's heroes. In mottled camouflage uniform, they were different from the plain green-clad soldiers. When leaving on a mission, M16s slung over their shoulders and the glint of machetes reflected in their eyes, they carried themselves proudly, upright and fearsome, the resounding stamp of their feet sending a warning to anyone daring to cross their path. These men were tough. When they returned after successes they ambled arrogantly into the base, smoking, shouting, laughing and slapping each other on the back. Their expressions, like their uniforms, were varied. When they weren't successful, those who returned shuffled quietly, dragging sadness, with heads low and shoulders slumped. Sometimes, of course, they didn't come back at all.

They displayed their bravado even when at play. One of their favourite tricks was the reckless practice of drinking from a glass holding a live grenade — the fit was so tight that the striker lever had no room to expand and detonate the weapon. Here were men used to cheating death in the jungle, yet even when safe they still chose danger to make them laugh and relax. For many of them, life was nothing but war. Their motivation was shown in the words *Sat Cong* — 'Kill Viet Cong' — tattooed on some of their chests and arms. Longy imagined that he too would one day decorate his skin, not necessarily to display such a brutal message, but to show that he was a soldier. Maybe the tattoo would depict a rifle, a plane, or even the love of a son for his mother.

When the commandos or regular soldiers told Longy about their battles and skirmishes, he listened intently, more so than he ever did in a classroom. Afterwards he'd look towards the hills and try to imagine all he'd just heard: crawling through the undergrowth avoiding bullets and spitting chunks of dirt and bark; creeping behind trees, holding your breath, and looking out at nothing, knowing you were being watched; hearing a branch crack, a leaf move, and shooting in blind hope. Ambushes, raids, and surveillance. Explosions, booby traps, and torture. Tears, blood ... death. Longy heard it all.

So why were they fighting? Because the Viet Cong were the enemy of South Vietnam and the Americans. But who were the Viet Cong — and why were they the enemy? Were they just like the Comanches shot by John Wayne in *The Searchers*? Many of Longy's earliest pro-American views were formed while peering through the projectionist's window in his mother's smoke-filled cinema. The 'bad guys' he saw may have looked different from the Viet Cong, but if they were all enemies of the 'good guy Americans' then weren't they all the same?

Longy's parents had already told him that the Viet Cong and the people in the North held different beliefs from the South Vietnamese. But what were beliefs and did they have something to do with the Army Catholic Church? Longy was taken there nearly every Sunday because his parents demanded that all their children show a belief in God. So was the war about God, then? Maybe the Viet Cong didn't believe in God. Didn't God love everyone regardless? Longy couldn't understand. At his age, he simply viewed the war as good against bad, us against them.

The five year old's only experience with the Viet Cong had been on the drive with his father after the Tet Offensive. He'd seen them from a distance when he and Hien drove past the prison camp on the way to the ARVN base; he'd heard them most nights when the *ttttt-ttttt-ttttt*, and *dddddd-ddddd-ddddd* kept him awake; and they crowded his thoughts when rumours spread of sightings of them in the plantations on the edge of town.

Then came the day he met one face to face — just the two of them all alone. There wasn't any need for alarm because Longy was outside Hien's office, where the VC was a prisoner tending to a garden flanked by a wall of used artillery shells. In his early twenties, he wore a dirt-red uniform and tyre sandals. He smiled politely, his yellow teeth bright against skin much darker than Longy had ever seen on a Vietnamese person.

'Do you live in the main street?' asked Longy, referring to the prison camp near the base.

'Yes.'

'How did you get here? By DC3?'

'I walked.'

'From the north?'

The prisoner nodded; Longy couldn't comprehend how many months the journey must have taken. They talked for a few minutes before Longy sneaked into his father's office and returned with a Salem cigarette. The VC accepted it gratefully, rolling it carefully into a rag and placing it in a pocket.

When he told the story at school, Longy instantly became a playground celebrity: 'Did you hear about that boy over there? His father's the Inspector General. He says he met a Viet Cong face to face!' Word spread from classroom to classroom. And with that word came reputation. Teresa had long instilled in Longy the need to earn the respect of others. It seemed he needed little help.

After spending one year at St Paul's he was transferred to Van Duc, a more practical school for the Nguyens because it was within a few minutes' walk (or still the occasional piggyback) from home. It was 1970, and Longy was now the oldest child in the household, as Lam had been sent to join James at school in Hue.

Van Duc was run by the Army Catholic Church. Apart from the absence of nuns as teachers, Longy didn't think it was any different from St Paul's. However, some of the students had a superiority complex and told their new classmate, '*Thanh Phaolo an cuc ga co*' — St Paul's eats chicken shit!

As he continued to grow in confidence, Longy started to tempt fate in the classroom. With a mix of mischief and exhibitionism, he resorted to writing left-handed — but only when he didn't feel the need to wield the pencil in his right. It all depended on which side he was using in his exercise book: left for left side and right for right. It was an amusing trick for other children to observe, although at one stage a girl started to cry because of the 'freak' sitting in front of her. It was also strange for the teacher to see a legible scrawl change to a miserable scribble in the middle of a sentence.

Longy was fast teaching himself many classroom shortcuts, and in the process discovered the art of negotiation. He knew there were students much brighter and more conscientious than he was, but they couldn't afford to buy their own books. On the flip side, Longy had the money, but not the scholastic inclination. So it seemed logical to offer the playground pitch, 'I can get you a book, if you will do my homework.'

Homework wasn't a nightly exercise, but to Longy any minute devoted to study outside the school gates was a waste of precious time. If he couldn't make a deal for someone to do it for him before he left for home, he did what many a conniving student does the world over: he left his books at school. Not only could he shrug his shoulders when his father asked, 'Where's your homework?', but by the time he returned to school in the morning the books were often missing, perhaps stolen by someone with a greater appreciation of education.

While Longy strode cockily towards, then past, his sixth birthday, the US continued its withdrawal from the south, and was joined by Australian troops. But the reduction in numbers didn't mean less conflict or controversy in either Vietnam, or across the world. In fact, 1970 was one of the ugliest years of the war. In a particularly sour development, ARVN and US forces launched operations into Cambodia in a bid to stop the movements of the Viet Cong and PAVN. This led to massive protest rallies in the United States and Australia.

The most volatile fuel for igniting public anger was the revelation of a 20-month cover-up involving the US military's involvement in a massacre at Son My, a supposed Viet Cong stronghold. As many as 500 women, men, children and babies were murdered. Some were speared by bayonets, others were shot point-blank or mowed down by machine-gun fire. Women were raped, livestock killed and dwellings destroyed. All sides committed acts of similar savagery, some of which will never be revealed. This war was as inhumane as any in history.

Such incidents battered the already bruised public image of the American GI, but in Pleiku a star-spangled-eyed boy saw a different side. The Americans had once helped some of his father's men fix the roof of the main building at St Paul's, and they came to the new school with chocolate powder and hot water, a sweetener for the times they pricked the children with tetanus and typhoid injections.

Longy saw the Americans as friends. His father talked about how they had improved the roads in Pleiku from uncomfortable stretches of dirt and mud to smooth ribbons of gravel and tar. They constructed new buildings and developed town water supplies. Most of all, they offered security. To see them sitting in the backs of lorries dressed in uniform, sleeves rolled up, arms bulging, Zippo lighters tucked into the sides of their helmets, and cigarettes 'real cool' in the corners of their mouths, they looked as though they were unbeatable. When these real-life heroes were added to the macho characters of John Wayne and others taken from the silver screen, it was comforting for a six-year-old boy to know the Americans were on his side.

Despite the constant presence of the war, Longy most frequently saw the Americans when they weren't in military mode. After school, he'd often slip past the guard at the driveway gate of the Nguyen home and hurry a few doors down the street to the Hoang Lan, a café that provided an entertaining insight into the war's extracurricular activities. He wasn't allowed inside, but never mind — there were enough sights leaning against walls at the front to keep him amused; namely, American soldiers with their shirts out and arms wrapped around Vietnamese women and teenage girls mostly dressed in skin-tight slacks and low-cut tops. There were wandering hands, legs entwined, and mouths working furiously together. And what they were doing with their tongues! Quite a show in a country in which public displays of affection were seldom seen.

Watching from the footpath, Longy could see glimpses of activity inside the Hoang Lan where women sat on the laps of soldiers, giggling, and saying in broken English, 'Baby want boom-boom?'

The air smelled of an acrid mix of body odour, coffee, cocoa and cigarettes. Occasionally fights would break out and spill onto the street, where Longy silently urged on every push, shove and punch from the nearest vantage point of a tree or Jeep bonnet.

He rarely spoke to the Americans. His English was limited to the odd sexual reference such as 'boom-boom' or descriptions of condoms nicknamed 'silver dollars' because of the colour of their packaging. And quite apart from keeping his mouth shut, he was smart enough to realise he'd be tolerated as long as he didn't get in the way. This was an adult's domain.

The Hoang Lan was also a popular place for Korean soldiers and those members of the Vietnamese military who could afford it, most commonly the ARVN's high-ranking officers, and the suave, sunglasses-wearing helicopter pilots who made heads turn when they arrived on their humming Vespas. There was, however, one prominent man who would never frequent the establishment: Inspector General Hien

Duy Nguyen. He indicated his strong church values by threatening to throw out any soldier who used a prostitute while boarding in the flats next to the Nguyen home. But this didn't stop the discovery of silver dollars on the premises, or on the streets. Whenever Longy found one, it ensured he'd be the centre of attention the next day at school.

By the end of 1970 Longy had a third brother, Linh, the seventh child in the Nguyen family. Teresa had used the *Cam le* epidural for the last time — her role of child-bearer was complete; but, much to Hien's chagrin, her penchant for smoking remained. Unwilling to upset her husband by lighting up in the house (this was, however, a common practice for Hien with his favoured Salem brand) Teresa resorted to having a puff only when outdoors. It wasn't unusual for townsfolk to see her rolling up a thick *Cam le* joint while sitting in her Jeep by the roadside.

Having two parents who smoked, and living in a country in which tobacco was a companion for all occasions, it was inevitable that Longy would shake hands with the habit at some stage during his childhood. Older sister Maria was the instigator. With the senior Nguyen children home on holidays, Longy banded together with Maria and James for an experimental drag or two in the family room. Cross-legged on the floor, hearts sprinting, and ears pricked for the rumbles of either parent's Jeep, they took turns inhaling from a cigarette taken from one of Hien's open packets. When it was passed to Longy, he eagerly guided it to his lips, and drew back as though sucking a pea through a straw. This wasn't going to be hard — he was just taking a breath of blue air, that's all. Wrong! Almost immediately he began to choke, then his shoulders shuddered, and his cheeks billowed in rejection. Smoke spilled from his mouth and his tongue absorbed a bitter, nasty taste. Yuk!

Amid further puffs and splutters, the sound of the driveway gate opening could have been missed, but the alert nicotine gang heard enough to know it was time to panic.

'Quick! It's Dad.'
Confusion whirled through the room.
'Put it out.'
'Where?'
'Here.'
The Jeep eased into its parking spot.
'What about here?'
'How about here?'
'That will do.'
Footsteps outside the front of the house.
'Oh no! Smoke!'
'Water!'
'Hurry!'

The front door opened, three children scattered, and Hien walked into a mist of disobedience. Which was the worse crime — his children smoking? The fact they'd hidden the evidence under a pillow? Perhaps it was the pillow catching alight? Or the fact they'd used water from the goldfish bowl to put the fire out.

Hien didn't punish them — it was part of growing up. It was no use sheltering his children from an everyday part of the culture. They had to learn and decide for themselves. Even a six year old.

Longy couldn't fathom why people smoked, but he reasoned the habit must be good because he'd heard some of the soldiers on the base say cigarettes 'warmed the heart'. He was yet to be entirely convinced, though, and was content for his contact to be limited to trips to the market with his mother to buy *Cam le* tobacco wrapped in banana leaves.

The market was the hub of Pleiku. About five minutes' drive from the Nguyen home, it was vibrant from dawn to well after dusk. Rows and rows of vendors sat, squatted and stood near goods that were piled on tables, or thatched leaf mats, or wooden trays attached to the backs of pushbikes. There were fresh vegetables and fruit, jumbled piles of greens, golds, reds, burgundies and yellows. There were chickens standing wing to wing in cages, so tightly packed that it was impossible to know which legs belonged to which body. There were tanks of catfish, crabs and prawns reeking in stagnant water. Dead, unplucked ducks hanging on hooks. Bunches of flowers. Herbal medicines to treat or prevent every possible illness. Shirts, shorts and sandals. Tailors, bicycle mechanics, and giggling children playing hide and seek. Men of all ages crouching in concentration over checkerboards, and wispy dogs with jutting hipbones, hungry eyes and noses to the ground in search of scraps. And all the while a patchwork of conversation, laughter and argument spread over the whole site.

Even during the wet season, when the downpours sent water gushing along the laneways, turning them into glue pots in which many a loose sandal was snapped or swallowed, the markets were always busy. Siestas in the heat of the day slowed business down, but few stalls ever stopped. To close down was to lose time. To lose time was to lose money. And to lose money could mean the difference between eating well or not at all.

It took little time for the market vendors to get to know Longy. Although he was the 'Inspector General's son', more people there knew him as 'Teresa's boy'. This was the environment in which Teresa earned respect, and she frequently reminded Longy: 'People live and die by their reputations. Be smart, be kind, and always repay your debts.'

At the market, Teresa could be trusted. She could take now, pay later — no questions asked. Her word was good.

Longy only understood this when he was allowed to go to the market by himself. Instead of money in his hand, he carried instructions from Teresa in his head: 'Go and get me some *Cam le* leaves. Tell the man I will pay him tomorrow.'

Longy always returned with arms full and, more importantly, the knowledge that not only did his mother have an enviable reputation, but she had incredible faith in her six-year-old son. Teresa had never allowed her other children to walk the streets unaccompanied at the same age. But now she was openly telling — in fact, ordering — the boy to tread a solo path. Had experience made her more lenient? Or was there some kind of instinct that made her loosen the hold?

Teresa was taking a risk, but her husband had already set the precedent by allowing Longy to wander freely around the ARVN base. If he was safe within arm's reach of live ammunition, he could surely stay out of harm's way among the watermelons, basil and chilli. What she couldn't know, though, was that the combination of the market and the military would create a dangerous dish ...

Longy may not have been enamoured of academic pursuits, but by his second year at Van Duc he had a commanding knowledge of both numbers and letters that emphasised his burgeoning interest in the war. As quickly as a GI could fire off a round, Longy could name the types of weapons he'd seen or heard: M16, M60, Colt .45, Carbine M1 ... It was a pity spelling and maths weren't as easy.

Longy's early fascination had been prompted by his father's Colt .45 pistol. Whenever Hien was in uniform the pistol would be with him, riding in a black leather hip holster, handle and trigger exposed, chamber and barrel hidden. It was a badge of power and authority; few officers had the same presence without one.

The Colt was often tantalisingly close to Longy. He could have easily taken it from his father's desk and shot a bullet into the air, just as he'd once seen Lam do, but there was more to shooting than simply pulling the trigger. There had to be the thrill of aiming at something, and once you fired the gun you needed to be able to shoot it again, and again. Just like the soldiers in the jungles did. *Ddddd-ddddd-dddd. Ttttt-ttttt-ttttt.*

But how could he do it? His father would never let him use the gun.

The market provided the answer. Amid all the produce were the products of the times: children who had no homes or parents, nor laws to obey. They were self-taught in survival: how to find food for the next meal, shelter for sleep, clothes for warmth. Ingenuity kept them alive. The oldest were in their mid-teens, yet they adopted the little gatherer of the *Cam le* leaves as one of their own. Longy, approaching seven years old, was entering another stage of his upbringing — learning the ways of the street.

He had no need for survival tips, but there was another subject that captivated him from the first moment he saw what clever hands and inventive minds could make. It seemed so simple: find two straight pieces from a discarded M16 magazine and tie them together to form a channel just wide enough for a bullet. Then attach a spring, and a strong rubber band to the end of the channel behind the bullet; bind your hand in thick rubber for protection; pull back on the rubber band, forcing it to stretch and gain tension over your thumb; insert a nail through the rubber band and spring; hold the contraption at arm's length, drop your thumb to release the tension, shut your eyes, and hope that the nail, speared onwards by the rubber band and spring, had the power to discharge the bullet but leave the hand intact.

The necessary equipment was easy for Longy to secure; all he needed was an afternoon at the ARVN base. Once that was accomplished he returned to a quiet spot behind the market and, with the help of his 'teachers', carefully constructed his first weapon, a handgun in the truest sense of the word. There was no holster, no officer, no Colt .45, but in a field surrounded by boys urging him on, Longy momentarily felt an additional bond with his father. He had power.

BOOM!

The firing was an anticlimax. He'd shot at nothing, hit nothing, felt nothing other than a rumbling numbness through his hand — his left hand. Would his first teacher have rapped him across the knuckles if she'd seen him?

Longy had the power, but he needed more. He had to have a target, something that was easy to hit and which would show the full effects of the blast. Preferably something that could be killed. He found it a few days later when playing at home in the kitchen with one of the market boys. There it was, high and dry on a tin tray — a catfish that was to be cooked for the evening meal. It could stay alive out of water for hours, and when the time came to kill it, the fish would probably fall to the standard practice of having its head cracked by the handle of a knife. So if it was going to die anyway...

Apart from ensuring that the house was empty, Longy made no preparations and certainly gave no thought to the aftermath. He simply loaded his gun and, when he was a mere metre away from the catfish, he aimed and fired.

BOOM!

The sound ricocheted off the walls; Longy's hand went numb; the tray, with a now sizable hole in it, spun across the room — and the unrecognisable catfish was no longer on the menu. Somehow neither parent found out about the incident, nor questioned the cook about the lack of flavour in the soup. Longy soon became known by the market boys as 'the executioner' — since men were allowed to shoot each other in war and the movies, Longy saw nothing wrong in roaming the streets and knocking birds off power lines.

Longy continued to bustle precociously through his childhood, while the war waded deeper into the unknown. Just how it would end, or when, no-one knew. The year of 1971 was marked by further international protests and troop withdrawals, and, following their attacks on Cambodia, US and South Vietnamese forces turned their attentions to Laos in another attempt to sever the Ho Chi

Minh trail. In Pleiku, Inspector General Hien Duy Nguyen remained busy developing, implementing and overseeing combat strategies. His role frequently took him away from his home for weeks on end, but by now his family had become well used to having a father and husband in absentia.

Occasionally Hien would cut his travel time and elevate an arrival home to grand proportions by ordering his chopper pilot to illegally land on the grounds at the Army Catholic Church. From there, it was just a simple stroll down the hill to his family. Testimony to the respect Hien had earned in the community, the helicopter's *whop-whop-whop* would sometimes bring the townsfolk hurrying to the church to deliver gifts to the pilot, with the message: 'Please give these to the Inspector General. He is a good man.' Fish, fruit, vegetables, chickens, woven mats — all were tokens of respect and admiration.

Hien wasn't necessarily out of town when away from his home for long periods. Sometimes he'd be trapped at the ARVN base for days, if not weeks. These periods didn't prevent Longy from visiting, and firmly ordering his father to 'ring Mum every day and tell her you love her'.

The trips also gave Longy the chance to stock up on supplies. Not only bullets and magazine pieces, but gunpowder to use in small bombs, and his favourite acquisition, smoke grenades, which offered endless fun when tossed from the mango tree into crowds of churchgoers.

'Don't you ever do that again!' warned Hien when he was first told of the mischief.

But Longy did.

'Please don't take any more smoke grenades out of my Jeep!'

But Longy did.

'If you must take them, don't ever throw them near a petrol tank. Always be careful!'

And Longy was.

Not that any victims of his impetuous attacks would agree, but he was always wise enough to assess the situation before acting. Too much risk meant no throw. Manageable risk meant wrap that grenade in your itchy hands, pull the pin and let it fly!

Here was a military-minded seven year old who was increasingly mapping his own path of development. Forget the conventional — kites, balls and wind-up toys; go and chase the thrills and dangers of living in a country at war. What about pain or being seriously wounded? Well, it hadn't happened yet, so that alone was a strong enough reason to continue, wasn't it?

School, however, was a hurdle. Longy overcame this by sitting at the back of the classroom; after waiting for his name to be marked off at morning roll call, he'd quietly slip out the nearest open window and dart away to his next adventure. It was a tactic that was used sparingly, though, because overuse would surely lead to discovery.

Longy considered education to be a time-consuming annoyance that was taken to a new, agonising level when his father sought additional help from a tutor, a middle-aged man who taught at another of Pleiku's schools. Once a week revision lessons were conducted in the Nguyen home. All progressed well for a few days, until an altercation between the learned and learner led to some angry exchanges. Hearing her son's screams, Teresa raced into the family room to see the tutor wiping blood from his face and Longy standing proudly in the corner. James's judo tips had proved their worth. The tutor, who was promptly sacked, would prove to be just one in a long line of brave educators.

Thankfully for both parents, Longy finally discovered a classroom he did feel comfortable in. One evening when driving with his mother, he pointed to a large timber house that he'd often passed on his way to the market.

'I really want to go there.'

Teresa pounced. Within minutes, she and her son were standing in a room dominated by the smell of sweat and dirty feet, and filled by sixty boys and young men working as one. Stern faces, tight fists and sharp, cutting movements — right arm forward, twist the hand, pull back; right arm forward, twist the hand, pull back ... The thumping of feet on the wooden floor pulsed through Longy's body. For years he'd seen the Koreans near home performing tae kwon do patterns, but the sheer weight of numbers here was forging a greater impression. He looked at his mother and grinned. Teresa smiled back, pleased at the thought that martial arts might instil some discipline into her boy's life and give him an outlet for his aggression.

Unlike the academic tutors, the instructor gained Longy's immediate respect for three reasons: not only did he have a black belt, he was also a second lieutenant in the military police, and he attended the Army Catholic Church. He was a sinewy man with thick black calluses on his knuckles, self-crafted medals struck by dedication to his discipline.

He taught two classes: one was for the white, yellow and lower ranks of blue belts; the higher blues and browns worked in the other. The students were aged between five and their mid-twenties; many of the older ones were soldiers. After being placed in the junior class, Longy concentrated on every single movement his instructor made. Left-hand block, then back. Keep the fists tight. And again. Left-hand block, then back.

'That's good, Longy. Very good.'

Nearing the end of his first session, Longy watched the higher-grade students spar with each other. Flashing head-high kicks, hands as fast as bullets, and nimble feet that could surely climb up and down the mango tree without ever being seen or heard. Longy resolved not to give up until he was as skilled as they were. A whole spectrum of belts was waiting — but first, he needed something else. That night Teresa made it, measuring, cutting, pulling, slicing and stitching, until the end result was ready to wear. Longy put it on excitedly. It fitted perfectly, but it made him itch — uniforms weren't typically made from hessian grain sacks.

The white-belted Longy literally threw himself into his classes. Whenever he hit the floor, he simply bounced back up with a grin. His energy lit up a room that could be darkened by the tears and tantrums of other boys.

He advanced quickly, and was soon ready for his first grading exam. If he graduated to a yellow belt, he'd be the youngest so ranked at the school, and that would elevate him in the eyes of his peers. His parents would be proud, and he'd also be one tiny, determined step closer to living up to his word to James that one day his waist would be wrapped in black.

Before that, though, he had the difficult and daunting task of trying to perform every pattern he'd been taught — hands, feet, body and mind working together in front of the instructor's critical, examining gaze. For some students it was sufficiently nerve-racking to force alert minds into forgetfulness and coordinated bodies into spinning disasters. Would he suffer the same ignominy? He stood in the middle of the room, just metres away from the instructor, whose expression and folded arms were as cold as the wooden floor beneath Longy's twitching toes.

'Begin please, Longy.'

Longy felt all alone. There was no chance he could use the lure of a new textbook to try to swindle someone else to stand the exam for him. He could rely only on himself.

Clench fists in front. Feet shoulder-width apart. Chin in. Look left. Turn left. Downward block. Hold it. One down.

Longy stared ahead as he launched into his second pattern. Step forward on right foot. Downward block. Swivel on foot. Each movement was precise and more confident than the last. Nerves? What nerves? Why should he be worried? He had been the centre of attention before ...

My mother's vegetable garden, vegetable garden, vegetable garden. Fresh and green. Fresh and green ...

In ten minutes it was all over. A few kicks, a few punches, a few turns, and then the toughest pattern of all — the holding pattern. Longy searched the instructor's face for some hint of approval, but received only the slightest of nods to acknowledge that the floor show was over.

'You will know tomorrow.'

Longy didn't realise the instructor was in a quandary. White or yellow? Should a reason be given? After much troubled thought and searching, he took a lowly white belt and hopped onto his motorcycle; he had an important job to do. Later that evening the instructor acknowledged the guard at the Nguyen gate and placed the belt in the letterbox. He rode away with traces of yellow paint still drying on his hands.

Duy Long Nguyen, the yellow belt. After he found his trophy in the morning, Longy proudly showed it off at Van Duc. It didn't matter that the belt was actually a white one painted yellow. That, in fact, allowed some embellishment of the story. If the instructor couldn't find a proper one, it was obvious that yellow belts were very rare, and Longy, at seven years of age, was in a class of his own.

Longy's reputation spread beyond the tae kwon do mats, and in the minds of many of his schoolmates he earned even greater recognition for his prowess in an arena where there was no discipline or rules, and competitors fought for their lives. During each wet season droves of crickets chirped incessantly, their presence inviting eager boys to come forth with sticks and ambitions. The boys would dig into every hole they could find, then reach into the sticky earth until they plucked out a handful of potential champions, which would be taken to school in matchboxes and tossed into their own theatre of war. The fights were one on one. Each boy would produce a cricket, then shake it up until it began flaying its legs in agitation. The combatants were then placed on the ground, flanked by their owners and a ring of boisterous spectators. A tangle of legs would follow, each new engagement bringing a cheer from the crowd until one of the fighters admitted defeat by turning its back and running. The victorious boy would pick up both the winner and loser; one would return to its stable to fight another day; the other would lose its head, placed in another matchbox to be carried in the pocket and displayed as a symbol of lofty schoolyard status, a position Longy rarely tumbled from.

He did, however, have a distinct advantage — not only did he have a shovel, but he discovered his own exclusive supply of prizefighters in an area where few townsfolk ever ventured. It was half an hour's walk from home across a few roads, along some paths, then onto a jagged, shadowy track that rolled towards the jungle, and a canopy of mystique.

His teachers had warned him not to go there, as the people who lived there were 'primitive, dangerous and not to be associated with'. Longy heard, but didn't heed. The curiosity he felt was too powerful to be ignored.

FIVE

At the End of the Track

They walked in single file to the market; wore brightly coloured hand-stitched sarongs; spoke their own flat, high-pitched language that town kids mocked; ate almost anything; and were regarded by many people in Pleiku as being primitive. These were the 'mountain people', or, as the French had called them, 'montagnards', a collective label for the tribes who lived primarily in the high country of both South and North Vietnam. The most populous tribes near Pleiku were the Jarai and Bahnar, both peaceful groups whose beliefs and rituals were based in nature.

Longy had taken his first, somewhat tentative, steps into the land of the Jarai when he was just six. What he saw — a naked young woman bathing in a stream — certainly encouraged him to return. When he told his mother where he'd been he was advised not to go again, but Teresa didn't stop her son altogether, reasoning that if he really wanted to do it, she should let him — it was just another stage of growing up.

Jarai villages were scattered all around the fringes of Pleiku. Longy chose the closest to home to explore: a small settlement nestled in jungle just a short stroll, or muddy slog during the wet season, from town. The journey began along a narrow dirt track that rambled hundreds of metres down an easy slope. On either side there was dense and often impenetrable undergrowth with long, snaking vines twisting around the trunks of trees; the tallest formed a canopy that dappled the sunlight in some places, and denied it altogether in others. In the wet season the air buzzed with mosquitoes, and there was a fresh, moist smell of wood and leaves.

The first signs of human habitation were the wisps of curling smoke that loitered in the shards of light along the track. The further Longy walked, the more smoke he disturbed. It wove round him, tickling his nose until its thin blanket met him in a clearing that was scattered with long bamboo-thatched huts raised above the ground by wooden stilts.

From the first time they saw their visitor, the tribespeople made him welcome; their smiles and warmth belied the widespread belief that all mountain people were '*moi*' — savages. Murderous intertribal battles had enhanced this image, but much of the picture was painted by political ignorance. Before the war, various governments had tried to suppress the indigenous people; in some quarters of the south the montagnards used guerrilla tactics to resist the Vietnamese majority. However, during the war they were suddenly recognised as being valuable to both sides — their knowledge of the jungles and, in some cases, their proximity to the Ho Chi Minh trail, led to their recruitment by US and communist forces.

The Jarai whom Longy visited were more interested in self-sufficiency than the war. Bare-breasted women in dark blue and black sarongs sat cross-legged in clusters, their nimble fingers busy weaving bamboo strips into mats, or, invariably, cradling babies. Older children slept or played nearby. The men, wearing only laps, used machetes and knives to carve musical instruments and weapons from bamboo and wood. Small and sprightly, they tiptoed through the jungle hunting pigs and deer. In the wet season they became fishermen, casting nets into rushing streams. At various times throughout the day and night they gathered in the centre of the village around a clay pot full of rice whisky that they sucked through reed straws.

Whatever the occasion, the Jarai always regarded Longy as one of them. During various celebrations he sipped their sour rice whisky, sang and danced with them, and listened to the shallow clinking of the string gongs and the piercing notes that whistled from the bamboo flutes. But he never understood what he was celebrating — because he didn't understand their language. He tried to learn a few words, but his attempts at rounding his tongue in an unusual way and speaking in a higher pitch tended to end in laughter and a smile of self-mockery.

Whenever Longy returned home from his adventures he was muddy or dusty from head to toe, prompting the curt demand from his mother, 'You like an ethnic! Go wash yourself.' Which he did, in either a steaming tub of water that was prepared by a house-assistant or, when he was hot and in a decidedly cheeky mood, he'd take a can of beer from the fridge and pour its contents over his head.

Teresa came to accept Longy's bond with the Jarai to the extent that she even made fun of it. Once when a Jeep-load of Nguyens passed some tribespeople walking by the roadside, Teresa said, 'Look, we adopted Longy from them.' For weeks afterwards, younger sister Thao was convinced her brother was a native mountain person.

Teresa had only one rule concerning her son's wanderings into the jungle: he was never to eat anything with the Jarai. It was one stipulation that he always obeyed — he had no need to challenge his stomach with raw pig meat when prepared meals were waiting at home.

Despite her somewhat poor regard for the mountain people, Teresa had reason to be grateful for one thing her son learnt from them. The first time Longy saw it, he thought it was just a game — one man repeatedly tapping points along another man's body with a ball of hardened sap that was attached to the end of a bamboo stick. Perhaps the men were secretly laughing at the musical instruments that they struck in similar fashion: *ping-ping-ping-ping-ping* up and down the spine and neck, across the shoulders, and out along the arms that were spread like a bird's wings.

Longy observed every detail with fascination: the speed and firmness of the taps; the repetition of taps on any one point; and, most importantly, the position of the points. This wasn't a playful, spontaneous pastime — this was an act of precision and purpose, a unique form of healing. It was Longy's introduction to massage. The boy sat for hours at a time, his eyes fixed on the healer's every movement and the patient's every response, whether a twitch, a flinch, a smile or a nod. Afterwards he'd go home and use his hands to practise on his mother. He'd search for the spots that he'd seen touched time and time again. It would be years before he understood the importance of the body's pressure points, but his enjoyment was immediate when he discovered he could ease the pain of Teresa's worsening rheumatism, an affliction she had endured since early adulthood.

'That is good, Longy. Yes, just there. Good boy.'

The irony of this activity was lost on Longy. At the same time he was experimenting with the softness of his touch, he was learning elsewhere that the manipulation of pressure points could be used in confrontational ways. While continuing to impress at tae kwon do, he watched older boys bring opponents to their knees with a simple pinch or the sharp dig of a knuckle. As with the Jarai, Longy absorbed all he saw, edging closer to recognising the potential power that trained hands could possess: they could fix, but they could also break.

New adventures, challenges and lessons beckoned him. Some, such as kangaroo-hopping Teresa's Jeep out of the driveway and onto the street, were fraught with danger. It prompted the house-assistants to whisper that Longy was *Quay* — a stirrer.

He made miniature bombs by cutting holes in table-tennis balls, packing them with gunpowder and attaching long wicks of string. Whenever a loud *boom* was heard near the track to the Jarai people, it was probable the little soldier had lit the fuse.

Longy also taught himself to swim. The first step was learning to tread water in the 2-metre-high iron tank at the back of the Nguyen home. From there he advanced to dog paddle, breaststroke, and eventually his own stiff-armed freestyle in the streams near the Jarai tribe. Every time he stepped into the water he felt a rush of excitement: he was a seven-year-old boy taking an exhilarating chance against nature, which provided him with a sense of freedom he'd never experienced before. The cool water always stole his first few breaths, then, when he plunged his body and head below the surface, he felt he was part of the stream. He'd lift his head to breathe, turn his arms, kick his legs and be swept away, piggybacking on the current. This was surely as good as life could be.

Longy was one of only a few boys who could swim, and one of an even smaller number who would tempt fate in the stream. That realisation slapped him the day he heard that one of his closest school friends had drowned after stumbling into deceptively deep water.

Longy could be almost anywhere, and doing almost anything. He had graduated from carrying goldfish with him to taking his dogs — Lu-Lu, a border collie, and Salem, a German Shepherd, whose name reflected the overwhelming influence of smoking in Vietnamese society. The dogs, with tongues hanging out and panting smiles, relished trips to school with their master. They sprinted ahead of him, took a sniff of the ground, then turned to see if he was following. They playfully nipped at his heels; they jumped at him until they slowed his progress enough to stand on their hind legs and rest their front paws companionably against his waist or chest; then they'd run ahead again, sniff, and cock a leg. When they reached Van Duc they'd be sent home, or, just as Sen the housekeeper used to do at St Paul's, they'd sit and wait patiently at the gate until Longy came back, which was often sooner than it should have been because of his deft positioning near the window at roll call.

The trio was most commonly seen together at the market, where Longy bought his mother's *Cam le* leaves and Tally-Ho cigarette paper. Sometimes, when the war caused road blockages between Pleiku and Saigon, there'd be a shortage of supplies, including Tally-Ho, which forced Longy to spend time cutting thin substitute strips from the stationery in his father's office at the ARVN base. While there, he collected bullets for his homemade gun; throughout his childhood he continued to shoot birds and, when the demand arose (although it was thankfully rare), dogs, so their meat could be served as a delicacy on special occasions.

Longy had become well known about town, and in one Jarai village in particular. His traits were increasingly apparent to those who knew him, or knew of him: he was strong, adventurous, independent, gregarious, curious, confident, cocky, daring, cheeky, resourceful, at times sadistic — and above all else, he was his own person. He was Longy.

By the start of 1972, Longy knew enough about the war to realise it was more than 'us against them — good against bad'. His views were still simplistic, and obviously blinkered by the pro-South, pro-American conversations he'd heard at home and in his travels, but he was old enough to form some opinions of his own. The conflict was about beliefs, but he now knew those beliefs affected the way he lived. Not only himself, but his family, his friends, the townsfolk of Pleiku, the mountain people, and even the Americans, although he'd heard his father say it was only a matter of time before all the GIs went home — which was something Longy couldn't comprehend.

With or without the Americans, the young boy wondered why the North wanted to change the lives of the people in the South. Wasn't the North happy? Why was it so different? Couldn't everyone live together? Amid the questions, there was one overwhelming certainty in his thoughts: when he grew up to be a man, he would become a general and drive a tank into the northern capital of Hanoi, and fight until he knew all the answers.

More questions were posed in March 1972 when the North increased attacks in both Corps I and II, and by the end of the month Southern bases were being thumped by rounds of artillery near the western border with Laos and the demilitarised zone at the 'seventeenth parallel'. PAVN forces moved south along the coast and the Laotian border, aiming to take advantage of the weakening presence of American forces.

Hien recognised that Pleiku was a potential target; fearing for his family, he made arrangements for everyone to go to Nha Trang, a relatively safe coastal city to the southeast. Within days, Teresa and her children were acquainting themselves with a new but temporary home near a sweeping beach. They were helped to settle in by one of Hien's closest friends, Major Ho Van Tinh, who provided the accommodation and treated the family as though it was his own. He was a small bespectacled man with a strong military presence. Longy nicknamed him 'Uncle Ovaltine', a play on words with his proper name.

Hien remained behind, working on strategies to counter the advancing PAVN in what was the most widespread outbreak of hostilities since the Tet Offensive. With the reduction of American troops, Inspector General Hien Duy Nguyen knew that the war was entering a most critical phase. Doubts were beginning to invade his thoughts. Could the ARVN continue without American support? And what would happen if it couldn't?

Hundreds of kilometres away, Longy was so happily distracted by fresh adventures that the war didn't seem as significant as it had been in Pleiku. Nha Trang was 'like a holiday camp full of swimming, fishing, and a bit of school'. He wasn't able to forget the conflict altogether, thanks to the constant sight of soldiers in the town and Teresa's insistence that the family repeat its oft-uttered prayer from the Tet Offensive: 'Please, God, look after our father, and let him come home to us.'

Hien flew in for several visits, but his time at home was brief: as much as he was needed by his family, his immediate priority was the war. The PAVN was trying to split Corps II into two distinct regions: the central highlands and the coast. Considerable advances had already been made along the coast, prompting intense discussions in Pleiku between the Americans and the top-ranking officers of Corps II, including Hien.

By April, sections of the highlands were under heavy attack; similar raids were also happening west of Saigon. Two months later, the 'Easter Offensive' was considered over. Due largely to US air power, the South had regained sufficient control to claim victory, but it was badly damaged by the losses — 10 000 men had been killed, and about 30 000 were wounded. After hearing of the death rate and the casualties, the destroyed towns and fragmented troops, Hien thanked God that his family had been out of the firing line. Whatever decisions he had made during the war, none had been more important than sending away his wife and children. In the shadows of this latest conflict, though, he feared it wouldn't be the last time he'd have to take such action.

After spending nearly four months in Nha Trang, the Nguyens regained their normal lives. The four oldest children returned to boarding schools, and Teresa took Thao, Linh and Longy back to Pleiku. The wet season had started. At night Longy curled on his bed under a mosquito net and listened to the rain roar on the roof above him. The sound comforted him and made him feel secure. He was happy to be home.

Longy quickly returned to his familiar ways. There were streams to swim, cricket fights to win, massages to give, school exams to cheat at, dogs to walk, *Cam le* leaves to buy, birds to shoot, the mango tree to climb, bombs to build, commandos to idolise, a brown belt to aspire to ... and there was also the one certain way of filling his parents with pride: upholding the Catholic faith.

Catholicism was introduced to Vietnam during the 1600s, when French, Spanish and Portuguese missionaries travelled throughout Indochina, and, despite being intrinsically different from the popularly practised Asian beliefs and philosophies of Buddhism, Confucianism and Taoism, it found a comfortable corner in a country that was crowded with ancient spirits and superstitions.

At the outbreak of the war, the South Vietnamese Government under the leadership of President Ngo Dinh Diem was pro-Catholic, and it remained so under General Van Thieu's subsequent rule. Although it wasn't mandatory for members of either government to be Catholic, it was undeniable that the followers of the faith had a much greater chance of walking the corridors of power or rising through the upper ranks of the military than those of other religious persuasions. If Hien hadn't been a Catholic, it's almost certain he would never have reached the position of Inspector General.

Both Hien and Teresa had been raised on a mix of fire and brimstone from the pulpit, and a firm insistence from their parents that God was almighty. It was a matter of accepted course that they handed down this version of the faith to their children. While the parents provided the routine, they needed the church itself to build and strengthen each child's relationship with God. For this they depended on Lieutenant Colonel Father Anh, the head chaplain of Corps II. He was a tall, striking man whose intelligence was underlined by his ability to speak fluent English and several mountain dialects. He was assisted by Father Chinh, a shorter man with brilliantine-glossed hair swept back in a trademark flick.

For longer than he could remember, Longy had attended church with some member of his family at least once a week. Now, leading up to his eighth birthday, marking the age at which he could take Communion, he was forced to increase the frequency of his visits to Father Chinh's classes, which were filled with fidgeting pupils who generally had no passionate understanding of the Catholic faith, nor any desire to learn about it other than to satisfy the wishes of their parents.

Longy tolerated the classes without ever enjoying them. What was it that Father Chinh kept saying about Jesus, the son of God, sacrificing his life to save not only Longy's soul, but everyone's in the entire world? Well, Longy had to make sacrifices too. While he was undertaking Bible study, praying and acknowledging God as his almighty Father, the world outside the Army Catholic Church was passing him by. He felt as though he was living within a hymn — slow, boring and out of tune when compared with the exciting hip-shaking, shoulder-wriggling, toe-tapping rock and roll songs that belted out from Pleiku's cafés. Nevertheless he persevered until the day shortly after his eighth birthday when, dressed in his church-best clothes — pressed tailor-made shirt and trousers, and black shoes — and standing in front of his immeasurably proud parents, he tasted the blood and body of Christ for the first time.

With Communion taken, it was time for the real honour, the true reward for his sacrifices. The next morning, without stopping for a mouthful of breakfast, Longy hurried to the priests' quarters at the rear of the church and impatiently knocked on the door. Father Chinh answered, raising his eyebrows in surprise when he saw God's novice servant.

'Good morning, Longy, what can I do for you?'

'Father Chinh, I want to be an altar boy, please.'

SIX

Good Morning, Pleiku

Longy's first happy brush with religion occurred when he was seven years old. Forever seeking new territories to satisfy his insatiable wanderlust, he risked roaming the grounds of the small nunnery behind the priests' quarters near the Army Catholic Church. Although he had whispered 'trespass' countless times when mumbling the words of the Lord's Prayer at Mass and at home, any possible understanding of the word he might have gleaned didn't prevent him from entering the forbidden domain. The nuns — small, delicate and peaceful — were a source of curious fascination, and not to be overlooked by a boy who was devoted to discovering whatever he could, with or without permission.

On this particular day he encountered more than he could have expected, or hoped for, when he climbed onto a brick ledge, peered through a window and was instantly intoxicated by the sight of a naked nun having a shower.

Needless to say, this wasn't Longy's last visit to the nunnery. Perhaps if Father Chinh had known of the clandestine peeps, he would have needed to give some thought to Longy's request to become an altar boy; armed with no such evidence, and additionally, a very good reason for the request to be upheld — Father Chinh and Hien were good friends — he granted Longy his wish.

Apart from martial arts classes, there was little else for Pleiku boys to do — certainly not much that Longy hadn't already discovered — so the role of altar boy was elevated to a much sought-after position. Fathers Chinh and Anh had a select group of boys who assisted in the day-to-day running of the church. Most of the duties were mundane: adjusting and tidying pews before services; sweeping floors; handing out hymn books; collecting money plates. However, sprinkled among the routine jobs were tasks that appealed to Longy, especially the highly responsible role of ringing the morning bells. This was the 5.30 alarm that many people in the town relied on in the absence of radios and clocks. After just weeks of performing the more menial duties, Longy was granted this honour; the fact that he lived so close to the church, and had reliable parents who would never dare let their boy sleep in, made him an obvious choice.

The night before her son's debut, Teresa was full of encouragement.

'It is very exciting — your first big job as an altar boy. We are all very proud of you. Be strong and ring the bells hard so everyone in the town can hear. We'll all be waiting. Now go to sleep, and one of the assistants will wake you in the morning. Good night, Longy. I love you.'

'I love you too, Mum.'

Longy slept restlessly that night. The slightest noise was enough to wake him and send him into a burst of panic, fearing that he'd slept past his big moment and left the whole of Pleiku asleep at a time when people should have been cooking, washing, cleaning, heading to the markets, and preparing themselves for the day ahead. A quick tiptoe to the nearest window and a long stare into the pitch-black darkness was enough to allay his fears and send him back to bed for another bout of fitful rest. After several false starts he woke in the early hours and, without consulting a clock or the darkness, he knew it was finally time to go. He dressed quietly; no-one had yet stirred in the household, and there was no need to wake anyone until he reached the driveway gate where one of his favourite guards, Con, was positioned, sound asleep. Longy nudged him gently.

'It is time for me to go and ring the bells. Can you open the gate, please?'

The guard nodded, rising stiffly from his chair and moving the gate wide enough to allow Longy to slip through onto the street.

The stillness was shattered almost immediately by the snap of a rifle bolt. Longy froze, his heart suddenly banging hard against his chest.

'What's going on?' shouted a man from the other side of the street, too far away to be seen.

Con reacted quickly, and calmly.

'It's only the Inspector General's son. He has to ring the church bells.'

The man walked towards them. He was barely visible in the dim light until he was only metres away. He was dressed in black, a night watchman who patrolled the streets and enforced the curfew. He looked suspiciously at Longy.

'Why so early? It is only three-thirty.'

Three-thirty! Longy didn't know what was worse — the sudden fright of having a gun pointed at him, or the glare he received from Con for the premature wake-up. For the next hour and a half he sought refuge and comfort in his old friend the mango tree until he had a legitimate reason to wake Con again. He then rushed to the church. Father Chinh was already waiting.

'Good morning, Father. Should I ring the bells now?'

'Not yet, Longy. You still have a few minutes. Sit down.'

From where he sat marking time near the altar, Longy could see the bell rope dangling like a loose thread in a room at the front of the church. High above it in the tower, three huge bells were waiting to mark their own time. Longy tapped his feet: the few minutes he was forced to endure stretched his patience intolerably. He looked at Father Chinh; one glance, two, three, then finally —

'Now, Longy.'

Longy rushed along the aisle, forgetting the decorum required in a place of worship. He launched himself at the rope, grabbing it with both hands and offering his entire weight to the great bells that shifted only very slightly, as though they needed a few last moments of rest to regain their senses and organise themselves.

Ding!

Longy pulled again with every ounce of strength and this time the bells answered with a much stronger song.

Dong!

Another pull.

Dong! DONG!

After tugging again Longy was lifted from the ground, the might of the bells too much for his small body to resist. He giggled as he was pulled up and down, and every few seconds his sandalled feet skimmed across the floor in an impromptu cha-cha.

Dong! DONG! Dong! DONG!

When the bells' momentum weakened, Longy gained enough purchase to pull hard on the rope again, hitching another ride. Swinging gleefully from side to side and listening to the clatter he was making, he felt he was the most important person in Pleiku. A whole town was in his hands. At the Nguyen home, Teresa smiled.

The bells rang for several minutes, and would have undoubtedly continued for much longer if Father Chinh hadn't asked his enthusiastic charge to stop. Later that morning Longy strutted through the Van Duc playground, boasting to everyone he saw.

'Did you hear the bells this morning? That was me.'

The enthusiastic bell-ringer never failed to uphold his dawn duties.

Not all tasks were as pleasant. One day at school, when storm clouds were piling up in the sky, Longy and another altar boy, Binh, were summoned from their classes by a nun telling them they were needed at the church quickly. They met a very solemn Father Chinh at the priests' quarters.

'You will come with me this morning, boys. Hurry and get your clothes.'

They rushed to the vestry and collected their red sarongs and white shirts, rolling them into balls and tucking them under their arms to keep them dry from the gusts of driving rain. They then scampered back to the school entrance, where they'd been told to wait.

'What do you think is happening?' asked Binh.

'I don't know. Maybe there's something special going on at the army base.'

One of the perks of being an altar boy was the weekly visit to the ARVN base to help the priests conduct services.

As the two soaked youngsters stood by the roadside, their hair clinging to their faces and their shirts glued to their backs, they watched an army truck come towards them and then slow down, its wheels throwing water from puddles that lay on the road.

'There's no room here! You'll have to travel in the back,' yelled Father Chinh, who was squeezed in between the passenger side door and a nun so tiny she was barely visible above the dashboard. Her white habit was dripping wet. The driver was a grim-faced soldier. On Father Chinh's direction, he drove the vehicle onwards once he saw his newest passengers had climbed safely aboard. There was no shelter for the boys; they stood on a tray surrounded by a skeleton of steel poles that usually supported a canvas canopy to cover combat men as they travelled to and from the jungles. Longy and Binh each clung onto a pole, turning their backs against the spearing drops of rain. The faster the truck went, the more fiercely the rain beat against them.

The vehicle laboured on for half an hour, banging, bumping and slipping its way over both bitumen and mud roads that eventually led to the hospital on the ARVN base. The rain had stopped and, as the truck shuddered to a halt, Longy was chilled by the sounds of uncontrolled weeping that came from the driver's cabin. He knew what it meant. It was just like the times he had heard mourners in a funeral procession pass by the Nguyen home on the way to church. But he was surprised that the noise came from the nun. Nuns weren't meant to cry — they were the givers of strength, never the receivers. How could Longy comfort this tearful, skinny little woman whose sharp bones seemed close to cutting through her fragile skin, adding to a pitiful image of complete and utter despair?

Longy and Binh waited in the back of the truck as they watched Father Chinh escort the tragic figure to a hut at the side of the hospital. They walked along a path, neither needing to stop to read the gloomy handwritten words on a sign that was wired to a gate: *'Nha Vinh Biet'* — 'Gone Forever'. Father Chinh and the nun were walking towards the morgue.

Next to the hut there was a canvas tent that neither boy wanted to go near. The stench of death and antiseptic was thick in the air, accompanied by the loud, haunting buzz of flies swarming around bodies that were piled haphazardly on top of each other. A small group of soldiers huddled outside, their hunched shoulders giving the undeniable message that they'd rather be anywhere else than here.

'One, two, three!'

Gathering strength between each foray, they'd rush into the tent, covering their mouths with handkerchiefs. Moments later they'd emerge, dragging a body behind them, followed by a mass of flies. More men would wrap the body in a blanket and carry it into the morgue. Both groups rested uneasily after each horrific trip. There were more physically demanding jobs than the hauling of the dead, but nothing could rival the dreadful anguish these men felt as their hands grasped the arms and legs of the fallen.

Longy and Binh were speechless, terrified, sick. They looked at each other, searching for understanding behind the shock. How could they ever accept or explain what they were seeing? To Longy, the most telling question reached far beyond this: how could any God let this happen? Or was this the punishment for all the soldiers who didn't believe? Surely the nun's loss answered that. Her brother, a commando, had been shot too many times to count the wounds. He was just one of thousands of victims across the country, good men who didn't deserve to die. God was wrong. Very wrong. Longy may have been an altar boy, but in his heart he knew he could never be a devout follower of the faith.

'Longy!'

'Yes, Father.'

'Come here, please.'

Longy looked nervously at Binh, then reluctantly stepped down off the truck and shuffled towards the morgue, which Father Chinh and the nun had just entered. If only something could swallow that path and disable him from going any further. A fly landed on his face. He slapped it away and, forgetting the poise he was meant to show as a member of the church, he began spitting as he tried to overcome the horrible taste of death. This was worse than the Jeep ride with his father after the Tet Offensive. Much worse. Since that first encounter with death, he may have learnt to understand it, but that understanding also gave him a greater appreciation of life, and in his final heavy-footed steps before reaching Father Chinh, he was scared by his thoughts of just how fragile life could be. During war, no-one was safe. Not even an eight-year-old altar boy.

Longy edged inside the morgue, and was so startled by what surrounded him that he desperately wanted to turn on his heels and run until he was home, safe with his mother. On every side there were rows upon rows of simply made wooden coffins holding bodies bound in white cloth. The nun was kneeling next to one that was draped with the South Vietnamese flag, its brilliant red stripes and yellow background in bold contrast to the black mood that engulfed the room. The nun, head bowed, hands clasped in prayer, and tears following a well-worn path down her face, was mouthing words in silence. Longy thought of his parents. If a nun couldn't handle death, how would he cope if either his mother or father died? He stood motionless for several minutes. He says now that he felt that a 'scar was being drawn on my whole life. Eight years old! I shouldn't have been there. It is good to be strong, but at eight years of age?'

Worse followed when the nun lifted her head. Her reddened eyes focused on Longy. 'I want to make sure this is him. Please, could you take off the lid.'

Longy looked at Father Chinh, hoping that he would see a shake of the head, but a nod plunged him further into fear. With trembling hands, and eyes turned away from the coffin, he did what he was told until he felt the gentle touch of Father Chinh's hand on his shoulder — the nun had seen enough; her only brother was indeed *Nha Vinh Biet*.

A group of soldiers, their eyes and thoughts masked by sunglasses, carried the coffin to the truck, then jumped into Jeeps that would take them to the Army Church in town. Longy and Binh returned as they'd come, holding onto poles in the back of the truck, but this time wishing they had the discomfort of rain stinging their faces instead of a crate of death that slid from side to side, leaking fluid that gave off an odour that overwhelmed even the billowing exhaust smoke and forced the two altar boys to gag with every breath they took.

When they reached the church, which was already filled with officers and soldiers, they ran into the vestry and crammed a thick block of incense into the censer that was to be used in the service. They lit it. An uncustomarily large amount of smoke poured out, realising the boys' hopes that its sharp, pervasive scent would override the stench coming from the coffin.

Amid the prayers and salutes that followed, the nun continued weeping. Her sorrow would be one of Longy's most painful memories of the war.

After the burial Longy asked Father Chinh to say a prayer over the grave of his friend who had drowned earlier in the year. The fear of mortality crowded his thoughts: wrong place, wrong time, and it could all be over ... Life wasn't fair.

Returning to the soldier's grave, Longy found that some commandos had gathered for their own impromptu service. Sitting around the fresh hump of red clay, they chatted, laughed, smoked, and drank until they teetered on the edge of inebriation. They left together at midday; the clouds cleared to reveal a sparkling afternoon. When Longy and Binh returned to school they didn't speak to anyone, didn't feel like speaking to anyone — couldn't speak to anyone. And nor could Longy gain solace that night by recounting the experience to his mother. Instead, he lay on his bed, pulled a blanket up over his head and hid from what remained of the most distressing day of his tender life.

He continued as an altar boy for several months. Certainly it was a position that commanded respect, but throughout his time as a servant of the church he constantly questioned the role of God. He believed because his mother wanted him to believe; he dared not mention his uncertainty to her, because he knew she drew strength and comfort from the knowledge that all her children would be accepted by the Lord.

But what would happen if the Almighty Father was short-changed by one of his children? Longy didn't give it a moment's thought the day he dipped his hand into a bag full of offerings after a service at the ARVN base. His reasoning was simple: he was thirsty and needed a drink. After helping the church, surely he was entitled to some little reward. He had a partner in crime, another altar boy, who was struck by guilt soon afterwards and blamed Longy for leading him into temptation. They argued, Longy walked off in anger, and his days in red and white were over. His parents were disappointed, but accepted his decision to quit; it was inevitable that his sense of independence, which was entwined with a growing strand of stubbornness, would sooner or later twist free. He still went to Sunday Masses with his family, and prayed each night with his mother, but beyond that God had no hold on him.

The time that had been devoted to religion was now filled with more enjoyable pursuits, although one was also bruising. Such was Longy's dominance at the tae kwon do school he was soon awarded his blue belt — minus the wet paint. Recognising that this pupil was years ahead of his peers, his instructor thrust him into a brown-belt group with youths twice his age. Suddenly, the strong frame that had dwarfed the boys he'd flattened in the novice class was no longer a weapon of intimidation, but a target that had to move nimbly and precisely to avoid being battered. His new combatants took no mercy on him, and on one occasion a group ambushed him, nailing him with several upward kicks to the base of the spine that caused him to buckle over, breathless and screaming. The immature pack act was a test for Longy's character; this was indeed a school of hard knocks, but no matter what the lesson, he refused to give in. His resolve was strengthened in the unlikely environment of his mother's hazy cinema, where he was mesmerised by the dynamic new star Bruce Lee, a kung fu fighter whose flashing fists and feet leapt from the silver screen into Longy's imagination. Motivated by what he saw, he practised every day, squeezing patterns and drills into any spare moment: a spontaneous kick while walking along the path to the mountain people; some push-ups in an alley behind the market; stretches against the driveway gate before going to school. Slowly, the cruel attacks of his tae kwon do seniors gave way to respect.

Longy was racing through childhood at a furious speed. Almost everything he learnt beyond his formal education at Van Duc pushed him, made him hungrier to know more. He pursued new knowledge with the attitude that there was no time to waste. In healing, he had progressed from firmly rubbing the rheumatic feet of his mother to experimenting with acupuncture on chickens. And he explored his own body. Just as a guitar player practises chords, Longy felt for tendons and joints, each becoming familiar to his touch.

In the swirl of his new experiences, he graduated from firing his handmade gun to joining hunting expeditions with soldiers using real weapons during the idle times of the war. When first invited on one of these trips, Longy was surprised how easily his father granted permission. Whatever concerns Hien may have had about his son's reckless adventures were countered by the trust he had for his fighting men. Once they were in the jungle, perched behind rocks, and staring down their gun barrels at deer drinking at water holes, they allowed Longy to squint down his own M1 carbine and squeeze the trigger.

BOOM!

Returning from his very first trip, he joyfully sat high in the back of a Jeep, unable to take his eyes from his trophies: the swinging carcasses of three deer that were tied behind him. 'The executioner' had left smaller game behind.

Dusk was the best time to hunt. Longy and the small group of soldiers left the ARVN base in the early afternoon and, after a two-hour journey, were crouching in their positions well before sunset. Depending on their tally, they either returned that night or next morning. Sometimes Longy would be dropped straight at school, waving goodbye to his fellow marksmen, then, his broad chest swelling with pride, he hurried to answer the breathless questions of his envious friends: 'How many did you shoot?'; 'Were you scared?'; 'What's it like firing a big gun?'; 'Did you miss any?'; 'Was it only deer you shot?'.

Longy basked in the attention. His listeners were eager to hear every word, and although his answers were usually similar from one trip to the next, only the most fanciful of imaginations would have conjured the story he returned with from one particular expedition.

It was a steamy afternoon on the fringe of the wet season. The hunters had been in position above a water hole for some time, but hadn't yet fired one shot. They crouched and waited, whispered and waited, watched and waited, but nothing happened. In more than an hour their only game had been the incessant mosquitoes that they pinned against their skin with soft slaps. The backs of their hands itched with bites, sweat dripped down their faces and bubbled annoyingly under their uniforms, and the rocks dug sharply into their knees. It seemed as though it was a wasted journey. Then, suddenly, they heard the snap of a broken branch. There was a golden flash on the far side of the water hole.

Ddddd-ddddd-ddddd!

The gunfire shattered the silence, chips of bark flew off trees, the soldiers shouted and pointed wildly, and Longy held his breath. It was happening too quickly to register.

'There, there!'

The soldiers scurried over the rocks and rushed through the undergrowth until the leader, a few steps ahead of everyone else, yelled triumphantly. At his feet lay the most treasured and incredibly rare prize for any hunter in the jungle: a fully grown male tiger. Longy stared wonderingly at the magnificent beast: fierce eyes; enormous head; sleek, muscular body; powerful legs; and a shining coat. Even dead he was beautiful.

To the soldiers, the unexpected trophy would bring prestige and considerable money. Not only the skin, teeth and claws could be sold, but also the blood, as well as various organs. The gall bladder was especially sought after in the mysterious circles of Eastern medicine.

They packed up immediately, and arrived back at the ARVN base yelling and cheering, as though their good fortune had turned the tide of the entire war. Longy, arms raised in a victory pose, was swept along by the emotions. This was a glorious moment that was crowned when the callow hunter was presented with one of the tiger's gleaming eyeteeth.

Such activities were welcome distractions for the soldiers in a war that was dramatically changing complexion. In August 1972, two months before Longy's eighth birthday, the last US combat troops had withdrawn from Vietnam (the last Australian soldiers withdrew by December). At his office on the ARVN base, Hien contemplated his position, knowing the war would be much harder to win without the Americans. Would he and his family still be safe in Pleiku? Should he seek to change roles — perhaps move to Saigon, where there was greater protection?

As he pondered his options, the focus of the war shifted from the jungles of Vietnam to Paris, where, in late January 1973, international participation in the conflict officially ended when the Paris Peace Accords were signed. Of the three million Americans who had served in Vietnam, nearly 60 000 had been killed. The direct cost of the war was $US165 billion. The argument as to whether the USA should ever have entered the conflict will likely continue forever.

During its involvement, Australia committed nearly 50 000 personnel and 496 were killed. New Zealand, South Korean, Filipino and Thai soldiers also lost their lives as members of the so-called 'Free World' military services.

A ceasefire throughout the south followed the signing of the Paris Peace Accords, and as both Southern and Northern forces considered what would happen next, Hien had already made a decision. He'd grown weary of the day-to-day tactical analysis, his mind had frayed, and he'd questioned his worth. So he accepted a demotion to lieutenant colonel and became a chief protagonist in the prisoners-of-war exchange program.

Longy recognised that this was a period of immense change. After all, it was impossible not to question what was happening when the GIs were no longer seen in Pleiku's cafés and there were fewer silver dollars to be found in the streets. Did this mean the war was over?

'No,' insisted Hien. 'The Americans have gone, but the North remains.'

There was just a brief lull before fighting resumed. The South continued to receive weapons, ammunition and fuel from the Americans, the North was still being given similar assistance by China and the USSR, and the whole of Vietnam continued to suffer. In reality, the Peace Accords had done nothing more than formalise the withdrawal of international forces.

For Longy, the greatest changes were personal, most notably the freedom he enjoyed the older he became. His wanderings away from home lasted longer, and he stayed out later, often defying the military curfew. Hien and Teresa had accepted that their son's character couldn't be shaped by conventional rules; he may still have been a boy, but he needed to be treated as an adolescent, even if that meant introducing him to habits that most parents tried to protect their children from. By the time he was nine, Longy was not only allowed to smoke cigarettes, but his mother taught him how.

'Don't suck. Just take a little breath, let the taste relax you. Don't be in a hurry to finish.'

Longy didn't like the overpowering *Cam le* roll-ups, preferring his father's Salems or 555s, and although he wasn't a regular smoker, there were times when he puffed with Teresa in the market or shared a cigarette with Hien as they drove through Pleiku, the sight prompting pointed fingers and pangs of jealousy from Longy's school friends.

However, his parents still had limits, which were abruptly reached the day Teresa disturbed a friend of Hien's bodyguards tracing a cannon on Longy's shoulder with a pen. A needle and unopened ink bottle were next to him.

'Stop that right now! And get out!'

There was no room for argument — no child of hers was going to be a walking monument to the war, or anything else for that matter. The tattooist apologised, packed his bag and departed, knowing that he wouldn't be back. Teresa stood glaring at Longy, hands on hips. 'You can do what you like in a few years, but not now.'

Her son looked sheepishly at the outline on his skin; it would rub off with some spit and scratching, but the lesson couldn't be erased. He'd learnt that, whether he had a tattoo or not, it was his mother who drew the lines, and there were times they weren't to be crossed.

Teresa may have been more lenient with her little favourite than any of her other children, but when she needed to she could still rule Longy with a firmness that was never questioned. She was proud of her son's development, but towards the end of 1973 she had reason to wonder about his future, and that of her other children. After spending nine years in Pleiku, Hien decided it was time to move his family away from danger. Or would they be heading towards it? Either way, Longy was about to begin a new life as far removed from jungle tracks, mystical tribes and open spaces as a nine-year-old boy could ever imagine.

SEVEN

Saigon

Bow-legged riders on pushbikes, clanking, shuddering and rattling over potholed roads; circles of serious men playing cards; laughing boys kicking soccer balls; girls in thin dresses skipping to the beat of clapping hands; women squatting by the roadside, bananas for sale at their callused feet. Mothers, fathers, grandparents, children, all staring from doorways. Dogs wandering, cocks crowing, cats slinking. Spices spitting, noodles simmering. Quacking horns and squeaking brakes. Coffee shops, cigarettes and rock and roll ...

Saigon: a world that Longy couldn't peel his eyes from as he sat in a truck winding through the streets towards his new home.

The 500-kilometre trip from Pleiku had taken the Nguyen family more than two days. At night, they'd slept on top of one of the four trucks that were laden with a jumble of pushbikes, pots, pans, crockery, cupboards, tables, clothes, photos — all the possessions too valuable or practical to leave behind. By day they sat in the trucks' sauna-like cabins, feeling every bump of the slow, twisting journey from the jungle highlands to the river plains. They'd been stopped and inspected by soldiers, and had been forced to make diversions, chiefly through streams and low rivers where bridges had been destroyed.

Now they'd arrived.

Saigon, divided into districts, was more readily recognised by numbers than names. The Nguyens moved into District Three, a bustling area of markets, travelling vendors and small street-level shops below family homes that extended up one or more skinny storeys. The buildings of wood, tin or concrete crowded together near the main road. Others huddled even closer along the warrens of narrow lanes in which there was little room for pedestrians to change their minds, let alone direction.

The Nguyens bought a grand, somewhat unusual house that had three and half floors, the half being wedged between the ground and first floors — it had just a 6-foot ceiling, high enough to enable the small Vietnamese to stand without hunching over but low enough to give a feeling of permanent claustrophobia. The building was on the corner of a main street and a lane that stretched for hundreds of metres and fed tiny dirt alleys that crept out of sight around dark, mysterious corners.

The family lived on the highest two floors. Longy was given his own room at the very top, an indication that he remained his mother's favourite child; apart from James, the others all shared rooms. Perhaps Teresa knew it made more sense to isolate her most rebellious son than have him distracting everyone.

Whatever the reason, Longy was pleased to have his own space, because it not only gave him freedom but the chance to house a collection of animals. Within weeks of his arrival, he had in his room: a tank full of goldfish; a sleek, black jungle parrot in a cage; and a lean American pit bull terrier crossed with a Chinese fighting dog that looked more criminal than canine. The dog was a replacement for Salem and Lucky — both had to be left behind in Pleiku, a parting that caused Longy considerable anguish. Without hesitation he christened the pit bull Lucky as well, a fitting name considering it had been taken out of a hovel full of dogs for sale in Cholon, the Chinese section of the city. Like Longy, Lucky was beginning a new life. It was a savage animal with a history of snapping and grabbing at strangers, but with the uncanny sense that dogs have, it realised Longy was a friend and quietened down in his hands.

Longy considered all his animals as a link to his time in Pleiku, and a bond with nature that he was determined wouldn't be erased by city life. If he'd had his way he would have owned an even greater menagerie, but Teresa firmly shook her head when her son made the request, 'Can I get a monkey too?'

Below the mini-zoo and family quarters, the half-floor of the home was used for the kitchen and house-assistants' area, and the ground floor was fitted out for Teresa's newest business venture, the 'Thien Ly', a coffee shop named after a local flower. Through her colleagues in Pleiku she'd developed a network of contacts in Saigon long before the family had arrived, and as a result her business had a ready supply of coffee drinkers soon after she opened the doors for the first time. Word-of-mouth enhanced the customer base; once it was known in the district that the shop was run by a respectable army family, it began to flourish at a time when similar businesses were beginning to struggle.

From morning to night the powerful aroma of thick black coffee drifted outside, reeling in many passers-by, especially high-ranking army officers and businessmen. Tea, chocolate and cans of fruit cocktails in sickly sweet syrups were also served. There could be as many as forty people crammed around tables at any one time. They shared jokes, laughed, smoked, whispered in corners, or simply rested, silently catching a breath before venturing out into the hustle and bustle of the streets. When Longy wasn't needed to work — he helped make the coffee, and was a proficient cleaner of cups, glasses and tables — he sat on a stool at the side of the room near a small fish pond that had been built because he'd asked for it. The pond wasn't just another example of how spoilt Longy was, but a display of obvious wealth — any business that could sacrifice valuable space for such a luxury was obviously in a comfortable position.

As he watched the goldfish darting and flickering in the water, Longy remembered his days at the ARVN base. Would he ever return?

'No. Pleiku was just part of your life. You must now move on,' said his mother.

That was somewhat difficult when he was further reminded of his past by the sounds of rock and roll that twanged from a reel-to-reel tape machine Teresa had bought, hoping to create an upbeat Western ambience in the shop.

Of all the songs on the tape, it wasn't a heart-starting piece that stirred him the most but a melodic wandering of happiness — 'What a Wonderful World'. The soft, flowing music and the gravelly tones of Louis Armstrong were comforting, although Longy couldn't yet understand the words.

At that time, the closing weeks of 1973, 'wonderful' wasn't a fitting description for Vietnam. Although some people remained optimistic the South would win, others believed any resistance against the North was simply delaying the inevitable. The communists may have held only a scattering of quiet, sparsely populated areas in the south, but what would happen if they tried to build up their depleted forces again and, with the help of Soviet and Chinese aid, launched further attacks? Amid the differing opinions, there was one certainty: never, ever, ever underestimate the capabilities of the North, no matter what the circumstances.

This didn't stop President Thieu from pushing troops into areas near Saigon, and south of the city along the Mekong River delta, in a bid to overrun the enemy. Although this was successful, there were worries that the ARVN forces had been spread too thin, leaving other areas across the South vulnerable to attacks. Thieu ignored the concerns.

A sliding economy was a more palpable indicator that all wasn't well in the south. In 1972 prices had risen by 26 per cent in Saigon, and were more dramatic in 1973 when inflation in the city rocketed to 45 per cent, and the price of petrol increased by 400 per cent.

The consequences of the Americans' departure had also impacted heavily on the South. When the troops went so did the dollars, leaving behind businesses, most notably bars and restaurants, that were forced to downsize or close altogether. This created a flow-on effect through the entire economy: jobs and money were becoming increasingly hard to find. As it struggled to adapt to its constantly devalued currency, Saigon also faced another problem: the influx of rural dwellers and peasants. Tin-hut shantytowns sprang up, and the amount of people living on the streets reached new, immeasurable levels. These weren't yet desperate times, but a growing number of people were beginning to knock on the door of despair.

Despite the difficulties, the Nguyens built a comfortable lifestyle. The success of the coffee shop was testament to Teresa's shrewd business sense. Whenever possible, she converted her profits into the more desired form of currency: namely, small rolls of gold that she hid at home. She remained the family's main money-earner as Hien, now ranked as a colonel, collected modest pay for his new role as a teacher at a college for high-ranking officers and chiefs of staff at Long Binh on the outskirts of Saigon. Nevertheless, his wage was considerably higher than that of the poorly paid foot soldiers, many of whom were trying to support families but found their incomes and morale being increasingly sapped by the state of the economy. This was as worrying a sign as any for those who felt the South was slipping into a dangerous state.

For a boy finding his way in a new and exciting environment there were much more important things to consider, like meeting people, making friends, and learning the ways of the city. With Lucky by his side, Longy explored different areas of his neighbourhood each day, always alerting his senses, gaining his bearings and taking note of everything he saw. There were the tight lanes which people used during the day to cut time off their journeys to the markets, and where more than an occasional cyclo-rider sought a quiet spot to sleep during the siesta heat. The same lanes at night became dark, treacherous stretches of uncertainty in which the only light to be seen seeped out timidly from underneath the closed doors and windows of nearby houses.

The people who lived in these lanes ate their fresh *pho* at their doorsteps, mended the chain or tyres on their pushbikes, strung washing across lines attached between windows, and always had one eye on the happenings in their neighbourhood. The peasant women sat like statues by the main road, their faces hidden under their *Non la*, the conical leaf hats that were held in place by chin straps made from sweat-soaked handkerchiefs or fraying pieces of string. There were men dressed in tailored shirts and trousers; they were wealthy enough to afford motorbikes which they wove through the traffic that was dominated by bicycles. Longy saw it all: the soldiers passing through in Jeeps; the shallow, stinking canal only minutes from home; the young men rattling sticks with bells, advertising their services as street-side masseurs; the lean, mean cocks in bamboo cages marking time until their next fight; the clothes shops; the cafés; the barbers; the drink stalls; the coconut sellers ...

Longy was never afraid to cold-sell himself, boldly walking up to anyone and saying, 'I'm Longy. My father is a colonel at Long Binh and my mother runs the coffee shop.' And with those words, Longy declared that a whole new cycle of his life had started.

Despite being so young, Longy was an imposing sight on the streets — a strong, confident boy with a dog that looked as though it could take a bite out of a tank if needed. Longy was eager to display this image of toughness because he thought it was the best way to earn respect. One morning within weeks of his arrival he finished his chores in the shop, kissed his mother goodbye and headed out for a typical day of discovery with Lucky. They turned left out the door, took a few sprightly steps, then left again into the lane. In the distance, Longy noticed a boy in shorts and a shirt walking towards him. He was a stranger — a threat, perhaps. Longy immediately saw the impending crossing of paths as an opportunity to stake his territory. He stopped, leant against the outside wall of his home, puffed out his chest and lifted himself to look as strong and confident as he could. Sensing his master's sudden tension, Lucky stiffened, pricked his ears and growled.

The boy approached. He was of similar height to Longy with broad shoulders and wiry, loose limbs; his angular face was defined by jutting cheekbones and a high, prominent forehead. He slowed and exchanged glances with Longy; then, before the two youngsters could contemplate what to do next, Lucky forced the issue by springing at the boy's waist. Longy did nothing, content to watch his dog snatch viciously at the air in search of the flesh of the panicking, back-pedalling victim. A piece of shirt was torn, and a swatting hand narrowly avoided the angry snap of teeth. The boy twisted and turned, dancing on his toes as his attacker barked and bit, bit and barked.

Then suddenly: 'Lucky! No! Down!'

The dog retreated to Longy's side.

'Sorry. I haven't had Lucky for long.'

The boy nodded, inspecting the damage to his shirt.

'My name is Longy.'

'I'm Truong.'

They shook hands uneasily, their first movements in what would become an incredibly close, heart-warming friendship.

Truong lived just 30 metres along the lane on the opposite side of the road to the Nguyen home, but his existence was worlds apart from that enjoyed by Longy. Truong was one of four children — two boys and two girls — in a fragmented family in which the mother and father had separated yet continued to live in the same tiny house that also sheltered Truong's paternal grandparents. His grandfather added further strain to the situation because of his addiction to opium.

Truong needed a good friend, and he found it in Longy. Their friendship developed as they spent more and more time together; many of their activities were impromptu, often starting when Truong appeared at the back wall of the Nguyen home and yelled to Longy from the laneway.

A grinning face would poke out from a bedroom window on the top floor of the home and announce, 'I'm on my way.'

When Longy wanted to make contact with his neighbour, he didn't waste time or energy sauntering down the alley — he simply used a slingshot cut from the flexible wood of a guava tree. From his window he could see his target: the solid steel gate at the front of Truong's home. Loading his weapon with a ball bearing — having obtained a ready supply from a nearby pushbike repairman — Longy ensured that there were no straying pedestrians, then drew back the rubber band, took aim and fired.

PING!

Within seconds Truong would appear, tentatively treading towards the gate while looking up at Longy's window, ready to duck for cover if he saw he was in the line of another shot.

Once they joined each other in the laneway they'd plan their day, then off they'd go, mischief often in their thoughts, and Lucky usually in a much more agreeable mood than when he had first cast eyes on Truong, trotting happily behind with tongue hanging out, part of a slobbery smile. They'd roam the alleys and streets; sometimes they'd just sit and chat or play soccer. This may have been a pleasant enough way to pass some time, but Longy was always eager for more daring pursuits; and although his friend was at first wary about following Longy's lead, both boys soon raised enough trouble in the neighbourhood to become known for the infamous thrill of stealing melons from gardens and throwing them at unsuspecting passers-by. They were boys being boys.

And Longy, being Longy, was always looking for more daring pursuits, even if it meant putting himself in danger and trying something alone. And alone was how he found himself the first time he was tempted to swim in the Saigon River, a muddy waterway that was hundreds and hundreds of metres across at its widest part. Unlike the undisturbed streams near Pleiku this river was never allowed to rest: it was churned by propellers of all shapes and sizes, from the homemade spindle-like contraptions fixed to the boats of vegetable growers heading to market, to the gigantic steel fans of the navy ships that powered up and down the channel. In addition to the traffic, clusters of weeds with long roots twisting below the surface made the river a dangerous playground for anyone bold enough to swim in its waters. But that wasn't enough to deter Longy.

'Come on,' he said to Truong, shedding his shirt and second-hand jeans.

'No, I'm not going in, it's not safe.'

Longy replied by rushing into the water and diving until he was out of sight. Truong waited anxiously for several seconds before he saw his friend's head burst through the water followed by the sound of a devilish giggle.

'It's beautiful. So warm.'

Dangers or not, Longy would never give up what became a regular pleasure. Sometimes he was content to float on his back near the water's edge; on other occasions he ploughed onwards until he was a mere dot that Truong strained to see when watching from the bank, or occasionally from the water when he dared to go in, always remaining close to the shore. On his return, Longy would frequently promise: 'When I grow older I will swim all the way to the other side and back again.'

Truong never doubted that his friend would; he had never met anyone like him, as he explains all these years later:

> It didn't take long for everyone to know Longy. Just a few weeks, and after a few months he was the king. He was very different. He had a very strong body. He was much bigger than many older boys. He frightened them. He walked the streets like he was the boss of Saigon.

Truong's ceaseless admiration, which at times bordered on worship, was enhanced by the stories he heard from his oldest sister, who attended the same school as Longy. This place of learning, Le Bao Tinh, was situated in a lane a few minutes' walk from the Nguyen home. As opposed to the vast space Longy had enjoyed at the schools in Pleiku, his new school was tucked behind walls that were topped with curling strands of razor wire glinting in the sun. The classrooms were in a multistorey block that overlooked a characterless quadrangle.

Longy and his youngest sister, Thao, were the only members of the Nguyen family who went to Le Bao Tinh; James and Maria were at university in Saigon, Van and Lam were at different senior schools, and Linh was still at home. Without his older brothers and sisters around, Longy considered one of his most important school duties to be protecting Thao, who had been the occasional victim of cruel barbs in Pleiku because she had a hare lip. Longy wasn't going to let this happen at Le Bao Tinh, and he was a frequent visitor to his sister's class between lessons. Prospective tormentors realised that if they dared so much as glance sideways at the girl, it was enough to make her big brother clench his fists and glare angrily.

Apart from the spontaneous playground spats in which boys kicked first and thought later, Longy was rarely confronted — his presence, when added to the stories that were told about him, was more than enough to demand respect. Some boys had seen him when he first displayed his ability at the local tae kwon do class, where he performed each pattern as though it was tailored just for him. Others had caught glimpses of him on the rooftop of the family home where he fought his shadow, practised moves by spearing his hands into a pole he'd covered in cloth, and did chin-ups on window ledges and bars. His appearance further enhanced the don't-mess-with-me image: he had hard, black knuckles; forearms that seemed as thick as some boys' legs; a powerful chest; and alert eyes that flitted from side to side, incessantly sizing up the situation.

However, there was another side to Longy that the boys didn't see, a gentler side moulded by Teresa. She frequently sent her son out armed with bags of used coffee and tobacco collected from discarded cigarettes that could be given away to the beggars and peasants living on the streets.

She was also kind to Lady Xoi, a middle-aged woman in a tattered plain tunic, tired *Non-la* and scruffy sandals who wanted to set up her cigarette cart directly outside the coffee shop. Other businesspeople had been known to shoo such vendors away; Teresa not only welcomed her, but refused to sell cigarettes in her shop because she knew it would affect the woman's meagre income.

'Why?' Longy asked his mother.

'Because some people aren't as lucky as us.'

While extremely influential, Teresa wasn't Longy's only teacher. Just a few blocks away from the Nguyen home was a barbershop owned by My, a quietly spoken man in his early fifties whose only vice was whisky. He was of immaculate appearance: his short-back-and-sides cut never had a hair out of place; his trim moustache was devoid of any errant hairs; he dressed proudly in crisply ironed shirts and trousers, and his black shoes were always shiny. In short, he was a prime advertisement for his business. He had lived his entire life in the area and knew the streets and its people as well as the scissors that seemed like extra fingers on his dextrous hands.

Longy had first gone to the barbershop during one of his explorations. After walking through the door, he introduced himself and, without invitation, sat in the shop, watching and listening. Much laughter and eager conversation bounced around the mirrored walls that captured a moment from a dozen angles. There were also silent times when My was a study of concentration as he edged his scissors along a fringe, or steadily worked a steaming cut-throat razor across an outstretched neck. Longy was most intrigued by the barber's practice of strapping a small vibrating machine to the back of his hand. The machine sent a throbbing pulse through his fingers, providing a vigorous massage for the customer's scalp, neck and upper back. It — and similar contraptions — was a legacy of the war, originally brought over by the American GIs.

In between these buzzing massages and the snips and slices, My and Longy talked, their sentences woven by questions and answers:

'Where have you come from, Longy?'

'Pleiku. How long have you been a barber?'

'Ah, Pleiku in the central highlands. I started long before you were born, and how many brothers and sisters do you have?'

'I have three brothers and three sisters. Maria is the oldest, she is nearly twenty. James is my oldest brother. Is it hard cutting hair?'

And so it went.

My was a very wise man. He thought carefully and spoke slowly, choosing his words precisely when offering advice: 'Longy, be careful of walking the streets at night. They can be dangerous ... Keep learning tae kwon do, it will help you in the years to come ... Never take your family for granted. They will always be there for you, whether in body or spirit ... Always be nice to girls, because there will come a time when you will fall in love, and they have good memories ...'

My's wisdom was combined with a caring nature, and Longy recognised someone he could listen to, learn from and trust. As time passed, he called his confidant and mentor 'Uncle Ba', a term of immeasurable respect: the use of 'Uncle' showed that Longy considered My to be part of his family; '*Ba*', the number three, referred to his level of importance (in families, the number two, *Hai*, is the highest level, normally reserved for parents; one is not used).

Longy also had another name for My, one which he only used when the two were alone.

'Uncle Ba, you are the "Street Master". No-one knows more than you do.'

In turn, the Street Master christened Longy 'Billy the Kid', in reference to the popular comic book hero named after the American Wild West outlaw. Longy wasn't on the wrong side of the law, but My recognised his cowboy-like qualities: he had a confident swagger, a fearless look, and a sense of adventure that wouldn't leave him out of place perched in a saddle, digging his heels into a horse galloping full speed across the plains of New Mexico.

'Here he comes, Billy the Kid,' Uncle Ba would announce every time the grinning boy walked into the shop. Longy became a regular visitor, arriving most mornings before school to check his appearance and listen to whatever the barber had to say. Then away he'd go, his hair shining brightly with brilliantine and his face fresh after an invigorating cleansing under a hot towel — the quintessential boy about town.

By the time he turned ten, nearly a year after arriving in Saigon, Longy had no regrets about leaving Pleiku. No matter what the time of day he was always busy, squeezing action out of every second. Sport in particular provided many hours of fun. He was a lively goalkeeper, highly sought after by the local soccer teams; he excelled at table tennis; continued to push himself further across the Saigon River; had flown through the blue-belt grades on his way to earning a brown belt in tae kwon do; and as a spectator he was enthralled by the strange matches he sometimes saw the Australian civilians play near the army college at which his father taught. These were highly physical encounters — when the players weren't kicking or carrying an oval-shaped ball, they were piling on top of each other in heaps. Longy doubted he'd ever have any reason or need to understand what he called 'olive ball', but he certainly enjoyed watching it.

When Longy's sporting pursuits were added to his work in the coffee shop, his wanderings with Truong and Lucky, and his time at school, he led a very full life indeed. He didn't seem to have a worry in the world: he was happy with his own existence, and all his family seemed content as well, especially his father, who was much safer than he had been for the past twenty years. Life was good. Or so he thought.

The reality was that Saigon was slipping further into an economic, social and military quagmire. The August 1974 resignation of US President Richard Nixon following the Watergate scandal placed further stress on the Thieu regime, which was claiming to be already struggling because of the gradual reduction of resources provided by the Americans. Nixon's departure hastened the process, as the new president, Gerald Ford, sought to distance his country from the war. Thieu insisted his military was short of ammunition, but a US inspection report suggested there were substantial stockpiles being kept near Saigon. Corruption in the military remained a curse, and consequently large amounts of petrol were siphoned off to be sold on the black market. The remaining fuel was tightly rationed — even the Jeep allowances for generals were dramatically cut. When combined with the inadequate, and at times impossible, maintenance of machines, the soldiers were forced to slog long distances on foot. They were thrust into fighting a poor man's war — which was an experience the Viet Cong knew well. All the problems were weakening Thieu's grip on power, but despite this and the growing push from inside the South for some sort of peace settlement, the president refused to act, clinging to the belief that the Americans would re-enter the war if the South Vietnamese position became too desperate.

The people on the streets of Saigon, however, were mostly unaware of how dangerous the situation was becoming. With little sense of their city's vulnerability, they continued to scrape together just enough work and money to provide for themselves and their families. It was easier for the middle and upper classes, many members of which still had viable businesses, although most weren't as profitable as they'd once been. These were challenging times. For the majority of Saigonese, life was about day-to-day and, occasionally, minute-to-minute survival, as Longy discovered one evening.

It was late. Only a few weak lights lit up the neighbourhood that was alive with meal-time chatter and laughter. As he often did, Longy was eating with Truong at the front of his best friend's home. They'd just finished playing soccer, and Longy hadn't yet taken his boots off — another sign of his wealth, because few boys could afford to play in anything other than bare feet. On the opposite side of the lane, in a two-storey wooden house, an old woman was preparing dinner for her family in a kitchen crammed into one corner of a room that was also used for sleeping.

Years of routine had shaped her every movement: she knew how to turn in the congested space without disturbing any implement, or knocking herself against a wall or shelf. But in recent times age had caught up with her, and she was no longer as nimble and sure of herself as she once was. Every day she was reminded of her mortality by a coffin that had been placed in the house in preparation for her death. Her time was running out, and yet she lived as she always had. Making dinner was just part of her routine: cut the vegetables, wash the rice, and place everything in pots to be brought to the boil on a small kerosene cooker. Nothing ever changed ... except for this time.

As she lit the kerosene cooker, the woman didn't give a moment's thought to the flowing tail of her *Ao dai* flicking around behind her — and skimming the flame. By the time she realised her clothes were alight, her movements had spread the fire to several parts of the kitchen. In her panic she tipped the cooker over, spilling kerosene and sending flames sprinting across the floor and leaping into other parts of the room, towards a drum of cooking oil.

Longy was midway through a mouthful of food when he and Truong heard the explosion. Longy was gone in a flash, his boot studs clopping on the tar across the lane and skimming the top of a gate at the front of the crackling house. He paused. An orange glow flickered behind a window and the air was thick with smoke. Just metres away an old man lay wheezing, unaware that his wife, who'd started the fire, was crawling towards him. Both were safe. Without a thought Longy dashed past them into the building, disappearing into the smoke that scratched his eyes and lungs, forcing him to squint and cough. He took a few steps and turned towards a staircase leading to the second floor. Through the choking darkness he saw two legs lying halfway up the stairs, the rest of the body shrouded in smoke. He rushed towards the screaming figure; it was a small boy. Longy grabbed him by the shirt with one hand, the other hand shielding his face as he dragged the child out of the house. In his urgency he accidentally trod on the head of the grandfather, who groaned but didn't move. Longy dropped the boy near the old man and turned back towards the house. By now the flames were licking both storeys and the dense smoke made it impossible to see more than a few metres ahead. It was too dangerous to attempt to go inside again.

Longy looked around him, but it was hard to distinguish anyone through the smoke and darkness. People had already gathered, and there was much pointing and shouting as men hurried off to collect buckets of water in a futile attempt to stop the blaze. In the chaos, Longy chose to sneak away and watch from a distance. The previous few minutes had been a high-speed blur. He'd acted on impulse. He didn't understand what he'd done until he returned home and told his mother. Even then, he downplayed the incident. He hadn't gone into the house looking to save lives, but had been drawn by the thrill of adventure, a new experience, a challenge.

The fire was extinguished only after the house had burnt to the ground. It was then the true extent of the damage was known. A woman had died — the mother of the boy Longy had saved. Amid the grief that followed, there was also curiosity. Who was the anonymous hero who'd prevented a second life from being lost? Rumours leapt across the neighbourhood as quickly as any flame. A boy fitting Longy's description had been seen entering the house, but the witnesses couldn't be certain because of the smoke and dim light.

Over the following days, Longy became used to answering the same question wherever he went: 'Was it you who went into the burning house?'

His response never varied: a shake of the head followed by a firm 'no'. He was afraid to acknowledge his actions because he was ashamed that he hadn't returned to the house in search of the mother. It didn't matter that he'd saved one life — in his mind, he should have saved two lives. Although Truong quietly alerted some people to the truth, Longy steadfastly refused to confirm it.

For those searching for the facts, there was a subtle sign of Longy's presence at the time of the fire. For days afterwards, the mourning grandfather sported dotted bruises on the side of his face which, upon closer inspection, resembled the pattern of boot studs.

As 1974 wound down, another incident offered more tangible proof of Longy's standing on the streets, and among his school friends. At just ten years of age he was invited to try for his black belt. For one of the few times in his life, he feared failure, believing that he was surely too young to succeed. But after arriving at the grading venue, an enormous hall on the outskirts of Saigon, he was encouraged by the presence of boys only a couple of years older than he was. There were about 300 hopefuls, a mixture of ages, occupations and belt colours all striving for greater rewards.

As Longy walked into the hall, a tiny figure in his stiff white canvas uniform — he had outgrown his initial hessian outfit — no-one seemed to take much notice of him despite the three stripes that ran across his brown belt, signifying an impressive rank for someone so young. Around him there were soldiers, university students, even priests, many of whom already had black belts hugging their waists. It was an intimidating environment.

Longy was placed in a group of boys mostly in their midteens. Sitting nervously in a corner of the hall, he watched the other aspirants going through their paces and waited for the words that would launch him into action.

'Duy Long Nguyen.'

'Yes, sir.'

An instructor stood before him, a third-degree black belt with a military presence who read a collection of other names from a piece of paper on a clipboard, each time stopping just long enough to hear the response of every boy before continuing without any hint of emotion: 'You will be paired off for two-minute rounds of sparring.'

Two minutes. More than enough time for Longy to be bashed. Each opponent in the rotation hammered him; the thud of feet hitting his padded leather helmet became uncomfortably repetitive. Longy was simply too small and not physically strong enough to match his rivals — but mentally he didn't buckle. He stood his ground, refusing to be scared by anyone and, despite being out-muscled, he landed enough blows to show he wasn't wholly out of his depth.

He further demonstrated his impeccable technique when he was required to break a roof tile with his fist and display his spin kick. Then followed the discipline: standing in front of the instructor and reciting, almost shouting, the rules he lived by every time he walked into a tae kwon do class: 'I respect my teacher ... I respect my opponents ... I respect myself ...'

Lastly he performed his patterns, the tireless hours of repetition on the rooftop of the family home having ensured that every single movement was as natural to him as breathing.

Then came the wait. If the two-minute sparring sessions had seemed painfully long, the two hours sitting outside the hall were insufferable. Longy passed the time by chatting to the other boys in his group. They quizzed each other as though they were students who'd just finished their end of school exams.

The boys' answers, and the endless minutes of uncertainty, created a maelstrom of worry for Longy. What would he say to his school friends if he failed? What would he say to his mother? Had he done as well as he could have? Was he really good enough to earn a black belt?

The questions were still tormenting him when everyone was ushered back into the hall. One at a time, names were read out by the chief examiner. Longy could barely wait any longer.

'Duy Long Nguyen.'

Longy sprang to his feet, his heart suddenly racing.

'Yes, sir.'

'*Huyen Dai De Nhut Dang.*'

The Chief Examiner acknowledged Longy with a brief nod, then called the next name without altering his impassive approach. Longy sat down quietly and looked around, feeling for the briefest of moments that all eyes were on him. He replayed the chief examiner's words: *Huyen Dai De Nhut Dang ... Huyen Dai De Nhut Dang ... Huyen Dai De Nhut Dang.* He couldn't believe it!

Huyen Dai De Nhut Dang: black belt, first degree.

EIGHT

The Fall

*'Fellow citizens, in the past days you have wondered
why so many people have quietly left the country.
I want to tell you, dear citizens, that this is our
beloved land. Please be courageous and stay here
and accept the fate of God.'*
DUONG VAN MINH, PRESIDENT, SOUTH VIETNAM, 28 APRIL 1975

If only the South showed as much fighting potential as Duy Long Nguyen, black belt, first degree. While Longy had every reason to be optimistic about his future conquests, President Thieu's corrupt and blinkered government was unwittingly leading its country into increasingly dangerous and unstable territory. The warning signs were all too apparent in December 1974 when the North attacked the Phuoc Long province 70 kilometres northwest of Saigon. By January 1975 Phuoc Long had fallen to the communists, who had used the attack to monitor the United States' response. Washington did nothing, prompting a growing feeling of optimism in Hanoi where the PAVN's commander in chief, General Van Tien Dung, was busy plotting a major offensive for later in the year, leading to what he planned would be their biggest and most decisive assault, in 1976.

In the weeks following its success at Phuoc Long, the PAVN built up its troops in preparation for attacks on Corps I and II. By March it had claimed the town of Ban Me Thout, 250 kilometres north of Saigon. President Thieu responded by making a critical decision that in effect rolled out the welcome mat to his enemies: he demanded the evacuation of troops from the central highlands, with the intention of redeploying them further south, closer to the more heavily populated and resource-rich Saigon and the Mekong delta. This left the north of the country, except for the coastal areas, poorly protected. It was the beginning of the end.

In mid-March Pleiku, the foundation stone of Longy's life, was abandoned. Highway 19, the main thoroughfare heading east to the coast, had been blocked by the Viet Cong and PAVN, forcing the ARVN troops to change direction and head south along a much smaller route. At first the departure went smoothly, but as the military convoys continued to roll out of town, the civilians who were left behind started to panic. Sensing they were in danger if they remained, thousands fled after the troops. Some were on foot, others on pushbikes or in motor vehicles, and all were transported by fear. No thought had been given to their reactions, and suddenly a road that was more used to the laboured grind of logging trucks became an artery clogged by panic and confusion. It was an irresistible target for the North.

Three days after the first troops left Pleiku, the PAVN launched artillery attacks along various sections of the route. The ARVN retaliated where it could. The conflict turned the road into a wash of red. Tens of thousands of civilians and soldiers were killed (estimates of the total amount of people travelling the route vary between 100 000 and 200 000) and for those who survived the bullets there remained the prospect of a slower death caused by thirst, hunger and heat exhaustion. There were similar retreats across other parts of the central highlands. In Saigon, the horrific images of the so-called 'convoy of tears' were shown on television. In the living room of their home, the Nguyens watched the fuzzy black and white pictures in disbelief. The grim reality was that the South was crumbling, and it was only a matter of time before the North was landing on Saigon's doorstep.

ARVN soldiers continued to retreat; others deserted their posts; civilians fled in immeasurable masses; and all the while, their enemies advanced. The imperial city of Hue soon tumbled, and in Danang desperate soldiers shoved aside women and children, trampling them in their haste to board departing aircraft. As planes taxied down runways, people clung to landing gear, wing tips, whatever they could reach; some were crushed, others fell to their deaths. In Saigon, the images bled across TV screens as thousands of families considered whether to flee or stay put to wait and see what would happen. Thieu's only response was to seek help from the Americans, but President Ford was unmoved. The United States was out of the war. Period.

By the beginning of April the top half of South Vietnam had come under communist control, and although no-one could have forecast the furious speed of the collapse, it was becoming obvious to the North that it wouldn't need to wait until 1976 to launch its all-out assault.

While television pictures and the crackling radio news of the BBC World Service painfully described nearly every incident to the Nguyen family, nothing underscored the gravity of the situation more than the unexpected arrival of Teresa's brother, Dieu. He was beyond tears: 'I've cried them all away.'

His wife and five children had arrived in Saigon after fleeing Hue by boat just before the arrival of the invading troops. Amid the swarm and panic of people leaving, somewhere, somehow, Dieu had been separated from his eight-year-old son, Tho, whom he now believed was dead.

Dieu was unable to be comforted, and unwilling to believe that he and his remaining family had a future. They arranged to live in a house not far from the Nguyen home. In the days ahead, the crowded living conditions couldn't prevent the emptiness they all felt.

Throughout all the dramas, Hien tried to remain strong for his immediate family and relatives. After the Americans had first withdrawn he had voiced his concern about dwindling supplies, but other than that he kept his fears and concerns to himself. He knew how serious the situation was and continually considered his family's position.

By now the ARVN's troops were hopelessly outnumbered — regular forces totalled just 90 000 against the North's 300 000 — and generals and other high-ranking officers were on the run, leaving behind a disintegrating rabble of soldiers. Equipment had been abandoned, stolen, sold on the black market or destroyed; refugees from the central highlands and coast were flooding Saigon; word was spreading that US embassy officials were planning to leave amid reports of 'black flights' arranged by the Americans to evacuate specially chosen Vietnamese; and then, on the evening of 21 April, President Thieu announced his resignation live on television. The Nguyen family watched the once incredibly powerful man tearfully read a prepared speech. There was disbelief, and they wondered what would happen now. Hien quietly contemplated their position. A fiercely proud and loyal man, he made his decision: they would all remain where they were.

Under new president General Duong Van Minh, hasty attempts for peace were made, but these were too late. Saigon was going to fall; it was only a matter of when.

Longy understood what was happening, but with the blind faith that childhood can give, he imagined the Americans and ARVN special forces joining together one final time to destroy the enemy and save Saigon — just like the endings he'd seen in his mother's movie theatre.

Throughout early April Longy had gone to school, but as the situation deteriorated after Thieu's resignation, he was barred from leaving home. Teresa had prepared, stocking up with food and water in case the family had to bunker down, as they had during the Tet Offensive.

Across Saigon, fear walked with every footstep. Each day there were reports that communist troops were moving closer to the edges of the city. Twenty-five kilometres away ... 20 ... 15 ... 10. Then, on 28 April, the day after a series of rockets had rained on the city, the North launched its only air strike of the war in a bombing raid on the airport.

By now, mass hysteria had gripped Saigon. Newspapers carried advertisements placed by Vietnamese women seeking foreign husbands, and Westerners in the streets were stopped by Vietnamese pleading to be evacuated, their demands encouraged by the news that the 'black flights' were no longer just a way out for selected people, but for anyone who was rich or persuasive enough to find an American sponsor. And on the city's outskirts long lines of people were coming and going, suitcases in hands, babies on backs, terror in every eye.

From his home, Longy watched storm clouds gathering in the distance. Crashes of thunder and ground fire from ARVN gunners boomed over the city, and fingers of lightning stretched across the sky as though trying to grab the US helicopters and planes that were full of evacuees counting every second to safety. On one occasion the thump of churning blades was much closer than normal; Longy looked out his bedroom window and saw a small chopper landing on a nearby rooftop where a group of white people, probably a family of Americans, scurried on board, soon to become a fading mark on the horizon.

Rooftops weren't only landing pads — they had become watchtowers for hastily assembled police units. One vantage point was on a building opposite the Nguyen home. Surrounded by sandbags, with their machine guns directed at the streets, patrolmen sat and waited. No-one knew just what would happen when the communists arrived. The pessimists suggested there would be widespread death and bloodshed; those with greater belief in human nature hoped a quiet surrender would offer the prospect of a relatively peaceful transition.

As the enemy closed in, the city was already pulsing with violence. Deserted businesses and homes were being looted, and sporadic gunfire punctuated both day and night. After one burst of bullets Longy rushed out onto the balcony.

'Get back inside!' yelled Teresa. But her demand was overridden by her son's curiosity. Longy looked down to catch sight of two ARVN soldiers sprinting away from a man lying dead on the street, blood from several wounds seeping onto the tar. The police from across the road were rushing down from their post, and by the time they arrived at the scene a crowd surrounded the body, including Longy, who'd sneaked out when his mother's back was turned. Weaving through the throng, he made it to the front. The man's crimson chest was covered in holes. His tailored shirt and trousers suggested he'd been in business. There was also a white strip of flesh above the man's wrist where once a piece of jewellery had sat. Through a gap in the crowd Longy noticed a scantily dressed, obviously poor man fastidiously inspecting a watch ... In these times, one person's misfortune was another's good luck.

The incident had been a distraction for Longy, who was growing restless being trapped at home when so much was happening on the streets. All he could do was watch and wait. As there was now no television reportage, the only reliable source of information was the radio.

By 29 April the skies were frenetic as helicopters ferried Americans and a few fortunate Vietnamese to US Navy ships offshore. The emergency evacuation codenamed Operation Frequent Wind was under way, and the anguish and desperation of those left behind was mounting beyond control. Thousands tried to scale the walls of the US embassy in central Saigon in a bid to reach the choppers. Nearby, charred remains of sensitive war documents spiralled into the air in columns of smoke. People gathered everywhere in the streets, beating on the vehicles that were carrying evacuees to fly-out points. A woman threw her baby at a bus in the hope that it would land inside, but it was crushed under the wheels. Others massed outside any building where they knew Americans worked or lived. On the rooftop of the CIA offices, a panicked crush pushed towards departing helicopters. Some people risked their lives by breaking cordons and launching themselves at the aircraft, hoping they would be dragged on board, others held onto the choppers' skids and were lifted above the ground, only to be dragged down by the chains of people hanging onto their feet. Vietnamese soldiers recklessly fired pistols above their heads, the shots barely heard above the screams and the whirl of rotor blades.

In the Nguyen living room there was quiet. Teresa knelt in prayer below a painting of the Virgin Mary, and Hien sat wondering about the fate that awaited him, and what it would mean for his family. Would he become a prisoner? Perhaps shot at point-blank range? He'd already heard the lengths that some soldiers were going to in order to avoid detection; none was more excruciating than the burning off of anti-North tattoos by pouring alcohol onto the skin then applying the flame from a cigarette lighter. Even if he had tattoos Hien would never have taken such a drastic, and questionably futile, step. Certainly some marks could be removed; army papers, uniforms and medals could also be destroyed; but, short of killing everyone, nothing would prevent traitors — those desperate and weak enough to change sides at the final hour — from providing whatever information they had to the new regime. This was simply a fact of war, one that Hien knew could destroy him.

'When the VC comes, what will happen?' Longy asked his father.

'I do not know, but let us hope that we will be happy and safe, and that we have each other.'

Hien's voice was strained. His bloodshot eyes peered through glasses that had become much thicker in recent times and deep lines of worry ran across his forehead. He was tired, and much older than he had ever looked before. Longy felt for his father, but he was also angry. Was Hien partly to blame for what was happening? Were the Americans? How could the ARVN allow this to happen? The South had always been going to win — Hien had told his son as much. Hadn't it?

By the early evening of 29 April, Saigon had plunged into new depths of destruction. Violent, angry mobs stormed through the streets, upturning vehicles and setting fire to buildings. Looters ripped homes apart, taking refrigerators, furniture, televisions, sinks, clothes, radios — anything that could be carried. Most damaging of all were the rumours that the communists were planning widespread carnage. But the truth was that the slaughter of a city had already begun.

Throughout the night, helicopters continued their shuttle runs between rooftops, runways and ships. More than 5000 Vietnamese were among the 6000–7000 evacuated by Frequent Wind. Many more thousands had left the city on barges and boats. The final tally of US-assisted evacuees during April 1975 was about 65 000. However, when the very last chopper left the US embassy just before 8 a.m. on the 30th, thousands more were stranded, their futures in the hands of their enemies who had just entered the city.

By that time, Longy had been awake for hours. Like many in this city of some four million people, he'd had a mostly restless sleep. After the final evacuation chopper had departed Saigon fell quiet — an unexpected twist considering the gloomy predictions by some residents that communist troops would make a bullet-studded entrance, shooting down everyone and everything in their path. But as the North's convoy of tanks and trucks approached the city centre, there wasn't the need to fire a single shot.

It was midday when the first tank crashed through the main gate of the Presidential Palace. Others followed, forming a semicircle in the deserted courtyard. Inside the palace, President General Minh waited to hand over power, but when North Vietnamese Colonel Bui Tin arrived, he shook his head.

'There is no question of you transferring power. Your power has crumbled. You can't give up what you don't have.'

The war was finally over. Estimations of the final Vietnamese death toll during the conflict vary greatly, but officially it is believed that the North and VC lost more than one million soldiers, and Southern forces suffered a quarter as many deaths. A further four million civilians were either killed or injured. Whatever the true figures, this was a tragedy of immense proportions.

Moments after midday on 30 April 1975, a blue and red flag with the yellow star of the Viet Cong was unfurled by a soldier standing on the balcony of the Presidential Palace. It was the 'Day of Great Victory' for the North, but resentful Saigonese labelled the fall of their city as 'National Hatred Day'. Communism had arrived, but the unity of a nation was very much in transit.

NINE

One Month in a Lifetime

Did you hear about the VC soldiers who broke into a house and assumed battle positions when they saw a fridge? They thought it was the entrance to a tunnel, so they shot it before opening it. And what about the VC who dangled a fishing line into a toilet bowl hoping to catch his dinner? Or the one who ran away when he saw the doors to an elevator open! Whether these jokes were urban myths or fact, it didn't matter to those Saigonese who considered the Viet Cong primitive.

Would they be dangerous, though? In the days immediately after the fall of Saigon, the streets and homes were full of fear. But Hien and Teresa decided life had to return to normal as soon as possible until they were told otherwise. This normality included opening the coffee shop, complete with Western music belting out. There was only one obvious change to the Nguyen household — after twenty years of military service, Hien no longer had a job to go to.

And he was in no hurry to reflect, nor look forward and seek other work. In this time of immense uncertainty it was best to keep a very low profile, especially for someone with such a high ranking in the ARVN.

Allowed back onto the streets the day after the fall, Longy didn't need to wander too far to see the signs of defeat. Just a few blocks away a South Vietnamese helicopter hung from the rooftop of a deserted building, and nearby some youths were hurrying away with drums full of the petrol they'd siphoned from an abandoned tank. Others laboured under the weight of huge artillery shells that could be cracked open and drained of gunpowder. These were unusual sights, but not surprising, as nearly every single thing was deemed valuable in the anarchic city. Looters overloaded their bodies and carts with every imaginable object: petrol tanks, boxing bags, tyre tubes, soccer balls, shiny black vinyl records, belt buckles, mirrors ... Nothing was worthless.

When outside, Longy spent much of his time with Truong sitting in the laneway in the shadows of the Nguyen home.

'Are you scared, Longy?'

'No.'

'How different do you think it will be?'

'I don't know. But Mum and Dad say there will be changes.'

Reconciliation was the main and most immediate concern of a military committee that was quickly established to govern Saigon. As Colonel Bui Tin had said to General Minh at the time of the fall: 'You have nothing to fear. Between Vietnamese, there are no victors and no vanquished. Only the Americans have been beaten. If you are patriots, consider this a moment of joy.'

Although 'joy' wasn't a word that readily sprang to the thoughts of many Saigonese, Longy did find humour in their situation. One of his earliest introductions to VC soldiers was the morning he watched two men in rubber sandals trying to ride pushbikes. They wobbled along, knees out, elbows tucked into the sides of their stiff bodies and white-knuckled hands wrapped tightly around the handlebars. They grasped at each tree or pole by the side of the road, never trusting their uneasy balance for more than a few metres. To the laughing Longy, it was almost impossible to believe that there were grown-ups who'd never set foot on a pedal in a country in which pushbikes were the hub of civilian transport.

These shaky two-wheeled adventures reflected how hard the Viet Cong had to work on the streets to be accepted by the Saigonese. The city's newest residents proved to be friendly and polite when they were stopped and asked questions by curious locals, yet they were also quietly ridiculed as being simple and stupid. They were unfairly considered to be socially inept and unable to think for themselves, as they invariably turned to the sayings of Ho Chi Minh and, occasionally, Karl Marx and Lenin. Understandably, they weren't trusted; yet despite all the negative views of them, they were widely admired — these were men who had fought so passionately for what they believed in, and had achieved so much with so very little.

In contrast to the Viet Cong, there were other so-called communists who deserved nothing but scorn. These were the 'April 30ers', mostly young men in their late teens and twenties who shifted their allegiances to the North as soon as Saigon fell. Some were power hungry; others didn't necessarily believe in communism but were encouraged by the prospects of a fresh beginning and the opportunities that might come with it, especially if they displayed unquestionable loyalty. They had an obvious presence on the streets, wearing red armbands and walking with an annoying air of self-appointed authority. They kept their eyes and ears open and reported back to command posts run by cadres, the leaders of the new police forces in each neighbourhood. Longy despised the April 30ers, but was warned by his father not to show any hatred towards them: 'They are very dangerous. Whatever you do, someone will know.'

Hien had been waiting for the rise of such an element. The April 30ers were traitors whom everyone needed to fear. Not only did they monitor the present but, unlike their superiors, they remembered the lives of people in Saigon before the fall. Hien knew he was in their sights.

There were others who were just as big a threat. 'Hunting dog' was a name that had long been used in Vietnam to describe a snitch, anyone who betrayed an individual or group by providing information to the perceived enemy, whether in a prison, a schoolyard, the workplace — even at home in a battle between siblings. Now, in a city racked by suspicion, potentially anyone could be a hunting dog.

Apart from the presence of cadres and April 30ers, the earliest notable changes on the streets of Saigon were symbolic ones. Households weren't just required to fly the Viet Cong flag, but each had to display a photo of Ho Chi Minh together with his famous saying: 'Nothing is more valuable than freedom and independence.' A forward-thinking entrepreneur near the Nguyen home benefited from the edicts. Having stocked up on VC flags and photos before the fall, he suddenly enjoyed a rapid trade. There was tremendous irony in his good fortune: 'Uncle Ho', the father of communism in Vietnam, had indirectly helped this small businessman make a considerable profit at a time when capitalism was the scourge of the regime Ho inspired.

In recognition of that inspiration, Saigon became Ho Chi Minh City. In each neighbourhood meetings were held almost daily by government-appointed group home leaders, who informed the heads of each household of the latest changes. No-one dared protest about anything. Further information was relayed by flat, scratchy monologues that erupted at any hour of the day through speakers wired to poles and buildings throughout each neighbourhood. Much to Longy's annoyance, one speaker perched on a rooftop next to the Nguyen home regularly burst to life at the rudest of hours.

During one blast it was announced that all former military officers from the South had to register with authorities. Hien discussed his options with Teresa, and both decided it was best that he go and tell the truth. Apart from shooting and killing thieves on the spot, the communists had shown no signs of violence since their arrival. It was too early to determine whether they really would adhere to their promise of reconciliation above all other measures, but Hien presumed he had a better chance of being treated fairly if he admitted to his past. If he didn't, it was highly likely the April 30ers or a hunting dog could expose the truth anyway, and that would surely lead to greater trouble.

However, by the time Hien arrived at registration at a local school the next morning, he'd decided to alter his approach, albeit slightly. When he filled out a form, he answered all but one question honestly: What was your highest rank? *Lieutenant colonel.*

The former Inspector General of Corps II instinctively knew that, sooner or later, reprisals would come; it stood to reason that the higher-ranking officers would suffer the harshest penalties. Hien's dishonesty was a gamble worth taking.

The government's quest for information didn't stop with the military. Over the following weeks cadres conducted a massive census, visiting every home. These were incredibly intrusive affairs: not only were the household heads asked about everyone living under their roof, they were encouraged to provide information about anyone in the neighbourhood. The hunting dogs were beginning to bark. It was hoped the extensive exercise would determine which people were potential dissidents and, alternatively, who could help in an official capacity. The knock on the Nguyens' door came a fortnight after the fall. Hien and Teresa gave honest, succinct answers about their family, but they wouldn't be drawn into observations concerning the comings and goings of their friends and neighbours.

Few in the area were at greater risk than Hien. With the exception of attending the group home leader's meetings, he chose to remain indoors. Word was spreading that the South's former government officials, businessmen and high-ranking army officers were being taken away to 're-education camps'. Little was known about these places, but Hien feared that the treatment would be cruel and that some who went would never return. Every day he prayed the communists wouldn't be interested in a lieutenant colonel. And every day he prayed the April 30ers and hunting dogs would keep quiet.

Longy was first made aware of the camps after the disappearance of a man from the district who'd been filled with his own self-importance. Before the fall he had boasted to everyone that he worked for the CIA; afterwards, he barely said a word. No-one knew for certain if he was a friend of the Americans, but it mattered little to the April 30ers who revealed the man's supposed past to the cadres. He was never seen again.

As time passed, Longy believed that his father would remain safe. He saw and heard the tears and anguish of families affected by the camps, and yet nothing happened to Hien. In contrast to the tragedies occurring around them every day, the Nguyens believed they were blessed. But then the announcement came, three months after the fall: 'All senior officers of the South will attend one month's re-education camp. This will begin in two weeks' time. Junior officers will attend a ten-day course.'

Hien was at home when he heard the crackle from the speakers. He showed no emotion; it was as he'd always expected. The only positive aspect was the camp's duration: one month would be tolerable. He immediately began preparing himself, the memories of his time as a prisoner of war twenty years ago had taught him what to expect. He bought dried fruit and rice, cartons of cigarettes, and an array of medicines and personal hygiene products that he wrapped inside a straw sleeping mat. He already had everything else at home: blanket, towel, toothbrush, toothpaste, soap, mosquito net, rain jacket, jumper, trousers, shirts, a bowl and a writing pad. He also decided he'd need two pairs of glasses: his everyday thin-rimmed steel ones, and a much uglier set with black plastic rims and thick lenses that gave the impression he was struggling with his eyesight much more than he really was.

Once satisfied that this was all he should take, he turned his attentions to a duty that needed James's help. Without the knowledge of the rest of the family, he handed his oldest son a mini Beretta pistol, his most treasured military possession: 'Hide this in case the communists come looking.'

That night, James slipped out of his home with the gun wrapped in a plastic bag smeared with oil. After tiptoeing into the darkness of the nearest laneway, he knelt next to a manhole that led to a drain at the back of the house. Quickly and silently, eyes shifting from side to side, he slid the heavy concrete cover back and carefully placed the bag on a narrow ledge about a foot below the surface of the street. Within seconds he was gone.

Half an hour later a boy squatted on a rooftop, running his fingers over the weapon he had just collected. The metal was cool to touch, yet there was an exhilarating warmth that came from holding something so powerful. After several minutes he carefully wrapped the pistol in its bag and placed it in a crack under the corner of the roof. He then slipped downstairs into his bed, grinning. In the room next door his older brother was asleep, none the wiser that the treasure he had hidden was no longer in the manhole.

Longy didn't know if he'd ever need the Beretta, but he gained comfort from having it so close, especially with his father leaving in a few short days. Hien had spoken little about his coming absence. During the war he had been away for longer periods than a month, but had never known when he'd be returning home; this time he did. The camp was just another stage of the North–South conflict that he had to endure. Provided he was treated reasonably well, he'd come back in the same manner as he planned to leave. There'd be no fuss, no tears. Teresa thought the same.

The morning of his departure, Hien put on a pair of black pyjamas and sandals. The farewells were mostly matter of fact: this was a familiar drill for everyone in the family. Longy watched his father and mother hug briefly, then, after a few words and nods to his children, Hien picked up his straw mat and hefty bag of supplies. Longy made his way to the balcony, from which he could see James waiting on a scooter on the street. When he saw his father emerge, Longy was struck by an urge to say goodbye one final time. He rushed downstairs as he heard the scooter's engine kick over. He sidestepped the tables in the coffee shop and burst through the door onto the street just in time to touch his father's hands with an outstretched arm. Hien turned; his eyes met Longy's.

'Be good to your brothers and sisters. And look after your mother.'

'Yes, Dad.'

'I will be back soon.'

Hien turned around, settling onto the scooter's seat with his bag and mat, then James eased the buzzing bike into the traffic. Amid other scooters, trucks, pushbikes and cyclos, the man with the billowing black shirt and trouser legs flapping against his ankles was soon out of sight. He was being taken to a central meeting point in District Twelve on the other side of the Saigon River. The direction his life would take after that was known only to the communists.

When Hien arrived, he noticed the look of resigned acceptance on the faces of the men being marshalled together. Put in a small group, he found himself among former generals and other men of only the highest ranks. As far as he could gather, there were no other lieutenant colonels. Perhaps the April 30ers or a hunting dog had spoken after all.

Hien shuffled into line, wondering what would happen next. One month. Surely he could handle that.

TEN

Uncles

Teresa, Thao and Longy watched the wisps of smoke curl into the air from the small bin at their feet in the living room. No-one had wanted to burn the handfuls of army photos, especially the most precious ones of Hien negotiating with the VC for the exchange of prisoners, but Teresa knew it was wise. The cadres had already gone through the house once to ensure that Hien had left for the camp. What would happen if they chose to come back again? Any reminders of the ARVN might be enough to warrant further penalties.

The ribbons from Hien's twenty-one medals were next to go. Teresa and Thao cut them into tiny pieces, then sprinkled them into the hungry flames. Longy held the medals themselves in his hands.

'They have to go too,' insisted his mother.

'In the fire?'

'No.'

Later that morning, the rewards for half a lifetime of devoted military service were wrapped in paper and discarded along with catfish heads, empty coffee sacks, cigarette butts and tins of condensed milk. Garbage.

Little relating to the army life of Inspector General Hien Duy Nguyen was kept. Teresa riskily decided to keep a few snapshots of her husband in uniform with the children, but apart from that a reversible jacket was the only other item of Hien's that remained. On the outside, it was coloured with the mottled greens, blacks and browns of camouflage; when turned inside out it looked like a civilian's black coat. The cadres surely wouldn't know the difference.

All that was left to do now was count down the days. Soon, the month was nearly over, Hien would shortly be home, and the Nguyens' lives would be back to normal — if there was such a thing as normal at this time of immense upheaval. The relatively peaceful transition period was making way for the early stages of a much more aggressive phase officially called the 'cleaning of the culture' which in the years ahead would be known in hushed tones as 'the change of life'.

People who were well educated or had held some reputable position in society were deemed to have 'unclean backgrounds' and were classed as unemployable. Some businessmen, the so-called 'unproductive capitalists', were forced to leave their homes empty-handed and fend for themselves on the streets. Others were marginally more fortunate, watching helplessly as soldiers and officials took away gold and everyday goods — refrigerators, televisions, washing machines, blankets, radios, furniture, clothes — anything at all that could be sold, sent to the north or used in the residences of the officials, cadres and corrupt businessmen who were becoming the new rich and elite. The upper and middle classes lost most in this brutal redistribution of wealth and position. The cost was tragic: suicides and alcoholism rose, and those who'd been happily established just months before were reduced to begging on the streets or turning to crime. While the rich tumbled, some of the poor began to climb as they were presented with better work opportunities, and for the first time in their lives they had small amounts of money to spend.

Many of the more dramatic changes affecting Longy happened at school, where classrooms were saturated in unbearable propaganda. New teachers had come from the north, and existing teachers were being retrained so they would espouse the values of communism. The first noticeable difference was the uniform: white shirt, dark pants or skirt, and the option of wearing a communist-red neckerchief, which Longy did not choose. This was the *Doi Vien* stage, the introduction to communism for primary school children. Each morning began with students standing at attention in the quadrangle and addressing a photo of Ho Chi Minh hung high above them on a building wall, reciting, 'Nothing is more valuable than freedom and independence.'

In the classroom, teachers insisted how grateful people in the south should be that they'd won the war against the Americans, reminding them that 'Everyone is now free and happy.'

It seemed everyone also had someone looking over his or her shoulder. Within days of resuming school, each student had to fill out a form about his family. In another time and place the questions could have seemed unimportant, but here they served a purpose, thickening the government's files: 'Where do you live? How long have you lived there? How old are you? How many brothers and sisters do you have? How old are they? What do they do?' and so on.

Longy provided only the briefest of answers, then paused to consider the toughest question: 'What does your father do?'

Longy looked around at his classmates, their shoulders hunched over desks, heads low, writing furiously. He twisted his pen through his fingers, then scribbled the only answer he knew: 'My father is in a re-education camp, and he will be home soon.'

But Hien wouldn't be. As his family anxiously awaited his return, he and a group of other officers were transported from a makeshift camp southwest of Saigon near the Ho Chi Minh trail to a boat that was heading north. Pitching and rolling over the waves of the South China Sea, Hien sadly realised his absence from his family wasn't coming to an end.

One month passed. Two months. Every day more rumours spread around the neighbourhood. Tearful, desperate women whose husbands had been taken away at the same time as Hien came and spoke to Teresa, each time telling what they'd heard: the men were doing hard labour in the jungles; they were being fed one sweet potato a day; hundreds had already died; others had been killed for being undisciplined. These whispers bred still more conjecture: the men had been moved to the coast, where they were working on fishing boats and living in awful, stinking, cramped conditions under decks for weeks at a time; hundreds more had died.

Teresa refuted whatever she heard. She believed her husband was still alive, and until she officially heard otherwise there was no need to heed such dreadful gossip. Her incredible strength inspired her children. No-one thought the worst — certainly not Longy, who believed his father was 'too tough to die'.

Scattered across remote locations in both the north and south, the camps held thousands of prisoners, all apparently being 're-educated' by long, continuous programs of indoctrination and, if the need arose, interrogation. In truth, many of them were little more than hard labour farms, and the duties of the men included clearing jungles and carrying logs, building other camps, digging canals and wells, and growing vegetables for the guards. Six days a week, more than eight gruelling hours a day in sickening heat and humidity. The work time didn't take into account travelling, which could include hours more of slogging through thick undergrowth and mud. Prisoners were punished if they were unable to meet the quotas that were ruthlessly set: some were forced to make up for their lack of productivity by working on Sunday, the rest day, and others were placed in solitary confinement, or beaten with anything from rifle butts to the thorn-studded branches of bougainvillea. Nutrition was poor — the men were given bowls of rice without meat or vegetables — and any semblance of good hygiene was rare in areas where there was little fresh or running water.

Some prisoners were moved to a new camp every six or so months to avoid familiarity with their surrounds and the likelihood of escape attempts. Living quarters were either huts or individual cells. There were no beds, no blankets, no pillows, no toilets, no medicine. Talk about life before the fall was banned; even singing and references to superstitions were forbidden. There were no charges, no sentences, and each prisoner entered a camp never knowing when or how he would leave.

Hien was taken to a camp in the far north that inmates surmised was close to the Chinese border. He was put in a hut with several others, including an old friend, Le Trung Tuong, a former brigadier general and commanding officer of the 23rd Division in Corps II. They slept next to each other, lying on their straw mats at the end of each day's labour, too tired to talk. Hien tried not to think about the life he'd left behind, nor did he choose to assess what might lie ahead. The present was all that he focused on — survive it, then move forward with faith and hope.

In Saigon, Teresa continued to turn her back on neighbourhood gossip. She considered the only reliable source of information to be the BBC World Service which she listened to at night, barely turning the volume of her short-wave radio above a murmur. When not listening, praying or enduring fitful bouts of sleep, she occupied herself by working long hours in the coffee shop. Apart from watching the communists take away the reel-to-reel tape machine soon after Hien's departure, she lost nothing from her business. No doubt it helped that she'd already given away furniture to local cadres who welcomed her generosity and, in turn, didn't trouble her.

As a result Teresa was able to keep the coffee shop running, an incredible achievement in an environment of swirling inflation in which many goods, including coffee, were scarce. Her success was due in no small part to that all-important word she'd driven into Longy's thoughts ever since his youngest years: reputation. The network of contacts and friends she'd built up was so extensive that she never needed to whisper in too many ears before she received what she wanted. At a time when Vietnam was being swathed in communist red, it helped to have some undetectable threads leading to the black market.

However, for every reliable supplier there were dozens of others, hustlers whose reputations only stretched as far as the next ounce of gold. There were sharp, slick teenage boys, dressed in jeans and creaseless shirts. They rode scooters, their throttle-twisting wrists glinting with Seiko or Omega watches. They could be violent, sliding into an alley at one end with a clean machete and leaving at the other with a blade dripping in blood. As long as they offered some of their profits to the cadres, they were protected by the blind eyes of authority. Then there were the older hustlers, more humbly dressed men in plain trousers and shirts. Having learnt their business before the fall, they relied on their street wisdom to adapt. They were aided by their many contacts and their uncanny ability to survive. Then there were others still, those so desperate that they walked the streets yelling, 'We buy gold, any gold! Necklaces, rings, teeth!'

Longy was warned about them all by his mother, but contact was unavoidable, as they gathered in the coffee shop — a suitable meeting place for deals to be discussed — and when storms struck they sought shelter under the shop's front awning. The sight of them scampering across the street, pulling raincoats or shirts above their heads, was the signal for Teresa to keep a closer eye on her son: 'They have bad habits. Don't you go near them.'

Longy was only allowed to watch from a distance as the men discreetly swapped goods under tables, or exchanged information with as little as a nod or a hand gesture. This wasn't enough to satisfy his curiosity, though. The more he saw, the more he wanted to know. How did these people find anything they needed to? And where did they go? One day he would need to discover the answers.

Longy was now eleven years old. The three months since his father's departure had ground by without a single word from the camp, and the boy was becoming increasingly bitter towards the communists. Despite his mother's ability to sustain her business, he'd watched other families suffer, slowly drained of their fortunes, assets and, most sadly, their enthusiasm for life. People who'd once smiled on the streets now walked by with heads hung low, sorrowful eyes and no spring in their steps. The strongest managed brave faces, but these masks hid immense pain and anger.

It was impossible for the city's residents to comprehend how drastically and abruptly Saigon had changed. Even during the unsettled times of the war the city had always enjoyed a vibrancy and zest, an energy all of its own. But now in some quarters it was slowly rotting with sadness and resentment. Those people trusting enough to share their views with close friends asked the same question time and again: 'If peace was meant to bring us together, why are we now more divided than we've ever been?'

The strategies to destroy Western influence were extensive: music, magazines, books and even comics were banned; newspaper publishers who had operated before the fall were shut down; and international journalists remaining in the city had their work censored.

Other changes ripped apart the old city's very fibre: the judicial system was suspended; police stations were torn down; and prison gates were flung open, allowing inmates to flee without fear of recapture. The administration of law was temporarily based on public trials and executions. Thieves comprised the vast majority of the accused, stories of their misdemeanours and subsequent deaths invariably dominating the front page of the new official newspaper.

The conversion of currency was one of the more dreadful changes. With next to no warning, residents were informed by authorities that 500 piasters of old money would equal just one meagre new piaster. Entitlements were determined by the numbers living in each household. People queued with bags full of money only to be told when arriving at designated exchange points that any money above their allowance was worthless. As a result, gold became an even more valuable currency.

More aware of what was happening around him than he'd ever been in his life, Longy allowed his bitterness to grow into anger. He knew families who hid gold under pots; he saw hustlers thinning petrol with kerosene; he felt the presence of secret police peering from behind corners; and he heard the hiss of escaping air from pushbike tubes repaired so many times that patches rose above the rubber like tumours. He hated what the VC, the communists, the PAVN, the North, the NLF — whatever you wanted to call them — had done. Most of all he hated them because they had taken away his father. One month! Liars!

Resentment. Anger. Rage. And now, Longy sought revenge. The first marks were left at school, where teachers entered classrooms to find blackboards covered with the obvious scribble of a child: 'Down with communists!'

He chose his moments carefully, slipping into rooms before school and between classes. He was never caught, although it's likely some teachers knew who the culprit was, but as not all teachers were hardline supporters of communism perhaps they felt sympathy for a boy who was searching for guidance in the absence of his father.

Other children in similar positions also sought vengeance, but weren't always successful. One boy's mother was summoned to school after her child had been discovered defacing the storybook *Bo Doi Ve Lang* — *Army Boy Comes Back to Village*. The offender had added one word, '*Du*' — the army boy had come back to fuck the village. Despite the complete disrespect shown, the boy was scolded but not punished. Students who strayed outside the narrow corridors of strict discipline were considered too young to know better. This approach adhered to Ho Chi Minh's belief that 'It takes ten years for a tree to grow, but one hundred years for a human being.'

To Longy, every branch of his education was decidedly prickly. Students were encouraged to write Ho Chi Minh sayings at the top of each page of their books, and when writing stories, or answering questions, it was expected that they praise communism. They were taught politics, and were endlessly told that 'Americans are evil'. To emphasise that hard work was 'held in honour', students were periodically arranged in groups to strip bamboo that would be taken to factories where adults continued the 'productive labour' process by making furniture and curtains.

Longy held such practices in contempt. His lack of regard for his education was further heightened by the cruel statements that some of his teachers made in front of the class: 'Longy, your father is a bad man. He is a criminal. You must be grateful that Ho Chi Minh's teachings won't let this happen to you.'

Longy, however, continued to rebel. Next he vandalised the toilets, hurling large rolls of firecrackers into the weak clay bowls that were concreted in the floor. The shattered remnants and walls covered with reeking splodges of sewage were his way of saying, 'Fuck the school, fuck the communists, fuck everyone!'

The absence of Longy's father had changed his life. He didn't care what happened to him; he just wanted to show that he hated the VC for what they'd done. Fury was beginning to drive him. Fury of thought, fury of action, fury in the speed at which nearly every sleepless minute passed.

The banning of tae kwon do classes further angered him, but at least he could still take part in informal tangles on the streets, which became somewhat therapeutic for him. Some exchanges were purely recreational, a hobby that had passed the hours for young and old — a flying spin kick, a hurried deflection, then both combatants on the ground laughing. Other duels were more serious as each protagonist flew into action determined to hurt and beat his rival, to ensure a higher position in the chain of respect. There were also the brutal gang assaults between older youths. There were no rules in these fights — fists, feet, bamboo sticks and knives were all fair weapons.

Whatever the fray, crowds invariably gathered to watch. Amid the cheers and gasps from the packs of adolescents, old women squatting in the doorways of their homes yelled in disapproval, 'Go home and help your parents. They didn't bring you up like dogs!'

No-one ever took any notice, not even the cadres who only occasionally broke up some of the more violent disputes. In the scheme of all that was happening in the city, these mostly adolescent altercations were trivial.

Longy relished these spats as both a spectator and a participant. His black-belt reputation frightened off many would-be opponents, but others took their chances. Starting metres apart, eyes firmly fixed on each other, they'd spin, kick and punch until one conceded defeat. Yet to graduate to gang fights, Longy was rarely troubled in the one-on-one altercations. He was much stronger, more determined and skilled than others his own age, and even some who were several years older. His viciousness was obvious to anyone who saw him launch into an opponent. There was a glint in his eye, the hint of a smile when he landed a stinging blow.

He was relentless. Seeing his rival hurting relieved some of his own emotional discomfort.

Longy's successes further enhanced his reputation. Walking, almost strutting, with the fearsome Lucky by his side, and the ever-present Truong reminding all within earshot that his friend was 'the King', Longy had outgrown his reputation as a boy who could fight. Now, he was a boy who *loved* to fight.

On the incredibly rare occasions when he fought at school, Longy needed just a few kicks or the flash of a hand to dismiss most challengers. Longer scraps risked the intervention of teachers and an ensuing disciplinary hearing between staff and the offending boys' parents. When Longy did get caught it was difficult for Teresa to take time away from the business, so Uncle Ba accepted the role of surrogate parent. He'd leave his barbershop to attend the hearings, then he'd return and wait for Longy to visit him after class. His advice never varied: 'There will be times when you will have to fight for your honour and your worth, but most of these will not be at school. There is no need to fight there unless your reputation demands there is no other way.'

Uncle Ba was one of the few people Longy listened to. Ironically, the barber only ever raised his voice to ward off other boys fighting in the streets outside his shop, crying out, 'Get away! There is no need for that here.'

No-one ever disobeyed.

Teresa was comforted by the knowledge that Longy and Uncle Ba had developed such a strong, earnest relationship. She trusted the barber, but she couldn't wholly trust her son. This was in no way an insinuation that Longy lacked love and respect for his mother, but an indication of his free spirit. Since his youngest years it had been impossible to watch his every move. Now, in this changed city, the best supervision could only be asked for in prayer: 'Please, God, look after Longy.'

Teresa feared for the safety of Longy more than that of any of her other children. There was no question that he was going to find greater trouble the older he became. That was why Uncle Ba was so important: in the absence of Hien, Longy needed a father figure.

The responsibility wasn't shouldered by Uncle Ba alone. In the slum-ridden bowels of Cholon, Longy shared a bond with Hung, a known eccentric who was as different from Uncle Ba as the politics that had split Vietnam were from each other. Where Uncle Ba was solemn, reserved, cautious and polite, Hung was expressive, loud, impulsive and crass. At the front of his home he had a Christian cross, a statue of a buddha and numerous figures of Hindu gods. He considered religion a lottery — the more tickets he held, the better chance he had of being looked after by a greater force. His speech was littered with obscenities, and he smoked opium in the afternoons, curling on his side and taking long, slow breaths through a pipe. However, for all his differences, he shared some significant similarities with the barber. He too was referred to by Longy as both a 'master' and an 'uncle'. Such was the respect he commanded, he was known throughout his neighbourhood as 'Uncle Nam' (Uncle Five).

In his fifties, with grey hair shorn to a stubble, Uncle Nam had an endearing, seemingly permanent smile. He was immensely strong, his enormous forearms and long, sinewy fingers hinting at what he did for a living: he was a masseur. During the war he had been a nurse for the ARVN, and he had since returned to the art of massage and practising Eastern healing. His home smelled of a pungent collision of herbs that were used to treat every possible ailment, including Teresa's arthritis.

Longy had first met him before the fall when Teresa sought a remedy for her son's swollen, stiff knuckles — the result of too much tae kwon do practice.

'Either you have very weak hands, or you hit too fucking hard!' joked Uncle Nam, who sent Longy home with an oil mixed with rice whisky and herbs. 'Soak your hands in it every day for half an hour. Do it for only a week because there is much *Ma Tien* in the oil. Too much of that can make you sterile. That is not something a young boy wants to be!'

The stinking concoction worked. Intrigued by the speed at which his hands healed, Longy wanted to know more. He soon returned to Uncle Nam with a general muscular soreness from playing soccer. Whether the pains were from physical exertion or simply signs of a boy growing into a youth's body didn't matter. After a traditional Eastern manipulation of the back and neck — *Crack! Crack! CRACK!* — Longy was fixed again. There was no need to convince him of the power of touch, and this was just another lesson in the art that had fascinated him since he'd sat wide-eyed in the villages of the mountain people.

Uncle Nam was a most willing teacher, happily massaging Longy while answering all of his apprentice's questions.

'There is no mystery to what I do, Longy. There is just experience. You must do it over and over again.'

And Longy did. Whenever he was taught a new technique, he returned home to practise. He spent many evenings quietly experimenting on his mother, accompanied by the distant voices of the BBC World Service. He stood, he crouched, he knelt; his fingers, knuckles, elbows and heels all became keys that were needed to unlock the pain in deep, aching joints. Occasionally Teresa screwed up her face, but the agony she endured was always worth it for the relief she felt afterwards.

'You are very good, Longy. You must keep doing this. It is an art. You are very lucky — you are blessed with a skill.'

Longy needed no encouragement. Through Uncle Nam he was already learning about medicines and oils, the properties of herbs and how they should be used. Once he visited 'the Master of Cholon' complaining of being cranky and frustrated by even the smallest of worries.

'Are you sleeping well, Longy?'

'No.'

'You are fatigued. You need *Jen-shen*.'

Jen-shen was the Chinese word for ginseng, meaning 'shaped like a man', in reference to a typical root structure of one of the most powerful and popular of all Eastern herbs. In either powdered or solid form it was considered a panacea for the entire body, and was commonly used as an upper, especially for the elderly.

Uncle Nam's supply of *Jen-shen* came from North Korea, where the plants grew wild. After the precious roots were harvested they were dried in the sun until rock hard. The older the ginseng, the more valuable it was considered. Uncle Nam gave Longy some strips wrapped in newspaper, along with instructions: 'Chew them for about a week. During the day you will have much energy; at night, you will be tired and relaxed. You won't be cranky any more. It will also help you get bigger and stronger.'

The plant's initial sweetness and bitter aftertaste didn't appeal to Longy at first, but once he recognised he was indeed feeling calmer and sleeping better, he always ensured he had some of the herb in his pocket. As time passed, he also noticed how strong he was becoming, how his body was thickening and hardening — becoming *Jen-shen*.

Longy's impressive growth spurt was in vivid contrast to the decline of thousands of men across Vietnam in the re-education camps. In the deep north, a gaunt and seemingly muscleless Hien threw every ounce of his skin, bone and willpower at each torturous day. Around him men had already died, and others were so weak and ill that their existence was measured only in hours. Forget the rigours of war — this was the harshest fight for survival most ARVN officers had ever known. Sweat, blood, stench, vomit, chills; jungles, mud, mosquitoes; loneliness and madness. Desperation and depression. Suicide. Constipation, malnutrition, and infection ... Nothing was easy; little was bearable; every moment was a challenge.

Despite it all, Hien was managing to cope. He had lost weight, and his eyesight was deteriorating, but he wouldn't let go of his faith, believing God would guide him through. And now, after nearly a year of incarceration, there was some hope: the inmates had been granted a significant privilege. Before indulging in this luxury, Hien reflected on his awful existence, then thought of his family. Did they still think he was alive? Did they know where he was? There was much to tell them about the month he'd been away.

ELEVEN

Hitting the Streets

Longy had never seen his mother so emotional. Since the postman had delivered the mail that morning the single sheet of paper had been read, folded, unfolded and reread dozens of times by everyone in the family. Now, Teresa stood alone in the living room, the crinkled letter in her shaking hands. She looked at the Virgin Mary and whispered, 'Thank you.'

Teresa held the letter to her face and smelled it. She stared at it, running her fingers over every word. She imagined the man who wrote it. Then she wept some more.

Different feelings and thoughts had swirled through her mind all day. Anger, anguish, helplessness, despair, disappointment — but, most of all, relief. Hien was still alive. But she cursed the communists for their lies. One month had turned into a year — and there was no indication of when it would be over.

The letter hadn't contained significant detail about the camp, other than the vague description of its location: 'we are living in hills in the far north'. Hien wrote that he was being treated well, and was fit and healthy, but in the context of the rumours in District Three that men in the camps were suffering and dying, could this really be believed?

Of all the information contained in the letter, there was only one statement that could be confirmed. Hien revealed that he'd hidden some cash in the top pocket of his reversible army jacket: 'You may need to use it if times become very tough.'

He obviously didn't know that money had been revalued, and the thick roll of piasters that was indeed in the jacket was worthless.

Hien had no idea just how dramatically life in the south had changed since his departure. While he battled through each day, thousands of people were undergoing similar problems in 'new economic zones' that were being established in rural areas outside Saigon. Families were allocated small parcels of land to grow rice. They lived in basic huts, there was no running water and no infrastructure to maintain the instant communities that developed. Some businessmen were sent to these zones as punishment for their capitalist sins; other, poorer people volunteered to go. Despite Teresa's protests, her brother Dieu, still grieving over the loss of his son in Hue, decided he and his family would start again in one of these zones.

Privacy too had been shoved aside. In an extension of the activities of the April 30ers, households were randomly checked at night by the cadres. A loud thumping knock on the door would be followed by the stern, authoritative voice of an officer demanding a head count of everyone under the roof. If the number he found didn't tally with the household's official papers, countless questions would be asked, and if he was not satisfied with the answers, the officer would return with his superiors. It wasn't uncommon for people to be taken away and locked up for days while the cadres reviewed the infringements.

Vietnam was officially unified under communist rule in mid-1976. This prompted a new wave of escape attempts. People with enough gold to buy a boat, or at least the right of passage on a boat, risked their lives in clandestine operations all along Vietnam's east and south coasts. If they survived long enough to sneak past coastguards and ruthless Thai pirates, they still had to endure unpredictable, often violent ocean waves. Then there were the atrocious conditions on board. Sometimes hundreds of people were crammed shoulder to shoulder, knee to knee below filthy, stinking, sweltering decks. They were barely able to move beyond the appointed spots where they ate, slept and, in the most appalling circumstance, were also forced to urinate and defecate. Yet they considered that the risks were better than the lives they were leaving behind. Their destinations were varied — Thailand, Singapore, Malaysia ... anywhere there might be hope of a fresh beginning.

At night, Teresa listened to the tragedies that were spelt out on the BBC World Service. Boats were found wrecked and abandoned in the South China Sea. Hundreds, thousands of lives were lost. Was it worth it? The mother of seven, and the wife of a prisoner, had no answer. She had the gold to help her children flee, but she didn't know whether the time was right, or whether it ever would be. There was only one certainty: any attempt to flee would have to be made without her, because she had to wait for Hien.

Nineteen-year-old James was in the most precarious position of all the Nguyen children, because he was old enough to be called into the army. It was a possibility neither he nor Teresa wanted to consider. But despite this, Teresa held the greatest fears for Longy, who was nearing his twelfth birthday. He should still have been a carefree boy, but he'd shed his childhood as though it were a dirty shirt that needed changing. The fact that he was now tall and broad enough to wear James's hand-me-downs added

LONGY'S PARENTS:
TOP Lieutenant Colonel Hien Duy Nguyen just before his promotion to Inspector General of Corps II
BOTTOM One of the few remaining photos of Teresa and Hien together

TOP Two-year-old Longy in an outfit specially made for him — military stars were hand-sewn by his mother onto the collar, and a dragon was embroidered over the chest
BOTTOM The Nguyen family outside their Pleiku home. Back row (from left): Teresa, Maria, and Hien. Middle row: Lam, Longy, James, and Van. Front row: Linh and Thao

Two Familiar Sights:
TOP Longy in his customary position, between his parents in his father's army jeep
BOTTOM Close by his mother's side, on a rare holiday to Dalat

TOP A family picnic at Lake Bien Ho, Pleiku; from left: Van, Teresa, Lam, Linh (in nappies), Longy, a house assistant, and Thao (James and Maria were away at boarding school)
BOTTOM Tree-climbing was a favourite pastime for Lam (left) and Longy

A proud Teresa on the day of Longy's communion at the Army Catholic Church, Pleiku

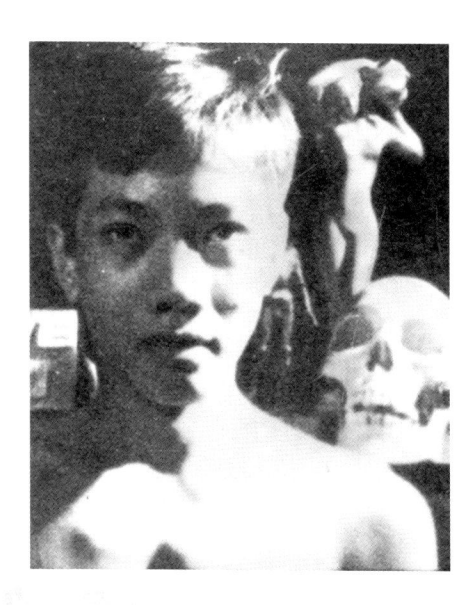

TOP Thirteen-year-old Longy with black eyes and a fractured cheek after a street fight in Saigon
BOTTOM The Laemsing refugee camp in Thailand — most of these huts each housed at least ten people

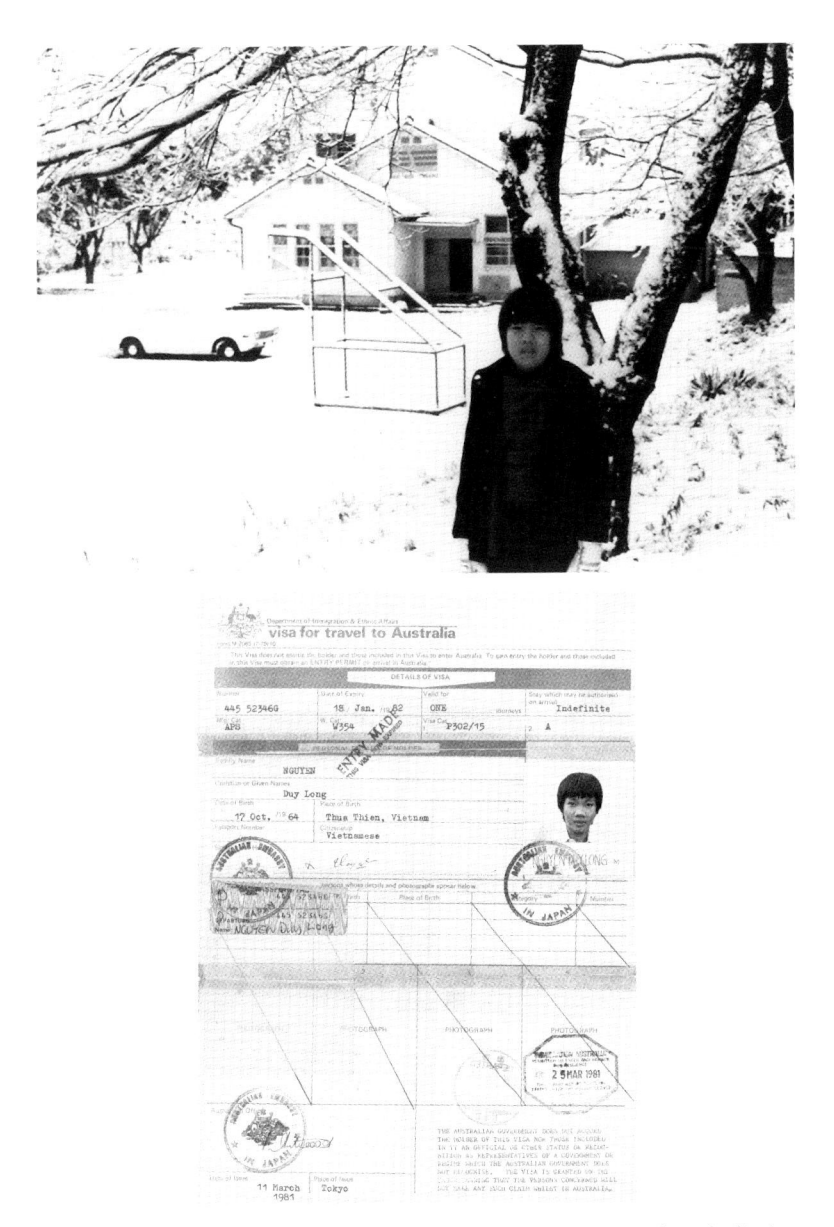

TOP Snow! A very cold Linh Nguyen stands in front of the Vietnamese refugee facility in Tokyo — Longy placed a South Vietnamese flag on the roof of the residential building
BOTTOM Longy's 'Ticket to Lucky-Land'

TOP Sixteen-year-old Longy just weeks after his arrival at East Hills Hostel, Sydney
BOTTOM The Hung Vuong tae kwon do class in Cabramatta — Longy (second from the left, second last row) was one of four black-belt instructors

to the impression that he was no longer a boy. If he continued at the same rate of growth it wouldn't be long before the idle attire in Hien's wardrobe could be unfolded.

The bustling pace of Longy's physical development was laborious when compared with the changes in his mental state. These were what disturbed Teresa the most. Already people in the neighbourhood were asking her, 'What will happen to Longy when he's a bit older? He had better behave.' But it was too late. Unwilling to learn at school, her son had shifted his education to the streets. He was spending more and more time away from home, and on the rare occasions he was there, he spent hours practising tae kwon do and karate. Sometimes when she walked out the back of the house for a quiet *Cam le* cigarette, Teresa heard the repetitive thumping of Longy's hands and feet on the rooftop. It was impossible to know which direction her son's life would take, but it was becoming increasingly obvious that it wouldn't be a peaceful journey.

Although she wouldn't always agree with what her son did, she knew she would always support him. Too many horrible events since the start of the war had taught her how brittle life could be. Only recently, she and the whole neighbourhood had been rocked by the cruelty that one wretched woman had suffered. Her husband had died in battle years earlier, leaving her to bring up their only child, a boy who wasn't much older than Longy. Mother and son were incredibly close. They lived in a small one-room house, minding their own business and finding whatever means they could to survive. They could be seen walking the streets together, holding hands, guiding each other through the challenges and hardships they faced. But then they had an argument — their only argument. The boy rushed from the house, threatening never to come back. He stayed out after the curfew, and still hadn't returned by sunrise. When daylight began spilling onto the streets, the boy's whereabouts were all too painfully revealed. Longy was one of the first to hear the news. By the time he reached the scene on the back of a friend's pushbike hundreds had gathered, their whispering voices drowned out by the uncontrollable sobbing of the boy's mother. Her son would indeed never go home again. As many people did, he had spent the night sleeping under a truck, nestled against a tyre to stay out of the wind and rain. In the morning, the careless driver had rolled his vehicle back without starting the engine, nor looking underneath for sheltering sleepers. It was an avoidable death — but so many were.

Teresa wondered how she would cope if something similar happened to one of her children. She could never be prepared for such a tragedy, yet she partly expected it with Longy. The older he became, the more at risk he would be, God help him.

The early signs that he was sliding into street life were subtle. After leaving for school with just one pen, he'd return home with a different, more valuable one. This was the reward for a successful day of trading, when a boy's success depended on his ability to talk up the items he wanted to swap. No money changed hands — words were the most valuable currency. Banned at school because of its apparently capitalist tone, the activity was forced underground, where slang words and whispered messages were used to arrange meetings of boys in quiet corners. Pencils, pens, notepads and comic books were among the most popular items. Inevitably some exchanges led to disagreements and fights, but Longy, with his formidable physical presence and black-belt reputation, was rarely involved in these.

Most importantly, Longy knew how to give the impression that he was being out-thought. There were many times when boys walked away believing they'd had the better of the negotiation, only to see the item they'd parted with being exchanged for twice as much in the next deal. Longy was one of the best dealers; he was smart, smooth-talking, confident and imposing — all the makings of becoming the type of person his mother continually warned him about: a hustler.

Much to Teresa's relief, though, Longy was content to keep his business inside the school gates for the time being. This was only because he had so many other distractions. Among his latest was the perilous pursuit of raiding guava and mango trees surrounded by electrified wire. With Truong on the ground holding pushbikes for a quick escape, Longy climbed up the trees, deftly avoiding the rings of wire to pluck as much fruit as he could carry inside his shirt. He'd either give the rewards to Truong, take them home, or, if wanting to impress, offer them to girls at school.

Of all his activities, Longy was never more excited than when playing soccer. Every possible space in the neighbourhood became a potential playing field: small, dusty parks with scatterings of grass; courtyards; roads; and the laneway alongside the Nguyen home, where Longy would kick his leather ball against the wall and wait for enough numbers to arrive to start a game. Youths passing on pushbikes and scooters would stop, and after rolling their trouser legs up to their knees they'd line up for shots against their fearless opponent, who'd protect the wall-cum-goalmouth with endless energy. The pieces of skin that peeled off his hands, elbows and knees were the marks of his determination — no pain was great enough to stop a ball skidding through.

If his ability on the tar and the grass was worthy of recognition, his ability on the glass was worthy of greater accolades. As popular as soccer was, it was a poor cousin when compared with the grand and profitable pastime of table soccer, which turned even the quietest laneways into rollicking venues of banter and bluff every lunchtime. Tables were set up at the front of businesses or homes. Covered with a glass surface, they featured eight rows of small wooden figures attached to horizontal rods running above the table. By twisting a rod a player could swing the row of stiff figures forwards or backwards, either kicking the marble-sized plastic ball or allowing it to pass through to the next row. This was a game of reflexes and anticipation. A player stood at either end of the table, controlling four alternate rods each. Similar to pinball, this coin-operated game delivered a new ball to the table each time a goal was scored. It was accepted that the loser would be the one to pay.

Players always bet against each other, and with the best matches drawing boisterous crowds, gambling between onlookers was inevitable. Just as in real soccer, Longy was a star performer. Playing with his shirt off, sweat glistening on his chest, he was able to assert his authority with a flick of the wrist, a quick glance at his opponent or some well-timed sledging.

He became known as Long Thien Ly — Longy, the boy from the coffee shop. Such was his reputation that he often had to handicap himself by swinging his wooden goalkeeper's feet skywards and declaring: 'I won't use him. You have an open goal to shoot at.'

Not only was his team one player short, but his family found itself with an empty seat at the dinner table, as Longy forewent meals to chase goals and money. Annoyed with her son for being absent at the one time of day when the Nguyens all gathered together, Teresa usually ordered Thao to go and find her wayward brother. And Longy always came home ... eventually. By that time his family had invariably finished eating, and the only heat coming from the table emanated from Teresa's simmering temper: 'We must eat as a family. That includes you, Longy.'

Torn between the two different tables, Longy rushed between matches and mouthfuls. He survived indigestion, but was sometimes left with a bitter taste when he was swindled. Table soccer was renowned for its sharks: young men who'd arrive from other neighbourhoods with unknown form and reputations. After throwing a game or two, giving every impression that they weren't the least bit skilled, they'd then reveal their true abilities in displays that would bewilder their opponents and fleece many a coin from honest punters. Longy was plundered occasionally, but the older he became, the more aware he was of the ploys. Table soccer reflected the golden rule of the streets: never trust anyone you don't know.

Over the following months, Longy continued to learn more about both the streets and himself. Missing his father, he went through patches of anger and resentment, sadness and loneliness. Whatever his feelings, he sought comfort and confidence outside his home. He still spent time with Teresa, but he was selective in what he told her. This was his way of being protective, adopting the age-old approach: 'What she doesn't know can't hurt her.'

Yet Teresa found out more than her son knew through her contacts. 'Longy was raiding melons with Truong today,' she'd be told. 'They say Longy can nearly swim all the way across to the other side of the Saigon River'; 'Longy won a fight today' ...

At night, as she lay down to receive her soothing massages, Teresa reproached Longy for his behaviour: 'Your activities are no good for my blood pressure. You know I don't like you swimming in the river, and you must be careful in your fights.'

'But everyone fights.'

'It's not the fighting that worries me. It is who you fight with, and what that may lead to. These are dangerous times, Longy. Everything you do is being watched. When you grow up you don't want to be taken away like your father.'

Yet Longy continued his street education with vigorous enthusiasm, his senses alive to everything around him. He took special notice of boys he hadn't seen in the neighbourhood before. If their hair was wet and well groomed it was likely they lived close by, because long journeys in the heat would have both dried their hair and ruffled their appearance. Then there were the schoolgirls, mostly from the poorest of families, who hid behind trees on busy roads. Their positioning intrigued Longy, until he realised they were waiting for male customers to masturbate in exchange for money or a small parcel of food. There were the youths who made stamps out of candles to be used on forged documents. There were the men who wrapped black-market goods in newspapers; the women who brewed rice whisky to sell; and the children whose parents only allowed them to play in the laneways when the cadres weren't anywhere near. And there were the peasants, the April 30ers, the cadres, the seedy hustlers, the street gangs, the hunting dogs, the mourners, the disabled veterans ... And then, the men and youths who'd become Longy's most recent source of fascination: the cock fighters.

Cock fighting was a popular and profitable pastime in the laneways of Saigon. Through word-of-mouth, people gathered to gamble illegally on these gruesome contests that often led to the losing bird lying in blood, its neck slit by the metal spurs attached to its rival's legs. These were horrible affairs, yet they offered the chance of some quick money and, for the owners, considerable prestige. It was a sport of the times.

Perched atop a light pole, or sitting on a window ledge, Longy had the perfect vantage point to observe all that happened. Others took their places on poles, around corners and in buildings, to act as lookouts for approaching cadres. Below, as many as 100 or more people formed a ring, leaving a space of just a few metres in the middle. Inside it stood the owners, birds under their arms, ready for battle. The cocks were ugly specimens. Standing as high as a man's knees, they had long, lean bodies. Their necks, heads and legs were plucked free of feathers, leaving angry red skin that the owners toughened by rubbing with rice whisky and herbs. In addition to their regular diet of grains and rice, many were fed meat to give them a taste for blood. In other words, they were conditioned to kill.

Before each fight the owners would agree on the betting terms, which were usually 'winner takes all'. The money, or sometimes gold or jewellery, would be given to a neutral person to mind. Other wagers were laid between the onlookers; their odds and conditions varied. The owners would strap a spur to each leg of their bird. These were sharp 3-centimetre-long hooks made from bike spokes or fence wire. Once they were in position, all was ready.

'One, two, three!'

The cocks would be thrown into the fray, each furiously flapping its wings and stretching out its legs in an arc, looking to land a blow with the spurs. Some fights lasted just seconds, others stretched on for ten to fifteen minutes or more. In the closest of tussles the birds would lock onto each other's necks with their beaks and try to bring their legs around in a slicing action across the neck or chest. They tried aerial assaults, jumping and flapping a metre off the ground. Drops of blood and feathers would land on the cheering spectators as dust swirled at their feet. When the birds' wings became locked together each owner would break them apart and quickly spray them with water before allowing the contest to resume. Losses either came through death or when a bird was too injured or tired to continue. Together with his wad of earnings the winner took his bird home; the loser's bird, if it had been killed, would end up in the dinner bowl.

These cruel and brutal events had been an intrinsic part of Saigon's street culture for generations. For a boy who only a few years earlier had proudly carried a formidable collection of cricket heads in a matchbox, the world of cock fighting was too exciting to be ignored.

However, Longy had to be patient. Before he could enter the domain of 'dignity, prestige and reputation' he needed the key ingredient behind any successful cock fighter: money. And although he was learning to store away the cash he won at table soccer, or had been given by his mother, or earned in the coffee shop, he didn't have a sustainable flow. So the solution was obvious — Longy the hustler was about to hit the streets.

TWELVE

Poultry Pugilism

In the early months of 1977, Longy had a problem: who would let him in late at night when he came home from his rookie hustling? It used to be Maria, woken by the sharp taps of pebbles hitting her bedroom window. But she was now living in a new house a few hundred metres away from the Nguyen home. The oldest child in the family had married David, a teacher, who'd endured his own hardships when he was part of the 'convoy of tears'.

As Teresa adapted to having one less person under her roof, Longy was busy building his small empire. Advancing from trading pens and pencils, he began dealing in pushbike parts, one of the street's most valuable commodities. His time spent listening and watching the hustlers near the coffee shop proved priceless. Once he learnt the value of goods, he knew whether a seller was telling the truth or bluffing. Then, adopting the basic rule of buying low and selling high, he haggled, and found he was able to return home with more dong — the new currency — in his pocket than when he left.

Because he was so widely known throughout the neighbourhood, and was also willing to knock on doors well outside his local area in search of goods, Longy developed a network that could provide him with everything he needed: ball bearings, frames, handlebars, spokes, tyre rims, pedals. There was nothing he couldn't obtain. All he needed to do was whisper to the right person 'What do you need?' or 'What do you have?'

It was a difficult challenge for someone so young, but, as with his life in general, Longy was years ahead of his age. With no fear of being captured after curfew, he ducked, darted and scurried through the alleys and lanes at the oddest of hours to make a deal. When he returned home, his well-directed pebbles inducted Thao into the door-opening role vacated by Maria. The creaking sound of feet scaling the stairs past Teresa's bedroom seemed to shout in the darkness, but the daring entrepreneur was never caught. If Teresa had been woken by her son's unpredictable movements, she never mentioned it — this was just another stage she had to accept. Whether she liked what was happening or not, Longy was now beyond her control.

The irregularity of Longy's hours meant he sometimes missed school, preferring to rest all day to save energy for his exploits at night. In the privacy of his bedroom he stored his profits in a hessian bag that fattened to the extent that he jokingly boasted to Truong, 'Look, I can do weights with it!'

The size of the bag contradicted the tenor of the times: a smirking twelve-year-old boy doing arm curls with a sack of money in his very own room in a big house, while so many homeless people were barely able to drag their feet through each day because they had so little cash and food. Yet again, Duy Long Nguyen was showing how different he was from everyone around him. There was indeed only one dragon.

In his wheeling and dealing Longy was certainly helped by the neighbourhood's respect for the Nguyen family, as some locals were willing to provide him with business because they felt sorry for the position he was in without his father. But he would have succeeded regardless of this, because of his gregarious nature and willingness to try to gain the confidence of the people he met, including the cadres and local patrolmen who became used to the chatty boy's endless questions, laughter and well-timed cheek. The apparent friendliness not only earned Longy the trust of his enemies, but gained him knowledge of their routines, habits, personalities and weaknesses. Of course, he could never completely protect himself from the hunting dogs, but knowing as much as he did was an invaluable asset. On the few occasions he was caught on the streets at night nearing curfew, he knew to offer simple excuses: 'I just wanted to see what was happening on patrol. I wanted to go for a walk.'

'Well, get home and walk there,' the patrolman would reply. 'You have a big home and stairs.'

While his false naivety and innocence were useful camouflage for his activities, he knew they wouldn't be tolerated when he was a bit older. The more streetwise he became, the more tactics he'd need to develop if he were to avoid capture and punishment.

Inevitably, Longy's pushbike trade turned into an avenue of much greater enterprise. By the time he was thirteen, his contacts were like the streets of his neighbourhood: he had his main routes, the regular suppliers who quietly and safely provided him with whatever he needed; then he had the alleys and lanes, the smaller dealers who could neither be seen nor trusted around the next corner. Together, they were part of a maze leading in many different and dangerous directions, some towards cogs and chains, others towards antibiotics or coffee. There were distributors for all types of Western medicine, jeans, sports shoes, watches, petrol, machinery parts ... the list was endless. It seemed as though nothing was impossible to acquire if the connections were good enough and the price was right. Most critically, those involved all had to be willing to take chances, which emphasised another basic principle of business: the bigger the risk, the bigger the return.

To Longy, risks were just part of the adventure of life. Here was the boy who'd dared to walk the jungle tracks to visit the mountain people; who'd fired bullets from a homemade gun that could have easily blown off his hand; who'd taught himself to swim in turbulent rivers; who'd stolen from the church plate; who'd been beaten and bruised by youths at tae kwon do sessions; who'd rushed into a burning house; who'd criticised the communists in the classroom. Here was the boy, now a teenager, ready for more exploits.

Finding suppliers and buyers was the relatively safe part of any trade. The biggest peril lay in the transportation of goods between the two parties. When he was unable to work under the cover of darkness, Longy hid the contraband under his clothes, or used banana leaves or pig intestines in a tray on the back of his pushbike. When demands were high, he sought help from a ready group of younger boys who milled outside the Nguyen home waiting for Longy to appear and request their services. They called him '*Dai Ca*' ('big brother'), much to the annoyance of Teresa, who realised that in effect her son was building his first gang. These boys in tattered, dirty clothes and bare feet were the sons of poor parents who had to use whatever means possible to earn enough money to raise their families; putting their children in danger was an unavoidable risk. They all worked alone when working for Longy — only one person at a time delivered goods to a drop-off point, using different routes. No-one was ever caught. In return, they were well paid and often supplied with food and drinks from the coffee shop, unbeknownst to Teresa.

The boys were on the bottom tier of a simple gang structure. On the next level, directly below Longy, were the 'lieutenants', a group of older youths responsible for protection, enforcement and intimidation. Like the younger boys, they were mostly from impoverished backgrounds, and a few of them had lost brothers during the war. They were a formidable sight: some had long hair flowing to their shoulders; others exposed their lean, sinewy frames by not wearing shirts; and at least one had a tattoo of a buddha on his forearm. They became known as the 'Long Thien Ly Boys' — Longy's coffee shop boys. The fact that most were in their mid-teens showed how Longy's reputation was growing — he was beginning to command and demand the respect of those older than him. Teresa's dragon had all the makings of a leader: intelligence; cunning; daring; confidence; energy; and the ability to inspire those around him. Above all, he could fight with the best.

When needed, the lieutenants would wait for their boss outside the school gates to whisk him away on the back of one of their scooters — to deals, table soccer games or, if the situation arose, fights to bloody the knuckles. Longy's hustling, and his mere entry into adolescence in this environment, ensured that violence would be at the front line of his teenage development. The playful, recreational spats he'd enjoyed when younger had surrendered to his loss of innocence. If he was willing to hustle, he had to accept that the tiny alleys he did business in weren't nearly as narrow as the brittle edge he walked between safety and the danger of potential death. In the milieu he now inhabited murders weren't necessarily common, but were rarely unexpected. News of each killing was discussed and dissected over cups of coffee, whirring pushbike chains, footsteps to the market. Most were considered an accepted part of life. Only the most callous or inexplicable killings incited vengeful anger across the whole neighbourhood. One such incident involved a young woman, Le, who'd been viciously stabbed. Her killer was never found, the reason for her death was never known, but her memory lives on — to this day, the passage where she died is known as Le's laneway.

Every street, every lane, every alley, every building held horrible secrets, many of which had been born out of gang attacks. There were many reasons why blood was spilled: to assert authority; to satisfy ego; to maintain or boost reputations; to rob; to seek revenge; to intimidate; to settle a dispute over black-market goods or territory. There were also conflicts fuelled by hate, sheer desperation, a sadistic love of violence, and utter boredom, where youths went searching for trouble simply to pass the time. Longy and his lieutenants knew all the reasons and all the idle boys.

Whenever they entered a foreign neighbourhood, whether by foot or scooter, Longy's gang carried machetes, knives and chains that could crack through a bone with one furious swing. Longy had his own special weapon that he hid beneath his underpants — his father's loaded Beretta, which he decided he'd use only as the very last resort. His boys were his main protection; they were willing to gamble with their lives to defend one another. Their attitude reflected Saigon's street culture: 'Your business is my business. Your problem is my problem.' In reality, it was simply a variation of a universal theme: always look after your mates.

No-one needed more protection than Longy. This was purely because he was the person who arranged the deals and brought in the money. So if he was hurt, everyone suffered. He mostly used the lieutenants for intimidation, to stake a claim on a new black-market territory or to exact payback for deals in which he'd been cheated. Violence was just a standard part of any job. At the very least, bruises appeared; at the very worst, bones were broken, flesh was sliced, blood was lost. Although he never shirked a one-on-one contest, Longy really didn't need to become involved in any brawls. Like his father before him, he directed operations from behind the main line in his own kind of war. The little soldier had become a little general with soldiers of his own. He was thirteen.

These were just the formative stages of Longy's involvement in the gang lifestyle. If his reputation continued to grow — which seemed to be a certainty from the moment he secured his first fighting cock — he could expect heavier violence, and more lucrative black-market deals.

An owner of one of the neighbourhood's most renowned champion fighting cocks lived just a few minutes' walk from the Nguyen home. Longy had badgered him for weeks about buying the bird, a feisty fighter undefeated in twenty-one match-ups. The owner wouldn't be swayed by money, but when his young daughter fell ill with a chest condition he contemplated his position and made a request: 'Longy, if you can get me some antibiotics I will think about swapping the bird.'

There was a catch to buying Western medicine. Finding a supplier was easy enough for Longy, but in this seedy business of cheating, corruption and double deals, he had to make certain he was paying for an authentic product: it was a common trick for capsules to be filled with milk powder or cornflour. Before any sale, Longy with his lieutenants standing threateningly by his side, carefully unscrewed a sample of pills to both taste and smell their contents. With these precautions in mind he negotiated with a reputable dealer and returned to the owner of the cock with a bag full of bargaining power. Minutes later he was walking home with a bamboo cage swinging from his hand, carrying the latest member of his animal menagerie.

Teresa shook her head when she saw her son approaching: 'If you are going to fight that bird, I don't want to know about it.'

Longy grinned, then strutted through the coffee shop knowing his prized possession would turn heads and encourage chatter. He took the cock to its new home on the rooftop, and watched as it poked its head from side to side, its alert eyes taking in the strange surroundings.

Cocks were named according to their owner and colour. This apparently simple task created a problem for Longy. What to call a bird with an iridescent sheen of mottled browns, reds, purples, oranges, golds and specks of black? After some considerable thought, he made his choice: Longy Ga Chuoi — Longy Banana.

Within days, Banana had two more birds, Black and White, to keep it company, and their owner had a new companion who knew as much about poultry pugilism as anyone in the neighbourhood. Achay was about ten years older than Longy. He was a short, stocky, eternally optimistic young man whose passion for fighting birds was juxtaposed with his love of tai chi. The sight of him easing his body into a gentle flow of morning movements was the cause of much merriment for Longy, who mocked, 'That is an old man's martial arts. That's for girls!'

When not at peace with himself, or at war in a laneway littered with feathers, Achay mended pushbikes. Longy had first encountered him when on a typical meet-and-greet wander through the streets.

Once they were linked by the common bond of cock fighting, their friendship strengthened to the extent that they were together as often as Longy and Truong were. They'd sit and smoke by the roadside, excitedly talking about the last battle they'd seen or rumours of the next one. Achay was a veritable wealth of information. It seemed to Longy that there was nothing his friend didn't know.

Achay had helped choose both Black and White in a painfully fastidious selection procedure. He watched the birds for hours, silently analysing every feature, the thoughts winding through his mind like his limbs moved through tai chi: were the birds smart on their feet? Did they have strong legs? Did they have an alert, angry look in their eyes? How did they react to noise? A sudden clap of the hand? A loud whistle? Undoubtedly the most important of all questions was: how did they react to other birds?

The answer lay partly in the intriguing theory that cocks had good memories. It was widely believed that one badly injured in a fight would never forget the colour of its opponent. To ensure there were no mental scars, Achay taught Longy to test any bird he was considering buying. All he had to do was hold it against the cages of every different-coloured fighter he could find. If it bristled and threw an intense stare at its opposite number, it had the vicious streak needed. If it showed little reaction at all, it was too placid. And if it flapped its wings and twisted in sheer panic, one could presume it had been beaten before.

Longy devoted every speck of spare time to his stable of fighters. After feeding them each day on grains, meat and water, he rubbed them with rice whisky and herbs. These weren't just slap-and-dash affairs but precise massages using knuckles and tips of fingers, the same techniques first taught to him by Uncle Nam that Longy continued to use nearly every night on his mother — and now on the birds. He searched their muscles for scar tissue to break down, and stimulated the blood flow and energy systems of his ungrateful clients, who squirmed under his armpit and pecked at his hands.

When the rooftop became too hot and lacking in shade, Longy took his caged collection into the laneway, where the birds provoked considerable comment from passers-by. Later on he would use this display time to advertise his birds to rival owners seeking a fight.

His very first match-up was organised by Achay. Not surprisingly, he was unable to find an opponent for Banana — the champion's formidable record was too well known and revered. So the honours belonged to Longy Black, who was to fight another black cock.

Word spread quickly through the neighbourhood. Yes, Longy could hustle. Yes, he could fight. But could his birds? He barely slept the night before the contest. He was nervous, an unfathomable feeling for someone whose life overflowed with confidence. But now his reputation was about to be determined by something out of his control: two birds surrounded by a ring of noisy onlookers.

The fight had been arranged to take place in a laneway on the other side of the neighbourhood, well out of both earshot and eyesight of Teresa. After sneaking downstairs with Black tucked under his arm, Longy hurried to meet Achay on a hot and hazy afternoon. A group of boys trailed behind them, their feet slapping hard on the street in a frantic but futile attempt to keep up. This wasn't unusual — wherever Longy went, a burgeoning number of people followed. Not just boys, but youths and men who sniffed out the slightest opportunity to gamble. To see Longy holding a bird on the back of Achay's scooter was an irresistible invitation.

The laneway was no different to any other in the neighbourhood. It was narrow, dusty and surrounded by a jagged mix of single- and multistorey dwellings, their shadows leaning together as though conspiring about the fight's outcome. The inhabitants peered from their windows; some ran outside to have a closer look at what was going on.

Longy was immaculate. In what would become his typical uniform for these events, he wore jeans and a crisp white shirt, the most inappropriate colour considering the blood that was probably about to spurt forth. However, to the newest owner of a fighting cock, it was all about image — he had to look sharp and smart.

Negotiations for the fight didn't run smoothly. Longy was adamant that no spurs or knives were to be used. It was going to be a clean fight, which would mean it would take longer but there was much less chance of death. Losing a bird on debut wasn't an option. The rival, a hardened owner in his thirties, finally agreed.

The laneway heaved with people. The lieutenants were there in numbers, so too a handful of smaller boys who were puffing after chasing their 'big brother' all the way from the coffee shop. Longy appointed four of them to be lookouts for cadres; cock fighting wasn't illegal, but gambling was. As bets were made in the swelling crowd, the two owners handed their money to an old man well used to playing the banker. It was winner-takes-all.

Holding their wriggling combatants in front of them, Longy and the older man crouched down at opposite ends of the ring. Their birds scratched their claws into the dirt in angry anticipation. Both knew what lay ahead. Longy felt his heart thumping, and sweat slipped off his brow.

'One, two, three!'

Longy released his grip, the birds launched at each other, and the crowd hooted, clapped, laughed and whistled.

For the next half-hour, the fighters showed no signs of weakening. They kicked, they flapped, they scratched, they pecked. The crowd moved with them, shuffling backwards and forwards, bending around light poles and walls, giving the stars enough room to perform. All the while Longy watched, waited and hoped.

Then, suddenly and unexpectedly, he could smile. To everyone's surprise, the rival bird had turned its back and scurried towards the nearest jungle of legs it could find. This was the sign of defeat. Longy leapt forward and grabbed his weary fighter. Black offered no resistance, giving the impression it was relieved to have finished its work and could now relax in familiar hands. As quickly as the crowd had gathered it dispersed, leaving Longy and Achay to count the winnings.

Upon arriving home Longy rushed through the coffee shop, past Teresa, who gave her son a stern look of disapproval. Once on the rooftop he checked Black's mouth and throat, as dried blood had been known to choke birds if it wasn't cleared. He carefully prised open his bird's beak and blew softly into its mouth. He then rinsed it with water, cradling his fighter in his lap as though it were a baby. He also looked for wounds on the bare skin and underneath the feathers. Black had only a few nicks which would heal themselves, but in future fights Longy would use both salt and needles and thread to repair more serious injuries. Finally he poked and prodded his bird's body for signs of bruising or tenderness that would need additional rubs in the days ahead. Black flinched when touched in a few spots on its legs and chest. It was behaving like an athlete does on a massage table after playing a game, and Longy was certainly behaving like a trainer. Over the following days, Teresa's objection to the fight was shown by silence, a sure indication of her displeasure.

Longy soon strengthened his cock-fighting reputation when he arranged a contest for Banana. The appearance of one of the neighbourhood's most successful birds ensured a larger than usual gathering, this time much closer to the Nguyen home in a courtyard near Le Bao Tinh School. From the front of the coffee shop it was possible to see part of the crowd along an alley. Teresa didn't look.

As opposed to the debut fight, Longy accepted that spurs and knives would be used, but he didn't expect the request for a handicap. The rival owner had made the reckless decision to try an untested bird and suggested it was only fair that Banana be strapped with just one implement instead of the usual two. It made no difference in a ghastly, one-sided affair that ended with a deadly, swooping slice across the neck that twenty-one birds had suffered before. Banana was victorious once more.

On the way home Longy assumed his victory position on the back of Achay's scooter. He held his champion under his arm, while the limp and bloodied body of the loser, tied to the vehicle, swung behind him. Careful not to antagonise his mother by bringing back a dead cock, he asked Achay to detour via the home of Lady Xoi, the woman who sold cigarettes at the front of the coffee shop. As they passed Longy reached back, grabbed the bird and flung it over the fence into the yard. It would be good soup meat.

At night, when he massaged Teresa, Longy never spoke about cock fighting. They mostly talked about the abysmal conditions in the neighbourhood. Whole families were surviving on one meal a day. The food was basic: mixed rice and *Rau Muong*, a vegetable that became synonymous with the poor. Some of the most impoverished were forced to eat *Bo-Bo*, an unhusked grain used to feed animals. When buying food Teresa felt embarrassed that she was still able to afford such luxuries as meat, which she hid under vegetables on her way home from the markets.

Despite the absence of her husband, she realised she was in a fortunate position in so many ways. Her children were well provided for, and the home and coffee shop had been maintained without too much interference from the communists. Over the years of smart, hard work she had managed to save considerable amounts of gold — nest eggs for her family. In recent times she'd used a small part of her wealth to help fund the escape attempts of reputable businessmen she'd dealt with. In the right circumstances, she would offer her gold on the agreement that she received the same amount back before the escape took place. This was all about trust and respect, traits that had been the bottom line of all her operations since her earliest years in Pleiku.

As she heard stories of the growing number of escapes, she realised it was only a matter of time before her generosity would be needed much closer to home. Sadly this became all too apparent when James received the letter he and his mother had been dreading: he was to join the army and, without any training, be sent to the Cambodian border, where the Khmer Rouge were launching spasmodic attacks on Vietnamese villages. He had only two weeks to prepare. The similarities to Hien's departure were haunting, but unlike last time, Teresa wasn't going to accept it. She was angry and defiant. Her husband was gone, perhaps never to return. There was no way that she would ever allow the family to lose another.

James, too, had no intention of going. He was a peaceful, quiet young man, a dedicated university student, a devout Catholic. To send him into the jungles to stare down the barrel of a rifle was as incongruous as it would have been for a VC to drape himself in the stars and stripes. Countless people had already fled from army duties, but their actions had led to the punishment of their families — it was known that the government sometimes retaliated by taking away a parent or other children to work in labour gangs or the new economic zones. Therefore, James needed a plan that would protect both himself and his family. In contrast to Longy, he thankfully didn't draw any attention to himself when he walked the streets; this anonymity was in his favour. He was just one of thousands of people trying to make the best of his situation. He lived simply, dividing his time between his studies, family, religion and, most significantly, his girlfriend, Thu.

Thu's family lived in another district of Saigon, well away from the Nguyen home ... perhaps far enough to enable James to merge into society without fear of being identified. After considering all the possible repercussions of doing this, he formulated his plan. It was risky, but surely not as dangerous as the Cambodian border.

On the day he was to join the army, he did as was expected. He packed his belongings, farewelled his family, then headed for the registration point. After arriving, he joined hundreds of others in the same unfortunate position. The registration went smoothly: name, age, address. After this was over, he acted. Amid the long queues, the shouting officials, the swirling commotion, he walked away. No-one noticed him. No-one would have expected such an audacious move. That morning, James left his family to join the army. That afternoon, he left the army to join a new family. That night, Teresa cried. Her eldest son was gone, but he was safe.

Within a few days there was a loud knock on the door of the Nguyen home. The cadres had come to search for the missing soldier. Teresa was cool and implacable: 'He has gone. I haven't seen him since he went to join the army.'

The cadres looked in every room, then departed without any answers. Teresa allowed herself a little smile. In these times, James's successful disappearance was a significant victory. However, she was also struck by sadness and an overwhelming sense of loss. Slowly, her family was being pulled apart. Her husband and two oldest children were no longer under her roof. Would anyone else be going? Van was helping in the coffee shop; Lam, Thao and Linh were at various stages of their schooling; and Longy was ...

Teresa knew only too well what needed to be done.

Someone else was indeed going to leave.

THIRTEEN

Gone Today, Back Tomorrow

Death, robberies, starvation — Longy had come to expect that anything could happen on the streets of Saigon. Only recently he'd watched soldiers shoot dead a truck driver who'd refused to slow down for an inspection. Nothing would ever surprise him, but as he walked home from school he was puzzled by something he'd never seen before.

There were young guards everywhere. Their emotionless faces were in sorry contrast to the weeping inhabitants pleading for sympathy from the doorways of their houses. It was March 1978 and an anticapitalist campaign, primarily aimed at the ethnic Chinese, had begun.

Factories were closed and thousands of private businesses and properties were confiscated as the government began a new round of labour reform. Cholon was hit savagely. Longy heard stories of people shooting themselves, or jumping to their deaths from buildings. Tens of thousands of others fled, taking their chances on the open seas instead of going to the new economic zones.

The despair on the streets convinced Teresa that she had made the right decision. Two months earlier, she'd heard whispers in the coffee shop. After making some discreet inquiries, she acted quickly. She paid four ounces of gold to the men involved, then revealed everything to Longy that night while being massaged.

'I have arranged for you to be part of an escape attempt that is being planned. You must go, Longy, because life will be bad for you if you stay here. The older you become, the more dangerous it will be. You will be a target of the regime. I don't want that to happen. This is your best chance for a happy future.'

Longy didn't want to go, but once he realised his mother wouldn't be swayed, he accepted her decision. And it changed his outlook. For the next two months he cut back his activities on the streets, preferring to stay close to home. At an age at which many youths distance themselves from their parents, Longy turned the other way. He spent longer hours helping Teresa in the coffee shop; he linked his arm in hers when they walked to the markets; he massaged her more; and he even slept in her bed, cuddling close to her, telling her how much he loved her, how much he'd miss her. All of a sudden his sense of adventure had weakened; the wandering street kid realised the most precious miles were all travelled at home.

As the days passed he was torn between a rising swell of excitement about what lay ahead and an unrelenting sadness for what he would leave behind. He couldn't tell anyone outside the family. Not even Truong. Any escape plan had to be a closely kept secret to avoid detection from the authorities. The locals too posed a threat. Once hearing rumours of an attempt, people had been known to try sneaking on board the departing boat, or blatantly scrambling onto the deck in a pathetic bid for mercy.

Eventually word of the attempt came a few weeks after the ostracism of the Chinese had begun. The boat would leave in two days' time from My Tho, a village in the Mekong Delta, three hours' drive south of Saigon.

That night, in a steamy cranny under the roof of his home, a contact forged Longy's papers. Anyone wishing to travel outside the city needed the correct documentation from the authorities. Approval was mostly given for work reasons; rarely for family commitments. With only a single bulb emitting a quivering light over his work, and paying meticulous attention to detail, the forger wrote that Longy was required in the Mekong for a labour project. The forgery was completed when a stamp carved from a candle was delicately placed on one corner.

The following day was full of farewells and sheltered truths. Longy visited both Maria and James to say goodbye. He didn't cry — the reality of what he was about to do had not yet struck him. He also saw Uncle Nam and Uncle Ba. He told them that he was part of an escape attempt, but he didn't mention any other details. He didn't need to. Both men seemed to know.

'May you find happiness,' said Uncle Ba.

'Be strong and true to yourself,' said Uncle Nam.

Of all the people he visited, his time with Truong was the toughest. He so desperately wanted to share his secret with his best friend. Would it really hurt if he did? He fought against himself, before finally admitting, 'I am going to be part of an escape attempt.'

'When?'

'I don't know, but I think it will be soon.'

There was a sense of acceptance from Truong. He had known the time would come when he would have to wander the streets without Longy. There was no jealousy, just an acceptance of the situation. The Nguyens were wealthy enough to afford escape attempts; it was different for Truong's family. They used whatever money they had to survive. They had none to waste, and certainly none to save.

Longy left Truong as he had hundreds of times before. There was no emotion, no hug, no hint that this could be the last time they'd ever see each other.

'We'll get together soon,' he told his loyal friend.

'OK.'

After Longy returned home, he massaged Teresa longer and more sensitively than he'd ever remembered doing before.

'What do you think it will be like, Mum?'

'It will be hard, Longy. There will be many dangers, but you will be with good men. They will look after you.'

'Why don't you come? I will miss you.'

'You know I have to wait for your father. But I will be with you in spirit and prayer. We will always be with each other, Longy, even when we're apart. You must understand that this trip is for your best. Your life will begin again; it will be full of happiness. And knowing that brings me happiness.'

As he curled up next to his mother for the very last time, Longy found it impossible to sleep. He tried to imagine the boat. Would it be like those big US Navy ships he'd seen on television — strong and sturdy, the type of vessel that made him feel safe? And what about the ocean? He'd seen it when his family had lived in Nha Trang, but he'd never voyaged on it. He'd heard awful stories about people getting so sick that they spent their entire time vomiting. When they stood up their legs wobbled and their whole world spun out of control. It sounded like the behaviour of the American soldiers he'd seen zigzagging along the streets of Pleiku after they'd had a fix of heroin. Then there was the destination. Where, in fact, were they going? What was the plan? Maybe it would be safer to stay behind — at least he knew Saigon. And his family was there. Why leave them? Especially his mother, whom he loved more than he did his own life. And what about his father — would he ever see him again? Would the image of Hien riding away with black pyjama pants flapping be the final memory Longy would ever have of him?

The questions whirled through Longy's mind until sunlight crept into the house. The next few hours hurtled by. Worried that he would have little food on the trip, he ate a huge breakfast. Despite the summer stickiness that would send the temperature to 100 degrees in the heat of the day, he dressed in two layers of clothes: trousers and T-shirt underneath, an old pair of jeans and a shirt over the top. The discomfort he felt was countered by his belief that he was prepared. The extra items could become blankets or pillows at night, or if he needed the money he could perhaps sell something. He may have been escaping Saigon, but he was taking his hustling skills with him. He wore leather shoes and took just one piece of jewellery, a necklace with a cross that his mother had given him years before.

He left the rest of his belongings to his sister Thao: a few ounces of gold, money and sunglasses. She would arrange for the cocks to be sold at a later time. He kissed his youngest sister goodbye, then hugged Lam, Van and Linh. Everyone was crying. Longy too felt tears welling, but tried to control them as he approached his mother. They stood apart from each other for several seconds, looking into each other's eyes, trying to read what the other was thinking. Then they hugged. It was an all-encompassing embrace of arms, emotions and nearly fourteen years of love. Longy could no longer hold back his tears.

'I want you to come.'

'Remember, Longy, I will always be with you,' Teresa replied.

Indeed she would be: Longy had tucked a tiny photo of his mother into a pocket of his jeans, its smiling image so many emotions away from the tearful face that Longy couldn't bear to leave.

As they broke apart, Teresa gave her son a hand-sized object wrapped in plastic.

'Chew on this if you are tired or feeling sick.'

It was ginseng — Uncle Nam was there in spirit too.

'Now go. God will look after you. We all love you, Longy.'

'I love you too.'

Longy didn't look back as he walked down the stairs, but once on the street, which had come alive with the morning, he turned to see Thao and Linh crying on the balcony. He smiled weakly, then lifted his head and footsteps and hurried towards the nearest bus terminal.

He waited for half an hour, wondering what his family was doing. Was everyone still crying? What would Thao do with the cocks? For a brief moment he thought of returning home to be hugged again, to massage his mother as though nothing had ever happened, to smell the sharp scent of steaming coffee, to share a cigarette with Achay, to go looking for trouble with Truong. But he couldn't. No matter what he'd done to anger, frustrate or disappoint Teresa in the past, nothing would affect her more than if he turned his back on the opportunity he'd now been given. He needed to treat it as an adventure. And as a gamble, but one with much greater rewards than a few dong tossed across the glass after a victory in table soccer or an ounce of gold won in a cock fight. He couldn't go back. Not now. Not later. Not ever.

Once the bus arrived he settled into a seat and stared out the window at the city he knew: the markets, the canals, the bikes, the beggars, the twisting lanes, the hustlers, the gangs, the table soccer, the cocks in bamboo cages, the women squatting by the roadside eating *pho* ... He'd seen every scene hundreds, probably thousands of times before, but this would surely be the time he'd remember above all others.

In the centre of the city he needed to catch a 'Honda taxi' to another bus terminal on the outskirts of the city. More images flashed by, more memories: the fenced-off mango trees he'd climbed; the red, dusty field where he'd played soccer; the deserted bars where once the GIs rocked and rolled; the Presidential Palace that had surrendered to communism. Staring at the stark face of the past, Longy knew his mother was right: it was time to look ahead at a new life, a new beginning.

The second bus trip lasted three hours. It was a rough and bumpy journey over potholes and corrugations on roads that still had gaping wounds from the war. The cluttered streets of Saigon had made way for rice and vegetable fields, buffaloes, and villages of decrepit wooden houses with tin or coconut palm-thatched roofs and shutters which were either closed or partially open, winking at the day. Similar structures existed along the tributaries of the Mekong, but here they hitched up their floorboards to reveal long, skinny stilts standing in the muddy water. Washing dangled from lines of rope strung between poles, and cane fishing baskets, weary from overuse, sat slumped together on walkways that led down to platforms where boats were moored, bobbing up and down with the gentle swells caused by continuous water traffic. Broad-nosed wooden boats with flat open decks and rickety cabins chugged along, powered by weak motors. Peasant women in leaf hats gripped bamboo poles, pushing them into the murk to move their narrow fruit-laden vessels.

After getting off the bus at My Tho Longy was met by a teenage youth who took him to a noodle shop, where he was told to wait. An hour passed before he was approached by a man whose shady smile exposed a sprinkling of gold teeth that matched his necklace and the numerous chunky rings on his fingers.

'Are you Long?'

'Yes.'

'Come with me.'

They bounced along dusty paths on a scooter until they reached a tin hut at the water's edge. Longy followed the man inside to find nine other people already waiting. There were a few nods to acknowledge the newest arrival, but nothing was said. Longy sat down, looking at the others in the room. All were adults, except for one boy about five years of age sitting next to his mother with his legs neatly folded. Everyone was dressed in simple peasant clothing. Once he was settled Longy spoke quietly to the man next to him and discovered that the clothes were a façade — these people all came from wealthy, powerful backgrounds. One was a former doctor in the ARVN, others were businessmen.

It was mid-afternoon and very hot. Longy felt clammy and dirty under all his clothes. But this was the least of his concerns in a room crowded with anxiety and fear. Each person was lost in his or her own thoughts. It was likely they had three common themes: don't get caught; get on the boat at all costs; get to safety, wherever that may be.

They were told they would leave at night, when the chance of a successful escape was greatest. They would board a riverboat and when closer to the sea they'd be transferred to a fishing vessel with a narrower, sharper bow, designed to handle open waters. All they had to do was wait. And wait. And wait.

By sunset there was little noise other than the gentle lap of water and the creaking of the hut's tin in the cooling air. Time dragged, prompting a growing edginess as people began to shift about, walk around the room and whisper to each other. Only the child slept.

It was well after 2 a.m. when machine-gun fire splintered the silence. Shouting erupted between men outside the hut. Longy reacted quickly. He crawled out of the room and sneaked to the back of the hut, where he rolled through a door and pressed himself up against an outside wall that faced the river. He didn't care about anyone in the room; he needed only to look after himself. There was another round of gunfire. More yelling. Louder. Angrier.

Longy listened. The man firing the bullets skywards was the local cadre, demanding higher payment if he was to ignore the escape. He wanted the gold immediately, but that was impossible to arrange without more escapees.

'You only have ten people. You should have forty!' shouted the cadre, who was obviously being paid per head.

In the silence that followed, Longy decided to stay where he was. He lit a cigarette and wondered if the attempt was over. Word didn't come until sunrise, when he heard footsteps behind him. It was the man with the gold teeth.

'I'm sorry — the attempt is off. You will have to go home.'

Longy showed no emotion. He walked inside, said goodbye to the others, then headed for the local bus terminal. Although disappointed, he was also overcome with relief because he could go home again. Perhaps his one and only chance of a better life had gone, but he didn't give it much thought; at that very moment there was nothing more important to him than being with his mother.

He arrived back in Saigon by early evening. Despite all he had endured, Longy strolled into the coffee shop with a grin.

Teresa was startled: 'What happened? You didn't run away from it, did you?'

As Longy told his story, the dramatic adventure began to affect him. Two days without sleep, a false farewell from his family and the stripped promise of a new life suddenly weighed heavily on his eyelids.

'Go to bed. We will talk when you wake up.'

In the morning his first task was to retrieve everything he'd given Thao. However, within two weeks the gold, money and sunglasses were back in his little sister's hands as he once again said goodbye. Since her son's return, Teresa had worked hard to find another way for him to escape — she wouldn't rest until Longy was safely out of Vietnam.

This time he travelled a few hours northeast to Phuoc Long, a coastal settlement. He had new papers but, just as had been the case in his first attempt, he wasn't stopped by any official. Wearing two sets of clothes, carrying the photo of his mother and some ginseng, he arrived in the evening and was taken straight to a 14-metre boat that had been specifically built for the escape. It was planned that forty people would go, but as the passengers began boarding numbers soon swelled beyond 200. Nearly every part of the deck was covered with people either pleading to be taken or telling lies that they had already paid their gold and were entitled to be there. The situation was hopeless. The boat was so weighed down it was barely able to float, let alone travel anywhere. After futile attempts by the organisers to sift out those who shouldn't be on board, there was only one course of action: abort the attempt.

Again Longy returned home with a grin. Again he reclaimed his possessions from Thao. And again Teresa began searching for another escape for her son.

The third bid was again in the Mekong delta. All began well when about fifty people departed on a riverboat in the early evening. Longy sat quietly by himself. As had rapidly become customary, he thought more about what his mother would say when he returned than how she would react if she ever received a letter from him from a distant country. The vessel slipped further into the night. It was still in a tributary, but before too long it would be in the Mekong itself. From there, everyone would be transferred to a fishing boat for the run towards the open sea. It was the furthest Longy had come, yet he refused to believe he was heading to freedom. Considering his previous two attempts, it stood to reason that sooner or later he'd be returning to Saigon. Low hopes left no room for disappointment.

It was after midnight when the boat slowed and turned into the Mekong. The captain cut the engine, allowing his craft to drift with the current while he used his torch to flash a coded message into the blackness. Nothing happened. He tried again. Still nothing. The passengers began to murmur. The more time passed, the louder the chatter became. After nearly an hour two crew members jumped into the water and swam ashore. They returned another hour later with the news that the 'big boat no good'. The captain and crew had apparently been arrested and the boat confiscated by the coastguard. Longy shook his head; perhaps his mother just had to accept that a free life for her son wasn't meant to be.

Over the following months Longy's life was a revolving door of escape attempts that always ended back where they started. Despite her frustration, which was magnified by the rising despair and hardship that was everywhere around her, Teresa refused to be beaten, telling her boy, 'It will happen, Longy. If we want it badly enough, we can make it happen.'

In between his cameo disappearances Longy returned to his familiar ways, and his successes earned him enough money and gold to buy a symbol of his status — a 90cc Honda. Where most scooters burped and hiccuped with less than 50ccs, this machine roared with a modified exhaust that thundered out the declaration that not everyone was struggling to make ends meet. From the moment Longy kicked it over with his adidas sports shoes (acquired on the black market), the bike was heard on the streets long before it was seen.

The scooter wasn't the only ostentatious example of Longy's incomparable position: he had his shoes, his Levis, his Lacoste shirt complete with the embroidered alligator over the chest. And then there was his watch. Not just any watch, but a Casio with a digital display screen, a striking metal band and rows of buttons that comprised a calculator.

The way Longy obtained the watch showed just how slick a hustler he had become. He wanted it as soon as he saw it on the wrist of a flashy teenager in the coffee shop. With hair slicked back, a shining gold necklace and smart

Western clothes, the stranger was obviously a hustler from another neighbourhood. He oozed confidence when he sauntered across the room with his girlfriend, heading for the best table, the one nearest the fish pond.

Longy wasted no time in approaching him.

'That's a nice watch. I haven't seen one like that before. Do you have any others?'

'No, they're very hard to get.'

'How do you get them?'

Surprisingly, the hustler answered without a moment's hesitation. He had connections in Thailand who arranged for the watches to be brought into Vietnam by foot over the Cambodian border. The boy's openness was a weakness: any smart businessman knew to keep quiet about where and how he obtained his goods. Longy soon learnt other valuable snippets from this loose-lipped hustler. He was indeed from outside the neighbourhood, had been doing business on the streets for a few years, and was a keen gambler. It was this last point that triggered Longy's idea.

'So you like cock fights?'

'Yes.'

'I have a cock fighting today. A very good one. Very sharp, very quick. It's going to win easily. Some good money to be made. You should come.'

The hustler nodded, which immediately created a significant problem — Longy hadn't arranged a fight at all.

After promising to return to the coffee shop as soon as he could, he rushed out to find Truong in the laneway. Within minutes the two chuckling friends had developed a plan. Longy's youngest bird — by this time he had six — was a striking black specimen that on looks alone was a champion. However, unbeknownst to anyone apart from the two schemers, it had an injury, the result of a thoughtless game that Longy and Truong had played. One tossed the cock from the rooftop while the other waited below. They laughed every time they saw the bird flutter in panic and hit the ground in an awkward twist of wings, body and feet. Longy hadn't realised how much damage was being done until the cock began limping on one foot. Although he tried to fix the problem, his fighter had a permanent injury that severely affected its prowess in the ring.

While Longy hurried back to the shop, Truong sought out a friend who they'd planned to be part of the attempted sting. He had an ungainly-looking cock that, if put side to side with the lame bird, would appear to be hopelessly outclassed. However, it could fight well, and if all went to script it would win easily. Soon afterwards, Longy marched into battle with the hustler and girlfriend by his side, the injured cock under his arm.

'Everyone should bet big on my fighter because it's unbeatable.'

The hustler needed no convincing, but had little money with him.

'That doesn't matter. Maybe you should use something else. You can't lose,' boasted Longy, who proved his confidence by placing a large winner-takes-all bet with his knowing opponent. As he'd hoped, the hustler was swayed by the action, and was encouraged further when he compared the two birds. Longy's splendidly shiny black combatant was taller, stronger and more alert than its motley-coloured rival — this would surely be a lopsided contest. The naive hustler needed no more proof before recklessly following Longy's lead and laying a bet with the rival owner — his watch against a substantial amount of cash.

'You won't lose,' chirped Longy again.

The fight lasted just minutes before the black bird landed once too often on its sore spot and limped towards the safety of the crowd that had inevitably gathered. Longy feigned disappointment. He picked up his bird, looking at its foot in theatrical disbelief. Then he turned to the hustler:

'I'm sorry — it has a very bad bruise from kicking so much. Not good.'

To his credit, the hustler didn't protest. If placed in a similar position, others would have reacted violently, perhaps calling their gang to seek some sort of revenge. However this young man simply walked away, giving no impression that he'd been swindled.

This was the only time Longy accepted defeat in a cock fight. In the future, whenever his birds lost he'd take the failures to heart, especially when deaths occurred. Sometimes he would barely speak for several days. But there was no need for despair this time. After returning home with his beaten bird, he later met his smiling opponent and collected his reward ... he would never again need to ask someone else for the time.

The watch, the souped-up scooter, the clothes, the shoes all combined to present an image of a flamboyant, precocious youngster who was fast beginning to think he was untouchable. His reputation had been inflated even further by his success as a table-tennis player. At his mother's insistence he'd taken up the government-run activity to allegedly show his support for the communist infrastructure. Teresa considered it a way to counter some of his less respectable activities. From the moment he picked up the bat in his left hand — no-one here was going to hit him with a ruler or cane for not wielding it with his right — he showed the same coordination and skill he'd brought to his other sports.

Because of his competitive nature he was devoted to practice, spending at least an hour every second day at the Luu Luyen Club, an eternally hectic complex that had more than a dozen tables side by side. Day and night, players of all ages pinged forehands and backhands, cut deceptive slices and spins and unloaded smashes. Amid the metronomic clip of balls on bats, shoes squeaked, bare feet thumped and sweat dripped into small pools on the wooden floor.

Longy was trained by a cagey player and gambler called Son, who was in his thirties and still quick and nimble around the table. For three dong an hour he taught his student all the finer points of the game: how to trick an opponent with the amount of spin or slice on a ball; how to serve; how to read the opponent's game; and where to stand. Son was as keen a teacher as Longy was a listener.

On his way to the club, Son would ride via the Nguyen home and yell from the laneway, 'Longy, time for training! Hurry up!' They'd then ride to the club together.

There was no-one prouder than Son the day Longy reached the semifinals of a district tournament for 16 to 19 year olds. He'd pushed into the older group because it was easier than entering the under-16s where competitors were eligible only if they wore the red kerchief of communism. It wasn't the least surprising that Longy was able to hold his own against the seniors — after all, he'd done it in every other part of his life. However, when he finally convinced officials that he should be allowed to compete in his proper age bracket, he was knocked out in the first round.

As Longy says now, the tournament was 'an act to gain acceptance and get into the good books of the communists'. He didn't care what they thought, though — he only did it for his mother.

By this stage, tae kwon do had been allowed to resume. Longy returned to classes wearing the same uniform he'd worn before. It had yellowed considerably; the only sign of its previous bright white colour was a small square on the chest where Teresa had unpicked a miniature South Vietnam flag that had been sewn on by Maria years earlier.

Longy still loved martial arts. Under Uncle Nam's tutelage, and with impromptu lessons from people he'd met through the black market, he'd expanded his repertoire to include karate. However, when it came to practising tae kwon do as a communist-organised activity, his interest faded just as his uniform had. He attended only a few classes before deciding his main fighting would be done on the streets. There was also the schoolyard, but contests there against Longy were now almost unheard of. No-one wanted to make any trouble ... unless his name was Nguyen Chien Thang.

Nguyen Chien Thang, better known as 'Victory', was a hardened street kid and the most feared bully at the school. Feeling that some of his playground power was being eroded by the regard in which Longy was held, he sought the only remedy he knew — he challenged his rival to a fight. Longy couldn't refuse. Reputations and large egos were at stake.

They agreed it would take place before school the following day. There'd be no weapons, no lieutenants ready to pounce. It would be one on one; the winner would be the last man standing. Longy considered it to be just another street fight, except this one would be in a barely used classroom on the fifth floor, the very top of the school's main building.

The next morning Longy walked through the gates and the deserted quadrangle and up the winding flights of stairs to find Victory already waiting for him outside the classroom. Without acknowledging each other, they entered. The room was crowded with youths who'd heard about the fight. Many were standing on chairs and tables that had been pushed to the edge of the room to form a ring in the middle. A buzz of excitement and anticipation bounced off every wall. No-one knew who would win but, regardless of the result, this was an event that would be talked about for weeks.

Dressed smartly in jeans, shirt and adidas shoes, Longy looked as though he was on his way to a cock fight, except that this time he was the cock. He pushed his way through the ring, looking at the faces around him. He felt the electricity, the tension written on every face. He took his shirt off, exposing his broad chest and shoulders. Victory didn't remove anything, but beneath his shirt was a chiselled body every bit as strong as his opponent's. This was an even match-up.

They stood just centimetres apart, staring viciously at each other, each trying to reach behind the other's eyes and into his thoughts to create that last fleck of doubt. Neither gave anything away for several seconds, until they each took a step back. The room fell silent; there wasn't even the sound of a single breath. Both boys waited. Longy's heart thumped, his palms sweated, and his eyes never lost focus against the cold stare looking back at them. Was it only a second? A handful? He'd lost all sense of time when he decided to strike first. He turned, twisted, let loose, and —

It was over. Just one kick spinning to the head, heel against cheek, and Victory lay on the ground writhing in pain. Everyone was stunned, including Longy, who'd expected to win, but like this? He stood stiffly, wondering what to do next. Perhaps a triumphant thrust of arms into the air? Or perhaps just walk away without celebration, knowing that in this situation humility packed the strongest punch.

As he heard the squeaking of chairs and felt the ring close in around him, he moved towards the sorry figure who was now sitting up with bowed head in hands.

'Is it over?'

Victory nodded with a wince.

A few hours later when he returned home for lunch and siesta, Longy was met by Truong outside the coffee shop.

'I heard the news, Longy. One kick! You are the King.'

With his ego intact, and others' estimation of him another notch higher, Longy indeed felt powerful. There was no-one in the neighbourhood who could touch him. No-one could beat him. No-one could outsmart him. Most of all, he was afraid of no-one. He was the King indeed.

FOURTEEN

The Nicotine Gang

Longy was standing in the laneway with his cocks when the four strangers on scooters stopped next to him. The biggest, a fat youth in his late teens, dismounted from his bike with considerable effort, slipping off the back of the seat in an awkward shuffle. As his machine's suspension sighed with relief, he waddled towards the birds in the shade of the Nguyen home. He was obviously a powerful figure in his own neighbourhood. Apart from several necklaces and rings he had a Rolex watch, its thin gold band like a piece of string around his massive wrist. Without any hesitation he walked straight to the cage holding Banana and declared, 'I want that one.'

Banana had by now become Longy's 'image bird'. In the last eighteen months the champion had only fought on a handful of occasions, its notoriety having frightened away every cock owner in the area. Although Longy had grown attached to his top fighter, he recognised its greatest worth was no longer in the ring but in the hip pocket of a prospective buyer.

'He's a very good bird. He's unbeaten. He's not cheap.'
'How much?'
Staring at the bulky figure in front of him, Longy knew exactly what he wanted. He expected some spirited bargaining, but he wouldn't move on his price — it was a take-it-or-leave-it proposition. Surprisingly, the teenager didn't haggle at all. After he'd paid quite happily, he rode away with Banana on his well-cushioned lap, leaving Longy with another watch to add to his collection.

While cock fighting remained important to Longy, it was in the shallow end when compared with the black-market operations that quite literally stretched as far and wide as the Saigon River. To Longy it seemed a lifetime ago that he had stood at the edge of Pleiku's volcanic lake, Bien Ho, and wondered if he would ever be able to reach the other side. If he was back there now, he undoubtedly could. The boy who'd taught himself how to tread water in a tank could now 'swim like a trout' all the way across the swirling waters of the Saigon River. It was after one of these arduous journeys that he plunged deeper into the far murkier waters of the black market.

He met a group of lithe, athletic youths who were as comfortable in the river as Longy was in laneways and alleys. Born and raised in huts along the banks, the 'river boys' not only treated the water as their playground, but also as their territory. They readily accepted Longy the outsider, though, because anyone who was strong enough and brave enough to swim from the other side was worthy of immediate respect, recognition and, above all else, consideration for one of the slickest operations in the city — the smuggling of Western-brand cigarettes.

Longy was invited to visit the mastermind of the business, a 'madam hustler' called Trang. She was a comfortably large middle-aged woman with long grey hair tied up with a bow, her husky voice stained by nicotine.

With sharp eyes she looked at Longy from top to toe. Wearing only shorts, he cut an impressive figure.

'The boys tell me you are a very good swimmer,' she said.

'I swim a lot in the river and in pools. I enjoy it.'

'The boys' word is good enough for me. They wouldn't have brought you here if they didn't trust you. They will let you know when the time comes.'

Through her legitimate business, a dank little restaurant near Saigon's docks, this feminine Fagin befriended many of the seamen from visiting cargo ships. Those she trusted became part of a network of international suppliers who'd collect bulk loads of cigarettes from the various ports they stopped at, most notably Singapore. After hiding the contraband in their quarters, they'd wait until they entered the Saigon River before taking the next step. In the meantime, Trang would use contacts at the docks to find out when each ship was expected. The day before an arrival, she'd inform the river boys.

When told he was needed for the first time, Longy was abuzz with excitement. This was a new challenge, an adventure with rich rewards. It was just after sunrise when he and three other boys churned through the river's glassy stillness a few kilometres away from the docks. Once in the middle, they trod water and waited. Every few minutes they had to swim back against the current that gently carried them away from their designated spot. It was hard, tiring work. Finally, just when it seemed their heavy legs and arms would force them back to shore, a wave of fresh energy swept over them when they saw an approaching ship. The vessel was moving quickly and easily, as though it were skating across the surface. As it came closer, its immense size awed Longy. Staring at the gigantic bow heading towards him he suddenly felt tiny, insignificant and very, very fragile. For the first time since he'd accepted the job, he realised he was risking his life. If he tired, or didn't watch the ship's progress, he could easily find himself directly in its path with nowhere to go except under it, where he might be chopped up by a propeller.

The ship powered nearer. Longy's heart raced at the same furious rate as his egg-beating legs. The bow was adjacent to them. He looked up. And up. And up. For a moment he was lost in wonder at the daunting size and magnificence of this hulk.

'Longy!'

He turned to see the boys paddling towards a plastic bag bobbing in the wake. Another one plonked into the water. Then another. He collected the parcel nearest him, checked that it was watertight, then searched for any others. He looked back through the frothy path to the ship that no longer seemed so imposing as it dwindled into the distance and he imagined what it would be like on board — there could surely be few safer places anywhere in the world.

Pushing their contraband in front of them, Longy and the boys swam back to shore. They chatted and joked, their mood reflecting their success. They had made it, and would soon be richer. They gave the bags of cigarettes to another youth, who was responsible for delivering them to Trang's various hustling contacts. Each step was part of a smooth, well-organised operation.

Longy quickly became one of Trang's most valuable links. His exceptional swimming ability and the respect he commanded from others ensured he was sought for many jobs. All were physically demanding. Sometimes he and the boys paddled out with banana stump leaves to rest on. On other occasions, when a ship was really late, they took turns swimming back to shore for a rest. However, they never failed to be in the right spot at the time of the drops.

Western-brand cigarettes fetched high prices on the black market. To see a man with a packet of Marlboros or Dunhills in his pocket was to see someone of wealth and prestige — or, perhaps, a cadre who'd been bribed by Longy to ignore his wanderings after curfew.

Cigarettes weren't the only products considered to be almost as valuable as gold. One day after visiting Uncle Nam in Cholon, Longy was approached by a thin, balding man who'd heard of his reputation and said, 'I will pay you very well if you can bring me as much *Amanhang* as you can. I need a constant supply.'

Amanhang, a thick paper used as a protective coating for machine parts, was extremely valuable because it helped preserve engines on many escape boats. Sensing a lucrative opportunity, Longy went in surreptitious search of a supplier. This was fraught with danger, because the only places that made the product were government-operated factories. Such was the desperation of the times, however, that workers were willing to gamble their lives by stealing whatever they could from the sweatshops.

After whispering in doorways, murmuring on street corners and coffee shops, and quietly slipping dong into pockets, Longy found someone who could help him. He arranged a meeting, and once trust was established he was told of the daring workers who stole *Amanhang* by tucking sheets under their shirts and wrapping rolls around their legs inside their trousers. All the goods were delivered to a central point for distribution; it was here that Longy eased his way into the operation. Buying up to 40 kilograms of *Amanhang* at a time, he carted the precious cargo under banana leaves in pushbike carts. He either worked alone or with only one or two people. Each load was sold at a marked-up price to the contact in Cholon. This was a profitable business — rewarding enough for one of Longy's lieutenants to buy a brand-new bike after running just one deal.

Longy primarily used his growing earnings to buy goods that enhanced his appearance: clothes, jewellery, shoes — even Old Spice deodorant, another highly sought-after Western product. He also bought flowers and perfume for his mother, and was frequently giving away shirts and cigarettes to Truong. But although Longy enjoyed spending, he also knew how to save. Apart from his hessian bag of cash, he hid gold in a nook between bricks in his bedroom wall, and also used Uncle Ba to mind his riches. On the rare occasions his cash flow dried up, he rarely needed to look further than his best friend. Truong may have had little money at the best of times, but he was always willing to offer whatever he had because, 'Longy always looked after me, so it was my duty to look after him when I could. It made me very happy.'

However, neither Truong nor anyone else could provide Longy with what — or, rather, who — he missed most: his father. It had been more than three years since Hien had gone away to be re-educated. His letters, which came every few months, were brief and devoid of emotion or meaningful news. He always stressed that he was well, but unless his family could see him in person they found this difficult to believe.

Each letter fuelled Longy's utter contempt for the communists. When the need arose he was able to talk, smile, laugh and joke with them, but this was all a façade. Underneath it a simmering, rebellious teenager was planning revenge. He knew only his dreams would ever allow him to curse and scar every single follower of Ho Chi Minh, but surely there were ways he could leave a mark beyond his scribbles on a classroom blackboard.

Lying awake at night, he toyed with the fanciful idea of driving through the streets in a tank, gunning down anyone in a uniform. Or perhaps he could sneak into the Presidential Palace and use his father's Beretta to shoot government officials. Or maybe he could ambush cadres as they walked along the dark, squalid alleys that he knew so well. A chain; a machete; bare hands — he could kill them any way he chose.

Longy's frustrations rose with each letter his mother received from his father, until finally, towards the end of

1978, he couldn't control his actions any longer. No-one knew his plan when he shuffled into line in the school quadrangle for the daily assembly. Victory Nguyen was next to him (since their fight, they'd become good friends; Victory had even worked as one of Longy's lieutenants). A prefect was in front of them. It was the same every single day. As the national anthem screeched out from the speakers on the main building, this prefect would stand at attention — head straight, chest puffed, legs together, arms stiff as rods by his side, his extended chin jutting above his beautifully tied red kerchief. Longy detested the model pupil. But today would be different.

The quadrangle was crowded with hundreds of students. Each line was flanked by teachers who all stood looking at the elevated picture of Ho Chi Minh that hung from the main building. Apart from the odd fidgeting hand and shifting foot, all was still. Longy wondered just how dramatically he could shatter this frozen moment. His eyes fixed on the back of the prefect's head, he gritted his teeth, clenched his fist and waited for the sounds that never failed to spit venom into his thoughts. First came the crackle of the speakers. Longy held firm. He had just seconds to wait. One. Two. Three. Four ... The anthem began; the prefect opened his mouth; but before he could make a single loyal sound he was falling, his head in a spin. Longy looked around quickly. One down. Now he didn't care who he hit. In a raging burst, he chopped anyone within reach. Two, three, four people were down. Five! Six! Seven! Eight! He was stunned. How could the numbers be falling so quickly? He found the answer behind him. Victory Nguyen was making his own brutal statement. Bodies hit the concrete, blood flowed from noses, girls screamed, Longy and Victory continued swinging. And all the while, the anthem played on.

After the pair was subdued by a group of teachers, the tally of children who'd been hit was well into double figures. Longy was told his fate would be decided at a teachers' meeting that night. He didn't care. And nor did he worry what his mother would think when he went home and told her during siesta.

Teresa wasn't surprised. The incident simply hastened her search for escape opportunities. Now that Longy had so blatantly shown his disregard for the government, it was just a matter of time before he would be targeted for some God-forsaken duty that could ruin his life forever. At best, he had just two or three years of relative freedom. At worst, rules could suddenly change and he could be taken away in a heartbeat.

After the meeting, a teacher hurried to the Nguyen home to tell her friend Teresa that an unprecedented decision had been reached. Education was considered the essential tool in shaping the beliefs of any child or adolescent; the classroom was where a captive, impressionable audience could be successfully taught the values and practices of communism. It was expected there would be moments of misbehaviour and lapses of immaturity, but this fitted in with Ho Chi Minh's belief that it took a man 100 years to grow. But to do this?

Teresa calmly accepted the decision: 'You have always been very different, Longy. You are who you are.' And being who he was, he decided he had another statement to make. He prepared for school the next morning, dressing in his best Western attire: perfectly ironed jeans, a brand-new long-sleeved white shirt, and his sports shoes. Then he added the telling touch — he shaved his head, a contemptuous act recognised as showing complete disdain for those in control. From the moment he left the house his defiance prompted the shaking of heads, hurried whispers and disbelieving stares. These continued after he arrived at school. As he walked proudly and arrogantly between clusters of students, there were murmurings from all across the quadrangle.

A special assembly was called to announce the punishment for the fight. Longy was summoned to stand on a stage next to the headmaster in front of every pupil while the incident was recounted in bullet-point style. It was though he was on trial.

At the end of the monologue the headmaster said the word Longy had been waiting for: 'Expelled.'

Longy turned on his heels and walked silently across the quadrangle, knowing that nearly every eye was fixed on him. As he strolled out the gate he felt thoroughly satisfied that the education system's last memory of him would be the back of his shiny head.

His action made no difference to his mother, who knew there was only one way of changing her son. By now he'd been involved in a handful of unsuccessful escapes, but Teresa hadn't given up hope that sooner or later he would be free. Only then would he be forced to look at his life differently.

When she heard of a friend's plan to try escaping from My Tho, the scene of Longy's very first attempt, she decided it was time to become more involved. She travelled to the Mekong village to inspect the boat the escapees would be transferred to once they were approaching open water. Teresa was impressed: it was a restored 15-metre fishing vessel with a new engine. She asked questions about the journey. How many people? Forty. Where were they heading? Malaysia. Who was captain? An experienced, knowledgeable seaman. Would there be good food supplies? Rice had already been packed, and pork meat and crackling would be wrapped in banana leaves to be stored on the day of departure. Each answer encouraged her — it seemed nothing had been overlooked. On her return home she told Longy to prepare himself yet again.

'The boat looks good, Longy. It will take you far. This will be very different from your previous attempts.'

'How can you be so sure?'

'I just have a feeling. Plus, this time James is going with you.'

The brothers travelled together from a bus terminal on Saigon's outskirts. On their arrival at My Tho they discovered a mixed group of families, single middle-aged men and a well-known musician.

The early stages went as hoped. After leaving My Tho on a riverboat they linked up with the refurbished fishing vessel in the late afternoon. The transfer went smoothly. Within hours they were in open water. There had been no police, no coastguards. In all his previous attempts Longy had never seen anyone relax, but now, sitting shoulder to shoulder under the deck, rolling over a gentle swell, the people struck a mood that was as buoyant as the boat itself. They even began to sing. The journey may have been heading into the unknown, but the fact that everyone knew what had been left behind was worth celebrating. They were free.

Longy thought of his mother. He wanted to throw out his arms and give her one final hug, telling her how much he loved her. It had been difficult for him to appreciate her perseverance and urgency in arranging his escape, but as he felt the sheer ecstasy of the people around him in the grainy darkness, he was beginning to understand: his mother loved him too much to keep him by her side.

He was so relieved that James was with him — there was no better person for the situation. James had grown into a quiet, peaceful, yet assertive young man who could distance his emotions from his thoughts. He was as rational as Longy could be irrational. It was more than likely that, over the days or weeks that it took for the boat to reach safety, the two intrinsically different brothers would need to draw strength from each other.

They settled down and rolled with the hours that passed late into the night. After the singing had finished people fell asleep, or whispered to one another, often discussing their lives, both past and future. Despite the discomfort of being wedged together in a space that was beginning to reek of body odours, excrement, food and saltwater, no-one seemed to mind. It was the price of freedom.

By the earliest hours of the morning, few people were awake. Only the engine's chugs and the creaks from the hull interrupted the quiet. Everyone was at peace with the rhythm of the ocean. The fact that the swell was becoming bigger was nothing to worry about; it was perhaps cause for greater relief because it meant the boat was well into international waters. However, no-one below deck was experienced enough to know what was coming next.

BOOM!

The boat lurched from side to side.

BOOM!

People tumbled across one another.

BOOM!

Screams pierced the air. People scrambled. Fear and panic showed in every face. The engine stopped and the captain yelled. The boat had been hit by three rogue waves; they needed to assess any damage. Now! Right now! The reality of the situation was lapping at the feet of a group standing below the hatch: the boat was taking in water. Rapidly.

Someone hurried onto the deck with an armful of clothes and food that he hurled overboard. Others followed. Some cried. Others clutched onto rosary beads and prayed. And others used buckets, cups, whatever they could find to bail out the water that was knee-high and rising. Longy and James squeezed each other's hands and huddled together. There was no need to speak. They read each other's feelings through their contact. Longy's thoughts flashed back to some of the happy times he'd shared with his mother: the picture theatre at Pleiku; the trips arm in arm to the markets; singing 'My Vegetable Garden'; the massages; the late-night talks; the coffee shop; the unconditional love ... it was all over. He vomited, and the stench of spew and saltwater triggered a chain reaction as person after person threw up. Longy had never felt sicker, or sadder, in his life.

Panic steered the boat for half an hour before it was noticed that the water wasn't climbing any higher. On closer inspection, no holes were discovered in the hull — the water below deck had come through the hatch during the knockdowns. This may have been an obvious source of relief, but it was countered by the irreparable damage caused by human instinct. In the haste to keep the boat afloat, no-one had thought to keep any food supplies at all. Without them there was no possible way they could continue. After a brief discussion the shattered captain started the motor and headed back to Vietnam.

Yet again, Longy was going to surprise his mother.

By this stage, the exodus of so-called boat people had reached crisis point. In November 1978 the world was shocked by images of 2000 hungry, thirsty, desperate refugees on board the Panamanian freighter *Hai Hong* that was anchored off the Malaysian coast. The tragedy was underscored by a simple message that hung over the freighter's side: 'Please rescue us.'

Sadly, it was soon revealed the passengers had in fact been ferried to the freighter as part of an operation involving southeast Asian businessmen, shipping companies and the Vietnamese government, which was eager to rid its country of the ethnic Chinese population. Although the government denied its involvement, the truth was all too apparent: the lucrative enterprise of people-smuggling had begun.

It wasn't an isolated incident. As the United Nations and Western countries reviewed their refugee policies, the South China Sea became a theatre of political and social catastrophes. In addition to the large commercial operations, hundreds of tiny boats rolled and pitched under the weight of hope and despair. Some made it into a neighbouring country's waters only to be turned back or towed beyond the boundaries by that country's naval or coastguard vessels. Awake to such ploys, refugees risked their lives by purposely destroying their boats at the right moment in a last-gasp bid to be saved. Many crews on passing international freighters refused to help, aware that there was no guarantee that could off-load any people they picked up, no matter how dire the situations may have been. Although estimations vary greatly, it's reasonable to suggest that tens of thousands drowned during the 1978 exodus.

In December of that year, the gravity of the situation was magnified when Vietnam invaded Cambodia. This was in response to the Khmer Rouge's ongoing attacks along the border between the two countries. Although the action ended the 'Reign of Terror' in which more than a million people were murdered under the leadership of brutal dictator Pol Pot, it also increased the refugee flow across Indochina. Whether by foot or boat, there were masses on the move. If Longy or any other members of his family were to flee in the future, they would have to do it in peak hour.

FIFTEEN

The Wrong Side of the Law

Teresa could barely see Hien's letter through her teary eyes. She'd read it so many times that she knew every line virtually word for word. After three and a half dreadful years, she could finally go and visit her husband at his camp in the mountainous jungles of the far north. She began preparing immediately. First, she decided Thao should go with her — her daughter would provide both much-needed company and an extra pair of hands to lug a heavy sack of medicines, rice, ginseng and cigarettes. Choosing her youngest daughter had been a matter of deduction: Maria couldn't go because she had a new-born baby to look after; James was in hiding; Van needed to run the coffee shop; Lam, like James, had left home to escape army duties; Linh was too young; and Longy was at an age that would perhaps attract undue attention from various authorities along the route, if not gangs looking for trouble.

After two weeks away mother and daughter returned

home physically and emotionally exhausted, but nonetheless they'd been encouraged by Hien's good health and positive mood. Although he talked sparingly about camp life, he said he was being treated well and was managing to survive better than most. Sadly, he was only allowed to see his wife and daughter for a matter of hours in a special visitors' hut before he had to return to his living quarters.

The trip proved a distraction for Teresa — for at least a month she wasn't preoccupied with trying to help Longy escape. Once back in Saigon, however, she yet again searched for opportunities. In contrast to his mother's frustrations, Longy could see the funny side of what had seemingly become an unbreakable cycle. Whenever he left Saigon for an attempt he told his family, 'I will see you in a couple of days.'

By early 1979 he had said goodbye and hello again on no fewer than ten occasions. As soon as he was back he returned to street life, which had come to occupy far more of his time following his expulsion from school. He also had the added distraction of his first serious girlfriend, Lan, a tall elegant teenager he'd met with the river boys at Lady Trang's. Until now his relationships with the opposite sex had been only experimental flings, the highlight being the afternoon he lost his virginity to a house-assistant in his bedroom. But Lan was different. Longy enjoyed her company; he visited her at home, and relished the days he doubled her through the city on his scooter. This was a strategy adopted by any smart male: in a country where close physical contact in public was rare, bikes were the vehicles of accepted intimacy. With Longy gripping the handlebars, and Lan holding tightly onto his hips and pressed side-saddle against him, there were few better ways to have a date.

Of all his more regular street activities, none was more important than his long-standing duty of buying Teresa's

Cam le leaves from a middle-aged couple who lived not far from the Nguyen home. The routine was always the same: Longy would knock at the door and wait for the cover of a peephole to slide back; an eye would appear in the gap, cautiously inspecting the visitor before the door opened. This was typical behaviour in a violent neighbourhood divided between peaceful people wishing to mind their own business and gangs who wanted to know and rule everyone's business.

In all his trips to the couple, Longy had never experienced any trouble. He always came and went quietly, never loitering in the treacherous alleys, not stopping to talk to anyone. This was not his domain, nor had he any intention of ever making it his. Nevertheless, on one sweltering evening in early April his presence was enough to prompt a territorial response. He was walking home along a shortcut, a back passageway adjacent to a canal, when suddenly — *thwack* — he was ambushed. A second later he was buckled over on the ground, gasping for air, suffering from a flying side-kick to his back. He looked up. A Cambodian youth in his late teens was standing over him clutching a bamboo baton. Four others were a further step behind. There were soon ten, then more. Hopelessly outnumbered, Longy had no time to consider his options. He sprang to his feet, burst through some of the gathering gang and dived into the canal. He held his breath, slipping through the filth for several seconds. His knee was burning, his back and lower ribs ached, and his thoughts were as scattered as the *Cam le* leaves that were bobbing on the surface. When he nervously raised his head through the water he could only vaguely make out the outline of the Cambodians on the bridge above him laughing. They'd had their fun.

After returning home Longy patched up his knee, changed his clothes and ran to Uncle Ba's. When he arrived out of breath and rattled, he should have known that the

'Street Master' would have already heard about the incident.

'You mustn't go back there,' said the barber. 'It will only cause you more pain and trouble.'

'But —'

'No, listen to me, Longy. Remember what next week is?'

'What?'

'It is the Cambodian New Year.'

Uncle Ba curled his lips into a smile; he had said all he needed to. Longy considered what he'd heard, then, after some time, he grinned. During the New Year celebrations hundreds of Cambodians would walk between two Buddhist temples for traditional ceremonies. Their route was always the same, which meant they had to pass through Longy's neighbourhood.

Over the following days, Cambodian youths entering the foreign domain in ceremonial sarongs were randomly attacked. They were always outnumbered and surprised. Longy didn't lift so much as a finger in anger — his lieutenants did all the damage. Watching from a distance, he thought how beautiful revenge could be.

The most serious repercussion was that Longy needed to discover a new *Cam le* supplier. For someone who could find anything he wanted, it wasn't a difficult task — certainly much easier than Teresa's ceaseless efforts to get her son safely out of Vietnam. Her latest bid was her most costly and desperate: she applied for Longy to become part of the commercial smuggling operation. Although the government still refused to admit it was helping, the fact that official approval was needed showed the hypocrisy of the situation. Only ethnic Chinese were allowed to apply, but this was easily overcome if the appropriate people were bribed. After enough gold had filled the pockets of the greedy registrars, Longy was put on a waiting list under the Chinese name Ly Seu Long. It was no coincidence this was the same Chinese name as Bruce Lee, one of Longy's movie heroes.

In case regulations changed, Teresa considered it necessary for her son to be integrated into the Chinese community. So he began living with a handful of authentic ethnic Chinese on a boat about half a day's travel from the Nguyen home. There were similar vessels moored on the other side of the Saigon River. Each had a few full-time residents, but on any given morning hundreds of others would arrive to listen to an official read out a list of names. Those announced would be given a departure date and boat number. They were the lucky few.

While waiting for his 'lottery ticket to freedom' Longy hustled, went to the local markets, made new friends, and occasionally travelled back to visit his mother, Lan and Truong. Mostly he passed his time swimming, spending many lazy hours drifting with the currents. This was when he was most at peace with himself and the world around him.

On one such outing he met Hoang, a typically lithe, athletic river boy who was as much at home in the water as he was tending to his family's small vegetable plot. A mischievous teenager, he was well known for his penchant for hurling stones onto the roofs of the huts that overlooked each bank. Standing on the shore in a pair of wet tattered shorts he'd whirl like a discus thrower, launching his missiles towards the rows of ramshackle tin. He would grin if he heard a shatteringly loud clunk, but if he saw an irate homeowner storm out and shout abuse he'd break into uncontrollable fits of laughter and perform a celebratory dance on tiptoes. It was Hoang's favourite pastime, and he threw so many stones that it was possible to see where he'd been recently by the absence of smooth stones along the shoreline.

However, his mood changed one lunchtime when he and Longy decided to swim across the river to the markets. They dived off the side of Longy's boat and began churning through the water, turning the trip into a playful race.

Shoulder to shoulder, stroke for stroke, they were nearly halfway across when Hoang pulled up and started screaming, '*Du! Du! Du!*' — 'Fuck! Fuck! Fuck!'

Longy stopped and began laughing. It appeared his friend had ploughed his hand through a badly decomposed animal — but on second glance, how many animals wore trousers and a shirt?

'*Du! Du!*'

Longy felt sick. Despite knowing that hundreds of people washed and defecated in the water every day, only now did he feel like 'the dirtiest person in the world'. Nevertheless, he persuaded Hoang to pull the body back to shore. The river boy did all the work, clutching the shirt with one hand, pulling himself along with the other, and swallowing the occasional mouthful of water.

'*Du! Du!*'

Once on land they left the body and headed for the nearest police post. Nothing was done — the body of an unknown man wasn't worth investigating. Maybe he'd drowned, maybe he'd been killed, maybe he'd been tossed off a boat after dying naturally. Who really cared? Anonymous death was common in Saigon. Even Longy considered the episode just another experience in his life. He certainly wasn't as badly shaken as Hoang, who returned home to boil up an overpowering concoction of lemongrass and chilli that he soaked his hands in all night. He was adamant for several weeks afterwards that he couldn't rid his skin of the sickly smell. During that time, the river stones gathered along the water's edge and the tin huts stood unmolested.

Hoang drifted out of Longy's life like a banana leaf riding the river's ebb tide. They saw less and less of each other, until the day came when their time together reached a predictable end. After four months of watching other boats leaving, heaving with people, Longy was told the smuggling program had been cancelled without notice. As had become customary, one of the unluckiest, and perhaps one of the most reluctant, escapees in the city went back to his mother and retrieved the burgeoning collection of money and goods that he always left to Thao.

More failed escapes followed over the next few months. On his fourteenth attempt Longy was again accompanied by James. After leaving Tra Vinh, another settlement in the Mekong delta, they were squashed together with forty others under the deck of a 14-metre boat. Longy's space was so confined that he had to keep his head turned on an angle to avoid hitting a piece of overhanging wood. Amid the stench, lack of food and maddening whines of children, they reached the ocean ... but had to turn back when they couldn't find their transfer vessel. James was furious. It was after this that he made his decision: why not organise his own attempt? Teresa needed no persuasion. She was eager to fund the project, and soon afterwards James had bought a boat through family connections in Chau Doc, a town on the Hau River near the Cambodian border.

Lam joined him to work on making the vessel fit for sea travel. In the meantime Teresa decided there'd be no more escape attempts by Longy until the family could try together. Despite the veiled excitement and anticipation, there was also a strong feeling of intense sorrow, because everyone realised that Teresa would remain behind unless Hien was released. If all the preparations went well, the departure was still at least six months away, but no-one realistically expected the head of the Nguyen family to be a free man by then.

At fifteen, Longy was of an age where he was beginning to readily appreciate the sacrifices his mother was making for him. It annoyed him that he might never repay her. Then again, perhaps he could. But how? There had to be something beyond his love, occasional work in the coffee shop and the nightly massages he gave. In his delinquent wisdom he decided there was an answer, albeit a risky one.

Although Teresa never openly discussed her financial dealings, Longy knew that his mother was owed substantial amounts of gold by a number of families who had been involved in escape attempts. Without her knowledge, it was time for Longy to become her debt collector.

He discussed his plans with Xuan, a district police officer he'd befriended in the coffee shop. Xuan was easily identifiable because of his black lips, which he blamed on the malaria he'd caught while fighting near the Ho Chi Minh trail. He may have been a member of the communist constabulary, but he was never far from swinging the other way if the right money was offered.

Early that evening he and Longy stood at the door of a single-storey home in District Eight. They knocked, then casually walked into the main living room where a group of adults was sitting on the floor eating dinner. In one corner a toothless old man with thinning grey hair and a craggy face sat silently in a chair. Xuan ambled over and stood next to him while Longy politely introduced himself. He was calm, neither lifting his voice nor showing any anger in his eyes or his movements. He didn't want any trouble; he simply wanted to do his job as quickly and quietly as possible.

Standing in the centre, he addressed each person one at a time: 'Where is the gold that your family owes my mother?'

One at a time, the same answer came: 'I don't know.'

With each negative response, tension grew. Hands and feet shifted and eyes stared at the floor.

Click!

Longy had heard the sound enough in the past to know what it was. He spun around, as screams filled the room. There, in full view of everyone, the old man sat petrified, the barrel of a Colt .45 pistol in his quivering mouth. Xuan stood over him, one hand on the weapon, the other holding the back of his victim's head.

'Xuan!'

The corrupt policeman didn't move.

'Xuan, please!'
'Someone must have the gold. Where is it?'
'No, Xuan!'
'Where is it?'

The front door banged open. As it slapped hard against the wall, a group of patrolmen charged in with rifles raised ready to fire; they'd heard the screams from the street. Longy and Xuan froze, staring at the barrels that were pointing directly at them.

'Out now!' yelled one officer.

Within minutes they were in the back of a truck heading towards the nearest police station. When they arrived they were taken into a room empty of furniture.

Xuan was furious with the young men who'd arrested him, shouting '*Du Ma!*' —— 'Mother fuckers! If you hurt this boy, I will hurt you. You fucking lowlifes! *Du Ma!*'

Longy said nothing. He wasn't scared, but he was worried. Neither he nor Xuan had been asked yet to explain what they'd been doing. The police knew enough already from what they'd heard before they stormed into the house. The fact that gold was involved ensured the incident would be investigated, but perhaps not for legitimate reasons — it was likely the officers wanted to fill their own pockets.

After several minutes the station's commander entered the room. He looked the apparent criminals in front of him up and down, then spoke only to Xuan.

'Do you know where the gold is?'
'No.'
'Well, I think you should both go to headquarters then. That might help you.'
'*Du Ma!*'

The commander smiled, arrogance painted on his face as he walked out.

Longy turned to Xuan and whispered, 'What's headquarters?'

'Prison.'

SIXTEEN

Doing Time

Nhất nhật tại tù thiên thu tại ngoại
'One day in prison equals 1000 days on the outside'
VIETNAMESE SAYING

Longy already knew stories of men being murdered inside for as little as a plate of food. With that knowledge shuddering through his thoughts, he stood outside the cell where he was going to spend his first night in gaol. A guard opened the door into darkness. Body odour and the awful smell of urine and faeces escaped.

'In!' The guard directed Longy with the point of his rifle.

In response, Longy took a step forward. The door slammed shut behind him. He took another tentative step, unable to see anything.

'So, have you have been busted?'

The voice came from a corner. Longy stood still, waiting for his eyes to grow accustomed to the lack of light. Slowly he started to see the outline of a man lying on the ground.

'No, I've done nothing wrong. I shouldn't be here. I'll get out soon.'

'We all hope that.'

'What are you in here for?' Longy asked

'Robbery and murder.'

The prisoner shifted position and fell silent. Longy tiptoed to the other side of the tiny room. He wanted to be as far away from human contact as possible, even though this meant sitting wedged against a wall next to a stinking toilet can. He spent the rest of the night listening to raspy breaths and the scurrying of rats and mice across the tin roof. He knew the guards had put him here to try to scare him into a confession. It wasn't going to work.

By early morning, dots of sunlight through the roof's nail holes were bright enough to enable him to scrutinise his cell mate. The sleeping stranger wore a torn and grimy shirt; his shorts were no better. They partially hid deep cuts and bruises that stretched painfully along most of his skinny legs. His face was pallid and drawn, making his age hard to guess. Perhaps he was as old as forty-five, perhaps twenty years younger. It was impossible to say. However, there was little doubt he had been inside for a considerable time: his sunken eyes and the taut skin across his cheeks told of a starving body struggling to survive.

Longy heard approaching footsteps. After a jingle of keys the door swung back to reveal a guard, his frame silhouetted against the sun.

'Duy Long Nguyen, come with me.'

Walking ahead of the guard along a corridor, Longy was directed to another door which opened into now familiar darkness and stench.

'In,' the guard ordered.

The windowless cell was just as small as the previous one, but this time there were two men squeezed inside. Excited by the arrival of someone new, they happily introduced themselves. Their friendliness belied their situations: both had been charged with murder. One had been sentenced to life, the other to twenty-two years. They were waiting to be transported to Saigon's main prison, the infamous Chi Hoa. It was there that inmates grouped together the words love, money, prison, crime and death — TÌNH TIỀN TÙ TỘI TỬ — the five Ts that, years later, would have such significance for the Vietnamese gang culture in Australia.

Unlike those in the larger cells, these two inmates were allowed to have matches to light the crude cigarettes they made from cheap tobacco and dried pumpkin leaves rolled in newspaper. Longy listened to their stories, which were mostly made up or grossly exaggerated — they relied on their tale-telling to keep their sanity, although some yarns were so nonsensical that Longy wondered if madness had already taken hold.

He stayed there until the early evening, when a guard took him away. They went outside, where the fading light warmed and freshened Longy's face. Tired, dirty and hungry — he hadn't eaten for a day and a half — he relished the chance to walk, and to breathe clean air. But this was just a teasing thimble's worth of freedom, as he was soon put into yet another cell. About three-quarters the size of a tennis court, it was horribly overcrowded. In every direction there were rows and rows of men sitting, staring, sleeping or talking. In the dry heat most were shirtless, their sinewy torsos covered with welts from insect bites; some had needle marks on the veins of their arms; others had bruises that could only come from severe bashings. Their faces looked hollow and sinister in the eerie yellow light thrown from just a few flickering fluorescent tubes on the ceiling. In all there must have been about 200 inmates; most were between twenty and forty years of age, only a scattered few were older, and as yet Longy hadn't noticed anyone as young as him.

Whether or not he was struck by paranoia or the frightening reality of the situation, he suddenly felt he was the centre of attention. Wherever he looked, he saw people eyeing him up and down. Each inspection was blatantly obvious, as though it was a way of asserting early authority. These were hardened stares from hardened men. Longy dared not fix his eyes on anyone. Instead he continually scanned the room, trying to look comfortable in his surrounds without appearing overly confident — a cocky kid could be knocked down to size in the mere shadow of a passing second. He wondered what sort of crimes these men had committed. Hustling? Theft? Murder? No doubt all of them. God, what was he doing here! As he walked along the first row, he overheard whispers: 'We have a new ghost, we have a new ghost.'

He looked around for welcoming signs, but saw nothing other than tragic faces. Most inmates were lethargic, even slothful. There were the rare vociferous few who strutted around with chests out, randomly shouting obscenities for no apparent reason. One in particular, a muscular young man, seemed to be the self-appointed king. No-one spoke to him unless he spoke first.

After walking past some relatively comfortable prisoners who had their own food and cigarettes, Longy slowed near a cluster of ten or so men who were obviously near the bottom tier of the cell's hierarchy. They had nothing other than the clothes they were wearing and the straw mats and hessian bags they had to sleep on. One of them pushed himself to his feet.

'You want to stay here?'

Longy nodded.

'Well, you must fight then. Fight him — he's your age.' The leader stepped aside to reveal a youth whose frame had been whittled away by malnutrition.

'I can't, I'll kill him,' protested Longy.

'No, no, no — let's go, let's go.'

The entire group was now standing, excitedly pushing straw mats into the shape of a ring. With a look of resignation the youth stepped into the makeshift arena. Longy was shoved forward until he reluctantly faced his opponent. He felt sorry for him.

One kick was all it took for the youth to crumple to the ground. Everyone cheered and clapped. It didn't matter that the fight was so brief and lacked any fury; it had served its purpose of initiation, and also provided the inmates with a distraction from their mundane existence.

Invited to join the group, Longy was told little about life in the cell, the inmates still too wary of the 'new ghost' to drop all barriers. Nevertheless he learnt enough to know it was against regulations for inmates to discuss their offences with each other, although this was impossible to enforce. Unless a guard heard a stray whisper or was tipped off by a hunting dog, there was no way of knowing what anyone spoke about. In the congested space where each person practically lived under the armpit of the next, crimes and form were common knowledge. The most powerful man of all was Luong, the imposing young man whom Longy had already noticed. He was facing the serious charge of stealing three bars of gold from an elderly woman. Theft was considered by the government to be among the worst offences.

Longy was told he was one of only three 'boy prisoners'. He'd already come into unfortunate contact with one; the other was just twelve, a street kid who'd been inside for five months for killing his grandmother with a knife. The wretched urchin hadn't been to court, and no-one knew whether he would ever go — there were no rules for someone so young.

Little else was discussed, apart from sleeping arrangements. One of the older men pointed to a tiny space between two others.

'You stay there. And if you want some advice, it would be wise if you don't sleep on your side.'

'Why?'

'Because it is easier that way for someone to drive a chopstick into your ear if they want to kill you.'

Longy tried not to react. He lay down, resting his head on his rolled-up shirt, staring into nothingness. But snores, sneezes, coughs, wheezes and the repugnant smells of unhygienic living were all around. At least he could be grateful he was well away from the cell's only toilet, a small corner area with two holes in the floor above a pit brimful with waste.

He was too frightened to sleep. He lay on his back, arms folded across his chest, not daring to shift onto his side. Although the lights would stay on all night, they were so weak that darkness still engulfed the room. Unable to see beyond a few metres, Longy stiffened against the slightest sound or movement, unable to escape thoughts of some gruesome figure sneaking across the floor with a chopstick. He tried to calm himself by thinking of his mother. The guards said she had been informed. But had she? How could he trust men known by the inmates as *Bo Lat* — feral cows? Maybe no-one would really know he was here. And how long would he be here? Perhaps he would never be allowed to leave. God curse him for taking Xuan with him. Where was Xuan, anyway?

The hours crawled by until fingers of sunlight began stretching across the cell from the tiny windows along each wall. Careful not to disturb his neighbours, Longy sat up and looked around him. As the light strengthened and the clattering noise of freedom on the streets grew louder, the prisoners began to stir. At seven o'clock conditioning had taught everyone to form a weary, silent line that shuffled towards the only exit, a door where an officer stood listening to each prisoner shout his number as he went past.

'One, two, three ...'

Upon reaching the outside, the squinting line stretched towards a nauseating sight: men squatting six at a time over toilet holes on a pontoon atop a filthy pond. Longy moved closer, sickened by the splash and snap of catfish bursting through the water to catch the faeces.

Afterwards, the line turned back to the cell.

'One, two, three ...'

Back inside, Longy sat quietly in his spot. It was time to look, listen and learn. Only a few fortunate prisoners had their own food for breakfast, mostly dried noodles or fruit provided by family on weekly drop-offs.

At eleven o'clock a handful of prisoners was chosen to collect bowls, chopsticks and large pots of *Bo-Bo* from the kitchen. They distributed the food on their return, ensuring each chopstick was accounted for when eating was finished. There was sadness and desperation in the ways the prisoners ate. Some devoured their food, shovelling whole handfuls into their mouths at a time; others picked slowly, almost eating grain by grain, trying somehow to enjoy and prolong each skerrick. Longy felt every bit as desperate as those he was watching. He forced himself to eat his meal slowly, but even then the final mouthful seemed to come just a few methodical chews after the first. The meal was meagre — it was no wonder there were so many jutting bones and ribs.

Soon after Longy had finished eating, a guard summoned him to the door, where he was given a cloth bag.

'You are very lucky. Someone from your family came.'

It was Hong, Van's boyfriend. Relieved that his family knew where he was, Longy hurried back to his place to inspect his gift. His mother had packed him a feast. He licked his lips at the sight of two succulent pork rolls and a handful of sticky rice wrapped in banana leaves. He could have eaten everything right away, but he restrained himself, knowing that it was best to keep reserves for when his hunger was unbearable. There was also a carton of local brand cigarettes and a toothbrush with toothpaste in a steel container.

The parcel lifted his spirits. By early afternoon he felt comfortable enough to work his way around the cell, introducing himself to anyone he thought might be open to conversation. Amid the cold-shoulders and grunts he moved towards a 'five-star corner', well away from the toilets and directly under a barred window which offered a breath of fresh air and freedom. Two inmates smiled and beckoned him to come closer. They all sat down and exchanged introductions. The older, Tuan, began rubbing his neck, rolling his head from side to side. Without asking, Longy risked reaching over and kneading his fingers and knuckles deep into the tender spot.

Tuan nodded his head gratefully. 'Oh that's good, very good. Please don't stop.'

For the next few hours they chatted about their lives while Longy worked away. Tuan was in his sixties. He was short and wiry with hunched shoulders, a bent back and a face lined with deeply defined wrinkles. He'd already been sentenced to several years' imprisonment for his role as mastermind in various black-market operations. He said his crimes were theft and extortion, although Longy assumed it was highly likely that a man in his position had also been involved in gang murders. It was best not to ask, but wait to be told. Tuan's friend, Nha, with a strong muscular build and cheerful face, was at least twenty years younger. Inside for several months, he was waiting to appear in court on the charge of stealing truck parts. If he was found guilty, it was likely he'd be sent to Chi Hoa.

Their conversation flowed until the early evening, when it was time for the evening *Bo-Bo*. Afterwards Longy returned to his sleeping spot, eager to have some of the food his mother had sent.

'*Du!*'

The bag had been ransacked. Everything was gone.

'*Du Ma!*'

He shot accusatory looks at everyone in the corner. He stormed from person to person, standing angrily in front of them with clenched fists and a temper ready to explode. But he was ignored. It had all been seen before. A new, naive prisoner with no sense of value for his belongings was easy prey.

Longy felt a hand on his shoulder. He swung around, half expecting to launch into a fight, but he relaxed when he saw Nha.

'Why don't you come and stay with us? There is room for you,' he said.

'But my food ... Some fuckin' lowlife —'

'It's gone, Longy. You should have been more careful.'

Longy thought for a moment, then nodded. He should have been pointing the finger at himself for stupidity. Leaving goods unprotected in a prison of all places! He had only himself to blame.

That night, feeling secure in his new position between Nha and Tuan, he slept remarkably soundly. If he needed any further proof that he'd been accepted by the two friendly men, it came the next morning when he was offered some steaming noodles which not only satisfied his hunger but also his curiosity as to why some inmates, including Tuan, were given bowls of hot water by a particular guard. It was all a simple matter of bribery. Each week when a member of Tuan's family dropped off a parcel of food and cigarettes, the guard was secretly given a few dong to ensure Tuan received some basic comforts.

This preferential treatment didn't extend to personal hygiene, however. From where he sat eating his noodles, Longy could hear the splash of water in a block behind the cell where female inmates were allowed to wash each morning. It was only possible for males to be granted the same privilege if they became hunting dogs. To most, there was no choice to make: it was better to be dirty than to be scum.

Listening to the enviable sounds of cleanliness, Longy was interrupted by a guard at the cell door.

'Duy Long Nguyen!'

'Yes.'

'Come.'

He followed the guard into a hut where two officers stood in their standard khaki uniforms, loaded AK47s slung over their shoulders. Despite their formal appearances they were friendly and polite, acknowledging Longy with slight smiles.

'Please sit.'

Longy eased down cautiously on the room's only chair, behind a table that had a blank piece of paper, a jar of ink and a pen.

'You will write everything that happened in the house where you were caught. Do not leave anything out. Why you were there. Who you were seeing. Who you were with. And where the gold was. You must tell us everything — for your own good.'

Longy had been preparing for this moment. Despite the possibility that Xuan had been questioned elsewhere in the prison, Longy had to take a risk by concocting a story that would protect his mother — if it was known that she'd been lending gold, she would become a definite target of the authorities. Writing with more purpose than he'd ever shown at school, he made up the tale that he was trying to arrange his escape in order to join his girlfriend, who'd already successfully fled to Thailand. He missed her so much that he was willing to try anything to see her again. Hence, he'd gone to District Eight to ask his grandfather for money to fund the attempt, but had come away empty-handed. Becoming more agitated, he remembered hearing of a family in the area who could assist escapees. After securing Xuan's help, he visited the family in one last hopeful bid of securing freedom. It was at that stage that Xuan pulled out the Colt .45.

Once he finished writing he handed one of the guards his work; without having the chance to wait to monitor any reaction, he was taken straight back to the cell, where he immediately told Tuan and Nha what had happened.

'Be ready,' warned Tuan. 'They might ask you to do it again to see if you will change your story. You must know your story well. Practise it in your head all the time. They will only become suspicious if it changes. And that's when you will get your *Café da*. And no-one wants *Café da*.'

Café da, or iced coffee, was a popular drink on the streets, but in prison it was slang for 'having the shit kicked out of you by a guard'. Its use stemmed from the versatile word '*da*', which could mean ice, rock or, most significantly to inmates, a kick. Whenever someone was taken away by guards, it was assumed he was either going to be interrogated, or savagely bashed and kicked to the point where he suffered heavy bruising, cuts and, sometimes, broken bones. Hence *Café da*, the strong invigorating syrup that could kick-start a day on the outside, was unpalatable on the inside.

Another simple but effective practice was the interrogation technique in which guards would squeeze together two pens placed at right angles on either side of an inmate's finger. If enough pressure was exerted a bone could easily snap; the pain was extreme.

However, there was nothing more painful than the excruciatingly slow passage of time. Prisoners looked for any new means to help kill the endless days, weeks, months and beyond. Longy provided such a distraction. His arrival had prompted the predictable discussions about who he was, where he'd come from, what crimes he'd committed, and how long he would stay. But it was his ability to massage that attracted most attention, and subsequent respect, even from Luong, the cell king.

On Tuan and Nha's prompting — 'You should try to get on his good side as soon as you can' — Longy approached the most feared man in the cell when he was in obvious discomfort, gingerly running his fingers over the base of his neck. Longy presumed it was 'concrete flu', muscle soreness that came from sleeping in pools of sweat on the floor.

'You have a problem?'

Luong nodded, turning his head in surprise at being spoken to.

'Let me have a look. Lie down on your stomach.'

Luong did as requested. His curiosity to see what would happen soon turned to amusement when he was forced to tense his body under the weight of two feet walking along his spine. It was a peculiar sight. Here was the toughest, most distrusting man in the cell readily leaving himself open to attack from a virtual stranger. But the removal of Luong's pain guaranteed the tough guy would call on his magic-fingered colleague for days to come.

In the evening, Tuan received another massage. His twisted, leathery body was so worn by age and battered by prison life that Longy could only temporarily relieve pain, not remove it altogether. Nevertheless he rubbed, manipulated, pushed and pummelled for as long as the old man wanted him to. His methods were helped by a most unexpected source when a guard whispered through the window above him, 'Duy Long, I have something for you from Xuan.'

'Xuan! Where is he?' Longy sprang to his feet and looked through the window.

The guard shook his head. 'I can't tell you, but this comes from him.' The guard slipped a hot sweet potato through the bars and walked away. Longy returned to his spot and rolled the potato, while it retained its heat, across Tuan's neck. It would become a nightly habit: guard, sweet potato, massage. But never any word about Xuan.

The following days ground painfully by. Without any news about what was likely to happen to him, Longy was forced to endure days that could only be told apart by their names. It was an atrocious, appalling existence made more degrading by the sight of some inmates masturbating together. Others used rusty needles to inject opium into whatever receptive spots they could find, including beneath the tongue or into the penis. Opium had to be smuggled in. When it wasn't delivered by corrupt guards it was commonly hidden in food parcels, or wrapped tightly near the butts of cigarettes.

Apart from food, cigarettes were the most prized possession, but because matches and lighters were banned, enjoyment of a puff was hard earned. A group of long-serving inmates conquered the problem with an unbelievably laborious pastime that had begun some months before Longy's arrival. Collecting hair, and threads from the hessian sleeping sacks and clothes, the ingenious men had plaited together a string-like band that they wound into a tight coil with a protruding wick. It was no bigger than a fingernail. After they arranged for a sympathetic guard to provide just a few matches they carefully lit the wick, and from that moment on it was someone's responsibility to keep the slow-burning dot alive every minute of the day. Those in the group were virtually rostered on and off, often working two at a time to keep each other company as they gently fanned the coil and protected it from draughts. The tiny glowing thread was the saviour of every smoker in the cell. But using it came at a price: cigarettes and food were the accepted payments.

In this college of crime, where it was possible to be taught anything from theft to murder, Longy learnt most from the devotion, commitment and patience that was focused on the smouldering hair. To some of these men the coil was the centre of their existence. Longy didn't know whether to feel sorry for them or inspired by their dedication. Either way, he couldn't help but wonder what could ever possibly cause him to adopt the same resolute attitude. But perhaps it had already come; perhaps on fourteen separate occasions when he'd said goodbye to his family and embarked on an escape attempt. Next time he would know better. And he knew there would be a next time, because James was more driven to succeed than even the keepers of this incongruously symbolic flame.

Longy thought frequently of his family. He tried to imagine his older brothers sweating away the hours, working on the boat. He also thought of his mother; he pictured her on her knees praying to the Virgin Mary every morning and night, hands clasped tightly together, head down, pleading for her son's release. If there was indeed a God, Longy hoped beyond hope that now was the time Teresa would be rewarded for her impregnable faith. If he could be anywhere at this very moment, he wished he were home massaging Teresa's feet, listening to the BBC and pausing frequently for a drink — of all the food and liquid he could possibly miss, his greatest yearning was for a glass of Coca-Cola.

The young inmate's thoughts also wandered to his father. How in hell could he have survived in camp for so long? From a very young age Longy had considered the head of the Nguyen family to be the toughest of men, and now in the face of his own prison experience that impression was magnified. There could surely be no tougher person alive, nor could any son ever be prouder of his father. Longy gained strength from Hien's stoicism. If the Inspector General could make it, so could the Inspector General's little soldier.

In his second week of gaol Longy received another parcel from his family. This time every mouthful of food he swallowed, and every handful he offered to Tuan and Nha, made him intensely aware of protecting his belongings. Since the experience with his first bundle of food he'd seen thieves strike again, most often in the earliest hours of the morning when they scurried across the cell 'like rats', stopping to fossick through the bags of each sleeping person. Longy stowed his supplies under his hessian blanket. Aided by the additional vigilance of his two friends, his food was too well protected to be pilfered.

Longy knew he was lucky. He had considerate, warm-hearted people near him in prison, and on the outside a family who loved him. This was unlike most prisoners, who had little to return to on the streets other than the pursuit of more crime.

Each morning several inmates were washed and dressed in blue and white vertical-striped uniforms before they were taken away to appear in court. Their return was always greeted with widespread whispers of curiosity: 'How did he go?'; 'How long did he get?'; 'Does he have to go to Chi Hoa? Or is he staying here?'

One afternoon, the whole prison population was thrilled by the news that a known hunting dog had been sentenced to four years for armed robbery. He'd left for court believing he would escape punishment because of his willingness to cooperate. He returned an inconsolable mess, howling and moaning about his unfair treatment. No-one offered him any sympathy at all. But on most occasions inmates shared in the disappointment of those who were unable to beat their charges. The need to get out was the bond that melded everyone together.

There was no case more talked about than Luong's. For three days in a row the king of the cell went to the court and came back without news of his fate. On the fourth, his funereal walk with heavy feet, slumped shoulders and chin tucked against chest suggested the worst. Barely able to speak, he needed only to tell one or two friends for word to spread rapidly. This was the biggest story in the cell since the last chopstick stabbing some months before: Luong had been sentenced to thirty-two years, and would be on his way to Chi Hoa within days. In all likelihood the trip would offer him one last glimpse of the outside world before he began what was, in reality, a death sentence. Longy chose not to approach him. Instead he watched from a distance as Luong slid quickly into a desolate state of solitude, in sorrowful contrast to the intimidating tough man who had prowled around the cell only days before.

Longy continued to spend most of his time with Tuan and Nha. They sat in their corner, amusing themselves by whispering mostly dark jokes about their environment. Humour was essential to maintain their spirits. They made fun of anything: body odour; snoring habits; an inmate's limp; another one's lisp; a guard picking his nose; the screwed-up faces of those so constipated that they grunted and heaved over the toilets. Nothing went unnoticed.

Amid the sameness of each day Longy experienced some fleeting moments of difference. He shovelled coal that was used to fuel the cooking ovens, but he lasted only one morning before he sneaked away to rejoin his corner companions; he was also once directed by guards to roll ink onto paper strips that were used for finger printing. In return he was given a cigarette, a precious item for most prisoners but Longy already had a healthy supply — his entrepreneurial ability meant that nearly anyone wanting a massage had to pay a significant price. All were content to do so, although one elderly customer abruptly turned from giver to taker when he realised, just as Longy was about to light it up on the coil, that his payment had a hidden supply of opium rolled inside.

On the sixteenth day since his arrest, Longy was dozing in his corner when there was a booming knock on the cell door. The timing was unusual: most announcements or interruptions came in the morning.

'Duy Long Nguyen, get your clothes and come here.'

Longy felt a tingle of fear shoot through his body. He looked hopefully at Tuan and Nha for guidance, but they only shook their heads. Where was he going? He could only imagine he was on his way to a camp; it was all he could think of as he put on his shirt, the first time he'd worn it since his arrival.

'Hurry up!' shouted the guard impatiently. '*Dit Me may du oc tha!*'

Longy again looked at his companions, but this time he grinned. He reached over, kissed Tuan on the cheek and shook Nha's hand. Both men were happy, but Longy also sensed some sadness. He walked away, not wanting to look back, not stopping. He and the guard moved outside.

Behind them the door boomed shut. They continued walking, passing the cell and the women's block before they reached the front gate, a simple chest-high iron structure flanked on either side by a similarly tall barbed-wire fence. Another officer, with a rifle in his hands, sat watching from a small wooden hut outside the complex.

The escorting guard nodded at his colleague, then pulled back the gate, allowing just enough of a gap for Longy to slide through.

'Off you go.'

Longy was stunned. His fortunes had turned so quickly that he wondered if this was really happening. Or was it some awful joke that would end once he turned the corner to find a laughing guard waiting to take him back to his cell? He took a tentative step forward, then another, then picked up his pace. He kept telling himself to be calm. *Don't run, just walk. Don't look back, just keep going.* He reached the side of the busy street. No-one seemed to notice where he'd come from — he was just another person in the flow of a mild afternoon. Everything was as it should be. There were vegetable sellers; cyclo-riders; old women squatting and chatting; men drinking sugar cane juice; giggling boys scampering barefoot through the thick red dust. And there was soon a relieved teenager bouncing along on the back of a Honda taxi with the dry wind feeling fresh against his face. All he could think of were the sweetest words he'd heard in sixteen days: '*Dit Me may du oc tha*' — Fart-head, you can go home.

Once back under the family roof Longy enjoyed a steaming-hot shower, a simple pleasure that he would never again take for granted. As he meticulously scrubbed his body, he yelled to Thao and Van, 'Get me some food — I'm hungry!'

'Don't you dare talk to your sisters like that! You're not a criminal,' replied his mother.

But the food came anyway. Fruit, fish, rice, noodles, a bottle of Coke. By early evening he was clean, full and contented. After recounting his experiences to his mother, Longy went and told Uncle Ba what had happened.

'You are very lucky, Longy,' the barber told him. 'I know of men who have gone to prison for many months without ever going to court or knowing what would happen to them. Many just die or disappear. You are very, very lucky.'

The familiar sight of Longy strolling through the streets prompted most in the neighbourhood to believe the coffee shop boy had simply returned from another failed escape. No-one knew where he'd been. Not even Truong who, with a mixture of joy and disappointment, welcomed back his friend, admitting, 'I really missed you. I thought I'd never see you again. I thought you'd be in America disco dancing by now.'

Longy was barely able to sleep for several nights as he wrestled with the tricks played by his mind. Did he hear a footstep on the stairs? Was it someone coming to sift through his belongings? What was that crack outside — was it a guard cocking a gun? Where were Tuan and Nha? Why didn't they react whenever he rolled over? And why could he roll over? There surely wasn't room in his tiny corner. Did someone call out his name? Was he going to appear in court soon? In the darkness of his regained freedom, he was tangled up between reality and his imaginings. No wonder he'd heard stories of soldiers going crazy — there were few forces more powerful than the mind's ability to revisit the past.

It took Longy some weeks to overcome his flashbacks and fears. But once he did, he behaved as though he'd never been away. His return to street life frustrated Teresa, who was desperate for her wayward son to stay out of trouble until the time of the family's escape attempt. She'd hoped that his stay in prison would have scared him enough to pull him into line, but it seemed that he'd only learnt more bad habits. She tormented herself by questioning her role as a loving parent, her doubts fuelled by anxiety at what lay ahead. It was early 1980: four and a half years since Hien had been stolen away. If all went according to plan, in a few months the family would perhaps be split forever. God willing, most of the children would find freedom; but Teresa and Thao would remain behind, trapped by love and duty, waiting for a husband, a father, who might never be released. Teresa had experienced so many harrowing moments in her life, but this one could be worse than them all. She tried to remain positive and cheerful, but human frailty ensured that it was only a matter of time before her emotions overwhelmed her.

The inevitable happened one lunchtime when Longy returned home after winning a cock fight. All smiles and laughter, he cheerfully ignored the smatterings of blood all over one of his best-tailored shirts. But Teresa was furious.

'I hope you are thinking of your poor father while you're out there having so much fun,' she chastised him. 'Do you know how much of his life he's given to you and this family? I don't think you do. Do you know what you want in life, Longy? Do you know where you're heading? Do you want to go back to prison? Do you? Well, you're going the right way about it, and there's nothing I can do if you go back.'

The suddenness and sharpness of the attack unsettled Longy. Certainly his attitude and direction had been questioned before in softer, subtler ways, but this was an assault, a face-to-face barrage he'd never experienced. It prompted him to spend time by himself, thinking. He walked the streets, trying to imagine what Saigon would be like in a few years. Did he indeed know where he was going? Maybe his mother was right: maybe he would end up in prison as just another Luong or Tuan or Nha. Then again, he might be sent to a camp, or the army — or would he finally escape? He was confused. He needed support, needed some advice from someone who knew him but who was far enough removed to be impartial. Not Uncle Ba, not Uncle Nam, not Truong, not his girlfriend Lan, not anyone in Saigon. After some days of wandering and pondering, he had the answer.

'Mum, I want to go and see Dad.'

SEVENTEEN

The Camp

Longy looked at the fan specially prepared for his father. When it was closed no-one would know just how important it was, but when opened it stretched out to reveal folded notes of dong carefully placed between several pleats. This wasn't the only way to sneak riches past the guards: tiny pieces of gold had already been rolled up inside vitamin capsules. Together with the standard supplies of rice, dried fruit, ginseng, cigarettes, coffee, medicine, sugar, beef jerky and washing powder, they were packed into a huge sack made from an army tent. Dried fish were the last thing to be added — it was hoped the smell would act both as a deterrent to would-be thieves and give the impression that Longy was from a poor fishing background. He completed the impoverished image by wearing faded black trousers, a threadbare shirt and sandals. But the impersonation didn't go any deeper than that. In one trouser pocket he had a healthy bundle of cash and some gold. In another, next to a letter from his mother, he carried a special gift wrapped in a handkerchief. It had been prompted by Longy's nagging thought that he might never see his father again.

After applying to the local cadres, he was given a permit allowing him to leave Saigon; it was the first time he'd actually received a legitimate document to do so. Teresa stored this information away in her forever-scheming mind, because once Longy had visited his father permits might be easier to obtain in the future. And if the need arose, who would ever stop him swinging south for an escape attempt? It was worth remembering.

There were to be no deceptions this time, however, as Longy began the long, dangerous journey to the Doi Basao camp in the rugged far north. After saying goodbye to his family, he visited Lan.

'I will be back in two weeks. I promise.'

'And I promise I will be there at the train station when you come back.'

The first part of the trip was by train to Muong Man, northeast of Saigon. Every carriage seethed with life and desperation. Thieves and hustlers walked along the aisles, stealing and selling whatever they could in the dim light. There was no water, and the toilets either didn't work or were overcrowded with luggage or the passengers who filled every possible space. Longy found a spot on the floor where he sat on his sack, swaying to the rhythm of the journey, watching and listening for even the slightest suspicious movement. When the train rocked through tunnels Longy gripped his belongings tightly, aware of how vulnerable darkness made him. He didn't talk. It was best that no-one knew where he was going.

After reaching Muong Man in the early morning, he had to wait until the evening before boarding another train that would take him all the way to Nam Binh, southeast of Hanoi. For three days he watched the flashing countryside constantly change from flood plains covered in rice fields to hills thick with vegetation. The further he travelled, the more he noticed people living on the streets or in dilapidated wooden huts. Whenever the train pulled into a station, laughing boys would run next to the track throwing sticks and stones at the slowing carriages while scrums of hustlers waited to pounce on departing passengers or those hurrying outside to go to the toilet before boarding again.

When the train eventually arrived at Nam Binh, Longy swung his cargo over his shoulder and struggled out onto the platform and into the dusty chaos of hustlers, limbless beggars pleading for money, children playing games, and porters chasing business. He wearily pushed his way through, not slowing to acknowledge anyone until he reached the street where he bought some food for the next leg of his trip. He had barely slept since he'd left Saigon. He was tired and agitated, but he didn't want to rest until he was on a bus heading for his next destination, Nam Ha, in the highlands south of Hanoi.

Once aboard, he assessed the other passengers. Most were mothers and children with sad eyes and mouths that had forgotten how to smile. They wore simple clothes. At their sandalled feet were large bags and cases. It was obvious they were going to the camps as well. Longy felt safe enough to sleep lightly for a while.

When he was jolted awake he found he was covered in fine red dust kicked up by the wheels of the bus. He looked out the window. On either side of the bumpy road thick dark green walls of vegetation climbed skywards. In another time, another place, he imagined he could have been heading down a path to visit the mountain people. He spent the rest of his journey staring blankly, either looking back through his mind at his childhood or thinking ahead to the reunion with his father. Four and a half years had passed since he'd seen him in those black pyjamas; so much had happened since then. It would certainly be too much to talk about in the space of the few short hours visitors were allowed with inmates. So what would they discuss? Would they talk as though they'd never been apart?

Before Longy could find out he still had to complete a journey that was nearing a very dangerous point. He had been warned by his mother that when he reached Nam Ha he'd be engulfed by many impatient people demanding to be used as porters and guides. From this point on trips to the scattering of camps in the mountainous region could only be made on foot and on bike. To the jostling hundreds who gathered for the arrival of each bus, this was their only chance to supplement paltry incomes and help keep entire families alive. Every visitor had to be aware how desperate these people could be.

When Longy reached Nam Ha in the late afternoon there was anger on the streets. Just near the bus terminal people were pushing, shoving, arguing and pointing at something in the middle of the road. Ignoring the fingers that poked into his ribs and the shouts of people trying to attract his attention, he walked into the crowd holding the sack closely in front of him with both hands, to prevent someone ripping it away or slashing it with a knife. When close enough to see into the centre of the mayhem, Longy felt bile rise in his throat. A girl no more than five years old lay dead from gunshot wounds to her stomach. For some inexplicable reason, Longy couldn't take his eyes from her for several minutes. She was curiously dressed in a beautiful and obviously expensive silk tunic, yet she wore sandals that were held together by fishing line.

Eventually he moved away to a coffee stall, where he sat and thought of what he'd just seen. As he sipped his drink he overheard an old man recount the rumour that was swirling through the streets. The girl was apparently on her way to visit her father in a camp. Although she was from a poor family, her mother had scraped together enough money to buy her a special dress for the occasion. When they arrived at Nam Ha, a fight broke out between two men haggling for their business. Guns were drawn, shots rang out, and the girl fell to the ground, trapped in unforgiving crossfire. The mother slumped down next to her daughter, then ran screaming through the streets. She was yet to return. If the rumour was true, the girl hadn't yet been born when her father was taken away; this was going to be the first time they'd ever met.

At that moment, Longy felt closer to the girl than to anyone else in his life. He kept thinking of Ho Chi Minh's saying: 'There is nothing more valuable than freedom and independence.' What a lie! There was surely nothing more valuable than life. And in the aftermath of seeing another one senselessly lost, he sadly realised he'd never seen true peace. He began to cry. He had spent a good portion of his life portraying a hard, ruthless image, but underneath it all there was gentleness, a sense of compassion for his suffering countrymen on either side of Vietnam's festering political wound. Away from his family, away from the streets of Saigon, and away from both friends and foes, his true self was vulnerable. If this journey were forced to end right now, it had already been an experience that had forced Longy to discover another part of his character.

By the evening he'd regained enough emotional control to begin looking for a guide to take him on the final leg. Turning his back on the hustlers and desperadoes, he found a middle-aged peasant couple to help him. Together with their friend, a man of similar age, the husband and wife had travelled to most of the camps in the area, including the one where Hien was being held.

'It is a hard trip. It will take a day if we leave now,' said the single man.

They left in darkness, heading northwest into rolling hills along narrow red potholed roads. Each of the three locals had a pushbike. The wife rode by herself, the husband doubled Longy, and the single man had a rickety contraption behind which he'd attached a wooden trolley to carry luggage and food. They were kind people who made no mention of the war. It seemed to Longy that they were embarrassed by what had happened. He too felt moments of awkwardness, because it was likely the goods he was taking to his father amounted to more than these people currently possessed between them. They pedalled into the night, passing through small, sleeping villages. The few people who were awake watched their progress without changing their impassive expressions — this procession was an all too common sight every day of the week.

After several hours the travellers stopped by the roadside to sleep. Longy was assured all his goods would be safe without protection: 'No-one will trouble us. Most people who pass us here are doing the same thing we are,' said the husband.

They woke at dawn, and after breakfasting on cold rice they continued their journey. The guides asked Longy about life in Saigon, a city they considered another world away. They were also curious to know about Hien. How long had he been in prison? When would he be free? They spoke softly, almost apologetically; Longy was touched by their sensitivity and compassion. It saddened him to think how many similar people had been killed during the war. They were of his blood but the tie was weak when compared with the behaviour driven by political beliefs.

After hours of arduous travel the four were forced to walk a bumpy road winding to the top of a hill. Once there, they overlooked a valley of dense jungle with small patches of clearing and a few huts.

'Your father's camp is down the bottom of this hill. It is another hour's walk. We will wait for you here. Good luck,' said the husband.

Longy shook the man's hand and said goodbye to all three. He hurried away, the weight of his sack suddenly feeling light upon his shoulders. The path was so steep in parts that, combined with his heavy load, it pushed Longy into a run. He slipped, he slid, he tumbled.

The few huts in the clearing below were dominated by a large wooden structure shaped like soccer goalposts. A sign hung over the crossbar; this was the entrance to the camp. As he drew closer, he passed people leaving. There were women sobbing by themselves, and mothers holding back tears, biting their lips, trying to remain composed for the sake of the children clinging to their sides. It was right on dusk; specks of dust swirled into the air, adding a red tinge to a soft golden glow. But the beauty paled beside the sadness.

Longy moved on until he reached a group of guards in a hut.

'I'm here to see my father, Hien Duy Nguyen.'

'What are you carrying?'

Longy reluctantly handed over his sack. Although he couldn't prevent the inspection he was ready to protest, even fight, if anything was taken away. The guards examined every item. One pulled out a cigarette and ran it slowly under his nose to smell it. Another looked curiously at a bottle of vitamins as though he'd never seen anything like it before. To Longy's relief they skimmed over the capsules containing gold, and didn't bother opening the fan with its secrets.

While this was happening, prisoners walked past carrying a dead body. They placed it outside a hut, then walked away silently, solemnly. Longy returned his attention to the guards.

'So what about my father?'

'It's too late now. You will have to wait until morning.'

'Do I have to come back?'

'No, you can stay in the visitors' hut.'

A guard pointed to the hut next to the body. Longy walked over, keeping as far away as he could from the dead man. Inside there was just one room with a single bulb dangling from a wire in the roof. A few women sat on a bench crying. They were wives counting the hours until the all-too-brief reunion with their husbands. Longy's heart bled — he realised just how tough every single day must have been for them. And for his mother. Throughout the night they exchanged stories about their trips to the camp, about their husbands and the families left behind.

It was cold. Lacking a blanket, Longy curled himself into a ball at one end of the bench. His eyes were heavy, his whole body was leaden, yet he could barely sleep because of his shivers and churning thoughts, and the voices of the women. He tried to picture what his father would look like. Longy wondered if Hien was now thin, old, bald or weak, and if he had a blanket to keep him warm.

At sunrise he was stirred by the clinks of steel as two prisoners shovelled out waste from the visitors' shallow toilet. Longy couldn't watch. The dead body had stayed uncovered all night, a grotesque sight for visitors and a matter-of-fact statement for both guards and prisoners. Longy wondered how the man had died. He looked to have been only in his forties. The name 'Ho' had been painted in black letters across his yellow chest. Soon enough he would be anonymous, buried in an unmarked grave.

Longy hadn't yet been told when he would see his father. He contemplated washing himself, but decided against it when he saw some of the women return dirtier than when they'd left. They'd been forced to go to a creek a mile away through heavy jungle. The only other water was a drinking supply in a drum near the hut. Longy ladled some out in a cup made from a coconut and washed his face.

In the distance he saw a man in loose grey clothes walking towards him. At first he didn't take any notice, but as the figure came closer he noticed something vaguely familiar about the short, shuffling step. If that wasn't enough to ignite the memory, the glasses were. When their eyes met they both stood still, metres apart.

'I don't believe how much you have grown.'
'Dad!'

'You were a boy when I left. Now look at you — you're a man.'

Longy smiled when he saw the rubber tyre sandals on his father's feet.

'Have you turned into a Viet Cong yet?'

Hien laughed then hugged his son, neither allowing himself to be overcome with emotion. They then went and sat in the shade of a hut where Longy handed over the sack.

'It stinks! Are you sure your mother can afford all of this?'

'Yes. And she said not to give any of it away, especially the vitamins.'

'I could become a doctor with all these pills.'

'Don't forget what they have in them, and be careful when you open the fan too.'

Hien smiled knowingly, but his temporary happiness hid the harsh truths of his life. He was thin and had lost much of his muscle. He had little hair, his skin was blotchy, and his eyes were yellow and watery. Yet he assured his son that he was one of the luckier ones. He took advantage of his weakening eyesight by exaggerating to the guards just how bad it was. As a result he was considered utterly useless on the torturous work trips where prisoners were forced to cut down trees and lug timber on their shoulders back to camp, sometimes more than an hour away. Hien was able to stay behind to maintain a vegetable garden for the guards.

He lived in a wooden hut with a leaf roof, hidden in the jungle. Longy wasn't allowed to go there, but was assured by his father that conditions were 'good enough to survive'. Hien said he had a comfortable relationship with the guards and prisoners that was helped by his supply of gold and dong. Although he refused to talk in too much detail about his incarceration, he stressed that he was coping.

Others weren't as fortunate.

'Did you know him?' asked Longy, pointing to Ho's body.

'Yes, he was a friend.'
'What happened to him?'
'He killed himself on *Ba Dau*.'

Ba Dau was a tree-nut that when eaten in small pieces was a laxative, but in large amounts was poisonous. Ho had gorged himself on it after falling into a deep depression following his wife's recent departure. He told those closest to him that he wasn't strong enough to wait until her next visit; too many years of solitude had worn away his willpower.

Despite the desperate surrounds, Hien and Longy were positive. They mostly spoke about their family, and daily life in Saigon, although Longy didn't mention his expulsion, his time in prison, or his renegade activities on the streets. Instead, he cheerfully chatted about his sporting successes, and Lan.

'Did you know I have a girlfriend?'
'Your mother told me in one of her letters.'
'Her father is in a camp too.'
'You're lucky you're not married, because you'd have to go and visit him too.'

Hien chuckled. He wasn't just proud of his joke — there was an air of satisfaction that he'd retained his sense of humour throughout his ordeal. The prisoners who lost their ability to laugh were those most at risk of following Ho's path.

There was one subject Longy and his mother had decided he wouldn't talk about: the family's escape attempt. It was likely Hien would have accepted the news enthusiastically, but since there was a small chance it could prompt a feeling of some despair, it was best to make no mention of it. With that knowledge, Longy was torn by thoughts that he might never see his father again.

After spending an hour with Hien, Longy was told by the guards he had to leave. It was no use arguing. He nodded and faced his father, who gave him a letter for Teresa.

'Look after your mother.'

'I will.'

'And make sure you finish your education.'

Longy bit back on his words — now was not the time to say he'd finished his schooldays with a shaven head and a flurry of punches. He reached into his pocket and pulled out the precious gift in his handkerchief.

'I want you to have this.'

Hien unwrapped it carefully, but shook his head when he saw what was inside — a glittering Rolex watch.

'Thank you, Longy, it is beautiful. But we are not allowed to have watches here. Keep it for yourself.'

He folded the handkerchief over the Rolex, then handed it back. Longy said nothing.

'Now, you'd better go. We don't want to make the guards angry.'

'How will you get your sack back? It's too heavy for you.'

Hien smiled. 'Don't worry. I'll find help.'

They shook hands. Longy kissed his father on the cheek, then he turned and ran until he was outside the entrance. He didn't cry; he wasn't going to give the guards that satisfaction. But he did stop and look back one final time. In the distance, Hien was talking with some officers, probably negotiating a price for one of them to carry his new belongings. Even as a prisoner, the former Inspector General was trying to take charge of the situation.

Holding onto that image in his mind, Longy blindly began the climb back to the top of the hill where he knew his guides would be waiting to hear about his experience.

In his pocket, the Rolex moved with his struggling gait. Perhaps it was fitting that he still had it. Over the coming months, time would become much more important to him than it could be to his father.

EIGHTEEN

When the Time Comes

When Longy arrived home, two weeks to the day since he'd left Saigon, Lan was there waiting at the train station. She'd been true to her word. They walked next to each other until they found a quiet spot in a nearby market, where they hugged. Lan cried. The moment made Longy realise just how fond he was of his girlfriend. Yet there'd been times when he'd been unfaithful to her, or simply forgotten about her for days, even weeks, while he and his lieutenants roamed the streets. But then, he always wanted to come back to her, just like he had now. When away from her, he often spent dreamy moments wondering what she was doing, and questioning whether she was thinking about him, missing him. Maybe it was love, especially when he so desperately wanted her to be part of his family's escape attempt. It would only mean one extra spot on the boat. A slender girl could fit into any corner without making a difference.

But Longy had to keep his promise: only the family was to know. There were to be no exceptions for anyone.

After accompanying Lan to her home, he hurried off to the coffee shop. He raced through the door and leapt at his mother, hugging her with both arms and kissing her cheeks in a puppyish display of affection. That night they spoke in detail about Longy's trip. Teresa cried when she was told about Ho and the girl in Nam Ha.

'Does it make you realise you are lucky, Longy? This escape may be your last chance. You won't keep getting opportunities like this.'

Teresa told her son that preparations for the escape attempt were going well. James and Lam had begun installing a second-hand four-cylinder Kubota tractor engine in a special compartment in the bilge of the boat. Considering their lack of mechanical knowledge, and the fact the installation had to be secretive, they expected the process would take some months. To avoid suspicion they'd also put in a small outboard motor with a propeller at the end of a long thin rod — the typical amount of horsepower used by most river-goers. They'd moved downstream from Chau Doc to Can Tho, the busiest settlement in the Mekong delta, where they wouldn't be as conspicuous.

At the time the people of Vietnam were struggling to recover from one of the most horrendous periods since the end of the war. There had been chronic food shortages that led to famine in some areas; the economy had tumbled to such depths that Vietnam was now among the poorest countries in the world; basic health services had dwindled; everyday consumer goods were scarce; and general morale was miserable.

Longy, too, felt a sense of depression. Each passing day was one less he had with those who were the heartbeats of his existence: his mother; Thao; Lan; Truong; Uncle Ba; Uncle Nam; his lieutenants; anyone who'd been a part of his life. Unlike his other escape attempts, this time he had a strange feeling, an instinct, that he really was about to take the final steps away from his troubled homeland. Accordingly, he cut back his street activities so he could spend more time with his mother. Teresa capitalised on this. During the nightly massages, when she and Longy were alone, she stressed how her son had to make the most of every chance.

'If you do escape, you will have many more opportunities than you will ever have in Saigon. You have to be hungry for them. You have to go after them. There is no future for you here. Your future is in America, or another country a long way from here.'

In July, Teresa received word that James and Lam were almost ready. The brothers were satisfied they'd blended into Can Tho's river life and knew every muddy meandering they needed to. Overseas, the news was dominated by the US-led boycott of the 1980 Moscow Olympics. Sixty-five countries had withdrawn to protest against the Soviet Union's recent invasion of Afghanistan; only eighty nations were competing. Teresa watched avidly on the small black and white television in her bedroom. One night, with her eyes glued to the men's gymnastics, she spoke in awe of the agile competitors twisting and leaping across her set.

'Look at them — they are so strong, so good at what they do. We have no-one like that here.'

Longy stopped massaging her. He picked up his mother's hands, holding them for a moment.

'After I escape I will do everything I can to be like them. I won't be a gymnast, but I promise I will make a success of my life. I will do it for you. But please, please, come with us.'

'I can't, Longy. I want to escape, but even if I did my heart and mind would be here. I must wait for your father. I won't be happy until I see him free again. It's my duty to be here when that day comes.'

That was the end of the subject.

A few days later, Longy left the Nguyen home to make his most important contribution to escape preparations — he had to collect a sea compass on the outskirts of Saigon. James had already made the arrangements. It was a 'pay upon pick-up' deal, a simple matter of exchanging gold for the vital piece of equipment.

He took Truong with him, the pair zigzagging on a bike through the morning's traffic until they reached a wooden hut in an alley of aching dwellings and suspicious, narrow-eyed stares coming through windows and from behind corners. Longy surveyed the scene, searching for any signs that might trigger his sixth sense of danger. Satisfied that there appeared little to be worried about — it was impossible to appease all suspicions of ambush in such unfamiliar territory — he walked towards the hut. Truong waited behind, believing his friend was going inside to do business for his mother.

Longy knocked on the door, which opened just wide enough to reveal an old woman peering through a crack.

'What do you want?'

'My brother James sent me.'

The woman let Longy in while she called over her shoulder to someone in another room. A man in his early twenties appeared, and with no introduction, nor welcoming smile, he asked his visitor to pay before any exchange was made. Longy wasted no time — a fast deal was a good one. He dropped his shorts while he took out 2½ ounces of gold from a pouch tucked beneath his underpants, prompting the woman to look away. Hitching up his shorts, he then walked with the man to the nearest markets, only minutes away from the hut, where they watched a stallkeeper heat the gold before dropping it into a tin of water and acid. The gold didn't change colour — it was real. After returning to the hut the man slipped into a side room and returned with the compass wrapped inside a hessian bag. Longy inspected the steel object carefully.

Stolen from a navy patrol boat, it was the size of a 1-litre milk carton, small enough to be carried through the streets without attracting attention.

'Whatever you do, don't drop it,' said the man.

Longy slung the bag over his shoulder and returned to Truong, who knew not to ask any questions. When he returned home he hid the compass in his bedroom, unaware of his role in a tremendous irony. Here he was, a happy lifelong wanderer who was now the protector of an instrument that would hopefully offer nothing but clear directions to a boatload of desperation. To Longy, though, the safe acquisition of the compass meant just one thing: his remaining time in Saigon was evaporating quickly.

He rushed back onto the street to visit as many of his friends as he could. Uncles Ba and Nam had seen similar behaviour so many times before that they barely raised an eyebrow. Both shook his hand and wished him luck; nothing more needed to be said.

After whipping between his favourite shopkeepers, family friends and lieutenants, he devoted the entire afternoon to Truong. They rode through the lanes and alleys, skimming along side by side, chatting, laughing, occasionally stopping in the shade of buildings to whisper their hatred of the regime. Nothing was different from the way they'd enjoyed each other's company for years. Certainly Truong had no idea that this was perhaps his final ever outing with his friend. It was the way Longy knew it had to be. If he'd revealed the truth, he had no doubt Truong would be happy for him, but beneath the smiling face there would be enormous sadness. Longy couldn't bear to put his 'street brother' through such pain. Arriving in the laneway outside their homes, they parted, saying little:

'I will see you soon, Truong.'

'OK, Longy.'

Longy straddled his bike and rode off. If turning away from Truong had been difficult, his next farewell would be excruciating. The thought of leaving Lan behind had haunted him for weeks. Again he refused to surrender to his feelings, and only told her that he was 'going away for a while'. Lan was used to the intermittent absences, thinking Longy was probably preparing for a black-market run. This was nothing unusual, not disturbing enough to worry about. It was simply the way it was. Simply the way Longy was.

After he left her house, forcing himself not to look back, he suddenly felt utterly lonely and very, very insecure.

That night in the Nguyen house, Teresa tried to hide her sorrow. The family she had raised so proudly and strongly had long been fragmented by the times, leaving little more than memories for her to clutch onto. Whenever anyone left her nest she gave no impression that she realised she might never see that person again. Maria, Hien, James and Lam were already tucked into that corner of her mind's uncertainty; Van and Linh were soon to follow. As for Longy, he'd been farewelled so many times that she was beginning to wonder if there would ever be a final time.

As he massaged his mother's legs well into the morning's earliest hours, there was no mention of his imminent flight. It was a time to quietly, peacefully enjoy each other's company. Along the corridor, in another bedroom, Thao wept softly, burying her head in her pillow to stifle its sound. In a house that was once full of commotion, she would soon be the lone child. It was her choice to stay and look after her mother.

She wept again soon after sunrise when Longy went through the customary role of giving his little sister his money, gold and pieces of jewellery. The last gift he offered was beyond value: a hug that stretched from the arm's reach deep into the past. It was memories of goldfish in combat helmets, smoking in the family room, homemade guns, chilling beer-can showers, the nuns at St Paul's ... their childhood. They pulled apart silently. Longy turned to his mother.

'I love you, Mum.'

'I love you too, Longy.'

They hugged briefly — this wasn't the time for indulgent farewells. Longy broke away and began walking. Out of the living room. Down the stairs. Through the coffee shop. Then onto the street. There was no looking back. Apart from the compass that was wrapped in banana leaves, he had only his false papers and the jeans, shirt and shoes he was wearing.

Once on the bus heading to Can Tho he placed the compass at his feet, thus enabling himself to kick it away and deny ownership should there be any random inspection by authorities along the route. But by early afternoon, he arrived without any incident.

James and Lam decided that Longy would attract too much attention if he was seen with them. Instead he was introduced to Nam, a man of the river who Longy thought was at least sixty. He was still muscular and fit with strength and energy that could embarrass men many years younger. A relative of the Nguyen family, he'd become part of the escape attempt in a bid to help his daughter-in-law reunite with his son, who'd already successfully fled to America. Nam, however, had no intention of leaving.

'I am too old to go. My place is better given to a person who is young and has a future.'

After introductions were complete, Longy and Nam went secretly to a nearby field, where they dug a hole in which to hide the compass. It wouldn't be retrieved until the very last moment, when everything else had been meticulously prepared and checked.

While waiting for the day of departure Longy was to live with Nam in a typical river hut. Made of wood, with a thatched coconut palm-leaf roof, it rested on stilts that stood defiantly in the Mekong mud at the water's edge. Under the guise of being Nam's cocky nephew who'd come to visit from Saigon, Longy passed his time swimming and visiting the markets, where he began to learn and practise the local dialect. He also travelled with his caretaker on his fruit-seller's boat. Sometimes they passed James and Lam heading in the opposite direction. They ignored one another to prevent any chance at all of arousing suspicion.

However, Longy couldn't show the same restraint when it came to inspecting the boat that would soon transport him from his homeland. One morning when he was swimming, his curiosity overrode his willpower, and he sneaked aboard the moored vessel when his brothers weren't there. From the outside the boat looked 'shonky and poor', just like most other craft in the area. It certainly wasn't shaped for ocean travel. As opposed to the flat-bottomed, sharp-nosed fishing vessels that were taken into open water, this boat had a curved hull and broad bow. It was just 10-metres long, less than 4-metres wide — a meek creature when tossed up against the might of the sea.

The boat had three levels. The top deck had a small cabin at the rear, from which the craft was steered. Behind this sat the outboard motor, the 'fake engine' with its spindly propeller pole. The second level would house the passengers. There were no windows, no view of the outside world at all. Once on board, everyone would live together in semidarkness, crammed in the tight confines of a space that was just 6 metres in length and little wider than an average man's arm span. They would only be allowed into daylight to go to the toilet at the stern. On the third and lowest level, the Kubota engine had been installed on a platform about 50 centimetres from the bottom.

Longy was in awe of his brothers' work and commitment. Nothing had been overlooked. They had tested the boat extensively, taking it as far as the river mouth. Lam had even estimated how much oil would be used per hour under a variety of different conditions and passenger weights. It seemed to Longy that all was ready to go — yet the wait continued. It was up to James to decide when the attempt would be made, and Longy did not argue. He recognised that his oldest brother was indisputably in charge, and this wasn't the time to invade or complicate his thoughts.

Putting the boat together had been a monumental operation and the two brothers had thrown their lives into it. There had been times when they had run so short of money that they couldn't afford to eat. At one stage they tried to swap their digital watches for food, but in this socially sheltered, less developed part of the country, the locals refused to believe watches could tell the time without hour hands. They were more receptive to cigarette lighters, these amazing mystical devices that could throw flames into the air at the press of a thumb. James and Lam negotiated a healthy exchange rate: one lighter equalled five chickens. The locals thought this was a good deal, and never protested.

No matter how difficult conditions became, the two brothers never gave up. Lam recalls: 'It was all or nothing. The environment made us smart for what we had to do. We had to teach ourselves about anything we didn't know. We were motivated by freedom. We were going to make it. We had to. We didn't know where we were going — Singapore, Malaysia, Thailand, we didn't care. Just as long as we got out of Vietnam.'

They were boosted by the ceaseless support of relatives and close friends, a tight network secretly working together. Regardless of what was about to happen, Longy was immensely proud of his brothers. There was barely a spot on the boat that hadn't soaked up their sweat or creaked under the force of their straining muscles and single-minded determination.

Three weeks after Longy's arrival, the time had finally come. It followed three aborted attempts after confusion over numbers and the whereabouts of some passengers. Initially only twenty-five people were to go, but the final list had swollen to forty-seven — twenty-eight Nguyen relatives and nineteen friends. Longy was given the responsibility of meeting some as they arrived in small groups, primarily from Saigon. Three or four people came at a time, including Van and Linh, Maria, her husband, David, and their baby daughter, Noell. But there was no chance yet of a family get-together. As soon as people arrived, Longy and Lam took them away to carefully chosen taxi-men who were to look after their guests until the time of departure.

All had their own tragic stories, but none was more poignant than the recent life of Ho Van Tinh — Uncle Ovaltine, the former ARVN major who'd opened his heart to the Nguyen family when Teresa was forced to take her children to Nha Trang during the Easter Offensive. After he survived the war, Ho's greatest trauma still lay ahead. He endured many years in a re-education camp only to return home to find his wife had left him. Sadly, this was all too common for thousands of freed prisoners. Ho was shattered, seemingly beyond recovery. But his fortunes brightened when he fell in love again. Desperate for a new start, he unexpectedly arrived at Teresa's coffee shop seeking help, giving Teresa a chance to repay a personal debt. As a matter of family honour, two spaces on the escape boat were immediately reserved for Ho and his girlfriend.

Ho wasn't going to be the only military man on board. At James's request Uncle Ovaltine had sought the help of a former South Vietnamese naval officer, Hieu, whose presence and knowledge of the sea was expected to put everyone at ease. However, his arrival sparked some argument when he demanded he should be paid for his services. James disagreed, insisting the opportunity to escape to freedom with a wife and baby son was more than enough of an incentive.

It took a week for everyone to arrive. As James, Lam and Nam checked the boat and ran through the departure procedure, Longy grew increasingly agitated. His leisurely month in Can Tho had given him too many hours to ponder what he was leaving behind. Time and again his thoughts had drifted back to Saigon. Every moment the dreamy images of Lan, Thao and his mother came into his mind his feelings grew stronger, until he became convinced that there was just one foolish, selfish way of overcoming them. He had to go back for one last farewell.

James was furious when he couldn't find his brother. What on earth was he doing? The boat should have been on its way. Damn, Longy! Where the hell was he?

Arriving home, oblivious to the sparks he'd ignited in Can Tho, Longy breezed into the coffee shop as though he'd just returned from winning a cock fight. Teresa was stunned.

'What's happened? What's gone wrong?'

'Nothing. I just came back for a visit.'

'Longy!'

'One more day won't hurt.'

Initially he'd planned to come and go in a matter of hours, but he extended his visit when he saw Van's boyfriend, Hong, who was desperate to know where his girlfriend had gone. Longy was struck by guilt. He couldn't hide the truth from the man who'd delivered food to him while he was in prison. He made his decision on the spot.

'We are escaping soon,' he told Hong. 'I am leaving tomorrow for Can Tho. Van is already there. Do you want to come?'

There was no need for Hong to think twice.

Longy spent the rest of the day arranging Hong's false papers. By the early evening he came home to find Thao standing alone on the balcony.

'Longy, I don't know what is going to happen without you here. I don't know how I will cope.'

'It isn't too late for you and Mum to come with us. There is still room.'

'You know Mum won't go because of Dad. And it is my responsibility to look after Mum. We're staying here. We have to.'

Longy says that it was 'the most heartbreaking moment' of his life. During all his previous escape attempts there had always been a part of him that believed he would return, but looking softly at his sister's shadowed face, he had an overwhelming feeling that the sun was setting on his very last day in Saigon. This time would be different — he would either die or find freedom. Either way, he and the other escaping members of his family were leaving a void in which Teresa and Thao had to live, had to survive. Longy felt helpless.

Soon afterwards he crept into bed next to Teresa.

'This is very hard for all of us, Longy. But we are doing the right thing. You can only make me happy by making the most of your life — and you can't do that here. It is time to move on. We all must.'

Longy awoke early the next morning. He knew he should have immediately left for Can Tho, but he hadn't yet finished his work in Saigon. He scampered down the laneway to visit Truong. Few words were spoken; Truong needed only to look into his friend's eyes to know what was happening. These two had spent so much of their lives together that they instinctively knew what the other thought. False bravado prevented either from making a scene when Longy turned away.

He hurried home and leapt onto his scooter. A few minutes later he was sitting with Lan in the front room of her house. Choosing his words carefully, he tiptoed around the edges of the truth.

'If something happens to me, please look after my mother and sister.'

Lan began to cry; Longy wrestled with his thoughts. He so desperately wanted to sweep away all his secrets and deceptions, yet he couldn't find the strength to utter a single word.

'What's happening? Where have you been? What are you doing?' Tears flowed down Lan's face.

'I don't —'

'Longy!'

'I don't know whether I'll ever see you again, Lan. I'm sorry.'

There was silence. At that moment Longy didn't care about the escape attempt. Freedom — what was it? How could he be free if his mind was to be tortured by memories of loved ones still trapped?

Longy hugged the sobbing Lan, then left. Once on his humming bike, though, he looked back. Lan smiled weakly, the window she sat behind framing an unforgettable portrait. With that image clouding and crowding his thoughts, Longy opened the throttle and took off, hurtling along the laneway into an uncertain future.

He arrived home to find his mother asleep in her bedroom. He rubbed her rheumatic legs until she woke.

'Mum, I —'

'I know. It's time for you to go. Promise me this time you won't come back.'

Longy nodded. They hugged. Teresa pushed her son away.

'Go!'

Thao was behind him. Longy playfully pulled his sister's long hair. They both smiled. After so many dress rehearsals, he wanted to make this farewell brief — the longer it lasted, the more he would question his actions. He glanced at his mother.

'Go!' she said again.

Her son stepped back, disappearing from Teresa's view behind a wall that led up to his own bedroom and the roof. The roof! Shit! He'd almost forgotten! Longy raced upstairs to the cranny under the eave where he had hidden his most prized possession. He reached inside and pulled out his father's Beretta, which he tucked inside his underpants. He ran back down the stairs, forcing himself to pass Teresa's bedroom without stopping. He found Hong waiting in the coffee shop.

Longy hurriedly handed Van's bespectacled boyfriend his forged papers, saying, 'You will be travelling as a tax officer — you already look the part with your glasses! You ready?'

'I hope so.'

As they walked onto the street, Longy felt a pair of eyes piercing the back of his head. He looked up to the balcony where Thao was staring at him, biting down heavily on her lip. This time, she wasn't going to cry. Within minutes, she lost sight of her brother as he hurried away, Hong struggling to keep up.

They arrived in Can Tho just after midday. Hong was lathered in sweat, as much from his uncontrollable nerves as from the stickiness of the wet season. Longy told his travelling companion they now had to go separate ways. Hong was to go to the markets, where he would find a man wearing a white shirt with an odd black button — who was to be Hong's taxi-man.

'Tell him I am here,' said Longy.

For the next few hours Longy wandered the streets being 'cool and sociable' with the locals. Despite the urgency of the situation — by this stage James's anger at his nomadic brother was steaming above the local temperature — Longy wasn't in any mood to be rushed. If these were to be his final few moments on Vietnamese soil, he wanted to absorb them all: the wafting smells of simmering spices; puddles of water in the road; the frantic hand-waving banter between fruit-sellers and buyers; giggling boys and girls running in circles round their mothers; the lean, hungry-eyed dogs loitering near food stalls for scraps; even the relentless mosquitoes that left enormous stinging welts on the skin ... Longy wanted to alert his senses to every single second. This was what he knew. This was his life. A life he would not forget. Ever.

He made his way through the markets, where he bought enough fruit, rice, fish and whisky to stretch the sides of his sack. He planned to give everything to his taxi-man, a bonus in addition to the money each transporter had been paid by James.

While Longy was still shopping, several taxi-men had already begun their journeys with the small groups of people they'd been caring for. Stretched out over several kilometres of the river, the small craft slowly worked downstream, accompanied by the chugs of their feeble outboard motors. It would take at least three days of such travel before everyone would link up with James and Lam on the escape boat near the mouth of the Mekong.

Longy reached the house of his taxi-man by early evening.

'Is Hong here?'

'Yes. We've been waiting for many hours. We must go now.'

After loading the boat with the food Longy had bought, they slid into the fading light that was thick with humidity and swarming mosquitoes. The boat was a typical taxi vessel. About 3-metres long, it was so fragile that it rocked unsteadily against the slightest wake. Longy and Hong sat on narrow benches in the middle and spoke quietly about what might lie ahead.

Just before nightfall they were passed by James, Lam and Nam on the escape boat. James glared across the water at his younger brother. How dare he put the attempt in jeopardy! And who was the stranger with him? Longy knew he would face an angry inquisition when he and James came face to face in a few days' time.

As darkness fell, Longy's senses captured things he'd long taken for granted — the whispering splashes of water across the bow, slimy river weeds catching in his fingers when he dangled them over the side of the boat, the stars sliding in and out of sight behind the clouds. Despite all its problems, all its angry scars, Vietnam remained a hauntingly beautiful country. Regardless of what happened in the future to both the nation and its people, Longy knew he'd always consider it home.

Over the following days he tried to relax as much as he could. Each morning he swam, drifting with the currents, rekindling blissful memories of his mountain stream days in Pleiku. At other times he'd stroke to shore, then walk to the nearest markets where he'd wait for Hong and his taximan. There was no strict daily timetable for them, or anyone on the other taxi boats. It didn't matter how they spent their days, as long as they kept within reasonable distance of James's boat. There was no talk and little contact between people on different boats — they were simply individuals going about their daily lives, minding their own business.

By the afternoon of the fourth day they were nearing the mouth of the Mekong River, a renowned conflict zone during the war and now a highly dangerous area dotted with police posts hidden from view near the water's edge. If any boat aroused a mere whiff of suspicion it could be surrounded within minutes, and its passengers either captured or killed.

In the golden warmth of an August sunset, the Nguyen escape attempt was only just about to begin.

NINETEEN

Fear and Freedom

*'Happiness depends on being free, and freedom
depends on being courageous.'*
THUCYDIDES

The taxi-men guided their boats up to the escape vessel one at a time. Although the transfer of people was swift, there was still time for farewells. In the few short days that the passengers had come to know their temporary custodians, wonderful friendships had developed. Souls had been bared, secrets told, dreams dreamt. These were bonds that would last forever.

Longy was last on board. The sight of Van smiling excitedly was the only proof he needed that he'd made the right decision in bringing Hong. As people began settling below, Nam added final touches to the cabin and deck with his hammer and chisel. He worked quickly. The light was fading, yet at this crucial time darkness seemed to be dawdling. The lingering daylight carried a much greater risk of being discovered.

Sounds of music and laughter carried from the shore; it

seemed there was a concert going on. If good luck was with the escapees, the coast patrols might have taken the night off to join in the frivolities. Apart from the taxi boats fading into the distance, there were no other vessels in sight.

By the time Nam had finished his work the night had finally arrived, as had the time for the last goodbye. Tears flowed in the gloom. Nam's daughter-in-law was distraught. Every grown person on the boat felt her pain. After hugging her, Nam turned to move away, but he was stopped by a man holding a gold necklace.

'Please take it. Thank you for everything you've done. I'll never forget your kindness.'

Another person came forward. Then another. And another. More still. All offered gifts. Nam accepted each, wrapping them in a bag that he held tightly to his chest. He smiled gently and said, *'Thuong lo Binh an.'*

As he stepped down onto the only remaining taxi boat, he caught Longy's eye and silently wished him *Thuong lo Binh an* — have a safe trip. Then he was gone, another memory drifting into the night.

The silence was soon broken by the dull thump of the Kubota engine. Lam reappeared from the engine room covered in grease. He was tired, he'd had little sleep, but once the boat was beyond the river mouth he would be able to rest. It was then that the former navy officer, Hieu, would take over, under James's direction. Indeed, he was already seeking some control, asking for the sea compass to be installed in the cabin well before it would be needed. Once this was complete there would be little for anyone to do except look ahead into the unfurling night, and hope.

Longy chose to stay on the top deck with his two older brothers, Hong and Uncle Ovaltine. No-one ordered him below. James still hadn't spoken to him.

Below deck the conditions were cramped: shoulder to shoulder, knee to knee, no room to stretch out the legs, or stand up without hitting the roof. But no-one complained, even though piles of sugar cane on either side further restricted movement. These stacks served the dual purpose of being food supplies and ballast. The boat was filled with spiritual ballast, too, and amid the comforting rosary beads and silent prayers there was such a positive feeling that Lam felt it as 'an energy everyone could draw from'. Whether above or below, each person knew how important it was to keep the mood high.

The level of enthusiasm was boosted by the boat's progress. Despite fears that the departure from the river mouth would be among the most dangerous parts of the journey, it passed without incident. There wasn't a coastal patrol in sight. It was now just a matter of heading straight through till the morning, by which time Hieu estimated they'd be well into international waters.

It was a calm night. Longy looked back at the shadowy lump that was his homeland, thinking of his mother.

BANG!

Longy lurched forward, thoughts of his mother tossed aside by the boat's abrupt halt.

'We've hit something!' yelled James.

People clambered up from below deck, panicking, frightened. Longy reached inside his jeans and pulled out the Beretta. James stared in disbelief — he hadn't seen the pistol since he'd hidden it in the drain near the Nguyen home, but now wasn't the time to question how his brother had found it. Longy hurriedly handed the weapon to Hong before he stripped off his shirt and leapt off the back of the boat. The cold water seemed to suck out his breath as he plunged below the surface. Unable to touch the sea floor, he felt his way along the side of the boat. Suddenly, surprisingly, his feet reached sand. By the time he was at the bow, he was standing only waist-deep in the water.

'The nose is resting on sand,' he told the throng. 'It hasn't dug in, but I need help to move it. We have to push the boat back. The water's deep at the back.'

Only Maria's husband, David, jumped in.

'If we don't get help we won't be going anywhere. The tide is going out.'

No-one moved.

'Come on!'

In the uneasy stillness, Hong contemplated a drastic action. In one startling movement, he waved the Beretta threateningly above his head.

'If someone doesn't help I'll use this!'

There was a huge splash as bodies leapt into the water. Longy and his handful of freezing helpers threw their weight against the boat. It shifted slightly, then floated forward and kept going.

The grounding had been a silly mistake. Although they were well clear of the river mouth, they should have been prepared for the silt deposits that fanned across the ocean for kilometres.

Luckily, it was the only trouble they struck that night. As the sun peered over the horizon the next morning, Longy looked behind him. There was no land, no patrol boats, nothing but the ocean. It was impossible to believe they were all alone. Had they reached international waters? No-one knew. The plan was to head straight for another day, then turn right (west) and hopefully reach Thailand, or perhaps Malaysia. It had been considered too much of a risk to carry accurate maps, so James and Lam had relied on vague drawings they had made on rolls of paper which could be easily destroyed if they were captured.

In this daunting vastness, the monotonous chug of the engine was the most reassuring sound on the boat. As it told of smooth progress, James and Lam had the chance to rest. Both had worked themselves beyond the point of exhaustion.

Longy split his time between stints on the top deck and below, where he checked on every passenger. Despite his tiredness he couldn't sleep; his thoughts leapt back to

Saigon. If only his mother could be here right now to watch dolphins diving playfully in front of the bow, so effortless and uncomplicated. Longy envied them.

In contrast to the boat's joyful travelling companions, the water was frequently littered with clothing floating limply to nowhere. Each new lonely scattering was met with silence on the top deck, and a taut understanding that there was no need to discuss the sightings with anyone below. It was simply accepted that the owners of the belongings had either drowned or been rescued.

Several more hours passed without incident, until late in the afternoon when dark clouds began massing in the sky. By nightfall the sea's rhythm had changed from a gentle roll to a more ominous movement. This was the first true test for the boat. Time and again its bow lifted from the water, then rode the air for several seconds before slapping down hard between swells. Babies screamed; both women and men cried. Rosary beads were clutched between white knuckles, hands were squeezed and arms were wrapped together. The stench of vomit was rife; the smell of fear was greater. Hieu was one of the worst affected. Seasick, disoriented and afraid, he was utterly useless at a time when his experience and supposed calmness was most needed.

'You're meant to be a navy man!' yelled Lam.

'Yes, but I'm not used to being on a small wooden boat with only a torch and a compass to guide me!'

Lashes of water whipped the hull viciously. The bow rose and dipped again.

Boom!
Boom!
Boom!

As James huddled close to Thu, below deck Longy joined Lam who was wrestling with the rudder deeper down in the engine room. They stayed together, riding every bump and terrifying knock, watching and listening for cracks in the hull that would pose a life-threatening danger — a powerful leak could tear a boat apart with little warning. After all the risky situations he'd been in throughout his life, Longy had never been as doubtful about surviving as he was now. But he hid his fears. There was nothing he could do, after all. The fortunes of forty-eight people rested in the hands of fate.

Slowly, painfully slowly, the ferocious swells began to subside. By dawn the sea was relatively calm. Upon inspection the boat didn't appear to be damaged; the only wear and tear was on faces following the sleepless, panic-stricken night. Longy tried to lift the mood. He moved from person to person, smiling, laughing, and even making jokes about Lam's grease-covered face. Eventually he came to his oldest brother — the two still hadn't spoken to each other.

'I'm sorry, James.'

'How'd you know about the gun?'

'I watched you hide it.'

James smiled. He should have known! In the space of these few short words, any lingering animosity vanished. They had always shared a different relationship from others in the family. Longy firmly believed they communicated with each other as much through their thoughts as their words. There was never any need for long-winded chatter between them, but now, with their lives enmeshed in uncertainty, they opened up to one another. They reminisced about their childhood; talked about their concerns for their parents and Thao; analysed their previous escape attempts; and discussed what they'd do should they make it safely to a free country. Theirs was indeed a unique bond.

By now, Lam had turned the boat west. He was 'navigating by guesswork', in the absence of Hieu, who'd been sacked from his post after his performance during the night. Hieu was to take no further part in operations, his role now restricted to keeping his wife and child company below deck.

It was only mid-morning yet the sun was already stinging. Cups of water and coconuts were passed around.

No-one drank or ate excessively; moderation was essential in case the boat was forced to be at sea for longer than expected. But exactly how long was that — three days? Four? Perhaps it would be five or six. There was no way of knowing.

Nor was there a plan for what to do when something unexpected was noticed in the distance.

'Ship!'

People scrambled onto the top deck, their tiredness suddenly shrugged off by the thoughts of rescue. As the cargo vessel came closer, the mood shifted from restrained hope to feverish excitement. A T-shirt tied to the end of a sugar cane was waved frantically. Voices that only minutes earlier had been dry and feeble suddenly burst to life.

Maria's husband, David, who had little command of English, yelled the few words he knew: 'Come here, come here, come here!'

But the ship didn't. It changed direction long before its crew could have seen or heard any of the commotion. It powered away, its huge, formidable shape indelibly marked in the minds of everyone on the tiny boat that had been overlooked. Other ships were seen throughout the day. Some came close enough for their crews to see the frantic waves and jumps for attention, but none stopped — the sight of refugee boats clogging one of the world's busiest shipping lanes hadn't just become common, but was outright annoying for some operators. By sunset the Nguyen boat had only once attracted any sort of interest. It came from a shark that circled for several minutes before deciding, just as the ships' skippers had, that the wooden vessel and its cargo were of no value.

In the darkness that followed, the swells again became bigger. Or were they only imagined to be that way? At night the senses played tricks with the mind. The sound of every creak and crack was magnified, and every roll of the boat was threatening. Longy had heard fishermen talk of the sea as being a peaceful place, soothing and comforting. That was surely because the men hadn't ventured into the deepest waters, where land was just a memory. The South China Sea could be a temperamental beast. Its shallow waters, generally no deeper than 40 to 50 metres, were strongly affected by the winds. With little notice currents could shift, swells could rise to frothing white caps, and human lives became even more fragile in the overwhelming emptiness.

Longy wasn't frightened of the sea, but he had become suspicious of it. At night it was like a dark corner in a Saigon alley: it had to be negotiated with the belief there was always something, or someone, lurking out of sight, waiting to attack. Everyone realised that the further west they travelled, the more at risk they would be. But it wasn't only the conspiring elements that worried them. A few months earlier Thu had lost one of her brothers, chopped to death by Thai pirates. On that same boat, women had been raped. With those thoughts plaguing him, Longy slept fitfully. It was as though he was in prison again.

In the morning's earliest hours, he was shocked from sleep by a bright light on his face. He squinted, shielding his eyes with his hands. The light was coming from the cabin of a much bigger, sturdier boat that had pulled alongside. For one brief moment he thought it was a Malaysian trawler, but then the truth jolted him wide awake as the vessels banged together and three men leapt on board. *Pirates!* The men joined the boats with looping ropes that sprang from their hands so quickly that Longy barely had time to stand before the job was done. He was too weak to react as he would have done in a Saigon alley.

The pirates were all strong, sinewy, bare-chested men with tattoos on their forearms and knives tucked conspicuously into their shorts. They moved across the top deck with a confidence that indicated they had done this so many times before. Two went below, the other dashed to the cabin where Van was. Terrified, she twisted a ring off her finger and pulled out half an ounce of gold from under her clothing. She handed both over. The pirate shoved the booty in his mouth, perhaps to hide it from his partners in crime, who'd reappeared quickly, herding everyone from below onto the top deck. The passengers' fear grew with each step. Eyes were wide with horror. Thoughts of rape were in every woman's mind — in every man's, too.

Longy was pushed into the line. He felt his anger throbbing in pace with his pulse. Fuck these men. Fuck them! Submissiveness had never been his friend. He wondered what Uncle Ba would advise. Strike now? Impossible. Revenge at a later time, as with the Cambodian street gang? Not likely — there surely wouldn't be a later time. The Beretta? Longy hadn't seen it since Hong had flourished it in the air. God only knew if he still had it. It was no use trying to find out — Hong was too far away at the other end of the line. Longy felt hopeless. There was nothing, absolutely nothing he could do.

One at a time the passengers were marshalled onto the other boat. The pirates joked among themselves in a fast, clipped language only they understood. They laughed, slapped each other on their backs. About ten more appeared. It was only then that Longy noticed the skipper of the pirates' boat, hunched over the wheel in the cabin, approving the mayhem.

Longy looked at the more familiar faces around him. Each showed resignation. No-one knew what exactly would happen, but most expected the worst: theft then death, or death then theft.

In this air of fatalism, what happened next was almost absurd. The pirates brought out freshly steamed fish, which they encouraged everyone to eat while they leapt back on board the escape boat and searched for more valuables. The looks of resignation changed to utter disbelief and confusion. Was this the last supper? Or were they, oddly, hospitable thieves?

The pirates returned with their hands — perhaps one or two mouths as well — full of jewellery, gold and money. One also carried an *Ao dai*, which, with brief, unmistakable gestures he insisted Lam put on. If the serving of fish wasn't bizarre enough, the sight of a grown man fearing for his life while squeezing into a woman's clothing most surely was. The pirates laughed raucously; everyone else offered forced grins. In the middle stood Lam. Devout and loyal to his Catholic faith, he now knew 'what hell was really like'.

The pirates then began searching individuals. Bodies stiffened, eyes were either shut or stared blankly ahead, and fists were clenched so tightly that some fingernails drew blood from the palms. Only the pirates spoke, their voices occasionally drowned out by the heavy beat of their boat's idling engine. They moved casually from person to person, collecting everything from watches to money, necklaces and gold teeth. Some searches lasted mere seconds as victims surrendered their valuables the moment they were approached. However, this didn't prevent hands lingering on women.

Longy waited for his turn. He couldn't imagine this happening in Saigon: his pride and reputation would prevent it. Again he considered retaliation, but it was no use. He may have been the self-confessed king of the streets, but here he was quite literally all at sea.

Standing near Longy, a pirate was inspecting a wallet he'd just taken. He fingered it with some exaggeration before he opened it.

'Aaah!'

The pirate dropped to his knees, clasped his hands together and bowed his head repeatedly. Others rushed over to see what was happening. Once they realised, they too knelt before the face staring back at them — a picture of a buddha.

After regaining their composure they meekly handed back the wallet, but they didn't return the other items they'd taken. Under their religion they could expect some bad luck to befall them because of the bad deeds they had committed, but they seemed to be comfortable taking that risk. However, the sight of the buddha had been unsettling enough to stop them searching anyone else. Instead, in another weird twist, they happily tried to answer questions as to how far away they were from land. Smiling as though they'd done nothing wrong, they stretched their hands wide apart to indicate that terra firma was still several days off.

Their false friendliness didn't last long. In one final deplorable act they used a crane and metal chain to pull out the escape boat's 'fake engine'. Their laughter and the booming sound of their motor trailed into the night, leaving behind once defiant people. At least no-one had been hurt — they could probably thank a picture in a wallet for that — but in the inspection that followed, any slight relief turned to despair after it was discovered the boat was taking in excessive water. The bilge pump wasn't working properly, and the fan belt on the Kubota engine was beginning to tear. Lam was miserable: he knew his mechanical resourcefulness was going to be stretched beyond belief in the coming days.

More immediate intervention was needed, though, so a line was formed from the bilge to the top deck. People took turns bailing out the water in used oil cans that they passed along the chain until their hands were blistered and bloodied, their muscles cramped. No-one said what he or she was thinking. Trying not to draw attention to his actions, Lam began placing empty cans and sugar cane within reach of the several children on board. If the time came, he could tell them to use the objects to help them float.

The boat was making slow progress, wearily climbing every swell. This was a domain for only the fit and strong, but even they were struggling. The grinding hours and lack of sleep inevitably took their toll on Longy. He had blocked ears, swollen lips, and eyes stinging from the saltwater's whips. He found it hard to breathe and, worst of all, he was hallucinating. One minute he was fully aware of where he was, the next he was struck by panic and confusion. When he was lucid, he thought of his mother.

While others took rests, Hong, motivated by his inability to swim, refused to stop bailing. His extraordinary stamina and willpower defied the general mood — the positive energy that had been so abundant at the start of the trip had gone. Apart from whispered prayers, spasmodic snores and crying babies, there was little noise to accompany the tiresome sound of tin scooping up water. Sadness had not only engulfed the boat, but seemed to be steering as well.

Nothing had changed by daylight. As James and Lam tried to determine where they were, others squinted into the dazzling sun in a futile search for land. But there was nothing but careless winds, snapping fish, glistening water beneath a cloudless sky, and a fractured boat cradling forty-eight lives.

Then suddenly an object appeared in the distance. Could it be another ship?

It came closer. Yes, a ship.

Closer still.

A tanker.

Half an hour passed.

Closer still. Splintered hopes were swiftly mending. Longy joined the group watching every roll of 'the elephant approaching the mouse', as it seemed to them. It was heading towards them. Straight towards them. Surely they had been seen.

Then it began turning. *No, please no*. A slow, curving turn. Women were ushered up onto the top deck. Babies were held in the air. The shirt and the sugar cane were waved frantically. The tanker was still turning ... but not away.

'They're protecting us from the wind!' yelled Lam.

Closer still.

'Come here, come here, come here,' pleaded David.

Slowly it came alongside, its vast bulk squeezing out swells that rocked its tiny cousin sideways. Longy looked up in awe — it was the biggest ship he'd ever seen.

Faces started peering over the side. Maria held baby Noell above her head and shouted. Suddenly a rope ladder was tumbling down the side of the tanker, unfolding and banging against the iron. Excitement bubbled. Dry throats crackled with laughter. If Lam had thought everyone had been in hell just hours before, he now felt they were close to heaven.

Yes, they'd been spotted, and a ship was now at their side, but they hadn't yet been rescued. Above them a crew member was raising just one finger in the air, then pointing to the ladder. If the interpretation was correct, it seemed that a representative for the whole boat was being called for. James looked around, considering the choices. His eyes finally rested on Tranthi Dao, whose husband had fled to America several years before, leaving Tranthi to care for their daughter, who now stood looking wonderingly at the tanker and hopefully at its swaying ladder. Tranthi hadn't yet paid for the trip, but promised she would send money if she and her daughter ever made it to safety. James thought her to be a woman of her word. And at this moment, the only valuable words needed to be in English, which was likely to be the language most easily understood by whoever was waiting on the tanker. Having worked with the Americans during the war, Tranthi knew English well enough to hold a constructive conversation. She was the only possible candidate to scale that ladder.

Tranthi climbed one rickety step after another, her every movement watched anxiously from below and curiously from above. When she reached the top she was met by the Swiss skipper, a tall, bearded man in his fifties. No-one on the escape boat could see what was happening — they had to rely on the sounds of Tranthi's tired voice. Although her words couldn't be understood, there was no misinterpreting the theme: 'Please help us. Please!'

Longy stood patiently, wishing for rather than expecting a good outcome. He sensed similar feelings all around him. It was as though everyone was back in Saigon, listening to those cursed loudspeakers, waiting to hear whether loved ones would be called for army duty or taken away to be re-educated. But this time there was one poignant difference: no-one prayed to be overlooked.

A face appeared over the side of the tanker. It was Tranthi. She was smiling, laughing, waving her arms, jumping up and down.

'We are safe. We are safe!' she cried.

Cheers erupted, hugs swept from person to person, and the deck echoed with the sounds of hurrying feet. One by one they climbed out, only a few choosing to look back. David was the last to set foot on the rungs; he'd had to perform one final duty. Using a hammer and chisel, he cut a sizable hole in the bilge. By the time he was halfway up the ladder, the boat was rapidly sinking — the single sea burial of the voyage.

In the blur of emotions that followed once everyone was safe, Longy had one regret: somewhere in the froth below was his father's Beretta. It was part of him, a symbol of his life, of all the violence, the blood, the killings he'd seen. He paused, and thought again. Perhaps the Beretta was better abandoned.

Longy was about to discover a new life.

TWENTY

Looking for a Home

*A refugee, '... owing to a well-founded fear of
being persecuted for reasons of race, religion,
nationality, membership of a particular social group
or political opinion, is outside the country of his
nationality, and is unable or, owing to such fear, is
unwilling to avail himself of the protection of that
country; or who, not having a nationality and being
outside the country of his former habitual residence as
a result of such events, is unable or, owing to such fear,
is unwilling to return to it.'*
UNITED NATIONS, 1951 CONVENTION AND
1967 PROTOCOL RELATING TO THE STATUS OF REFUGEES

Longy couldn't believe it — this wasn't a tanker but a luxury hotel with Western cigarettes, spaghetti and meatballs, sandwiches, baked beans, coffee and ice-cold Coke. Then there was the bakery, the snooker table with chequer-like pieces instead of balls, the movie room, and lifts that zoomed between floors. The men were put in one gigantic room, the women and babies in another. They were fresh clean rooms with beds that had crisp sheets and pillows that were smooth and cool against the face.

How great life was. One minute Longy was drifting in 'a coffin on the ocean', the next — in bliss. The tanker, from Japan, was registered to the Sanko Steamship Company, one of the region's most renowned shipping lines. Longy shook his head again and again. To think he'd woken up hating the ocean. But now he loved it. He loved the whole world. At that very moment he couldn't even hate the Viet Cong.

As Longy rapidly and readily grew accustomed to the relatively luxurious life, it was a dreadfully different scene in Saigon, where a frightening storm had just rocked the city. Many houses had either been flattened by the winds or invaded by rising waters that had turned roads into rivers. In the safety of the Nguyen home, Thao sat holding her mother's hand. Teresa cried, fearing the storm had made its way to the sea, convinced that the little refashioned boat from Can Tho couldn't have survived such savagery. Teresa was inconsolable.

Out at sea, Longy stood laughing next to Lam in the showers.

'How are we going to tell Mum this? She won't believe us.'

'It's times like this I know there is a God,' Lam said.

Everyone did. Even Longy.

For the next few days the tanker glided over the water towards a port in Chon Buri, southeast of Bangkok. This gave Longy ample time to explore in his customary manner. Although the mostly Filipino crew was at first wary of this inquisitive youngster, they quickly warmed to him and showed him every part of the ship. Longy was fascinated by the engine room, an enormous steaming monster with a roar that could be heard some distance away, even in the confusing warren of narrow corridors. He frequently stood at the stern, staring down at the powerful white wake that laid a path to his past.

The refugees, as they now undeniably were under the definition of the United Nations, chatted excitedly about their futures. Longy dreamt of a life in the United States; he already had relations there who could look after him. Furthermore, was he not a friend of the American people? Perhaps he would meet some of the GIs who used to smile at him when he passed the Hoang Lan café in Pleiku. Surely they'd remember him. He would go back to school and learn about the Kennedys, rock and roll and baseball — all the subjects that were forbidden and condemned in Uncle Ho's classroom. But beyond that ... Would he still be the 'king of the streets' with his own cock fighters and lieutenants? Would he still have to fight his way out of trouble? Would he still win money playing table soccer? Swim across rivers? Ride a scooter? Go to the barber? The markets? Would there be *Cam le* leaves?

The arrival in Chon Buri further confused Longy. The tanker's skipper had notified United Nations officials of his passengers, but it wasn't simply a matter of going ashore, shaking hands and catching a plane to America. Everyone had to stay on board for another week while the obligatory paperwork was completed. Longy was frustrated, but he slowly accepted that this was part of the process, the transitional stage before dreams come true.

When the day of departure finally came, the words of a traditional Vietnamese thank you song drifted across the deck. Some of the tanker's crew wept as they listened to their departing guests' spontaneous performance. They'd grown fond of these boat people who had come aboard almost as wretched animals and would leave as inspiring examples of the human spirit. In a touching gesture, they forfeited some of their wages to give each refugee a gift of $US9. This brought more tears. Longy was also given a pair of jeans. He thought back to the Thai pirates. Bad karma, good karma — the world was driven by both. Just like the taxi-men of the Mekong, the Sanko men of the South China Sea would never be forgotten.

After shaking hands and smiling at indecipherable shouts of good wishes, Longy and the others climbed into a boat where UN officials, Thai police and a Vietnamese translator were waiting. Numerous forms had to be filled out and questions answered.

'Where are we going now?' asked Longy.

'To a camp,' said an official.

Longy immediately remembered his father — some camps weren't what they seemed. But the officials insisted it was standard procedure. The camp was just one of many across the region catering for hundreds and thousands of Indochinese refugees.

'Be grateful, you are one of the lucky ones.'

'Why?'

'Because you were found at sea.'

Under law, refugees rescued in international waters became the responsibility of the country that had technically saved them. In this case it was Japan, where the Sanko tanker was registered.

Ever since the fall of Saigon, the treatment and placement of refugees had become a highly emotive, contentious and insoluble political issue. Some refugees who had fled across land, or who had made it all the way by water to a safe country, had been inside camps for years without any indication of when, or if, they were likely to be resettled. It seemed the tragedies of war and ostracism hadn't ended at Vietnam's borders. No-one from 'Boat 48' — so called by UN officials because of the number of people on board — realised how fortunate they were.

'How long will we be at the camp?'

'Less than forty-five days. Then you'll be on your way to Japan.'

Longy smiled. He couldn't wait to write to his mother.

Teresa was no longer miserable: a few days after the storm she had heard a BBC World Service report that a group of Vietnamese had been rescued by a Japanese tanker in the Gulf of Thailand. There were surely many refugees gambling in the open sea at the time, but the knowledge that one boatload had been picked up was enough to give Teresa some hope. She listened to the radio every day, waiting for further news. She listened and prayed, prayed and listened. One afternoon she was interrupted by a knock on the door downstairs — a postman had come with a telegram. Teresa's prayers may have been interrupted, but they were also answered. She read the message again, then caught a cyclo to church to show the news to Father Chinh, a different man of the cloth from the one who'd been at the Army Catholic Church in Pleiku.

'This isn't a joke, is it?' she asked.

Father Chinh read the telegram and shook his head. 'No. I believe it's real.'

Teresa laughed, releasing feelings that had been trapped for years. Was it possible that happiness was magnified if a person had first suffered the deepest sadness? If so, at that very moment, there wasn't anyone alive who deserved to feel more joy than the mother who'd just read that her children were free. *Thank God*. And thank the skipper of the Sanko oil tanker who had not only made the rescue, but had sent the telegram. Obviously a kind, kind man. *God bless him*.

Teresa left the church within minutes. It was time to go shopping for cigarettes, vitamins and other supplies needed for the long haul north — Hien deserved to be told the news as soon as possible.

Another world of politics away, the bus carrying the members of Boat 48 drove into the Laemsing camp, several hours southwest of Bangkok. It was late afternoon. Longy's attention was first drawn to a large, drab concrete building with smoke escaping from chimneys. It was a crematorium, a conspicuous statement that conditions in the camp were too demanding for some.

Hundreds of people had gathered around the gate to catch a glimpse of the new residents. This was a daily routine for those anxious to see if friends or relatives were on board. As Longy stepped off he was struck by the pungent smell of salt air and sewage — the camp was right next to the sea. Huddles of bamboo, wooden and tin huts crammed laneways made from concrete or dirt. All the arrivals were placed in a large single-room building where they would have to wait until other dwellings became available, either through pure luck or the exchange of money. Luck was on the Nguyens' side when only days later Longy met a friend from Saigon who was soon leaving for the United States. He offered the family his dwelling.

The hut was near the back of the camp. As the Nguyen siblings made their way with just the clothes they were wearing and a few ounces of gold, they were stopped and asked questions by people eager for any news from home: 'Where have you come from?'; 'What was it like in Saigon when you left?'; 'What are the communists doing now?'; 'Did you have to go to the new economic zones?'; 'Do you have family in the re-education camps?'

Others watched from their doorways or as they leaned against fragile, muddy walls. Longy guessed there were thousands here. Three, four, five, maybe more. It wasn't so much a camp but a town.

The Nguyen hut was near the sea and adjacent to stinking pontoon toilets similar to the ones Longy was forced to use in prison. Made from bamboo, the dwelling had a single dirt-floored room to accommodate all ten people (James and Thu; Van and Hong; David, Maria and Noell; Linh, Lam and Longy). They slept on bamboo bunks; there was no power or running water. Food, utensils, cooking and heating oils could be bought at shops and stalls outside the camp or from vendors who visited each day.

Others from Boat 48 settled nearby. None was happier than Tranthi Dao. On arrival she was informed she and her daughter had already been approved to enter the United States; they would leave within days. Although the wait was longer for the Nguyens, time passed quickly. From the very first morning Longy established a routine of waking early and going for a swim in the sea. At high tide it was even possible to dive into the water from the hut. Afterwards he'd wander through the camp, introducing himself, chatting to everyone.

There were many nationalities and cross-sections of life. Although the Vietnamese were dominant, there were also Cambodians, Laotians and some Chinese. Longy befriended an elderly South Vietnamese couple who had been in the camp for nearly two years. Their tragic reality was that the husband was likely to die there. A chronic asthmatic, he wheezed so loudly that his distress could be heard from the other side of the road. There were also those from the north who kept to themselves, fearing that widespread exposure would lead to conflict — bashings were common in some parts of the camp where gangs operated as though they were still in Saigon's alleys. Longy stayed well away from these mostly teenage groups; he had nothing to prove. Considering the shortness of his stay, and the knowledge that his life was leading in a particular direction, there was no need to re-establish his street-king reputation. Maybe there would be a time for it in the future, but not now.

Instead he turned back the clock to his Pleiku childhood. He went to church with his family without a word of protest and, even more astonishingly, he joined the Catholic youth movement that assumed such responsibilities as street cleaning, clearing and digging drains. After a fortnight he advanced to one of the most sought-after jobs: working on the water truck. Nearly every day he'd ride with two local men, hanging off the back 'like a garbo', to a reservoir half an hour away. He never tired of the journey — each image flashing by was part of his education. There were fruit-sellers with golden pyramids of mangoes; barefoot boys playing badminton in the alleys; crowded rings of people cheering on kick boxers; petrol stations serving customers on sparkling new scooters; huge billboards advertising cigarettes; streets flowing with smiles; and, above all, no police or men in uniforms staring coldly from every corner. This was freedom; a liberal society.

Each time the water truck returned to the camp, Longy assumed a position of power, leaning against the truck, hose in hand, filling buckets for people jostling for position in a scrum of clinking metal, shoving elbows and the occasional expletive.

If only Teresa could see her son now — he was so responsible! Longy thought of his mother 'every second moment'. He prayed for her in church and wrote to her every day. He sent each letter from a post office just outside the camp, near Madame Noi's coffee shop, one of his favourite haunts where 1970s hits, from ABBA, Boney M and Tom Jones, belted out. His memories drifted back to his favourite coffee shop, 'Thien Ly'. He didn't know that since his departure from Saigon, Teresa had cut back the hours of her business, choosing only to open the doors when she felt like it.

As was his way in Saigon, Longy was well dressed in jeans, a shirt and proper shoes, thanks to money sent to the Nguyen family by uncles in the United States and Canada. Then, midway through their stay, they received a letter from Tranthi Dao who had arrived safely in America with her son. As James had always believed, the woman was indeed true to her word — the letter contained a money order for $US1500.

Longy begged his oldest brother to give him enough money to buy a tape recorder, but James controlled the purse strings tightly; this wasn't the environment for ostentation. Cash was used for essentials, and to help others less fortunate. In fact, the Nguyens quickly became known for their charity, offering food and cigarettes to people in need.

Longy grew to appreciate how lucky he was. He had everything he needed to survive comfortably and happily. However, he remained tormented by thoughts of those he'd left behind. When most troubled, he went to the front gate and joined the onlookers waiting for the arrival of a new group. Each time he heard the UN bus approaching, its gnashing gears acting as extra brakes down the hill into camp, he held his breath. Maybe, just maybe, he would see Lan. And then they could begin their lives all over again. Together. He always knew he wouldn't see her, but whenever a bus shuddered to a halt there was a brief moment, a flash of fantasy, when his world was almost perfect. He needed those times.

He missed Truong too. But perhaps Truong missed Longy more. A few weeks after the two friends had last seen each other, he had visited Teresa.

'Where's Longy? When is he coming back?'

'He's not. He's in Thailand, and will soon be in Japan.'

Truong held back his tears. He left the Nguyen home accepting time had to move on, but at least in his memories he could make it stand still.

However, Longy's days at Laemsing were coming to an end. United Nations officials had begun interviewing each member of the Nguyen family, a sure sign that a move was imminent. The questions were standard: How old are you? Have you ever had a serious illness? Where did you live in Vietnam? What do your parents do? How did you escape? Have you ever been a political prisoner?

On day thirty-seven, they received news that they were to leave the following morning. For the rest of the day Longy went around saying his goodbyes. Most were crestfallen affairs, the people remaining behind were pleased for Longy, yet disappointed they weren't in a similar position.

When the water truck drivers arrived to take Longy to the reservoir he shook his head and, using the familiar mix of hand movements, broken phrases and facial expressions, told them: 'No truck, no more. Me, Japan.' They hugged him and smiled; they were well versed in seeing water boys come and go.

That night the Nguyens threw a party for the friends they'd made. Over a few cigarettes and more beer than he'd ever had before, Longy floated through the evening, frolicking in the water, dancing in the hut, grinning and laughing. Life could hardly be better.

After further goodbyes the next morning, the family boarded a UN bus with about thirty others for a trip to a transit camp on the outskirts of Bangkok. They arrived in the early evening and were settled in a room full of other refugees in one of several accommodation blocks. The next four days were filled with interview sessions, health checks, injections and X-rays, and paperwork primarily undertaken by James. As part of a fresh intake of refugees under Japan's annual quota system, the Nguyens would receive accommodation, education, health benefits and vocational training. However, the family considered that the move would be a temporary one. James, in particular, was eager to explore settlement opportunities outside the Asian region.

Although Longy had his mind set on the United States as his final destination, at that very moment his main interest was in taking a journey to anywhere, as long as it was on a jet. He'd only ever been on a plane once in his life, when he'd travelled with his mother on a DC3 from Pleiku to Hue. Every time he heard a roar overhead at the camp, he stared in amazement at the enormous craft hanging in the air as though suspended from a piece of string. He couldn't wait to experience it for himself — it would, perhaps, offer the ultimate sense of freedom.

Amid the buzz of excitement amongst the refugees, there were the inevitable stories of tragedy. On one of his typical outings around the transit camp, Longy was introduced to two young Vietnamese sisters whose parents had been killed by pirates. Their only source of income was from selling noodles they cooked in a small pot, one of the few belongings they had. In a matter of days they'd be on their way to America — two lonely figures in a veritable flood of humanity.

Between 1975 and 1980 more than half a million Indochinese refugees had been resettled in countries of permanent asylum. The United States led the way. Canada, France, the United Kingdom and Australia were also significant participants, although the issue was so potentially explosive that there was always political pressure on each nation to increase its intake.

It was in this contentious environment that the Nguyens arrived at Bangkok's international airport. It was chaotic. There was a rolling squeeze of bumper-to-bumper taxis all bleating for business. Worried passengers burdened with luggage tried to calculate the few safe moments in which to open car doors and sprint to the footpaths. If they weren't hit by traffic, they were almost certainly swarmed on by porters. Once Longy was inside the vast terminal teeming with comings and goings, he stopped and stared in disbelief. What were those scoreboards above his head? They were certainly nothing like the old black wooden slabs with white number-cards that boys changed manually during soccer games in Saigon. These somehow clicked over at a furious rate without hands anywhere. The names whizzed by: London, Paris, Sydney, New York ...

After clearing immigration, Longy wandered through the duty-free shops wondering if it were possible that one day he would be able to come back here and buy whatever he wanted. A tape recorder. Electric jug. Toaster. Calculator. Perfume. A T-shirt with 'I've been to Bangkok' written on the back. Ah, capitalism ... how beautiful it was.

When the time came to board the plane, Longy, not wanting to miss a single second of this experience, was one of the first in line. It was all so orderly, but happily so. There were immaculately made-up women in uniforms smiling, inspecting each ticket. One at a time they allowed passengers to walk into a tunnel, which Longy strode purposefully through because he knew what was waiting at the other end. The rest of his family trailed behind.

The aircraft's cabin was like a 'luxury classroom with padded seats'. Longy sat next to a window, looking in puzzlement from the men outside on the simmering tar strangely waving table-tennis bats, to the uniformed women who stood at intervals in the aisles performing some sort of dance, pointing at windows, snapping open and shut little belts they pulled from overhead lockers, and waving picture cards of the plane above their heads. Few passengers seemed to pay any attention. Most were too busy unfolding newspapers. Longy thought this was rude. He watched everything.

He looked outside again — the ground was moving. How weird. No, no, the plane was moving! Slowly backwards. Then forwards, turning in a gradual circle until it straightened and stopped. Nothing happened for several seconds. Was anything wrong? Suddenly, there was a shrill song. The engines had burst into life. The plane jolted; the cabin shuddered; the overhead lockers rattled. The ground was moving faster and faster. The grass outside became a blur.

Longy felt an invisible hand press him against his seat. The front of the cabin lifted. Higher. Higher still. Longy swallowed. His ears popped. His stomach was light. Freedom was indeed an unfamiliar feeling.

TWENTY-ONE

Snow, Sumos and Sake

Osaka Airport was throbbing. There were people rushing, pulling, strolling, standing, laughing, talking, loitering. Hundreds of people. But there wasn't a solitary soul to welcome Japan's newest refugees. Not even a translator to help them understand the confusing jumble of symbols, numbers and arrows cluttering every wall.

The Nguyens entered into a busy hallway, struggling against the oncoming traffic. After several hopeless attempts to stop passers-by they reached an assistance desk, where they tried to talk with a puzzled official who answered every question with an apologetic shake of the head and a shrug of the shoulders. They needed to catch a connecting flight to Fukuoka. But how? Follow the arrows? The people heading left — right — straight ahead? In this land of democracy, the right to choose could be as frustrating as the rigid structure from which the Nguyens had escaped.

Eventually the official understood enough to guide this flustered group in the direction of their departure gate, but he warned them, pointing at his watch, that they needed to hurry because the flight was almost boarding. They began to run, threading their way through the masses who at every turn seemed to be flowing against them. They entered a long corridor, James urging everyone to quicken their pace. But Longy slowed. Could he really believe what he was seeing? Forget the flicking scoreboard in Thailand and the raw fish he'd been served on the flight — this was even more incredible. A television was mounted on a bracket above him. Not just any television, but one with colour pictures. Amazing!

'Hurry up, Longy!'

He rejoined his family as they breathlessly reached the departure gate just in time. Little more than an hour later they arrived in Fukuoka and, to their relief, were greeted by two smiling representatives of the small, local Vietnamese community. It was night-time. The air was crisp, and much colder than the shivering Longy had ever experienced. Apart from the jeans, shirt and sneakers he was wearing, he had nothing to keep him warm; his only other possession was a small bag holding scraps of paper with the addresses of friends in Saigon and those he'd made while staying in the refugee camp.

The family boarded a bus and Longy stared out the window at the clean streets that were scattered with neon lights blinking brilliantly from walls, rooftops and poles that speared into the darkness. Cars, scooters and trucks moved in neat, orderly rows, and although their horns squawked and squeaked regularly there was, nevertheless, a calm that was absent in the chaotic scramble of Saigon's traffic.

After reaching the semirural outskirts of the city, the bus turned into a driveway flanked by gardens behind which were a cluster of stone and brick buildings — a convent.

The Nguyens were met by the head priest, an elderly Polish man who shook each person's hand. A group of nuns stood next to him. Longy looked at them with some bewilderment. As opposed to the sandal-wearing servants of the Lord he'd come to know from his earliest days in Pleiku, these women wore black knee-high boots. He grinned. God moved in mysterious ways.

The refugees were shown to a demountable house where the men were allocated one room, the women and baby Noell another. Longy was too excited to sleep. He couldn't wait to begin exploring his new home, then he'd sit down and describe every little detail in a letter to his mother. He felt a 'happy sadness' in his heart. No matter how joyful his life would be from this moment on, it would always be anchored by the vivid, recurring memories of Teresa sitting alone next to the radio; Thao standing on the balcony biting her bottom lip to hold back tears; and Hien being driven away to go to camp, his pyjama pants flapping.

The next morning after breakfast, each member of the family was given additional clothes that had been donated by local charities. The Nguyens weren't the only beneficiaries, as there were other refugees already staying at the convent, all eager to meet the newest residents so they could swap stories about their escapes and discover if they had any common friends or connections in Saigon.

Longy spent the rest of the day wandering around the convent getting his bearings. The grounds were beautiful, dotted with red and crimson flowers and carpets of soft lawn. The scent of oranges from a nearby orchard drifted on the breeze. Longy took deep breaths of cool, untainted air. He felt very much alive, as vibrant and confident as he'd ever been. Despite this, he couldn't escape a reminder of the savagery of conflict. There was a hospital across the road that continued to treat people affected by the atomic bombing of Nagasaki during World War II. Although Longy would never see any of the patients, the sheer thought of the atrocity provoked memories of the horrible scars he'd seen on napalm victims in his homeland.

Not all memories were as haunting. After discovering a colour television in the recreation room Longy sat transfixed for hours, unbothered by the strange language that forced his imagination to play interpreter. He marvelled how the screen never went fuzzy from government censorship interference, as was customary in Saigon. Here he could watch whatever he wanted without fear of having his viewing cut short. There were dramas, sitcoms, game shows with loud hosts in outrageously bright suits and striped ties; soccer fixtures, stock reports, news bulletins; and, the most enthralling program of all, the movie classic *The Great Escape*, the ultimate prisoner-of-war epic with a cast that included Richard Attenborough, James Garner, Charles Bronson and Steve McQueen. Captivated by every moment of McQueen's frantic bid for freedom on a stolen German motorcycle, Longy imagined the Hollywood star in a real-life situation: 'All he had to do was jump a few fences to get away from the Germans — very different from escaping Vietnam on a pea-sized boat. He had it very easy!'

When he wasn't watching television or chatting with other residents, Longy spent time writing to his mother. Every few days he went to the administration offices to post a letter; each visit was filled with the hope that he would return with a reply. But as time passed he became resigned to empty-handed walks.

After three weeks the officials in charge of the refugee program deemed that Longy and his brothers were ready to take the first serious steps towards integration into the community at large. From then on they caught a bus each morning to a fruit cannery, where they worked from seven o'clock to mid-afternoon as members of a processing line. In a typical example of migrant employment across the Western world, their jobs required little interaction with others and no significant communication skills.

Despite the monotony of pouring buckets of oranges onto a conveyor belt for hours at a time, Longy enjoyed his role, the very first structured employment he'd been involved in. When he was in a mischievous mood he picked up his rate until Hong, with the responsibility of sorting the fruit, couldn't keep up with the flow. The sight of Van's bespectacled boyfriend swinging his arms and contorting his body in a futile effort to stop oranges cascading to the floor always brought chuckles from the youngest worker along the line.

In addition to the odd sneaky puff of a cigarette, the 45-minute lunch break was the day's highlight. Each employee was given a canteen voucher that enabled him to receive meat, a pickle and two raw eggs that could be stirred into a bowl of warm rice. Longy had such a good relationship with his supervisor that he nearly always received two vouchers. He only once forewent his meal, after he and the rest of the Nguyen contingent received their first pay packets. That day they rushed away to the local shopping plaza, returning three hours later overloaded with bags from their buying spree. The supervisor could only laugh. That night, Longy lay in his room examining his purchases. He wore stiff Levis jeans and a Lacoste shirt, listened to Western music on his Sony tape recorder and played with the buttons on his Casio calculator watch. Brand names had become his highly prized companions.

On weekends, when he wasn't needed at the cannery, Longy did odd jobs for the nuns, spending most of his time digging and weeding the convent gardens. Work had become a central part of his daily routine; after years of living by his own rules he was content to fall in line with others.

By now he was filling out and developing a muscular body; the physical demands of the cannery had helped sculpt a physique that was fast turning its broad back on adolescence. Longy wore tight shirts to give an inflated impression of the size of his chest and arms. With his hair flowing to his shoulders, he enjoyed overhearing the comments of other convent refugees that he 'looked like a movie star'.

If ever there was a reason to bask in the spotlight of the moment, it came soon after his sixteenth birthday while he made one of his regular walks to the convent's administration offices. As he entered, the nun on duty smiled. She knew no Vietnamese, but the glow on her face was easily understood — Longy had a letter. He slowly sliced it open with his fingers, then ran it under his nose. Every line and word, each corner and crease, was tinged with the fading scent of his mother. The news was simple, to the point and, as Longy expected, underwritten with stoicism.

> So there you are in Japan. I am very, very happy that you escaped. You now have a life ahead of you. Don't worry about Thao and me. We are well. Your father is still in the camp. I told him of your escape. He is very happy too. Be a good person, Longy. Help your brothers and sisters all you can. You are family.

Longy thought it was strange how life worked. He had grown up holding his mother's hands, massaging her legs, sleeping next to her, kissing her. Now, robbed of those loving touches, he turned to a single piece of paper for comfort. He folded it up, put it back into its envelope and placed it in his top pocket.

All the Nguyen children received letters from home over the following weeks. Longy responded immediately to all of his. He started to send money, not only for his mother but for Truong as well. On one occasion he sent a whole box of clothes to his best friend after spending his entire pay packet in a fashion store. Despite his largesse, he always had the smartest clothes for himself; his most extravagant piece was a snug-fitting leather jacket that became a second skin.

* * *

While Longy happily let time pass, James was busy looking beyond the convent and cannery. He had found out about a resettlement program for Indochinese in Australia. It seemed to offer substantial opportunities, including the chance of ongoing studies and education, something James considered most important for everyone in the family. Although Longy was still determined to eventually make his way to the United States, he accepted his brother's decision to apply. He then forgot about it for several weeks until James received notification that the application had been accepted. They were bound for Australia, a country they knew little about. Sydney — where was that? Melbourne? Perth? At least they had some time to learn. As part of the emigration process they would be relocated to Tokyo, where interviews would be conducted and mountains of documents signed. They were told it could take several months before they actually left Japan.

So once again the Nguyens were on the move. Within days they were heading to Japan's capital on a train that Longy found overwhelming. This was no rattler swaying like a villager drunk on rice whisky; it was a slick and smooth high-speed missile that turned the countryside, towns and cities into melting greens and greys as it flashed past. Longy expected he'd have time to wander off and stretch his legs when the train pulled into stations, as he had on the trip to visit his father. But it stopped only once during the entire journey, just long enough for new passengers to hurry on board.

By that evening the Nguyens had settled into a refugee hostel operated by the Catholic Church on the fringe of Tokyo's relentless concrete sprawl. They were all put in a single room that was drab but practical. It had a row of thin mattresses rolled out on the floor and a kitchen at one end. The bathrooms were outside along a corridor, near a community television room that Longy quickly discovered. It was here he spent his first few hours, flicking through the boundless channels, sometimes stopping to watch those funny fillers where products were endorsed, usually by rosy-cheeked children or housewives with false smiles.

These commercials weren't the only features of Japanese life Longy found unusual. Eating raw fish was still intolerable, and the practice of bowing the head when meeting someone left Longy swallowing giggles. However, nothing was as hard to adapt to as the weather. It was cold. Shivering was something that Longy had most commonly experienced when he was sick with a fever, but now, whenever he walked outside, his skin prickled with bumps and he had to clench his jaw to stop his teeth from chattering. How strange it was to see steam escaping with every breath. Wrapped in several layers of clothes, he felt cumbersome and heavy. His fingers, those supple tools used for breaking and fixing, were like rods of iron. At times he couldn't even feel them, they were so numb and clumsy.

The discomfort, however, didn't stop him from looking for a place that would enable him to return to familiar ways. Confident enough to wander outside the refugee facility, he was drawn to a group of boys racing remote-controlled cars along a footpath. They cheered wildly, laughing at every crash and bump. Behind them was a building with an empty corridor leading to a room that aroused Longy's curiosity. He knew exactly what it was. He crept in behind the juvenile grand-prix racers, who were too busy yelling at full throttle to notice the stranger in their midst. A few steps later he pushed back a door and entered a space fragmented by darkness and bright squares of sunlight coming from the only window. He was alone. He looked around. He smiled. On the far side of the room, he saw what he was looking for. Within minutes his gloves were off, his layers of clothes shed and the room's stillness was shattered by the sound of hands smacking into a punching bag. For the first time since leaving Saigon, Longy could practise his tae kwon do. Soon he would again have black, callused knuckles. Most of the time thereafter he had the gymnasium to himself, but even when not alone, he wasn't ever troubled or asked questions.

As he regained his fighting strength, his confidence grew. With this, his assuredness within the community developed and he again became a boy of the streets. He began introducing himself to people, waving his hands, pointing, smiling and using the sprinkling of Japanese words he knew, which he linked together in abstruse, comical sentences.

'Hello, my name is Longy. I like coffee.'

Perhaps it was no coincidence that his favourite haunt became a coffee shop, a social hub where he sat sipping on Fanta mixed with a few spoonfuls of condensed milk; the sickly sweet drink reminded him of similar ones concocted by the GIs in Pleiku's cafés.

With no fixed date yet given for the departure to Australia, Longy was eager to enjoy as much of Japanese life as he could. After his preliminary experiences in Fukuoka, he knew that the best way to achieve this was through working. Longy knew exactly the job he wanted. During his wanderings he had passed numerous building sites where fit, strong men in boots, overalls and helmets stood silhouetted against the skyscrapers. To Longy, real men in Japan were construction workers.

He sought the help of the coffee shop owner, a huge man whose chin was cushioned by rolls of fat. Longy indicated his intention by wrapping his hands around an imaginary jackhammer and began bouncing stiffly across the floor in a high-voltage charade. The owner threw back his head and laughed, his numerous chins wobbling. For effort alone, this cheerful Vietnamese boy deserved a chance.

The next morning the owner gave Longy a piece of paper with details of how to reach a work site near Tokyo's harbour. An hour later, after two train trips and a short

TOP The Breaker and The Fixer. Longy as a karate black-belt
INSET A 'fair-dinkum Aussie' in his much-loved green and gold colours

THE WHO'S WHO IN LONGY'S LIFE HAS INCLUDED:
TOP LEFT Olympic gold medal sprinter Linford Christie — 'the most flexible man I've ever treated'
TOP RIGHT Movie star Tom Cruise
BOTTOM LEFT 'The Body', Elle Macpherson
BOTTOM RIGHT Actor Brendan Fraser

TOP Laurence Fishburne before the premiere of *The Matrix* in Tokyo
MIDDLE With singer Deni Hines
BOTTOM Keanu Reeves and Hugo Weaving renew acquaintances with Longy at the launch of *The Matrix Revolutions* in Sydney

TOP Former Australian rugby league captain Laurie Daley
MIDDLE Two-time US Open tennis champion Pat Rafter
BOTTOM Famous boxing figure Don King and Félix Trinidad with Troy Waters and Longy

TOP With 'Uncle Frank' Lowy, one of the most important people in Longy's life
MIDDLE Treating Troy Waters
BOTTOM Between two of the fastest men on earth, Olympic silver medallist Frankie Fredericks and gold medal Olympian Linford Christie

TOP Olympic 100-metre champion Maurice Greene
MIDDLE Rugby legend Terry Hill, Longy's 'favourite walking injury'
BOTTOM Cardinal François-Xavier Nguyen Van Thuan, one of South Vietnam's most respected religious figures

TOP Longy and his lifelong friend, Truong, in the laneway outside their childhood homes where they caused so much mischief in Saigon
MIDDLE In 2003 Longy returned to Pleiku for the first time in nearly 30 years and he visited the nuns of a hostel for Mountain children situated behind his old school, St Paul's (now Le Quy Don) BOTTOM He sat in the same classroom where he spent his first year of learning. Little had changed, with the exception of the picture above the blackboard — in Longy's day it was a portrait of the then South Vietnam President, Nguyen Van Thieu (nowadays Ho Chi Minh stares out over proceedings)

TOP With his daughter Denica on her first day of school
BOTTOM With his two war heroes: his father (right) and former Brigadier General, Le Trung Tuong

walk, Longy entered a marina where a gang was busy knocking down an old house. Most of the men were in their late twenties or early thirties. All were muscular and athletic. Longy approached the supervisor, an older man with serious eyes. They used their hands and a notepad to communicate. Longy, forever the opportunist, was determined to have his way ... somewhere there just had to be a jackhammer. When asked if he'd used one before he shook his head but flexed his muscles, giving every impression he wouldn't have any problems.

The supervisor nodded, perhaps as much from amusement as acceptance. He motioned to a worker to bring over a jackhammer. The other gang members gathered close by, some smirking as they watched this would-be construction worker prepare for his moment of truth. Longy gripped the tool tightly, screwing his heels firmly into the earth. This surely couldn't be too difficult. If he could ride a 90cc scooter there was no reason why he couldn't handle a machine without wheels. His body stiffened. He glanced at the semicircle of faces, then took a deep breath and pressed the switch.

DDDDD-DDDDD-DDDDD!

The workers laughed, the supervisor frowned, and Longy danced a clumsy jig. The jackhammer seemed to have a mind of its own as it slipped across the stone it was meant to crack. Longy wrestled with it vainly. His forearms throbbed and his back and shoulders shuddered and twisted. He had no choice but to turn the powerful tool off. He'd been beaten in mere seconds.

However, he wasn't dispirited. After a few tips from some of the gang, he tried again. And again this cursed machine without wheels took him for a ride. Still, he wouldn't give in. He slowly grew more comfortable and confident. Despite his aching arms, he was soon able to control the jackhammer for long enough to break the stone. To Longy, just one small crack was like a canyon.

Longy's results may not have impressed, but his perseverance had. The supervisor arranged for a whole set of protective equipment to be issued: helmet, gloves, tool belt, kneepads, goggles. For the rest of the day, Longy duelled with the jackhammer while his workmates were given an extended course on the pronunciation of every possible Vietnamese expletive.

Longy arrived home that evening barely able to move, his pain made worse by the absence of hot water in the showers. He had finished the hardest day's work of his life, and it was worth every ache in his body. As he rolled onto his mattress he told his family: 'Being a construction worker is much better than being a soldier or cyclo driver.' A moment later, he was sound asleep.

He lasted just two weeks before he acknowledged that the job was too demanding for him. The communication barrier had added to the stress: although everyone on the site was cheerful and helpful, the lack of clear understanding sometimes led to confusion and disagreements. Try as he might, Longy was always the odd man out. For much of the time he felt lonely. However, there was little doubt he'd made an impression. After he finished his final day, he was taken aside to receive his pay. The supervisor counted out each yen note as he placed it in Longy's hand. When he reached the agreed amount he paused and smiled, then slapped down a few more notes.

Still with an urge to work, Longy tried his charades on the head nun of the hostel. Lost in the hieroglyphics of hand signals, the nun summoned a translator. The message was simple: no more jobs on a construction site; Longy now wanted to test his skills in a factory. Maybe he could help make a tape recorder, a washing machine, a car, or even a colour television. There could surely be few more prestigious positions in Japan.

Only a few days after leaving the jackhammer, Longy was standing in the orange glow of molten metal at a factory that made chains and plates for machinery. He had found his niche. After a brisk twenty-minute walk from home each morning he caught a train, then walked for a further twenty minutes before reaching the factory. He headed straight to the change rooms, where he had his very own locker which contained the signature items for any man of importance — overalls, boots, goggles and helmet.

The first steps onto the work floor were among the most enjoyable of the day, not least because the heat from the ovens thawed out any muscles and joints stiff from the winter's bite. He had a simple but exhausting job: straightening and cutting the rods that came out of the oven. He teamed with a stocky man in his sixties who'd been at the same plant all his working life. While sweating away they tried to communicate in short, animated sentences. They both laughed a lot, but understood little.

Shifts were divided into two four-hour sessions split by a lunch break during which 1000 men filled an enormous canteen area. Longy flitted from table to table, chuckling at the one Vietnamese saying some of his workmates knew from other refugees: 'Viet Cong are very bad!'

Longy loved his job. He never shirked the work, or the chance to do overtime, which sometimes meant he didn't go home between shifts. It was a common sight to see him wrapped in a cocoon-tight blanket, asleep on a girder in a quiet corner. He was never disturbed. Such was the Japanese work ethic that a sleeping man was acknowledged as one who'd earned a rest, not someone stealing time away from his duties. Longy never napped for more than four hours; his life in Vietnam had conditioned him well to short sleeps.

After receiving his fortnightly pay, it was usual for Longy to take the rest of the day off; the lure of buying electronic goods and new clothes was too great to be ignored. Shopping was his favourite hobby, an extravagance that prompted some outrageously immature behaviour. On occasions he threw away shirts after wearing them just once. Such frivolity was a novelty to him; after living in the tight squeeze of communist rule, it was time to loosen the grip. There was no reason behind it, he simply did it because he could.

He treated his first 'boom box' with considerably more respect. It was a silver Sony double cassette recorder with rows of red and green lights rising and falling to the beat — 'Fuckin cool!', he still remembers it. In the Nguyen family's room it became the 'refugee radio station', pumping out a ceaseless selection of Vietnamese songs and Western hits from the likes of Billy Joel and Elton John.

When not tapping to the hostel beat, Longy went in search of bigger, more enticing decibels. On weekends his sense of adventure led him to the discos and bars of downtown Tokyo. At first he was embarrassed about revealing his past, preferring to say in his broken language that he was a visiting Filipino sailor. But as his confidence grew, he told the truth to selected people, none of whom seemed to mind. In the pulsating atmosphere of glitter balls, smoke machines, spinning discs and sake, Longy was just another person out for a good time. He didn't need alcohol to feel he was part of the crowd. With a cigarette in one hand and a Coke in the other, he happily danced and chatted with anyone.

Longy was starting to feel very settled in Tokyo. Every day was a comfortable mix of familiarity and new experiences, none of which was more exhilarating than when he woke one morning to see tiny white feathers falling against the window.

'Snow!'

He sat watching through the glass with a cup of coffee, a cigarette and 'tingles all over'. It was just before Christmas; what a beautiful gift. As he walked to work he watched others in the streets leaning forward, burying their hood-covered heads into their chests. Longy pushed his hood back, walked tall, and let the snow drift onto his face. He rubbed his hands across his thin sideburns. He laughed. His mother would never believe he had hair that crunched! He was as far away from steamy Saigon as he could ever be.

Longy's thoughts barely strayed from his mother over the following days. After returning from work one night, he wrote her a simple letter with a tiding he'd always been able to wrap in a hug.

> *Mung Chua Guong Sinh* [Happy Christmas]. This time I can't say it to you, Mum, but my feelings are still the same. I wish you and Thao were with us now, and that Dad was out of prison, so we could all be here together.

As part of the festivities, the Nguyens were involved in a church pageant organised by the local Vietnamese refugee group. Longy helped James build and paint a set depicting a typical Saigon street scene, which included a small cooker mounted on the back of a pushbike. Unwilling to dance, unable to sing — the days of 'My Mother's Vegetable Garden' had long passed — Longy volunteered to be in charge of visual effects. Sitting on a stool out of sight behind the cooker, he puffed on two cigarettes at once and blew as much smoke into the air as he could. Only *Cam le* leaves could have made it more effective.

As 1981 began there was still no word about exactly when the Nguyens would leave for Australia. All the paperwork had been filled and filed, and the numerous medical examinations had been completed. It was, it seemed, now a matter of biding time. And Longy was happy to wait. Indeed, he was becoming so settled that he questioned whether or not he wanted to move at all.

The latest distraction helped to cement his feelings. Just a short walk from the steel factory he had found a karate centre. One evening when returning home, he went in and introduced himself to the instructors. Again the communication barrier was difficult, so Longy let his hands do the talking by launching into a series of tae kwon do patterns that impressed his audience. After much nodding and pointing of fingers, Longy was given an address on a piece of paper; he interpreted enough to realise he was being sent to a place where he could pick up a uniform. He returned a few days later dressed almost in full kit. Approaching the head instructor, he held out his hands: in one was a white belt, in the other a black. He shrugged his shoulders, indicating that he was unsure which to wear. The instructor smiled. After witnessing the precision of the tae kwon do routine, there was only one choice — this sturdy Vietnamese youth deserved a black belt. Longy then cheerfully went home and cut a small rectangle of yellow and three strips of red from two of his shirts. Maria sewed them onto his uniform over his left chest. The flag of the South Vietnamese was a much more prestigious symbol than any belt would ever be.

The new black belt practised at the centre twice a week. He never sparred, as classes focused only on patterns. There were other youths better than him, but no-one his age was as strong. At the start of each session he powered through 100 push-ups as many of his peers crumpled with exhaustion. He worked hard, raising an appetite that he satisfied on his way home with a plate of sushi and noodles, his acquisition of the Japanese palate a sure sign he was enjoying the Tokyo lifestyle. Yet he still missed Saigon. In a short letter to Uncle Ba he wrote:

> Here I am in Japan, home of the samurai. It is amazing, but sometimes I miss the life of the laneways. And I miss you. I will never forget those times.

The reply humbled Longy. Barely educated enough to write, the barber referred to himself in the third person. In

Vietnam, such a practice indicates only the closest of relationships.

> Dear Longy, Uncle Ba misses you too. He knows you will never forget him. You are always in his thoughts. Uncle Ba is very happy for you.

The letter was instantly one of Longy's most treasured possessions. Keeping it in his work locker, he read it every day; it boosted his spirits whenever he felt homesick or lonely. However, such feelings were becoming increasingly rare. He was comfortable wherever he was, whatever he was doing.

The coffee shop was his favourite place, with its wonderfully familiar environment. There were the sharp, sweet scents of ground beans, and that moment when a fresh brew was poured, sending up a lingering wisp of steam. There were chocolates, soft drinks, booming music, slaps on thighs, whispers in corners and, best of all, much, much laughter. The good old times were new again.

Once Longy felt at home there, he decided it was time others discovered his hands. The owner was the first to benefit. One evening while he was shifting his head from side to side in an effort to ease his aching neck, he was startled by the intrusion of unknown fingers prodding his injury. He turned to see a frowning 'Long-Key' carefully inspecting every vertebra. Bemused, the owner allowed the impromptu session to take its course. By the time it was over, his pain had gone.

A few days later, through hand signals and words, the owner indicated that he wanted to take his magic-fingered companion for a drive. Without questioning where he might be going, Longy readily accepted; perhaps this was the chance to see a side of Tokyo he hadn't yet experienced. Indeed it was. After turning through a maze of streets and alleys, they reached a building covered in brightly coloured writing. Longy presumed it was some type of club, like the discos he'd come to know so well. The similarities ended at the front door. Once inside, they walked along a corridor into a room that was filled with the biggest men Longy had ever seen. Some were blocks of muscle, others were layers of fat. Each man sat on the floor wearing a towel around his waist, so large that it could have been used as a bedspread. No-one said anything at the sight of their bewildered Vietnamese guest. The only sounds came from the slosh of soup and noodles and the grinding of teeth. Longy stood at the door watching for several minutes. No wonder these men were enormous: they were all eating their way through a king's banquet.

Eventually one looked in Longy's direction. He smiled gently, then, without speaking, he lay face down on the floor and pointed at his back. Longy took the hint. He tiptoed across the room, stepping over stacks of empty plates and bowls, until he reached his willing client. He knelt down and cast his eyes over the body next to him. Was this man real? He seemed to be more like a mountain. His back was nearly as wide as Longy's arm span. Surely any masseur's fingers would be worn to the palms by the time a job on such a massive body was finished. Where was the jackhammer now!

If he were to make any impression at all, Longy needed help.

'Hot. Hot,' he said to no-one in particular.

There were puzzled looks across the room. He pressed his hands against the nearest teacup. Nods and smiles followed. He soon received a hot-water bottle that he wrapped his hands around until he felt a familiar suppleness in his fingers. For the next hour he worked deep into the mountain-man's flesh and muscle, along the back, the hips, the hairless legs that were 'the world's biggest drumsticks'. The giant was silent and still throughout.

Longy finished with a smile, then waited for some reaction. The man beneath him smiled back, and bowed his head in polite acknowledgment. It had apparently been a job well done. Longy was chuffed: he had just massaged one of the most respected figures in Japan — a *sumotori* — a sumo wrestler. It wasn't every day he'd have that opportunity. Or so he thought.

The next night, he had just returned home from the factory when he answered a knock on the door to see the coffee shop owner with a refugee who could speak Japanese.

'Longy, this man said the sumo wrestlers want to know when you are coming back.'

'When would they like me to?'

Once told of Longy's answer, the coffee shop owner tapped his watch.

'They want you to come now.'

Longy was still dressed in his factory uniform when he arrived at a club that was even more luxurious than the first. It had spas, a dining floor and a locker room where the wrestler who'd been treated the night before was waiting. Longy went straight to work on him. Afterwards he treated a sumo with a swollen hand. Others waited patiently for their turn to be rubbed by 'Long-Key with the magic fingers'.

At the end of the night they gathered into a group, some pointing curiously at Longy's black knuckles. Without warning he jumped to his feet, and launched into a series of karate and tae kwon do patterns. Each precise movement was greeted with nods and whispered exclamations. When it came time to leave, Longy was inundated with gifts of food, towels, a carton of cigarettes, and an envelope containing a sizable wad of cash.

From that moment on, Long-Key was a regular employee of this sumo stable, returning every fortnight to massage body after body with his fingers, knees, elbows, feet. It was exhausting work, but Longy relished it. This was just another stage in his ongoing education about pressure points and the power of touch.

Inevitably, he was invited to go and watch the sumos in action. Sitting on the floor close to the ring, he saw the first two wrestlers approach, each dressed only in a thick belt and lap. It was difficult to tell them apart. Their hair was slick, tied into buns at the back. They had rolling, cumbersome gaits and held their crooked arms well away from their sides, as though they were carrying hefty tree trunks. Each step was watched quietly by the crowd.

Arriving in the ring, the wrestlers followed a series of religious rituals dating back hundreds of years to when matches were dedicated to the gods to ensure successful harvests. First they stomped their feet, then they accepted a ladle of water, before each threw a handful of salt into the ring to drive away the demons. After this they squatted in their respective corners and summoned the gods by clapping their meaty hands. Longy was mesmerised. He could feel the tension building. No-one in the auditorium moved, except for the two combatants, who turned their palms upwards to reveal they had no weapons. Then they stared at each other, cold intense looks that Longy had seen time and again in Saigon's alleys.

A referee, dressed in a decorative kimono and hat, stood holding a ceremonial paddle. After several minutes he faced the sumos and flipped the paddle in his hands. The contest was under way. A few seconds later it had finished. The loser lay belly-up in the middle of the ring; the winner was back in his corner bowing to the referee. Longy was astounded. All that build-up for so little action! A bit of a grapple, a quick push, and that was that. He had only known two shorter fights: his school encounter with Victory Nguyen, and his one-sided contest in prison.

Disappointed, Longy decided this sport was all about 'two fat men pushing each other around until one fell over'.

Perhaps that wasn't far from the truth: a match was declared over as soon as a wrestler was shunted out of the ring, or any part of his body, other than his feet, touched the floor. But the more Longy watched, the more he was enthralled by the explosive power on display. Initial contact was critical. A poor shove, a weak grip, and a sumo was beaten in a flash. There was no room for mistakes. Most matches lasted only seconds; the more demanding ones stretched to half a minute. Certainly none lasted as long as the pre-bout rituals.

Longy went along on several more occasions. He loved the atmosphere: the hushed voices of the spectators; the aroma of expectation; the traditions; the tension; the blink-and-you'll-miss-it contests. He wished he could explain to the sumos that he'd experienced it all before with feathers and spurs. However, unlike the cock fights, there was no need for lieutenants to be on the lookout, and cash could be bundled in pockets without fear of a nifty hand sliding in for the takings. What a wonderful way to live.

By March, however, it had come to an end. Although he'd been expecting the news for some time, Longy was still surprised when he finally heard it — Australia was calling, and in a few weeks the Nguyens would be starting all over again. They'd been given the choice of going to either Sydney or Perth. What was the difference? One was in the east, the other in the west. Other than that, well, who really knew? Sydney was the bigger city — perhaps there'd be more opportunities there for work and education and, hence, a better life. They'd heard that other refugees had already settled there successfully, so they would surely find some support when they arrived. Sydney it was.

Longy didn't care either way. He didn't want to go. He was tired of being on the move and had finally found stability in Japan. Why start all over again? The answer was, because James wanted him to — and no further discussions would be entered into.

So Longy began his well-rehearsed practice of saying goodbye. At the factory, he found it easier to tell his partner he was going to America, as that was a word the old man understood. They shook hands firmly, then Longy walked away without looking back. At the coffee shop, he tried saying 'Australia'. It was foreign to him, but the owner seemed to understand: he'd always presumed Long-Key was just passing through. There was another handshake, another silent departure. Longy didn't go to the karate centre. It would have been too difficult to explain to everyone. Only actions meant anything there.

After spending the final days packing — ensuring, above all else, that his boom box was securely wrapped — Duy Long Nguyen was ready, but reluctant. Late on 24 March 1981, he and his family boarded a minibus to take them to the airport. This time, however, Longy wasn't excited about boarding a jet.

TWENTY-TWO

Welcome to Australia

*'Sailing on a river should depend on its current;
living in a country, you must follow its customs.'*
VIETNAMESE PROVERB

The earliest record of Vietnamese arriving in Australia by sea dates back to August 1920, when a French ship transporting labourers from Vietnam to New Caledonia was blown off course during a storm. It sought refuge in Townsville in far north Queensland.

In April 1975, twenty-five days before the fall of Saigon, the first planeload of refugees landed, leading to some of the most emotional scenes ever witnessed at Sydney's international airport. All 215 of Australia's newest residents were either orphans or displaced children. Some were carried off the special Qantas flight in cots made from cardboard boxes. A year later, five young men, navigating from a page torn out of an atlas, reached Darwin in a decrepit fishing vessel. They were the first boat people to arrive in Australia.

At the time, the refugee issue was a political minefield. The recently deposed Gough Whitlam Labor government had provoked considerable public outrage with its opposition to substantial resettlement. The subsequent Malcolm Fraser Liberal government was more welcoming, partly because the exodus of Indochinese reached a new crisis point in 1978–79. By the end of the decade, Australia was accepting up to 15 000 Indochinese a year.

High emotions and divided opinions remained across the country. While humanitarians pushed for increased support, at the other end of the seesaw, 'yellow peril' extremists campaigned for the reintroduction of the White Australia Policy, which had been embodied in an outdated Act introduced at the turn of the century to restrict the number of Asian immigrants. One of its features was the 'dictation test', an unfathomable exercise which turned away any person who 'when asked to do so by an officer fails to write out at dictation and sign in the presence of the officer a passage of fifty words in length in a European language directed by the officer'. Incredibly, it remained in statute until 1958, but its talons still reached into the 1970s.

Oblivious to all the political and social rumblings, the Nguyens touched down in Sydney on the beautiful sunny afternoon of 25 March 1981. It took little time for the disgruntled Longy to find another reason why he wanted to be back in Tokyo. After passing through immigration without any trouble, he struck problems in customs when officers discovered a plastic rifle with imitation bullets and a pop-up telescope. James had bought it as a toy for Linh, but since Longy was carrying it, he was the one taken aside. The supervisor asked questions; Longy shrugged his shoulders — 'yes', 'no' and 'hello' were the only English words he knew well enough to use. The toy was confiscated. From his almost nonexistent knowledge of Australia, Longy expected people to be very helpful. After all, this land of 'kangaroos, beaches and beautiful women in swimmers' had supported South Vietnam during the war. The loss of the toy rifle changed his view.

Longy remained in a sour mood on the trip to 'yet another fuckin' hostel'. As the minibus drove through streets lined with warehouses and little apparent life, Longy complained to James.

'It's too slow here. Look — no people. I want to go back to Japan.'

'No, you have a better future in this country. Be patient.'

'But I was going OK in Japan. I had a job. I worked hard. I had friends. Things were really good. Why do I have to come here and do it all over again in a boring place that won't even let you have toys?'

'Longy!'

Longy said nothing more; he just looked out the window at the changing scenes. Beyond the warehouses were neat rows of single-storey dark brick houses with red-tiled roofs. Further out, the dwellings were different. They were made of wood and had tin roofs. Flowers lit up gardens which had squares of mown grass and footpaths leading up steps to front doors. Most homes had wire, wood or brick fences, and some, much to Longy's amazement, had long strips of narrow concrete that led down to huts where cars were parked.

The streets were orderly; the traffic flowed steadily, without the angry honks of horns, squealing brakes or impatient drivers sliding incessantly from one gap to the next. It seemed everyone had time, unlike Tokyo, where the clock was a constant agitator. There were fat men, bellies hanging over their shorts, walking dogs on long leads; and groups of mothers sitting in parks, bouncing babies on their laps, prams at their sides. Life seemed to be relaxed, but Longy still thought it looked boring.

After passing over the Georges River, with its banks of sleepily leaning trees, the bus entered a secluded pocket of suburbia: East Hills, about 30 kilometres southwest of the city centre. It was more blue collar than white, more fibro than double brick; it was a true working class area.

It was also home to a federal government–operated migrant hostel, formerly army barracks that were converted to accommodate immigrants arriving in Australia after World War II. It was one of more than thirty similar facilities across New South Wales; most were situated in or near Sydney. The Nguyens were allocated two small units. Longy was given his own room. Its cleanliness was soon hidden under discarded clothes, tapes and, of course, the boom box that took pride of place on the bedside table.

The hostel was considered a critical stepping stone in the immigration process, as it allowed recent arrivals to receive some resettlement education before they entered into the wider community. They were taught basic English and advised on accepted cultural practices. Indochinese refugees took up the majority of places, but there were also Europeans, mostly Polish. Some had been there for only a few weeks, while others had whittled away several months.

Longy was different from many at the facility. He was well dressed, had some savings, an untidy bedroom full of possessions and, most importantly, he had strong family support. In legal terms he was considered a 'detached minor', someone under eighteen years of age who was in the care of a close relative aged twenty-one or over. James was his guardian and received about $30 a week in a maintenance allowance which he wisely gave to Longy in small amounts.

Sadly, others in the hostel didn't have the same stability. A group of about thirty 'orphan boys' lived near the Nguyen units. They were 'unattached minors' with no parents or mature family support. Most had been in the hostel for several months, waiting to be resettled with sponsor families, or relatives if they existed. With little direction in their lives, they clung to their Vietnamese culture. They were tough, street-educated teenagers who solved disputes with their fists and feet. One youth, Mang, had a stubby finger on his right hand, a permanent reminder of when he'd cut off a joint in Vietnam to try to prove his innocence of a crime. The other dominant member, Phuoc, was short, stocky and strong.

It wasn't surprising that Longy befriended them. In Vietnam, perhaps, he would have been their enemy, but here, drawn together by background and circumstance, he was immediately accepted. With his broad physique, hair touching his shoulders, cigarette in his mouth and a look that could change from a clown's to a killer's at the turn of a head, he was every part the stereotypical Vietnamese youth who would soon enough be portrayed in the media as being the member of a 'dangerous gang element'.

The orphan boys steadfastly adhered to their cultural practice of protecting one another: 'You touch one Vietnamese boy, you touch the lot. You fight one, you fight the lot.' They never went looking for trouble, but were prepared, should it find them. The older boys, Longy included, all carried butterfly knives, which gave them a sense of security. They showed off to one another, flicking the blades out and slicing imaginary flesh. However, during Longy's time with them, they never needed to use the weapons for real.

Nearly every day they caught a train into the city. They hung their heads out the doorways of the tired red rattlers, breathing in the mingled scent of grease and electricity, laughing whenever their faces went frighteningly close to smacking into trackside stanchions.

The seedy inner-city area of Kings Cross was their favourite destination. It was always an irresistible kaleidoscope of colour and people: the bright lights of the strip clubs; the brawny men standing outside in tight T-shirts, their necks and fingers dripping with chunky jewellery and their arms a patchwork of tattoos. There were hookers with high heels, miniskirts, fishnet stockings, glowing red lipstick and billowing hairstyles that defied gravity; the back laneways where drug addicts slumped against walls, either desperate for their next fix or delirious after their last one. Longy loved it. Perhaps Sydney wasn't as boring as he'd thought.

Each trip was an adventure, not least the night Longy and four of his friends missed the last train home, forcing them to sleep at Tempe station. He wasn't at all worried. The prospect of a few hours' rest on a splintering wooden bench was 'like driving a Rolls-Royce after being on the back of a water buffalo' when compared with some of his risky slumbers in Vietnam. No-one was disturbed all night, not even by a passing police patrol. How wonderful darkness could be without curfews and ambushes. Sydney was continuing to improve.

By this stage he was about to begin an English Special Language (ESL) course at Casula High School, half an hour's bus ride from the hostel. The rest of his family was learning from home, but this didn't appeal to Longy, who wanted to be with the orphan boys who were already students. Dressed in jeans and a T-shirt — there was no requirement for a uniform — he departed for his first day of formal resettlement training.

That night, Longy returned from school and announced to his family, in English, 'Hello, my name is Duy Long Nguyen. I am sixteen years old.'

Lessons were intense: morning to afternoon, Monday to Friday. They were occasionally lightened by excursions to notable tourist sites such as the Opera House, or the Blue Mountains, west of Sydney. Most students were Vietnamese and aged between twelve and seventeen. There was only a handful of Europeans.

Once students had been assessed as having an adequate grasp of the language they were allowed to begin normal classes at the school. Longy was keen for this to happen sooner rather than later. Always polite and quiet, he worked hard. Outside classes he listened intently to people talking on television, and during his trips to Kings Cross he eavesdropped on street conversations — although some words he learnt were best left in the gutter. But how was he to know that there was a marked difference between saying 'It is very hot' and, 'It is fuckin' hot'? English was such a complicated language.

During breaks in classes the ESL students kept to themselves, well away from the general school population. They were the targets of jokes, particularly from a bunch of Middle Eastern boys who delighted in yelling out obscenities and making suggestive hand signals. Longy didn't understand what was being said word for word, but he understood the inference; for the first time since his arrival, he was experiencing racism. He watched others in his group being singled out for attention. And he waited, hoping that he would soon be the victim, because he wouldn't be as passive as his peers.

The inevitable moment happened when he was lining up outside his classroom at the start of a new day. One of the Middle Eastern boys walked past. Although still in his mid-teens, he already had a thick beard. He was tall and strong, his upper body a block of muscle. He stopped next to Longy and grinned. Then he put his fingers at the corners of his eyes and stretched the skin apart, making the typical schoolyard Chinaman's face.

'Fuckin' ching-chongs,' the boy sneered. 'Slopeheads!'

Then he ran. And Longy chased. They sprinted down the corridor and swung around a corner up a flight of stairs. The bearded youth quickened; Longy stayed with him. The youth thought he was safe when he neared the doorway to his classroom — just a couple more steps and he'd be out of trouble. But a second later he was writhing on the floor, his head locked between Longy's knees. He'd been felled by an elbow to the skull that he hadn't even seen, let alone had time to react to.

Longy contemplated what to do next. He looked behind him, expecting to see an empty corridor. But he should have known better. The orphan boys were standing there, led by Mang, anger in his eyes and a smashed Coke bottle in his hand. Further back a teacher was running, yelling, 'No! Stop it! Don't do anything. No!'

Longy waited until the teacher arrived, then he released his grip and stood up, dusting himself off. Although he knew little English, he had managed to speak in another way. His mother's voice was in his thoughts: 'It's all about reputation.'

He was led, with an interpreter, to an office where he pleaded his case to the principal, a man he knew only as 'Mr Koala'.

'I have come to a new school. I am in a new country. I am trying to learn and make my way. There is no need to tease me, or my friends. We just want to be left alone.'

'I've only one question,' asked Mr Koala. 'Would you do it again?'

'No, sir.'

'Good. Get back to class.'

There was no more teasing. Longy and the rest of his ESL classmates were even invited to play basketball with the Middle Eastern boys.

Although Longy didn't particularly enjoy his schooling, there was one definite reason to attend — Jolanta, a pretty blonde Polish girl. She was the only Caucasian girl in the ESL class, and each morning she and Longy caught the same bus from the hostel. Fuelled by the desires of a teenage male, Longy was desperately keen to know her better. He began by giving her flowers, and sitting next to her in the classroom, offering beaming smiles that couldn't be lost in translation. Their relationship was soon based on kisses and cuddles, but few words. Longy had his first girlfriend in Australia. Sydney was improving all the time.

The romance was a fleeting one. After Jolanta and her family moved to another hostel near the eastern suburb of Coogee, Longy faced the problem of distance and time-consuming transport. For three consecutive weekends he caught two buses, two trains and finished with half an hour's walk just to reach Jolanta's front door. He didn't try on the fourth weekend.

If only he could use the unregistered yellow Mini Moke that he'd bought for $50 from another hostel resident. Not confident enough to take his rusty machine onto the streets, Longy started, stopped and stuttered his way around the barracks, usually overloaded with orphan boy passengers. With legs and arms pointing in every possible direction, and the laughter of the passengers louder than the car's groaning horsepower, the Moke crawled along. Longy didn't care how slowly he went — it didn't matter. He had a car, and to the Vietnamese that was *Xitin*, or trendy.

However, Longy and his travel companions were eager for more. They wanted to experience life in the laneways outside the hostel. That would be 'very trendy', or 'fuckin' trendy', if using the Kings Cross vernacular. So they pooled their cash. Those who could also borrowed money from friends already established in the community. Eight hundred dollars later they visited some local second-hand car yards and returned with a two door, four gear, red Valiant Charger with mag wheels — 'very, very fuckin' trendy'. The car was unregistered, the drivers unlicensed, and the streets near the hostel were suddenly unsafe. This was the first step that would soon enough lead to Longy's view that 'White men can't jump, black men can't swim, and Asians sure can't drive!' Somehow, they avoided having an accident. When they cruised around, Vietnamese music blaring, engine thumping, they didn't have a care in the world. Life was great, and Sydney was no longer boring at all.

In the three months since his arrival, Longy had adapted well to his new environment. It certainly helped that he was still surrounded by Vietnamese, but he'd experienced enough of Australian culture to feel that his future would be brighter than he'd first imagined. Not even the 'fried chocolate meat', the dreaded lamb kidneys that were served at the hostel dining room, could deter him.

On weekends, he and his family visited white foster parents organised through government agencies or church groups. These kind and compassionate husband-and-wife teams opened their homes to many refugees. They became faces of familiarity, trust and knowledge. Longy discovered that Australians were generally relaxed. They didn't rush as the Japanese did, but they still managed to get their jobs done, mostly with smiles and good nature. They were happy people, which wasn't surprising considering their surroundings. The air was clean, and there was space — lots of space. Space bursting with colourful gardens and trees with silver-green leaves that rustled in the wind. Space with boys hitting balls, dogs running, and men listening to horse races on the radio with pens poised over their newspapers. Space with lovers kissing, parents scolding, and kites dancing across the sky. Above everything, it was space filled with opportunity. In a letter to his mother Longy wrote:

> I like Australia more and more. I will never forget where I came from, but I know this is my new country. If I learn hard, I think I will go to university. I will make you proud of me in my new home.

By the middle of the year that new home was made of fibro and tin and located in the western suburbs. With financial assistance from the federal government, the Nguyens could afford to leave the hostel. Maria, David, Noell, Van and Hong settled in Lakemba. Longy, his three brothers and James's now wife, Thu, rented a three-bedroom house at 32 Marnpar Road, Seven Hills. For the first time since he'd left Saigon, Longy had a roof over his head that he felt he could call his own.

By this stage his vocabulary had reached a level that only occasionally left him searching for words in everyday situations, such as 'Could you tell me when the next train is coming, please?'; 'Excuse me, where is the bus station, please?'; 'What time is it, please?'; 'Could I have three of those drinks, please, and a loaf of bread?'

However, he was still thousands of repeated sentences short of being ready to tackle wider education. He continued his ESL training, relocating to Arthur Phillips High School in Parramatta, which was closer to home. He quickly fitted into a group that, like his previous circle at Casula, was dominated by Vietnamese. Within a few weeks he was the most revered student in the class — but his status had nothing to do with verbs, nouns and adjectives.

One afternoon when walking to a sports session at the local swimming pool, Longy and a small group of his new friends were distracted by some loud bangs and cheers coming from a car park where they saw a youth jumping up and down on the bonnet of a vehicle. He was being urged on by a handful of others, a mix of Caucasians and South Americans. A gang. Without thinking, one of Longy's group chose an inopportune time to show off his English skills.

'Stop that! Don't do that.'

The youth did indeed stop, but only to jump down off the car and walk briskly towards the reluctant vigilantes. The rest of his gang followed. Longy didn't want any trouble, so he led his friends away. They turned a corner near a barbershop; Longy heard footsteps close behind him. He slowed, pushing his friends ahead of him; his Saigon instincts told him an attack was near. He turned. The youth who'd vandalised the car was just a step behind, shaping to throw a punch. But Longy was too quick. His left hand flashed forward. The youth fell to the footpath clutching his jaw, as his supposed mates sprinted away. Longy presumed he had frightened them off, but before he could enjoy his moment of triumph, he noticed a policeman approaching — no wonder the gang had scattered. It was too late for Longy and his friends to do likewise.

'So what's been going on here?' asked the constable.

In a comical combination of broken English and actions, the Vietnamese boys pointed at Longy's shaken victim and started jumping up and down.

'He hurt car! He hurt car!'

All six were taken to the local police station, where there were more excited explanations. After details were taken, all but the alleged offender were driven to the car park in the standard police force vehicle, a Ford F100 ute. Refusing to travel in the cage at the back 'like a criminal', Longy sat wedged between two officers on the bench seat at the front. It seemed more than a lifetime ago that he had travelled in a similar position between his mother and father on the way to family picnics.

An inspection found there were several dents in the car at the centre of the incident. The youth was subsequently charged and Longy and company returned to school as heroes. A few months later Longy received a letter summoning him to appear in court to give evidence; a cheque for $2.50 was included to cover travel costs. He dutifully turned up with one of his friends. They sat at the back of the room, listening intently to proceedings. It was all too confusing, but from what they could gather the youth pleaded guilty, and as a result they were not needed.

As they walked out, they were approached by a policeman sporting a big black moustache.

'I've been waiting for you two. It was my car that was damaged. Thanks for your help.'

They strode away smiling, chests out.

The incident had almost been forgotten about when James answered a knock on the door of the Nguyen home one evening. He was startled to see two police officers standing there.

'Is Duy Long Nguyen here, please?'

James turned, glaring back through the living room at his younger brother sitting on the couch. What had he done?

Longy approached with some trepidation. 'Yes, I'm Duy Long.'

One of the policemen extended his hand.

'This is just a thank you for all the work you have done for us. The police force is very grateful.' He gave Longy an envelope. 'Now don't spend it all at once!'

Longy waited until the unexpected visitors had gone then ripped open his gift to find a cheque for $200 for 'assistance rendered to police'. He laughed. James was stunned: the mischievous brother who'd spent much of his life breaking the law was suddenly its best friend.

Longy used the money to buy a set of weights, and sent the rest back to his mother with a little note: 'You won't believe what happened ...'

Teresa was never surprised by anything Longy did, though. She knew only to expect the unexpected.

TWENTY-THREE

To Educate and to Protect

Education: it was the buzzword in the Nguyen home. While James and Lam spent almost every day with their noses in textbooks, Longy was smart enough to realise he wouldn't advance as far as he'd dreamt unless he followed his older brothers' leads. He undoubtedly had the potential for a promising scholastic career. In his end-of-year report (1981) by the Parramatta school counsellor, he was recognised as 'a capable self-motivated student who has shown that he can certainly manage academic work. His attitude is to be a "self-starter" ... I feel he possesses an above-average IQ'.

Longy should have continued his ESL studies at the beginning of the 1982 school year, but he was impatient to begin mainstream learning. As a result he ignored the counsellor's recommendation that he attend classes at nearby Grantham High. Instead, the next step he took was literally just a series of steps, because the Nguyen home backed onto the playgrounds of Seven Hills High. Longy had only to climb the back fence to enter his new world of learning. In jeans, T-shirt, yellow jacket and sneakers, he walked out his back door and was soon standing unannounced outside the office of Mr Beuman, the school principal. He wasn't concerned that he had no appointment, nor anything other than the counsellor's report to support his case. He was simply doing what he knew best — Longy the 'doorknocker', the opportunist. The strategy worked: Mr Beuman was so impressed by this would-be student's gumption that he arranged immediate enrolment. The following day Longy began Year Ten, the final junior year of secondary education.

At seventeen, he was at least a year older than most of his classmates. Although the school had myriad cultures and races, Vietnamese students were relatively rare. On his very first morning while walking along a hallway, he noticed a youth sitting at a table outside the English teacher's staffroom, doing an exam. He had a mop of curly black hair, broad shoulders, skinny legs, matchstick ankles. He smiled when he saw Longy.

'G'day,' he said. 'You're new, eh?'

'Yes.'

'I'm Craig.'

'My name is Longy.'

After that, Craig Brown understood little of the garble he heard, other than the 'fuckin's' that were liberally sprinkled through every sentence. An Aboriginal, he'd been taught by his family never to judge people by their skin or looks. To him Longy was just another bloke, but perhaps an interesting bloke to get to know. In the space of just a few minutes, Longy and 'Browny' were forming a lasting friendship.

Others at the school also came to accept Longy, especially once it was learnt he was a boat person. 'What size was your boat?' they'd ask. 'How did you escape? Were you scared? Did you think you were going to die?'

Many students were keen to know if Longy could fight. Through movies and the media, they'd formed the clichéd view that all Asians were martial arts experts. Longy didn't disappoint them. An impromptu exhibition in the quadrangle warned all watching that Duy Long Nguyen wasn't one to tangle with.

Surprisingly, his physical prowess didn't extend to the school swimming carnival, which was held only weeks after his arrival. After negotiating the muddy, weed-infested waters of the Saigon River, he thought a chlorinated pool with lanes would be easy. But he didn't expect it to be so cold. It was freezing! He did manage to win his 50-metre breaststroke heat, but it was no use trying to convince him to dip his toe in again. Perhaps it would have been different if smuggled cigarettes were at stake, but the prospect of medals and ribbons didn't interest him at all.

Nevertheless, sport played an influential role in Longy's education. Unwritten schoolyard lore dictated that a boy was more likely to be admired if he was in the top teams, or was graced with the skill to produce a scything cover tackle or hook a bowler for six. Sport was also one of the easiest ways to meet people. Take a wicket, score a goal, serve a winner, share a joke — they were all occasions that invariably made Australians feel good about themselves. But this wasn't always the case for Longy. Some months after his tentative dabble in the water, he stood in jeans, shirt and bare feet at the starting line of a race at the athletics carnival. One hundred metres and nine flattened hurdles later he put his shoes back on, walked to the nearest shade and didn't budge for the rest of the day.

It was difficult for Longy to make an impression through sport because of his lack of exposure to the mainstream Australian games of cricket and rugby league. Instead, he chose table tennis for his Wednesday afternoon elective. Although some of his classmates considered it a 'poofter game' — real blokes only played footy — Longy soon earned respect when word spread that he could beat the supervising teacher. He didn't win all the time, but just once was enough for bragging rights.

However, Longy's true ability shone brightest in martial arts. This was recognised by his English teacher, who practised budokan karate. Invited to attend a few sessions, Longy became a regular, attending classes at a local club nearly every weekend.

Through his family's burgeoning Vietnamese connections, Longy had already begun instructing karate do at the Granville Soccer Club Hall every Wednesday night. His class was a cross-section of races and ages, including Browny and another friend, Brad, a short, stocky part-Aboriginal. They were frequently Longy's chauffeurs, picking him up from home and dropping him back afterwards.

After starting with a dozen students, the class swelled to more than thirty as people heard about the Vietnamese boy who was a 'gun with his hands'. Preferring actions to words, Longy silently led his students through vigorous hour-long sessions. With the sense of showmanship that had been with him throughout his life, he ended some evenings with a display of flying side-kicks and arm deflections that mesmerised his audience.

At first he couldn't have known how important this class would be to his future, but when pupils started asking for private lessons he realised he could make considerable cash-in-hand money. He also came in contact with a wider network of people, significantly, policemen and security officers. He taught them one on one in the playground of Seven Hills High or in the backyard of his home, where he set up a hitting post wrapped in cloth. Law enforcers in the western suburbs needed to be well prepared, because parts of the area were among Sydney's most troublesome crime spots; there were daily reports of robbery, assault, vandalism and motor vehicle theft.

The first sign that Longy was heading in a different direction from that of his studious brothers came when he accepted a security job at a car park near the Blacktown Ten-Pin Bowling Centre. For a dollar a vehicle he kept watch over the area several nights a week. Despite the suburb's rugged reputation, he only once had the need to defend himself, when a man tried to assault him with a screwdriver. In the flash of a hand the attacker was dispossessed of his weapon and wisely chose to leave without causing more trouble.

These extracurricular activities meant Longy could devote little time to his studies. His routine consisted of school, self-defence training, car-park security and sleep. He rarely did his homework, but it was never checked: his teachers understood that exceptions needed to be made.

The weekends were his only chance to relax. When not at budokan classes, he cruised the streets in a collection of *Xitin* cars owned by his Vietnamese friends. Increasingly they spent their time in Fairfield, a municipality moulded by an influx of European immigrants after World War II. Germans, Italians, Greeks, Yugoslavs — all had a strong presence. And they worked hard, many eventually owning their own small businesses.

Longy first visited Fairfield to make new friends at a migrant centre. Sitting on park benches, or in the hostel's dining room, he heard endless stories of heartbreak and tragedy. Two brothers told how they'd been forced to leave their father behind when they fled Saigon; their mother had died during the boat escape. Then there was the man with a miserable grey face and permanently reddened eyes — he'd fled without his wife and daughter and feared he would never see them again.

Despite such tragedies, people were managing to rebuild their lives, leaving the security of the hostels to settle in clusters in surrounding suburbs. Cabramatta was the centre of this new, sudden integration. The Vietnamese were drawn to it by affordable accommodation and the reasonable prospects of work at nearby factories.

On Longy's early visits here there were few signs of the so-called 'Asian invasion'. There was just one Chinese restaurant and a Vietnamese coffee shop in a business area full of fruit stalls, milk bars and fish'n'chip takeaway places. It was an area with little crime when compared with neighbouring suburbs. The police station certainly didn't reflect a trouble spot — it was a simple fibro house.

However, towards the end of 1982 there were signs that Cabramatta was changing. Tucked between the traditional European family businesses was a scattering of vegetable markets, noodle restaurants, fish vendors, jewellers, clothmakers, herbal medicine suppliers, even an acupuncturist. In this little pocket of Sydney, East was overtaking West.

Eighteen-year-old Longy had finished Year Ten. Although his lack of English comprehension prevented him from earning the School Certificate, he was rewarded with an encouraging reference from Principal Beuman, which read, in part: 'Academic progress has been such that Long should be commended for the supreme effort he has made.'

While school had been too demanding at times, Longy breezed through his other major exam of the year: the multiple-choice test for learner drivers. After securing his permit, he was allowed to use public roads when in the company of a fully licensed driver. That rule seemed a minor detail considering his previous stints behind the wheel of the now-defunct Charger. However, he was keen to adhere to the law and sought the help of his friend Lap, a former ARVN lieutenant who ran a snooker hall in Yagoona. Until then Longy knew little more about driving than pointing the car in a straight line and turning the wheel when necessary. With Lap at his side in a Toyota Corolla — a much too conservative car for Longy's liking — he was taught the finer skills: parallel parking; using the blinkers correctly; changing lanes; and making three-point turns.

After three months of practice Longy was confident he would pass the practical for his provisional licence. Driving the Corolla, he carefully negotiated every challenge the examiner demanded. When they returned to the motor registry Longy looked over at his marker, expecting to hear cheerful news.

'Unfortunately, Mr Nguyen, you have failed on three counts. Worst of all, you approached an intersection too quickly.'

Back in the car the cursing Longy was assured by Lap that he would succeed next time.

'A lot of people don't pass first go. It's just the way it is. You know you can drive — all you have to do now is learn to drive safely.'

Longy was still without his licence when school resumed. Under a special program for immigrants he was invited to start Year Eleven, the first of two senior years which culminated in the Higher School Certificate exams that opened the door to tertiary studies.

Longy still had hopes of going to university, but as he continued his hectic out-of-school schedule, it became increasingly obvious that it was going to be difficult. And this didn't take into account his social distractions which, when not involving cruising in cars, were invariably focused on going to parties with Browny and other mates.

Longy was astounded by how much alcohol was consumed at these get togethers. He'd seen the GIs in all sorts of conditions back in Vietnam, although they were older. But these kids in Australia? They were all so young, drinking themselves into oblivion, or at least until they threw up everywhere, which was considered a weakness when assessed in schoolyard postmortems. It was repulsive to see a teenager sprawled senseless in a corner, vomit drying on his chin and shirt. Longy was grateful he was never under pressure to conform. There were times when he did teeter towards light-headedness, but most of the time he held the same beer can all night and only pretended to be drunk. No-one knew the difference.

It wasn't the same with drugs. Longy shared the occasional joint, which was every bit as much a part of growing up as sculling a Tooheys or splashing some Coke on a Bundy. However, he didn't realise how much trouble marijuana could cause — but not necessarily from smoking it. When asked by Brad to look after a plant, Longy saw no harm in it and promptly put it in the garden at home next to Thu's immaculately tended herbs. He would have refused if it had been a poppy — he'd seen the damage opium could do — but marijuana ... Well, it surely couldn't hurt. Plus, he was simply helping out a friend.

A week later the Nguyens hosted a Sunday afternoon barbecue and invited their foster parents, Mr and Mrs John Smiley, a gentle, peaceful couple. As soon as John noticed the strange plant towering above the basil and rosemary, he calmly suggested, 'Longy, I think you should get rid of that.'

'Why? It's very healthy. I think its flower will be out soon. It looks very good.'

'No, Longy, I really think you should get rid of it. It's no good for you. It's illegal.'

Confused, but deciding not to protest any further, Longy ran to Brad's house a few blocks away. Brad returned and did as he was asked, ripping the plant out and hurling it across the back fence. Afterwards Longy went into his bedroom and flicked through the pages of his translation dictionary until he came across the unfamiliar word he'd heard: *Illegal: Unlawful, unofficial, illegitimate, criminal...* He laughed — this was probably the first time in his life he'd done something illegal without knowing.

Longy certainly adhered to the letter of the law when he next went for his provisional driver's test. This time he passed, walking away with a licence that he folded into his wallet. It was just a simple piece of paper with red print and a few typed words — it would have been easy to forge in another time and place.

He had now been in Australia for two years. The days were scurrying by, with little time for him to sit back and contemplate his past. He was too busy living minute to minute to wander for too long into his memory, other than to think about the loved ones he'd left behind. That changed when Browny took him on a two-week trip to the Aboriginal missions near Urunga and Coffs Harbour on the New South Wales north coast. This was Browny's home, a place he visited to be with his culture and his people, the Gumbainggir. The trip also gave Longy the chance to reflect. Under the patchy canopy of gum leaves and with the fine dust beneath his feet, he drifted back to the jungles near Pleiku and the indigenous people he once knew. Around fires at night he swapped stories with Browny's uncles and brothers, each acknowledging the other's heritage. They spoke about traditional foods and medicines, and of the Dreamtime. Longy talked of healing and martial arts; one evening he put on a display, astonishing the ring of watchers when he knocked a toolbox from the hands of a man standing on a milk crate. A spin, a kick, a spin, and he was back in the same position he started from without touching the ground.

Throughout his life he had collided with different cultures, but for those two weeks in the bush he was at one with the Aboriginal people there. It was a sense of belonging he already felt with Browny, although he could only acknowledge it by joking, 'You know, I reckon we're brothers.'

'Yeah, why's that?'

''Cos we got the same flat noses!'

Despite his efforts, Longy just didn't have an affinity for education. As the year progressed he fell further behind with his studies. By September he knew he couldn't go any further.

As opposed to his last day of school in Saigon, he left Seven Hills High of his own accord and with a flowing mane of hair. It hadn't been a tough decision. Although he wouldn't discount tertiary studies at a later point, for the time being he had decided on attending the 'university of life'.

This style of learning was destined to lead him into treacherous territory. It began when word-of-mouth provided him with a job teaching self-defence to the employees of a security firm in the Fairfield area. It was here that he established a number of contacts who offered him work as a 'protector' on a job-by-job basis. The work was varied: one day he'd be looking after a woman involved in a simmering domestic dispute, the next he'd be the right-hand man to bouncers at a nightclub. Violence was unavoidable and, as a result, more than a few drunken troublemakers had jaws and teeth rattled from being on the wrong end of a black-belt flourish. Longy was soon known by his colleagues as a 'dark horse', a valuable all-rounder who could handle any situation. In simple street talk, he was someone 'not to be fucked with'.

His transition from student to protector happened as quickly as Cabramatta shifted from West to East. In the shopping centre, the once familiar smell of salamis and cheeses was surrendering to spices. As traditional European-style businesses closed, Asian ones opened. Out with spanakopita and spaghetti, in with *pho* and catfish soup.

The footpaths burst into life. Once they were dawdling thoroughfares; now they were lounge rooms where old women squatted, chatted and cackled, and old men silently played chequers, their eyes rarely shifting from the board at their feet. Others found a space to sell the herbs and vegetables that they'd grown in their backyards or the planter boxes in their ugly red brick flats.

There was a new vibrancy, an atmosphere crowded with energy. Sandals slapped along concrete; music screamed from passing cars; laughter rang from coffee shops.

In this new mirror of Asian life, it was inevitable that gangs would develop. They were primarily made up of youths and men in their early twenties. Some grew out of boredom and frustration at a time when the unemployment rate among the Indochinese was about 25 per cent. After leaving the hostels they rarely received enough official support, both financially and socially, to raise them to a level where they could be justifiably confident about their new lives. So they found comfort in retaining their old ways, learnt on the streets of Vietnam. Other gangs were formed in the dingy back rooms of snooker parlours, where gambling was taking hold. Traditional Chinese games such as *pai kau* and *fan tan* (pea under the shell) were among the most popular. As the stakes rose, so did the debts. Gang members turned into debt collectors, knocking on doors and threatening the odd person to ensure that those in the black remained that way.

As Cabramatta changed, Longy's presence in the area became more prominent. Such was his martial arts reputation (he was now a black belt in budokan karate) that he performed a demonstration during a festival commemorating 'National Sad Day' on April 30th. He was also invited to teach a tae kwon do class at the local Catholic Church hall. His students were nearly all Vietnamese, including a quiet, well-mannered eight-year-old boy, Tri Minh Tran. No-one could have predicted what lay ahead over the next decade for this willing student.

All the teaching and protector commitments meant Longy was in perpetual motion from the earliest hours until late every night. But he wasn't satisfied. Typically, he went looking for more opportunities, and found them without having to leave his classes. When a pupil first complained of a backache, Longy knew it was time for the breaker to become the fixer. His business started with the treatment of a man on the floor of the Cabramatta Catholic Church hall, and soon spread into the living rooms of his clients. He charged $30 a session.

Without a car, he initially relied on his mates for transport, but with his flourishing income it was only a matter of time before he had enough money to buy his own vehicle, a second-hand Datsun 240Z. In the short space of a few months he climbed up the scale, buying and selling a 260Z, a 280Z and a Nissan 300ZX. In between these he briefly shifted allegiances to a blue Mazda RX7. He chopped and changed because of the sheer novelty of being able to do so. This was a symbolic time in his life. To some of his Vietnamese friends, the ownership of a vehicle was the indisputable sign of success. At nineteen Longy had apparently succeeded, but the wheels were only just beginning to turn.

Having a car gave Longy new freedom. He and his Vietnamese friends thought nothing of going anywhere for a party or a good meal. Even to Melbourne, some 900 kilometres away. They made the trip down the Hume Highway about once a month, with the music from their graphic-equaliser-enhanced stereos throbbing as loudly as the souped-up engines under letter-box bonnets.

By 1984 Longy had a white V8 Holden with a dual exhaust and modified carburettor. Of course, there was no question it had mag wheels, and the latest *Xitin* accessories, electric tinted windows — it was 'fuckin' hot, brother!' To have such a vehicle may have seemed ostentatious to some in the community, but to Longy the reason for his extravagance was simple: 'I deserved it.'

A flash car, a flashy personality. This blooming confidence and ostentation again highlighted the differences that had been evident among the Nguyens from the earliest days. As Longy's brothers continued their studies (Lam did his study in the garage for the sake of peace and quiet) they reflected the unobtrusive nature of most Vietnamese immigrants. Longy was altogether the exception. He needed the attention: acknowledgment was his fuel.

Longy had become so well known in Cabramatta that he was readily recognised by people who hadn't even met him.

His popularity and reputation meant he was never short of work, and even if he had been, he still had a lofty level of self-belief that allowed him to create his own opportunities. This was reflected one afternoon when he drove past the Woodland Road Primary School in Campbelltown, on Sydney's southwestern outskirts. In a rush of spontaneity he turned into the driveway, went to the administration office and asked to see the person in charge. After a brief discussion with the deputy principal, he was allowed use of the school hall to conduct tae kwon do classes two evenings a week. In return he did security work at the school when needed.

The sight of Longy instructing children was almost incomprehensible when compared with what was beginning to happen at the other end of the breaker's scale. In addition to his protector work, he had taken on debt collecting, primarily for businessmen. Some jobs were easy: knock on the door, demand the money, take it, then leave. Some turned into operations needing teamwork. One of Longy's favourite and most successful ploys was a matter of well-timed distraction. While some of his colleagues struck up a conversation with the inevitable protectors at the front of a bad debtor's house, Longy would approach from the rear, running and climbing through a number of neighbouring backyards until he reached the required back door. If there was no-one on watch, he'd boldly walk into the house in search of his man. The surprise element alone was normally enough for payments to be handed over. Of course, there were occasions when intimidation was needed — Longy's reputation was such that he rarely left without the cash.

After a brief stint in 1985 as a construction worker with the NSW Water Board, he took another step into the fringe of the underworld when he was offered protector jobs in Chinatown, a place where cash spoke loudest, yet its origins were frequently mentioned in hushed tones. Hidden among the many legitimate operations, chiefly restaurants, there were illegal gambling houses and drug suppliers. These were parts of intricate crime networks, including the K14 gang, a Hong Kong–based ring that smuggled in millions of dollars worth of heroin. In this environment, corruption and extortion were bedfellows and murders were common. The police were in an almost impossible position.

Longy sought security from the past, buying a Beretta that he tucked into an ankle holster underneath his jeans. Weapons were prerequisites for anyone involved at the street level; guns, knives, nunchukkas were all carried discreetly. With these came sadistic trademarks. Longy was soon told how to 'kneecap' a person: it was best to shoot down at the knee, rather than from the front. As a result, it was a known tactic for victims to be shot while squatting to inspect a deflated car tyre.

Longy wasn't deterred by the prospects of any such work-related injury. Not even when he once saw a man lying dead in the street — he'd heard gunfire and turned a corner to see a victim face down in a pool of blood. Sydney, it seemed, did have some similarities with Saigon.

But unlike Saigon, Longy adopted the attitude of 'what I don't know won't hurt me'. He would do the jobs without asking questions. Get in, get out, take the cash, move on. It was dangerous, but highly profitable — as a protector overseeing operations at a gambling house he could earn as much as 10 per cent of the night's total takings. Nearly all his jobs were in the evening. Most involved escorting various 'bosses' to gambling sessions, general functions, dinners and meetings.

When he needed help he teamed up with Jimmy, a strapping blond teenager raised in Belmore, the heartland of thuggery in the inner west. Jimmy had no fear, no inhibitions; he was the toughest of street kids. Longy enjoyed his company and, crucially in Chinatown where the golden rule was to 'always expect something to happen', he could trust his partner.

This trust was tested the night they were asked to protect a smartly dressed client for whom Longy hadn't previously worked. The fact that four protectors were being used was an indication this man was no ordinary player. He was driven from a pick-up spot in George Street to a restaurant known to be a front for illegal gambling. It was 11.30 p.m. in the middle of the week. The numbers of diners and passers-by were dwindling, shop owners had rolled down their shutters, neon lights were no longer blinking.

Longy, Jimmy and their associates waited in the restaurant foyer while their boss went upstairs. He returned minutes later, carrying a bag of cash. He waited for his protectors to gather around him. They stepped through the door.

Bang! Bang!

Longy ducked. The bullets had come from a Suzuki car parked just 50 metres away.

Bang! Bang! Bang!

Longy fell backwards, knocked by a bullet to his chest. He tried to reach for his Beretta. Now his leg hurt. And his hand.

Adrenaline charged through him. He sprang to his feet and covered his boss. The Suzuki sped away, tyres screeching.

'Longy!' came a cry.

'Get him out of here.'

The boss was hurried away through the shadows. Only Jimmy remained.

'Are you OK, brother?'

'I don't know.'

'Oh shit — look at you.'

Blood was seeping through Longy's shirt onto his leather jacket. He could hardly breathe.

'Fuck it!'

He stood up, hands pressing lightly against his chest. His car was only 100 metres away — just a short walk at any other time, but not tonight. He limped towards it, refusing to stop until he collapsed against the bonnet.

'Get in, Longy,' said Jimmy. 'Lie down.'

'Fuck that, I'm driving.'

Longy eased in behind the wheel, trying to calm himself before inspecting the wound. His right hand throbbed: a bullet had gone straight through the fleshy web between his thumb and forefinger. The top of his right thigh had also been hit close to the hip; a blob of crimson spread across his jeans. Both wounds ached, but he only had thoughts for the pain near his heart.

'Shit!'

'What?'

'I can see the fuckin' bullet!'

It was pressing against his chest, lodged in the zipper of his jacket. Longy cautiously peeled back each zipper tooth until the bullet dropped to the floor. He stared at the damage it had caused. The skin had been broken, but that was all.

Still in shock, he sped away, his right foot barely leaving the accelerator as he screamed through intersections, ignoring the traffic lights. He used his left foot to brake, his left hand to drive. Fifteen minutes later he was sitting in the family room of a close friend, a doctor in the inner west. Each wound needed only a few stitches.

'How fuckin' lucky am I? Saved by a fuckin' zipper!'

The incident made Longy consider changing his ways. He didn't want to end up rotting away tied to a slab of concrete at the bottom of Sydney Harbour or the Georges River. But, then again, this was the life he knew so well. It wasn't as though he'd only begun experiencing it since he moved to Australia. The art of survival had been a lifelong pursuit. It had made him who he was. Why change now after just one scare?

He was twenty-one years old. In addition to his growing massage clientele, he had good mates, fun girlfriends, a healthy supply of cash, and a succession of *Xitin* cars. Above all else he had a wonderful, loving family. By now he was living in Campbelltown with Maria and David and their children, Noell, Sally and John. Life was great.

And it became better still on a warm November afternoon when Longy visited James at home in Seven Hills. He found James in the kitchen, smiling and holding a telegram.

'What are you so happy about?' Longy asked his eldest brother.

'It's finally happened.'

'What?'

'Dad is free.'

Longy didn't know what to say. A sense of relief swept over him, mixed with some anger. One month it was meant to be! One fuckin' month! He tried to imagine what his parents were doing at that very moment. After ten and a half dreadful years apart, they had a lot of lost time to make up. Time that no-one knew was fast running out.

TWENTY-FOUR

Mum

Teresa had endured many hardships in her life, but right at this moment she felt she had nothing to complain about when compared with all the wretched people around her. In the five months since her husband had come back, she'd seen a sick man regain his health. Then she had her children. There was Thao, who had been so resilient and defiant. And the others who, although far away, were making a success of their lives: Maria with children; James and Lam both doing well at university; Van happily married; Linh top of his class at school ... and Longy? Well, Longy was Longy — he was busy breaking and fixing, as he always had been.

What more could a wife and mother want than the good health and happiness of her husband and children? Teresa was indeed grateful for what she had. She said her customary prayers then went to bed, and was soon asleep next to her husband. Thao, too, had turned in for the night. None of them heard the footsteps on the roof.

The next morning, the 18th of April, Hien woke early to go to church. Teresa was slower to stir: her arthritis never agreed with the morning. After dressing, she made her first painful movements across the bedroom into the living room.

Two storeys below, Thao heard the heavy thump of a body hitting the floor. She raced upstairs, colliding with two young men hurtling down in sheer panic. One raised a knife. Thao lifted her arm in protection, knocking the attacker off balance. He tumbled over. By the time he regained his feet, his partner had disappeared. Thao shrieked. Hearing the commotion, some men on the street tackled one of the assailants as he dashed outside.

Teresa was gasping for air when Thao arrived — she'd been stabbed in the chest. People rushed into the house. Some helped Thao carry her mother down the stairs. Someone else had called a cyclo-rider. Petrol was in short supply, so there was no chance of arranging an ambulance or any type of vehicle that would hasten the trip to hospital. The street was awash with curiosity and shock. An unseen bystander said, 'It wouldn't have happened if Longy were still here.'

Longy was playing with Maria's children Sally and John when the phone rang. It was 10 a.m; the caller was Lam.

'Longy, you'd better prepare yourself.'

'For what?'

'Mum has passed away.' Lam began crying.

'How?'

'I don't know. We've just received a telegram from Thao.'

Longy didn't know what else to say. He hung up; he stood still. He yelled, and slammed his fists into a wall. Then he fell quiet. He walked to his room and lay on the bed, staring at the ceiling as memories of his mother flashed through his mind: the coffee shop; the picture theatre; the pig farm; the *Cam le* leaves. He knew she'd been suffering from high blood pressure for some time. And the arthritis couldn't have helped. Perhaps the *Cam le* had killed her.

More fragments of Teresa's life floated through his memory: the fearful nuns at St Paul's; the picnic trips to the lake; the nights listening to the BBC World Service; the prayers to the Virgin Mary.

Lam rang again. The whole family had now been told; they were all to meet at James's home in Seven Hills. Longy was to drive his nephew and niece there immediately. When they arrived they were greeted by tears, hugs and a few gentle words.

Longy moved from person to person. He wanted so desperately to be strong. But he just couldn't be. This tough man of the streets was reduced to tears. He asked to see all the letters his mother had sent, all her photos.

The family was still grieving together late in the evening when they received a phone call from a relative in Melbourne.

'I am so sorry to hear the news. My thoughts are with you.'

'Thank you,' replied James.

'I can't believe she was killed.'

'Killed?'

In Saigon the street in front of the Nguyen home was crowded with curious onlookers pointing and staring, recounting and imagining. News had spread that the second offender, the one who'd successfully fled, had turned himself in to police. Piece by piece, the true story was coming out. The two men had climbed up a pole onto the Nguyen roof during the night. They stayed, waiting for the right moment to sneak downstairs and steal whatever money, gold and jewellery they could find. It should have been easy. Most robberies were. But this had all gone horribly wrong.

* * *

Longy slammed his foot on the accelerator, red-lining his Nissan in every gear. He needed time to himself. As he scorched through the streets heading to Cabramatta, he had only one thought in his mind: who murdered his mother?

For the next few hours he was a reckless mess. He fishtailed around corners, ran red lights, burned rubber. He knocked on doors, waking mates up. Their neighbours too. He didn't care. Fuck the world. Fuck everything.

His feelings turned to hatred. God was first to be singled out when Longy refused to go to the memorial service in Campbelltown on the same day the funeral was held in Saigon. How could he go to church, an alleged house of peace and security whose Father couldn't protect one of his most loving and devoted servants? God was a myth. Forget him. Religion was bullshit.

In the following weeks, Longy lost total motivation. He took his phone off the hook and ignored the mates who came to visit. He found most companionship in a boxer dog he bought the day after the funeral. He named him Nau, Vietnamese for brown, the dog's colour. Nau and his boss spent long hours wandering in bushland at the back of Maria and David's home.

Longy also tried to find comfort in martial arts. But he was confused. One day he wanted to become the best black belt he could, the next he thought of going back to school, or starting university. He forced himself to go to Cabramatta, searching for relief from his 'unfixable anger', but he was only tormented more. He detested people saying how sorry they were. They approached him at corners, in front of shops, in arcades, when he was in his car. They were trying to be kind, but he hated every one of them. After all, he and his siblings were so lucky because they'd gained freedom. But his mother? In truth, she'd sacrificed her life as soon as she chose to stay behind and wait for Hien's release. She could have been in Australia right now. Then nothing untoward would have happened to her —

Longy would have seen to that. But now it was too late. He had lost the most important and influential person he would ever have in his life.

Thao sat waiting in the courtroom for the judge to announce the sentence. Murderers were generally executed. The handcuffed men sitting across the other side of the room, heads bowed, deserved no less. Stand them in front of a firing squad; if given the chance, Thao would happily pull the trigger. Again and again and again. She wept. It had been harrowing to recall every detail. But it would be worth it. It would be satisfying to see the look on these men's faces when they were told they were going to die.

The judge waited for silence. Thao stared at the accused, then suddenly her eyes shot back to the judge.

Five years in a labour camp. What sort of justice was that?

Longy wandered aimlessly through the next few months. He stayed at Maria's, sometimes slept in his car, or camped in the bush with Nau. He didn't work. When he needed money, he asked his friends. He doubted his life would ever change.

Slowly, though, it did. There wasn't a defining moment when he realised he needed to snap out of his misery. It just came with the gradual passing of time, and the growing feeling that he wasn't alone. He'd always believed in spirits; now he knew for certain they existed. Wherever he went, whatever he did, he felt Teresa was with him. It was a powerful force, an inexplicable presence that inspired Longy to change his ways. He couldn't turn his life around immediately — maybe it would take some years — but at least he wanted to begin. He became an Australian citizen. He gave up working in Chinatown and Blacktown, and although he was still a protector in the western suburbs, he was more selective about the jobs he took.

He continued teaching self-defence, both to classes and individuals, but it was most rewarding when he worked on himself. It was therapeutic. He strived to become the fittest and strongest he'd ever been. He performed one-armed push-ups, chin-ups, and crunches that gave him that burning, satisfying pain felt only by those who have stretched themselves beyond their limits. He also had two crazy practices that were surely more frightening and damaging than beneficial. In one he smashed pieces of bamboo against his head; in the other he convinced a training partner to wrap a hand tightly over his mouth until he was on the edge of blacking out. Then he'd try to break free and overpower his partner with the little strength he had left. All this extreme training lifted his self-worth and belief which, until the last few months, had never been in short supply.

In the yin and yang of his life, Longy sought to balance his breaking with his fixing. He was hungry for knowledge about healing, massage, meditation, acupressure, acupuncture — all the techniques associated with the so-called mystical East. He read books, practising what he learnt on his household clients, and towards the end of 1986 his quest for learning took him to Thailand.

It was his first trip outside Australia since he'd arrived five and a half years earlier. As he flew over the South China Sea, he strained his eyes looking for a curled finger of land. Vietnam seemed so close. He wondered what every other passenger saw 30 000 feet below — probably just blue nothingness. To Longy, the water was a quilt stitching desperation, death, brutality, kindness and freedom all together. He wished his mother could have seen it. But instead Longy could only imagine her saying, 'Make the most of your every opportunity. And never forget I love you.'

TWENTY-FIVE

Healing Travels

The law of the gymnasium was written in every punch and kick that thudded into bags shining from overuse: work hard and maybe you will earn enough money to keep you going until your next fight. Kick boxing was not so much a sport as a vehicle of hope. Young men with hard shins and heads looked to the ring to provide for them. They came from the smallest villages and the cluttered streets and waterways of Bangkok to ride their luck on the canvas. Most departed with fat cheeks and thin pockets. In this environment, it didn't pay to pick and choose. A fighter always had to be ready, which meant he had little time to recover from injuries. As a result, a pair of healing hands was as powerful as any right hook.

Longy had arrived in Bangkok with a simple plan: if he asked enough people, he would surely find his way to a gym sooner rather than later. It took only one conversation at his hotel to be pointed in the right direction. The concierge introduced him to Johnny, a taxi driver who had a number of contacts in the kick-boxing industry. A small fare and big tip later, Longy was standing in a rotting brick building where tens of fighters were sweating through their routines. These men were tough; they had to be just to endure the techniques used to condition them. They showed no pain when they pressed their weight down forcefully on bamboo canes or bottles that they rolled back and forth across their shins. Longy — no stranger to pain himself — winced just watching.

It was, though, the subtler ways the fighters hardened their bodies that were of most interest to him. For this the kick boxers relied on a quiet fat man who sat at the back of the gym, a handful of bottles with tattered labels at his bare feet. These bottles hid secrets. They were full of oils and creams that he rubbed into muscles and joints to give them an added layer of protection, or to hasten their recovery from injury. His chubby hands reeked of his work. A sensitive nose could perhaps detect some of the ingredients, but beyond this they were a mystery.

Johnny introduced Longy to the master masseur. They swapped smiles, but little more — the language barrier made it too difficult. Each time the conditioner, as he was known, worked on a boxer, Longy learnt by watching and smelling. He came back every day for the next month, not so much to gain knowledge, but trust. While doing this he trained with the fighters, learning the ways of their sport, appreciating how fit and mentally strong they needed to be.

Longy's martial arts background fast-tracked him to the stage that he was able to compete in a low standard middleweight bout. He won, and claimed two more victories over the following days. But he rejected the invitation to fight in a more prestigious competition — he'd surely used up his share of luck already.

Despite this, it seemed that Longy still had some in reserve when the conditioner approached him just a few days before he was to fly back to Australia. After all the fighters had gone home, Longy was quietly shown how to concoct some of the oils that gave the fighters their bodies of steel. He still keeps these secrets today. All he'll reveal of that clandestine evening is that the herb ingredients were broken down by hand or rock, but never wood.

Longy arrived home to the news that one of the orphan boys had been stabbed to death in Cabramatta, which had grown into a dangerous suburb where gangs were trying to establish their reputations and extend their territory. Violence was the accepted means both to promote and protect their cause. To those involved, being without a weapon was akin to a carpenter having no hammer. A Beretta or blade were tools of the trade. So too chains, broken bottles ... even a fifty-cent piece could be lethal in the wrong hands.

The rise of the gangs from their relatively passive beginnings of the early 1980s coincided with a dramatic increase in gambling. The hundreds of thousands of dollars clinking into poker machines and spent at TAB agencies were matched by illegal betting in back-room casinos and card parlours. This activity attracted the loan sharks who circled, ready to capitalise on the desperate in debt with promises such as, 'I can give you ten thousand in cash today if you return fifteen to me by the end of the week.'

Extortions were rife, bashings prevalent and killings an inescapable product of the addiction to money that was destroying a suburb's once peaceful reputation. In surrounding areas and beyond, Cabramatta had been labelled 'Vietnamatta' — it was becoming an Asian slum that displayed the worst symptoms of resettlement. Sadly, this view tarnished those law-abiding, hard-working immigrants who opened their arms to opportunity and turned their backs on crime.

The respect he'd earned throughout the community enabled Longy to walk the streets untouched, and gave him the confidence to talk with anyone about what was happening on both sides of the law. He was in a rare and powerful position: people wanted to know him. This made him a potentially valuable resource for the police, who were struggling to manage the mounting problems in the community. Unless they could develop an understanding of the Vietnamese gang and crime culture, they would have little hope of breaking operations that were concealed by collective silence.

Longy first met with police in nearby Bankstown when he was invited to be part of a community representation to discuss street violence between Vietnamese and Lebanese gangs. He wouldn't comment on the structure of gangs — that was for the police to work out for themselves — but saw no harm in discussing the strength of the bond between members that was based on 'protect one, protect all'. He left the meeting knowing that little had been achieved. No amount of questions and answers around a table would solve the problem.

For Longy, there was a more troublesome issue — the increasingly fragile relationship between the community and the police. There was growing concern in Cabramatta that some officers were showing little courtesy and respect to residents, nor any willingness to develop a friendly rapport with them. People had complained they'd been pulled over for no apparent reason while driving; although they hadn't broken any road rules, they were subjected to blunt questioning which invariably led to implications that their vehicles were stolen. Rightly or wrongly, there was a perception that some members of the community were the subjects of undue police attention; committing as minor an offence as double parking was cause for concern that the offender would be continually hounded. Whether or not some stories were embellished didn't matter to people who had justifiable reasons to be suspicious of law enforcers — life under the communists had instilled that in them.

There were many good officers, but just as the 'Vietnamatta' label affected blameless residents, the bad police made the reputation on which everyone was judged. As a result, an 'us versus them' mentality developed. The majority of people, whether prepared to help police or otherwise, adopted the approach 'Say nothing of value to an outsider'.

Personally, Longy retained a comfortable relationship with the police. He didn't necessarily respect them, but he had no need to detest them. More often than not he laughed at their helplessness — how could they ever expect to control the criminals when they couldn't even find them? And even if they did, how would they ever get witnesses? Longy thought that was perhaps the reason why the police were so savage on parking offenders and other petty criminals — their behaviour was born of their frustrating inability to act when they really needed to.

In contrast to the state of Cabramatta, Longy had entered one of the most stable periods of his life. Driven by the 'duty and honour' to make his mother proud of him, he divided much of his time between martial arts and massage. Among the many people he met during this time was Wadie Haddad, a Campbelltown doctor. Recognising that Longy was eager to pursue a career in healing, Dr Haddad invited him to an international symposium on Eastern medicine in Sydney. The contacts Longy made encouraged him to make further travels to broaden his knowledge.

Consequently Longy revisited Thailand to learn about hot and cold treatments, different finger massage techniques and acupressure. He also spent time at kick-boxing gymnasiums but never fought again.

Longy was a keen student, captivated by the theories behind age-old healing practices. He learnt that the body consisted of a series of energy grids, or meridians. When blocked by scar tissue, calcification or excess lactic acid, these meridians failed to emit the power the body needed. It was the role of the acupressure specialist to break down the blockages and restore the flow. This not only required practice, practice, practice, but the best exponents had an extra sense, an inexplicable ability to understand each individual body. Longy had this skill. Within minutes of first touching a client, he knew what to do. Sometimes his actions were vigorous; on other occasions a firm palm was all that was needed.

Longy believed he possessed a unique gift that began where the theories and textbooks ended. He felt he had a special link with everyone he worked on. He was drawn to them, almost magnetically. He needed to touch, needed to make people better. He couldn't explain why, but he was certain he had found his calling.

This vocation took him to Hong Kong, where one of the symposium specialists had arranged for him to spend a week with a renowned master of reflexology (the practice of massaging points on the hands, feet and head). Cam Sieu was a small bow-legged man in his late sixties. He had recently retired after spending nearly fifty years working at a bathhouse. He had received no formal training; the skills he knew had been passed down through his family over generations. A man of few words, he communicated with Longy in short grunts. As payment for board and the knowledge he gained, Longy treated the master's neck, which had become worn by the years of caring for others.

Longy returned to Sydney knowing he was still a novice of his craft. It had already taken twenty-three years to reach this point, and there was still so much to learn. But as Cam Sieu had taught him, healing was best practised across a lifetime.

In comparison to his tumultuous past, nothing extraordinary happened to Longy between 1987 and late 1989. This was a time of almost methodical development in his life. He moved from Maria's house to nearby St Helen's Park, where he lived in a two-bedroom townhouse, with a backyard for Nau. The first items he bought were two enormous glass tanks that stretched along an entire wall. These were his 'aquatic televisions', filled with fish that he could sit and watch for hours on end, relaxing. Alternatively, he could exhaust himself in the garage, where he set up a gymnasium that included three punching bags of different weights. He kept one distinct link with his Chinatown past, inviting Jimmy to move in with him. Their upbringing on the streets was a bond between them — Longy recognised in his blond mate what he'd seen in himself in Saigon.

The two occasionally worked together in the western suburbs when Longy chose to venture outside his daily devotion to martial arts and healing. Considering the aggressive streak in his nature, it was impossible to leave his life as a protector behind entirely. He needed the balance between the two sides of his personality.

While Longy was content, Cabramatta was contentious. If the early 1980s had laid the foundations for change in this suburb, the late 1980s were building the empire — one which would be distinguished by bricks of heroin. Drug smuggling and distribution in Australia had primarily been the domain of the Chinese, but this was changing under the growing influence of organised crime and gang activity among the Vietnamese. It was inevitable that the white-powder trade would be too lucrative to be ignored. At first Longy heard little about the establishment of syndicates, but soon enough there were subtle street-corner conversations about the people involved and their plans to take their share of operations.

Some of the loudest whispers concerned rumours that a new gang of fearless and highly violent teenagers was being formed. No-one seemed to know much about it. Slowly, the answers became known amid rising levels of home invasions, vandalism and extortion. The gang was indeed young, its leader only in his early teens. Longy vaguely recognised his name when he was told it. Tri Minh Tran, the once quiet and polite eight-year-old boy in the Catholic Church hall tae kwon do classes. Tri had grown into a slender, long-haired youth of few words, yet with a charismatic presence that commanded respect among those his own age and older. He'd already been on the path of lawlessness for some years — he was just eleven when arrested by police for possessing a sawn-off shotgun. When thirteen years old, he threatened his teachers with a machete, and in late 1988 he was one of five people charged with the murder of a rival gang member (he was found not guilty three years later).

Tri had assembled a group of thirty or so core gang members, but there was speculation that as many as 200 were involved in various capacities. Longy considered the members he knew to be 'good, healthy kids who were torn between cultures'. None of them would have known that collectively they would be part of one of the most influential players in Cabramatta's immediate future: the 5T gang. The Vietnamese words for love, money, prison, crime and death that had been grouped together in the cells of Saigon's Chi Hoa prison were now rising as one frightening force on the streets of western Sydney.

The state member for Cabramatta, John Newman, was another local player with a leading role. The son of European parents, he had lived all but the first few years of his life in the area. He was an outspoken campaigner against gangs and drugs, his highly public stance attracting some support and creating many enemies. Certainly he couldn't expect to endear himself to the obvious elements when he made such provocative media comments as, 'The Asian gangs don't fear our laws. But there's one thing they do fear, and that's possible deportation back to the jungles of Vietnam, because that's where, frankly, they belong.'

Longy was first introduced to Newman when the politician attended a tae kwon do tournament. His greeting was short, but telling: 'So you're Longy. I've known about you for some time.' The two shared a common interest as Newman, an extremely fit man in his early forties, was a competent practitioner of karate. Longy was impressed by his stature and presence, saying now that Newman was 'the best-looking male politician in Australia. He put everyone else to shame.' Newman occasionally saw Longy at martial arts functions or on the streets, where he was always keen to ask questions about the community's mood and concerns. Longy replied with simple answers, never revealing anything the Member of the Legislative Assembly wasn't already likely to know. Crimes, criminals, names and places were never discussed.

After having breakfast one morning, Longy walked out of a noodle shop to see Newman hobbling towards him.

'What's up?' he asked the politician.

'I hurt my toe training. I don't know what I've done to it.'

Fortuitously they were near an Eastern medicine store. On Longy's advice, Newman went in and bought a certain herbal cream. Moments later he was sitting outside, shoe and sock off, grimacing as Longy applied a firm touch to the injury. When they parted company Longy walked away satisfied with his job, but annoyed his hand would stink of the herbs for the rest of the day. He knew there was no harm in helping the MP, but he was wary of being seen to be too friendly. He respected Newman for his determination, but also considered him 'ignorant, and either really brave or really stupid'. If the Honourable Member for Cabramatta wasn't careful, he would suffer much greater injuries than a swollen big toe.

The encounter was nothing unusual for Longy. He was proud he could mix easily with so many different types of people: politicians, businessmen, street kids ... Those who were closest to him would always remain so, even when thousands of kilometres away. Longy continued to send clothes and money to Truong. And then there was Uncle Ba, who had recently moved to the United States with his adopted Eurasian daughter, a product of the war, whom he'd cared for since she was just three years old. Sadly, the barber also took with him his ailing liver. He died with his daughter at his side. When Longy read the news in a letter, he spent the rest of the day by himself in quiet reflection. He thought he would never meet a kinder, wiser man.

By now Vietnam was slowly changing, pushing open a rusty door to worldwide exposure and recognition. In 1988 it had begun joint investigations with the United States into the thousand or more soldiers still listed as missing in action. In September 1989 it withdrew the majority of its troops from Cambodia, eleven years after first invading. International trade deals were increasing and travel restrictions were being relaxed.

On 27 October 1989, two events took place that held no political significance at all, yet they joined together people on both sides of the equator. In Sydney, Lam Nguyen celebrated his twenty-seventh birthday, and in Saigon, Thao and Hien Duy Nguyen stood waiting at the airport for the plane to land. Nine years after leaving, Longy was going home to see his little sister get married.

TWENTY-SIX

Coming Home

'Look at you — you're no longer a little girl!'
'And look at you — you're a man!'

Thao hugged her brother. She kissed him, squeezed him, pinched him, punched him, slapped him. Then she buried her head into his chest, and cried. Longy held her tightly, feeling the pain that had been inside his little sister for nine years. Hien stood next to them, tears blurring his glasses and rolling down his cheeks. A step or two away, Jimmy, luggage at his feet, cried too. He'd come to Saigon both for a holiday and as reassuring protection for Longy in the unlikely event that the local officials arrested him for returning to Vietnam.

Longy turned to his father. 'It's good to be home.'

As they embraced, Longy could feel every bone in his father's back and shoulders. Hien wasn't frail, but nor was he a strong man. His best years had passed, some of them left in the jungles of so-called re-education.

'So are you now a communist?'
'What do you think?'

Father and son laughed.

On the trip home Longy stared out the taxi's window at the streets that had been his playground and classroom. Apart from a few more scooters spitting out oil and smoke, it seemed as though little had changed.

It was early evening when they arrived home. Longy raced upstairs to his bedroom and pushed back the door, pausing in this opening to his past. He couldn't believe it — it was as though he was trapped in time. His goldfish bowl was still there, although now obviously empty; there was a stack of yellowing comics in a corner; his cupboard drawers were littered with torn and faded clothes; and in a jar next to the bed he'd outgrown was a handful of bicycle ball bearings. He grinned, spinning around to look at the back of the door. Was it possible ...? Yes! The slingshot was hanging from a hook, unmoved and unused since Longy had left.

Jimmy entered the room to find his mate blowing dust off a ball bearing.

'Look at this, Jimmy. I'll show you something.'

He loaded his weapon, opened the window, took aim and fired at a familiar gate.

Bang!

Moments later Truong stood in the laneway, squinting up at the window. The lowering sun masked his view of whoever had fired the shot. But he knew it could only be one person. He started to run, then sprinted as though he was back in his adolescence.

Longy ran down the stairs and darted outside. He turned the corner into the laneway just as Truong was swinging into the street. They started to laugh, hugging and hitting each other playfully in the arms.

'I can't believe it, Longy, I thought I'd never see you again,' said his old friend.

Truong — in trousers, shirt and tie — had become a schoolteacher, a position of considerable prestige in the communist structure. For the rest of the evening, he and Longy returned to old ways, whizzing through the streets in tandem on a scooter; Jimmy was forced to trail them on a pushbike. The sight of a muscular, blond white man in shorts and a singlet ensured the locals had an intriguing topic to discuss over their steaming noodles.

When he finally fell into his old bed, Longy couldn't sleep. Why waste time doing that when there were so many people to see, places to go, footsteps to be retraced? And amongst all the faces that came into his thoughts, one never left. When Longy first arrived home he'd expected to see his mother appearing from around a corner, or waiting in bed for a massage, or making a *café da*, or kneeling in front of the Virgin Mary. It was a strange feeling — Teresa seemed to have as strong a presence in the house now as when she was alive.

The next morning Longy was up early. Soon after breakfast he was on his way with Hien, Thao and Jimmy to fulfil the most important duty of his trip. They travelled for an hour before reaching a cemetery on Saigon's outskirts. Many of the headstones were overrun with weeds and blankets of rubbish. But towards the back, frangipani trees sheltered an immaculately kept grave protected by a waist-high green metal fence. Its concrete corner posts were topped with porcelain unicorn dogs that kept watch over the spirits. A cross rose above a headstone on which there was a small photo of a smiling woman — in stark contrast to the brutal end Teresa had met.

Longy walked to the grave by himself. He stood staring at the photo, remembering the last time he'd seen his mother alive, just before he left for the successful escape attempt. It had been so matter of fact. A hug, a few words, then he was gone. He had said goodbye to her countless times in his life, but only now it seemed real. He bowed his head. The smoke from the incense sticks in his hands drifted away as though respecting his need to be alone. He began to cry, softly at first, then harder, consumed by regrets that he hadn't been there to save her.

After three and a half years, the closure had finally come: Longy needed to tell his mother face to face that he blamed himself for her death. He had promised he'd always be there for her, but when she really needed him, where was he? In Australia, lapping up a rich free-and-easy life. He had been so selfish. Now, standing in front of her, he was asking for something he'd never wanted before: forgiveness.

Longy walked away with a weight lifted from his thoughts. Not only had he apologised, but he now knew where his mother was buried. In the future, whenever he needed to talk to her, he would picture her grave. It gave him comfort to know what it looked like.

He returned home to find Truong waiting for him: 'What are we going to do today? Where to?'

'The river.'

'What?'

'I want to swim it again.'

'Longy!'

'I need to.'

The Saigon River was as muddy and scattered with weeds as Longy had remembered it. He smiled when he thought how much his mother had hated him coming here. Now, for the first time, she could watch him. He hurried down the bank and surveyed the stretch in front of him. He was strong, fit, and aided by something he hadn't had when he'd negotiated this water as a boy. Back then he swam in shorts or jeans, but now he stood resplendent in a pair of bright yellow Speedos — Bondi Beach had come to Saigon.

By the time Longy was turning back after reaching the other side, a small crowd had gathered with Truong and Jimmy. They leant against their bikes, sat on the bank, squatted on rocks, drinking cups of coffee. Stroke by stroke, Longy loomed closer to the finish. He eventually arrived to the cheers, claps and laughter of the onlookers.

'Long *Ca Kinh*!' they declared — Longy the fish, the river king.

Afterwards the champion swimmer visited Uncle Ba's son, who was carrying on the family tradition in the same shop where, as in Longy's bedroom, time had stood still. As Longy sat in a chair, listening to the scissors snip and snap behind his ears, he noticed a group of youths outside, peering through the window. One of them looked at Longy as closely as he could before announcing excitedly to the others, 'Long *Thien Ly*! Long *Thien Ly*!' — it's Longy from the coffee shop.

The youths would have only been small boys when Longy had been at his prime on Saigon's streets. His reputation had indeed been powerful.

Throughout his stay, Longy was stopped wherever he went by people happy to see him. 'Welcome back,' they would say. 'Where did you go? I am so sorry about your mother ... Are you here to stay? ... I remember when ...'

A bicycle repairman, a noodle shop owner, a school girl, a street kid — they all remembered. As each one recognised him, Longy felt his stride lengthen, his chest fill. It was as though he'd never left.

However, there were some differences, both tragic and heartening. When he visited a familiar hut in Cholon, he was told by the residents that the previous owner had gone '*Mot Nam Mo Xanh*' (where the grass is green) four months earlier. There were rumours he had taken a liking to heroin, apparently shooting up nearly every day for years. His death surprised no-one. Except Longy, who thought Uncle Nam, his master of massage, would somehow live forever.

In the shadows of his sadness, he stood outside a home closer to his neighbourhood. He looked through the gate at the window that had once framed the most beautiful picture in his life. He waited for several minutes, hoping that Lan would glide into sight, smiling and waving as she once had. But she and her mother had left years before.

'Some say they made it to America,' said Truong.

'I hope so. I really hope so.'

The next month hurried by as Longy reunited with old friends, including his first tae kwon do instructor and some of his lieutenants. Others hadn't survived, killed as gang members in the laneways or as soldiers on the Cambodian border.

Thao's wedding ensured that Longy didn't reach only into the past during his stay. When he looked at his beaming sister in her bridal gown, he saw a little girl who was forced to grow up too quickly. Now she was a woman facing an exciting future, hopefully filled with happiness. Perhaps within a year or two she'd be cradling a baby. The only tragedy would be that the child would never know its grandmother.

Longy flew back to Australia with new enthusiasm. He remembered a lesson he'd been taught by Browny's relations on the Aboriginal missions: 'To know where you are going, you must first know where you've been.' It now made sense. His trip to Saigon had reinforced how grateful he was to be in Sydney. He left behind people who were silently rebelling against a system they would never agree with. True freedom and choice was only ever found in their dreams. But Australia was different. Longy had heard it described as 'the lucky country'. Better still, it was 'the lucky country with lucky people'.

TWENTY-SEVEN

Agent Longy

Longy ambled along John Street after having dinner with a friend. As he walked by the shops an ambulance screamed past. It stopped a block further up, beside a teenage boy lying unconscious on the footpath. It was 1990; drug use in public wasn't yet common, but there were too many signs suggesting that it was only a matter of time before it would be. Like a junkie after a fix, Cabramatta was spinning into the unknown and uncontrollable.

The 5T gang had established a stronghold, yet its operations remained mostly secret. There were rumours that it was smuggling in tiny amounts of heroin from Vietnam. The trafficking was still in its infancy, but no-one doubted it would grow.

Although Longy heard many whispers, he was too interested in his own activities to stop and contemplate Cabramatta's future. His massage business was taking him and his ageing table to countless households across the western suburbs. He'd also been offered security work in

Campbelltown, protecting Dr Haddad's surgery and a nearby pharmacy after hours. Occasionally he escorted the doctor on house calls.

In addition he conducted private self-defence classes in his garage gym, and trusted some of his clients, including police officers, to come and go as they liked. He'd often hear the roller door open late at night, followed by the repetitive thwacks of skin on leather.

Little else was new in his day-to-day existence. He kept in regular contact with his brothers and sisters over the phone, but visits were becoming increasingly random. They all had their own lives to lead, each a wonderful example of successful immigration. After completing his Bachelor of Business, James was studying for his MBA; Lam was working in the IT industry with a degree in computer science; and Linh was a medical student at the University of NSW. Maria and Van both stayed home to care for their children.

Single, and with comparatively little education, Longy remained the family's odd man out. Although he'd decided tertiary education was now a low priority, the same couldn't be said for his dalliances with the opposite sex. No-one stayed on the scene for more than a few weeks, until an unexpected meeting on the footpath outside Longy's townhouse dramatically halted the flow.

Ann lived next door. A petite blonde in her mid-twenties with shoulder-length hair and glasses, she was, in his opinion, 'a real good sort with a nice fit body', acquired partly from her days as a state ballroom-dancing champion. Raised in Sydney's northwestern fringe near Hornsby, she'd held a number of jobs after leaving school, her latest as the manager of a clothing store in Campbelltown.

She was quiet, yet assertive; Longy was impressed. The feelings were obviously mutual, because Ann eventually moved in with her new boyfriend. In the first few weeks her most tiresome duty was answering the door and phone to her partner's long line of female companions.

'I'm sorry,' she'd tell them. 'That's all over now. I'm his girlfriend.'

Longy kept his private life very private. Even some of his closest mates didn't know for several months that he'd entered a de facto relationship. It was the way he liked it: 'My business is no-one else's business.' With a girlfriend, a house, a dog and steady jobs, Longy had become a regular Sydney suburbanite. And this was the way it stayed during the early 1990s. Life was simple and smooth.

The same could not be said for Cabramatta. By 1992, users and dealers were travelling from all over Sydney and beyond to visit what had become the home of Sydney's drug trade. Glazed eyes and swaying bodies weren't restricted to the back streets, but were in full view of the main business community.

The 5T gang had cornered the market with high-grade heroin that it sold at the same price as a lower-quality product being offered elsewhere. Costs were reduced because the 5T sold directly to the street, cutting out middleman dealers. Longy knew boys as young as twelve who were involved. The gang members lived together in small flats where they rotated their working hours. While some slept, others roamed the streets looking for customers.

Longy tried to keep his distance from the problems, but his respected position in the community made this impossible. Despairing businessmen sought his advice over 5T members who stole whatever they liked, threatening violence or vandalism if there were any protests. Others wanted to know how they could stop junkies from shooting up in the doorways of their shops, and even in front of their houses. The saddest stories were of parents seeking children who'd run away. Unable to ignore their requests for help, Longy began walking the streets quietly asking questions, looking for any possible leads. The ad hoc work was at first voluntary, but it soon developed into a consuming pastime after more parents sought help: some were looking for runaways, others were concerned their sons and daughters were falling into the wrong company. Without intending it, Longy had become a private investigator. Complete with cups of coffee and hamburgers, 'just like you see in the movies', he staked out houses and flats and secretly followed teenagers through the streets. He became a family informant, perhaps the closest he would ever be to a hunting dog.

In order to legitimise his operation, Longy enrolled in a private investigator's correspondence course based in Brisbane. In the meantime he continued basic surveillance operations, but refused to accept any adultery cases; teenage runaways made up the bulk of his work.

He had mixed success. When he found runaways, most had no intention of going home. They were too heavily involved in the drug and gang culture to return to the staid and structured ways of adults whom they believed didn't understand them. In one sad case Longy tracked down the son of a highly respected businessman. He was shooting up in a hotel renowned for bathroom junkies. The revelation prompted the distraught and desperate father to send his boy back to Vietnam, hoping this would change his habits. It only hastened the slide: the access to heroin was easier, and the cost was less.

In the space of little more than a decade, Longy had seen Cabramatta become as much Saigon as Sydney. When sitting in a car one evening eating a pork roll, he and a friend heard a gunshot near the Mekong Club, a popular gathering place. They watched a group of security guards rush around a corner out of sight. Then came the screams and yells. Sneaking out to have a look, Longy saw a teenage boy dead on the street. As a crowd gathered, a girl pushed through the scrum and knelt down next to the body. She cradled the boy, rocking him in her arms, crying. Longy had seen enough. He turned away, thinking, 'Why do I have to go through this again? This is too much.'

It saddened him to see Cabramatta become headline fodder for the media. The suburb was demonised as the centre of lawlessness, reported as drug infested, violent, corrupt and, most distressingly, full of Vietnamese who were unable or unwilling to adapt to Australian culture. Unfortunately, decent, honest, working people also gained an undeserved reputation. Thus they too were among the victims.

The 5T gang caused much of the negative publicity. Members were described as incorrigible murderers, scourges of society. Yet Longy saw a different side. He was always treated with respect and courtesy by anyone in the gang. Perhaps this was partly due to Jimmy, who had 5T friends. However, it was probably more to do with the reputation Longy had built up over his thirteen years in Australia. His status was never more evident than when he was at an Asian social night in early 1994 at the University of NSW. After talking with a group of Vietnamese students, he was approached by a sharply dressed, long-haired teenager with the 5T insignia tattooed on his left forearm. There was respect in the youth's very first sentence when he addressed Longy as 'Uncle'. It was Tri Minh Tran.

They spoke for several minutes, just small talk about the night, the people and the university. After agreeing they'd keep in touch, Longy departed with the impression that the 5T leader was a 'cool, smart, good-looking guy, but too young to organise business'.

The 5T continued to prosper, the drug problem also flourished, police numbers increased — they had risen from thirty-two officers to ninety in six years — and John Newman continued to seek solutions, both quietly and in public. The opposition to his stance was as obvious as it was foreseeable: windows in his electorate office were smashed and his car was paint bombed.

On Monday 5 September 1994, the honourable member for Cabramatta left an ALP branch meeting at the Cabra-

Vale Ex Services Club. Twenty minutes later he entered the driveway of his home. Hearing her fiancé arrive, Lucy Wang went outside and stood waiting to help with the tarpaulin that Newman threw over his Ford sedan each night. There was a sudden loud crack. Lucy looked up to see a man in a hooded jacket standing at the gate only metres away. There were more cracks. The car's back window shattered. Then the man was gone, speeding away in a vehicle that had its headlights off. Newman staggered towards his partner.

Longy was sitting at home watching television when he saw the words stretch across the bottom of the screen: John Newman was dead.

He hurried to the phone and began ringing his friends. Theories leapt across living rooms all over Cabramatta and beyond: Chinese immigration protection; corrupt politics; political enemies; drugs; the 5T gang. Longy was stunned, yet at the same time he wasn't surprised.

The next afternoon he was visited by a friend, a police detective he'd been training in self-defence.

'So what do you know, Longy?'

'Only rumours. Could have been a lot of people. I don't know.'

'Really?'

'I don't know.'

They drove past the crime scene and surrounding streets to 'feel the tension'. There were few locals about. Longy felt angry when he saw all the media crews, wishing they would sometimes come out to his suburb to do a good story. Cabramatta was going to cop yet another public battering.

As police, journalists and the community tried to piece events together, Longy reflected on the death of the fifth dan karate practitioner cum-parliamentarian. He didn't feel upset. Newman knew the risks he was taking — although extreme, murder was an occupational hazard for a politician treading such dangerous territory. It would take seven years before local businessman and Newman's renowned council enemy Phuong Ngo would be sentenced to life for masterminding Australia's first political assassination. He still claims he's innocent. David Dinh, the accused shooter, and Quang Dao, the accused driver, were acquitted. At the time of writing, no-one has been gaoled for pulling the trigger.

While Cabramatta faced a new struggle for credibility, Longy returned to his regular routine. He finished the year on a rewarding note when he acquired a Diploma of Massage Therapy. He may have considered it 'just a piece of paper', but it was another step in the right direction.

However, the path to his calling continued to have distractions and detours that increasingly frustrated him. As 1995 began, Longy was tiring of the runaround nature of his work. At 7 a.m. he was at home for a private self-defence class; 8.30 a.m. — Seven Hills for a massage session; at 10 a.m. he was in Blacktown for more healing; 11–2 p.m. saw him in Cabramatta again to search for, say, the missing son of a prominent textile businessman; from 3–5 p.m. he was at home for own training; 6 p.m. — Ryde for a massage session; 8 p.m. till midnight was Campbelltown for security work. At 1 a.m. he went home to sleep. It was so monotonous, day in, day out. The venues and jobs changed, but the hours stayed the same. They were exhaustingly long.

Longy contemplated taking a holiday by himself to Queensland's Gold Coast. He needed a break, or at least a change of routine. It came most unexpectedly with no beach in sight and with familiar elements that he thought he no longer wanted to be part of — crime and cops. It began when he was approached in Cabramatta by a hysterical man about to appear in court.

'The police say I stole a car,' he told Longy, 'but that is bullshit. They bashed me.'

In the same week one of Longy's friends was charged with indecent assault, an offence he vehemently denied committing. Longy didn't know who or what to believe. However, he'd heard more than enough stories over the years to know that in amongst the good officers were some 'bad attitude cops' who could twist the truth to suit their purposes. Without any proof to counter the charge, he went to Campbelltown police station and boldly complained, showing little fear for his own position.

'I'm fed up with corrupt cops. It's your word against ours. It's not fair.'

He received a sympathetic hearing from a duty officer who acknowledged the complaints in writing. The next day Longy was surprised to receive a phone call from Ian (not his real name), an Internal Affairs agent.

'I would like to come and talk to you.'

In his living room that afternoon Longy spoke candidly to Ian; he considered he had nothing to lose. His knowledge of his friend's case was limited, and adorned by some emotional embellishment, but as the discussion spread into wider issues, Ian was interested in what he heard and recognised the considerable value of developing some sort of working relationship with Longy. They spoke on several more occasions over the next month. At the start of one meeting, Longy astounded Ian when he produced a sharpened fifty-cent piece from his pocket.

'I could kill a man with this,' he told the agent.

'How?'

With the mere snap of a wrist he sent the coin hurtling through the air until it speared into a tree trunk 5 metres away. It had lodged 2 centimetres into the wood.

'See, very easy. In the wrong hands, very dangerous.'

Lethal weapons aside, Ian was most impressed and intrigued by Longy's perception and understanding of a wide variety of issues concerning police work in the area. When coupled with his knowledge of the Vietnamese community, he was indeed a valuable resource, or, as technically termed, a 'community source'. When asked if he would like to become more involved with Internal Affairs, Longy immediately responded, 'I am not an informer.'

However, Longy was assured he would never be asked to turn against his own community. He was solely to be used for providing information about police corruption and misbehaviour, whether it was rumour or fact. Longy obliged. Because of secrecy provisions, not much can be written about his participation, which continued intermittently over some years. He was involved in cases at many levels. On a relatively minor scale, these were incidents such as drunken officers refusing to pay bills at local restaurants, and others pulling over and harassing drivers without due reason. On a higher level, he contributed to investigations involving brutality and corruption. He participated in stakeouts, and was even a bagman in a sting. On one operation he commented on how easily police could have been overcome because of their apparent poor handling of their weapons. He also suggested things such as integrity tests long before they were officially introduced. Ian acknowledges that Longy was 'ahead of his time'.

Because of his contribution and knowledge, he wasn't valuable only to Internal Affairs, but also to the New South Wales Independent Commission Against Corruption. In 1994 Justice James Wood was empowered to investigate 'the existence and extent of corruption in the NSW Police Service, and other related matters'. For the next two and a half years, the Wood Royal Commission was never far from the headlines as it uncovered 'endemic and systematic corruption'.

Longy was wary when first told by Ian that the Wood Royal Commission wished to interview him. Despite his friendly relationship with Internal Affairs, he'd retained a general mistrust of the police and had no desire to reveal what he knew to a room of strangers. However, Ian gently persuaded him that he didn't have to say anything he wasn't comfortable with. Eventually he agreed.

The first meeting took place in a secret location: a motel room in the western Sydney suburb of Bass Hill. It didn't begin well. Longy refused to answer questions from the two male interviewers unless Ian was present. The IA agent had been forced to wait outside, but after a few hasty phone calls he was allowed in to listen, provided he didn't speak.

For the next hour Longy was quizzed about police behaviour in the south-western area, particularly in Cabramatta. He gave little away, toying with his interviewers by pretending he didn't understand English well. He spoke slowly in confused sentences as though he was searching for words. His fear of being 'burnt' had overridden any willingness to provide information.

Longy left satisfied that his lack of help would ensure he wouldn't have to go through the rigmarole again, but a week later Ian told him, 'They want to see you again. This time I can't go with you. It's bigger. It's with Virginia Bell.'

Virginia Bell, one of five counsel assisting Justice Wood, was renowned for her thoroughness and forthright questions. She would later become a judge of the NSW Supreme Court.

On the morning of the interview Longy had yum cha with Browny and another friend in Chinatown. He was then dropped a block away from the meeting place, the Hilton Hotel in George Street, and he told Browny, 'Make sure you ring me every ten minutes to see how I'm going.'

After walking into the foyer he was ushered into a lift by a man in smart civilian clothes with a backpack over a shoulder. Longy said little until he entered a room where Bell was waiting, sitting behind a table. Longy thought of his time in prison. Was it possible he was about to suffer *café da* at the hands of this seemingly polite woman? It was a bizarre thought, but nevertheless it crossed his mind.

Soon after the questions started, Longy's phone rang.

'Sorry, excuse me.'

'G'day, brother, it's Browny. How you goin', mate? Everything all right?'

'Yes, yes, fine.'
'Good. I'll ring you soon.'
'No worries, brother.'

The phone call set the pattern for the interview. Bell asked questions, Longy answered them blankly. *Ring! Ring!* Browny asked questions, Longy answered them cheekily. It seemed a pointless exercise. After half an hour Bell thanked Longy for his time and offered him use of the room because it had been booked for the day.

'Does a woman come with it?' It was the most enthusiastic response he'd given. This time he departed knowing he wouldn't be called back again.

Longy was undoubtedly his own man, living and behaving the way he chose to. Although he gave nothing to the Wood Royal Commission, he remained a willing contributor to Internal Affairs, occasionally causing concerns with his gung-ho attitude to danger. These worries were heightened when he contacted Ian one evening to say he'd been shot at. He was on a regular security beat in Campbelltown when a car turned a corner towards him. Moments later he was hiding behind his four-wheel drive after hearing the dull thudding sound of a silencer. The bullets hit the road and the car sped off. After making some subtle and fruitless enquiries in the area, he convinced himself he was simply in the wrong place at the wrong time. However, it's probable he was the intended target. Because of his work as a private investigator? His security work? Debt collecting? Internal Affairs? It could be one or all of them.

If those behind the shooting intended to make Longy change his habits, it was an utter failure. He maintained his regular routine. His involvement with IA had further cluttered his hours, yet provided the relief from monotony he'd needed.

However, the attempted shooting wasn't to be the only unexpected twist to his life at the time. In early August

1995, Longy was doing some private investigator work at a hotel renowned for junkies and gangs when he saw Tri Minh Tran. The 5T leader was keen to talk. Longy detected that 'something wasn't right' when Tri told him about a growing restlessness in his gang. He said there were fights between members, and he wasn't talking as much any more to his right-hand man, Madonna. Longy was surprised, because in his occasional meetings with Tri since the Asian night at the University of NSW, Tri had never spoken about the 5T to him at all. Longy had actually felt sorry for him, thinking him 'a good kid trapped in a bad life'.

A few days later, in the early hours of Monday, 7 August, twenty-year-old Tri was murdered, shot twice in the head after opening the door of his Cabramatta flat. In the hail of bullets one of his lieutenants also died and another was injured. As police began investigations, Longy launched his own, returning to the hotel where he'd last spoken to the 5T leader. He met a teenage girl who had a connection to the gang. She was limping with a swollen ankle. In return for treatment, Longy sought information. He was told little other than it was rumoured that Tri knew his killer well — why else would he have opened the door? It was said he was also shot in the hands as he tried to protect his face.

Gossip spread that Tri had been killed because he was about to turn police informer over the Newman murder. Longy didn't believe it — if the 5T leader was going to do that, he may as well have turned the gun on himself. Reflecting on his last conversation with Tri, he presumed a jealous or power-hungry 5T member had pulled the trigger. This was one of the main theories pursued by the police, but no-one was arrested. Cabramatta's wall of silence was impenetrable.

Together with John Newman, Tri Minh Tran was the highest-profile victim of a suburb that had lost its way; the politician and the gang leader had finally discovered some common ground. Longy was unsettled enough by the Tri shooting to periodically search for answers, but he found out nothing. Even to someone on the outer fringe of Cabramatta's gang culture, there was no way into the middle. It was easier to move in police circles, which by now had offered another unpredictable turn that would change Longy's life dramatically.

TWENTY-EIGHT

Making the Grade

Longy laughed at the false papers, thinking that perhaps he hadn't moved so far from the days of forgeries in Saigon. Since becoming involved with Internal Affairs, a bogus address had been placed on his driver's licence, just in case a vengeful cop decided to go looking for him. In official police files, his residence was listed in the eastern beach suburb of Maroubra, at least an hour's drive from his St Helen's Park townhouse. The only slight hitch came when it was time to renew his security licence, an obligation that normally required going to the police station nearest to home. To uphold his residential deception, Longy made the trip up the Hume Highway, through the city and along Anzac Parade to Maroubra, when realistically he should have only had to travel a few blocks to present his papers.

The Maroubra police station licensing officer was none the wiser. To Constable Sean Garlick, Duy Long Nguyen was just another name to be processed. For his part, Longy thought this muscular officer might have been a part-time bodybuilder. His upper body was strong and thickset, but he presented a less formidable image when he rose stiffly from his chair and walked to a photocopier.

'You injured your back?' Longy inquired.

'It's a bit sore.'

'Too much time pumping out.'

'No, I play football.'

To the majority of back-page readers, Sean Garlick wasn't a policeman but a prize Rooster. He was the captain of Sydney City, one of twenty teams playing in the Australian Rugby League's first grade premiership, the sport's most prestigious club competition. As any player would, he carried a few bumps, bruises and niggling injuries. Longy hadn't heard of him, but he recognised the opportunity.

'I have a look at you. You will feel better.'

To Garlick's bemusement, this chatty Vietnamese man who was very hard to understand began poking and prodding him, running his fingers along his arms.

'You very tense. I help you. Five minutes, that's all we need, five minutes.'

Just like some other men as far away as a Tokyo coffee house and a Saigon gaol, Garlick was curious to see what would happen. Ignoring the vulnerable position he was putting himself in, he lay face down on the floor in full uniform. Amid interruptions from his amused colleagues, including the duty sergeant who was nonplussed to see one of his officers on the ground wincing, Garlick surrendered to Longy's touch. When the brief session finished, he stood up feeling remarkably sprightly.

'Mate, that's great!'

'You still need more work.'

'Do you have a clinic?'

'My clinic is any time, anywhere, any place. I can come to you.'

That afternoon after work, Garlick received a longer treatment on his back and shoulders at his home. It was a painful hour of feeling sharp knuckles dig into muscles and tendons. But all the agony was worth it when he was able to practically stroll through his team's evening training.

Afterwards, he rang Longy. 'I feel great. It's the best rub I've ever had. I really feel great. You'll have to come to the game on the weekend.'

Longy didn't need to be asked twice. Sitting in the stands at the Sydney Football Stadium, he rode nearly every second of the Roosters' match. His eyes only strayed from the action on the field when players limped to the sidelines, leaning on the shoulders of their trainers. Rugby league, the game Longy called 'olive ball' years ago in Saigon, was a brutal contact sport, a war where the only weapons were powerful bodies thumping angrily into each other at full speed. To the players it was about tries, goals and tackles. To Longy it was about torn groins and hamstrings, strained ligaments and dislocations. It was a massage therapist's utopia.

He met some of the Sydney City players afterwards and, boosted by Garlick's high praise, found himself with an immediate new stable of clients. In an extended job interview over several weeks, Longy proved his worth to a number of Roosters, including high-profile stars Adrian Lam and Tony Iro. He frequented training sessions, homes and games, where he sat in the crowd behind the player areas with one eye on the action, the other on limps, carried shoulders and stiff necks. Initially he wasn't accepted as a member of the support staff, but he was nevertheless allowed to attend to players provided he didn't interfere with the team's smooth running. Occasionally, enthusiasm and naivety swept him across that line. After watching Iro hobble from the field during one game, Longy leapt the fence and began working on the star's injured hamstring there and then.

The response from the startled officials was predictable: 'What the ...!'

The rapport Longy struck with the players saw him move from grandstand to sideline, and also into the highly guarded inner sanctum of any team: the dressing room. Amid the smell of linament, the sounds of studs tapping the floor and the slaps of well-wishers' hands on backs, Longy quietly helped some of the players prepare. Most of his time was spent with Garlick and Adrian Lam. He stretched, rubbed, bandaged, motivated ... at times he couldn't help but think of the cock fighters he'd groomed in Saigon. He considered himself 'part of the furniture', even travelling with the players on the team bus to and from games.

The players swore by him. Garlick in particular had a special reason to endorse his new friend's skills. Only hours before one game he'd been battling high temperatures, aching joints and stomach pains from a virus that he thought was going to sideline him. Longy thought otherwise. After numerous cups of herbal tea and a short, sharp session on the table, receiving some intense treatment near the liver, Garlick wasn't only well enough to play but he went out and set a club tackling record.

As the season progressed, word spread along the dressing room grapevine of this funny Vietnamese bloke with the incredible hands who had helped the Roosters: 'Mate, he's a legend. He got me back playing when the physios couldn't ... You'll hurt like hell on the table, but Christ you'll feel a million bucks after you get off it ... I can't understand a word he says, but he's bloody good ... He's about the only bloke I'll ever let touch me!'

Longy's appointment list grew almost daily as players from other clubs approached him: Mark Coyne, the St George captain; the Johns brothers at Newcastle; Steve Walters in Canberra. Garlick, too, received a growing number of requests, not only from players, but also friends and family. Longy fitted them all in, driving from one end of Sydney to the other. Knees, backs, hips, headaches, jaws, shoulders, ankles, fingers, arms, necks — the works.

Amazingly, he did a considerable amount of the work for little or no money. He considered his time to be an investment. Once he established a strong network, he could then move forward and grow a business. In the meantime, his security work kept the money flowing in. Towards the end of the league season he realised he couldn't stretch himself any more. From a chipped thumb at Kogarah to a grade-one medial knee ligament strain at Bondi to tendonitis in the shoulder at Brookvale, he was spending as much time clocking up kilometres and flipping through pages of his street directory as he was leaning over his clients. He needed to either slow down or have a central place to work from. There was only one choice.

In his casual, just-a-handshake-deal manner he made an arrangement with one of his clients, Genevieve, who lived in a terrace house in the inner-city suburb of Paddington. What began with treatments on the living room floor progressed a few steps out the back, through a courtyard, down a steep flight of stairs, into a garage cluttered with a drum kit, storage boxes and paint tins. This wasn't necessarily perfect, but it was good enough for what Longy needed. His clinic was born.

The clinic could be entered from the stairs or from a roller door facing a typically narrow Paddington alley. The room was modest. It had a toilet and shower in one corner and no windows. Longy bought a hydraulic table that could be pumped into several different positions. He put this in the centre of the garage and placed a small couch along one wall. The only other notable feature was a set of bamboo blinds in front of the roller door.

He still made house calls, but the Paddington clinic quickly became the centre of his operations. Many of the initial clients were Genevieve's friends. They would enjoy a cup of tea in the 'waiting room', a space flowing into the courtyard, then walk — or limp — down the stairs for their session. Some left chewing on a piece of ginger or ginseng, moving more freely than when they'd arrived. As much as it was a clinic, it was also a social club, a cheerful place to come and pass the time.

Only a short stroll from the Sydney Football Stadium, its location was perfect considering Longy was treating so many Sydney City players. After having a disappointing 1995 season in which they failed to make the play-offs, the Roosters regrouped for the following year, boosted by the news they'd signed one of the game's biggest names, Brad Fittler, who inevitably followed his team-mates to the clinic door.

In June attention turned to the representative games, where the showcase was the State of Origin series between New South Wales and Queensland. This was the sport at its best. The promoters pumped the angle 'state against state, mate against mate'. From the die-hard followers all the way to those only vaguely interested in league, this contest demanded complete and utter loyalty. It was either 'Go the Blues!' or 'Up the Maroons!' There was no middle ground, no each-way bet, no sympathy for the bastards on the other side of the border — unless you were a pressure-point manipulator with, literally, a hand in either camp. Because of his friendship with Adrian Lam, a Queenslander, Longy was invited to be part of the 'Banana Benders' preparations for game two. He worked on several players at the team's base in Bondi, receiving $210 a day and a tracksuit and training gear, which meant more to him than money. With an irrepressible grin, he proudly wore his uniform everywhere — or, at least, when he was in the presence of the Maroons.

However, Longy also quietly slipped away to the Blues' base just a few beaches and ragged cliffs away in Coogee, where players, including Fittler and Laurie Daley, were waiting. To Longy, the only division between north and south existed in Vietnam. When it came to football he was loyal to injuries and individuals, not teams and traditions.

So he happily attended to both sides of the border. His only dilemma was remembering to change from one team tracksuit to the other somewhere along the route.

These uniforms were priceless to Longy. They weren't so much symbols of state representation as trophies of hard-won acceptance — Australian acceptance. An Asian had made it into a traditional domain of Aussie brawn and bonding. Forget the certificates and passports, these layers of polyester, zippers, emblems and endorsements said more about being a dinkum bloke than any piece of paper ever would. New South Wales went on to win the series, but Longy didn't blink at the result — he'd already enjoyed his victory.

A few weeks later Australia played Fiji in a test match in the steel city of Newcastle, two hours' drive north of Sydney. As the players lined up for the national anthem before the game, Longy was only a few steps away on the sideline, stiff and upright, staring into the night sky.

'In joyful strains then let us sing, Advaaaance Austraaaaalia Fairrrr.'

The anthem faded away with the fireworks. Applause rang around the ground; the players loosened up, clenched their fists and shouted last-minute instructions; and Longy stood quietly. He was wearing his Australian tracksuit; this was a moment to be savoured. In some small way he felt he was giving something back to the country that had provided him with a second chance at life. He was an Aussie product made in Vietnam. There was no-one prouder in the stadium.

He'd initially gone to Newcastle to treat Fittler for a finger injury, but predictably he was soon entrenched in the hotel camp, cheerfully going from player to player, offering his services. Terry Hill was one to benefit. The rugged centre was struggling with a shoulder injury that threatened to end his season on the operating table. After watching Longy work tirelessly one afternoon at the Australian team's hotel, he felt a little guilty asking for treatment, but was quickly reassured, 'No worries, brother. Come on.'

With herbal oil, hot water, a towel and his table, Longy launched into his work as though he was just beginning for the day. Two gruelling hours later, he cleaned his hands and said, 'That's it, we do it again tomorrow.'

Hill was amazed. Longy had barely stopped throughout the entire session. In truth he hadn't rested all day, not even for lunch. And yet he hadn't complained, or asked for as much as a glass of water.

'Longy, mate, how about you come downstairs and I'll shout you a feed.'

'No, I pay for you.'

'Get out! You've just worked solid on me for two hours. I owe you.'

'Are you sure?'

'My oath!'

It was the beginning of a 'pick'n'stick' friendship. When Longy returned to work for Sydney City after the test, he always reserved time for his new mate at the rival Manly club. Hill's shoulder was, in league vernacular, a 'one game at a time' proposition, but with Longy's touch it held together, defying one surgeon's belief that reconstruction was the only option.

In a test of Longy's allegiances, the Roosters and Manly met in the first round of the play-offs. The Sea Eagles won, but Hill was forced off after tearing ankle ligaments. The early prognosis from the specialists wasn't good: 'You mightn't play again this season.' He had two weeks to recover for his next game — the race against the clock had begun. In between his commitments to Sydney City, Longy worked on Hill every day for hours at a time. His only tools were his hands and hot water.

While Manly had qualified for a week's break, the Roosters were back in action for the second round of the play-offs in a do-or-die game against St George. The bowed heads and silence in the dressing room afterwards told of their fate. While the players sat sombrely in front of their lockers, slowly peeling off their socks and tossing them away into a corner together with their premiership dreams, Longy contemplated his future. Would he be back here again next year? In the darkness that defeat can bring, it wasn't the time to ask. After a few handshakes and promises to keep in touch, he left with a jumper given to him by one of the players, Paul Dunn. Perhaps it was the negative mood that affected him, but he couldn't stop thinking he wouldn't be back.

He'd barely driven out of the Sydney Football Stadium's car park when his phone rang: 'Longy, brother.'

'Terry Hill! How's your ankle?'

'It's going OK. Listen, now that you're finished up with the Roosters, come to Manly.'

'Next year too far away to think about.'

'No, now. For this week, and the rest of the season.'

It wasn't a difficult choice. Because of his connection with Hill, Longy had already met many of the Manly players and coach, Bob Fulton. It wouldn't take him any time to adjust. The main priority remained Hill, who didn't run with the team at all in the week leading up to the game against Cronulla. Longy cancelled all his appointments to concentrate solely on an ankle with a grade-one tear of the lateral ligament. Only two days before the game Hill thought he had no chance of playing. On game eve, Longy worked on him for several hours until midnight. He slept over. The next morning he woke early to continue the treatment.

'You will be right, brother. I will get you there. You will play.'

With the help of the standard painkilling needles in the dressing room before kick-off, Hill ran onto the Sydney Football Stadium turf to be greeted by a thunderous roar from Manly fans, who until that moment hadn't known whether or not their star was playing.

Hill played well, the Sea Eagles won, and the race began again for the grand final in seven days' time against St George. The media pounced on the story. It was an angle that could be followed all week, building the drama of the season's most important game. And that was even before Hill revealed the role of his unsung helper, the Vietnamese refugee boat person with the magical touch. By the next morning Longy could barely take a breath between phone calls from journalists seeking interviews, players wanting help, and members of the general community desperately needing cures from all sorts of afflictions, from sciatica to bunions, arthritis to swollen knees. Longy had arrived on the public stage.

At the same time, Hill awoke to find his ankle swollen beyond recognition. Together with team doctor Nathan Gibbs, renowned as one of the best sports medics in the country, Longy launched into the most demanding challenge of his time as a healer. Hot water, ice-packs, hands. Hot water, ice-packs, hands ... He moved in with Hill and his young family, working late into every night. Hot water, ice-packs, hands. Hot water, ice-packs, hands ... By mid-week the swelling had gone down, but Hill still found it difficult to walk. Hot water, ice packs, hands. Hot water, ice packs, hands ... By Friday, two days before the game, Hill's range of movement had returned, but he still hadn't run with the team. No-one knew whether he would play.

On grand final day, Longy sat next to Hill on the team bus for the forty-minute trip from Brookvale to the Sydney Football Stadium. Outside car horns were tooted and people decked from head to toe in Manly colours waved maroon and white streamers.

'Go the Eagles ... Go get 'em, boys ... Onya, Terry ... Belt the shit out of 'em, Manly!'

The mood on the bus was varied. There were quiet players with eyes shut and headphones on; some stared out the window; others, like Hill, were upbeat, chatty and dosed up on one-liners. When they were close to the sports ground, the streets filled with fans yelling, cheering, and, if dressed in the red and white of St George, abusing: 'Manly suck! Up the Dragons!'

When the players reached their dressing room, the mood changed. There were no more smiles, no jokes, little laughter. Above them the stadium rumbled with expectation. As soon as the players settled Longy began working on Hill, dipping his hands in a bucket of hot water then firmly pressing them around the ankle. He rolled it, pulled it gently, pushed firmly. Hill bit his lip. The pain eased after he was 'needled up' by Nathan Gibbs. He was then strapped up and sent on his way to the warm-up area, where he ran with the team, a rare sight in recent weeks. Longy watched every step nervously; he wasn't alone. It seemed that every official had at least one eye on an ankle that had been spoken about from office to pub, press box to playing field. There were no problems. Hill was ready. The team was ready. The time was ready.

When the players filed out of the dressing room into the tunnel, Longy stood at the door, slapping everyone on the back. He felt his heart thumping; he was as anxious and excited as any of the grim-faced thirteen about to run on.

Manly was under self-imposed pressure after losing the previous year's decider to Canterbury. Victory wasn't a dream: it was a demand. The signs were promising at half-time. The Eagles were ahead 14–2.

Back in the dressing room, Longy asked only one player one question. 'How is it?'

'It's going all right, brother. We'll get through.'

And they did. When the siren sounded, Manly had won 20–8. In the exuberant, champagne-soaked celebrations that followed, Longy hung back until Fulton urged him to join the lap of honour. He was barely noticeable in this swaggering huddle of ecstasy. The players brushed the hands of cheering fans leaning over the fence, they sipped from magnums, hugged each other, laughed, joked, uttered the odd expletive. They straggled along, basking in every second. They headed behind the southern goalposts, then swung along the eastern touchline.

'Hey, Terry.' Hill swung round to see Fulton, laughing.
'What?'
'Look at that!'
Hill followed his coach's pointing finger to the big screen.
'You're kidding me! What a bloody classic!'
There was Longy grinning in the centre of the picture, holding aloft the premiership trophy, the JJ Giltinan Shield. Since he'd begun working with Hill he'd refused to accept any payment. Now, he was enjoying his reward. There were 40 000 people around him, roaring, clapping, crying. Some were asking who was the little Chinaman with the ponytail crashing Manly's parade. He was Duy Long Nguyen, a Vietnamese boat person who had never played rugby league yet had one of the sport's most gifted pair of hands. He was proud of his grand final role; no-one could deny how important he'd been. He thought of his mother. If ever there was a time for her to be proud of him, this was it. It was one of the happiest moments of his life.

Longy enjoyed more celebrations in the dressing room, and on the team bus back to the Manly Leagues Club, where thousands of fans were waiting to back-slap and booze into the early hours. This wasn't the scene for the nondrinking Longy. He slipped quietly away. With the day still fresh in his mind, he wanted to go home and share his stories with Ann, and show her his lasting memory — another priceless tracksuit to add to the collection.

TWENTY-NINE

Pressing the Flesh

What a body! It was all that Longy could think when he saw the shirt peeled off. Outside the massage tent, as the wind whipped whitecaps across the water, the ground announcer struggled to be heard above the jet engines from Sydney Airport.

'Welcome to the Botany Bay Gift, where one of the world's true sporting superstars will be in action this afternoon.'

Linford Christie lay down on the table. Longy wasn't overawed; the muscle under his fingertips may have belonged to a former world and Olympic 100-metres champion, but there was no need to change his style. He happily chatted away, laughing at his own jokes. Christie, well used to carnivals loaded with accents, struggled with the occasional word but understood enough to have a conversation.

It was February 1997 and Longy had his first overseas client. Most of his other clients at that time were local and national sportsmen. Apart from the growing list of footballers, he treated boxers Troy Waters and Shannon Taylor, former Formula One motor racing world champion

Alan Jones, touring car driver Glenn Seton, golfer Rodger Davis, and Melbourne Cup-winning jockey Jimmy Cassidy. Singer Deni Hines, television presenter Deborah Hutton, media personality Kerri-Anne Kennerley and Queen's Counsel David Bloom had also been on his table. Business, which operated solely on word-of-mouth and contacts, was flourishing. Perhaps the greatest endorsements of Longy's ability were the referrals from existing clients to friends: 'You should go and see this bloke — he's fantastic. But don't tell anyone, because he's getting really busy. We don't want him to be too hard to get to!'

People rang from interstate seeking cures for terminal diseases. They'd heard of the 'miracle worker with the magical powers'. Longy turned those cases away, saying, 'I can't play God.'

One of his greatest strengths was the recognition of his limits: 'If I can't fix, I don't touch.' And yet people still rang in the hope that he could.

The speed at which word spread shocked him. It had been less than two years since he'd first met Sean Garlick. That seemed a whole stadium full of massages ago. Now that he was so busy with his healing, his security and private investigation work had all but gone. He still did the occasional job, but by the time he generally finished his last clinic appointment or house call each day, he only wanted to find a pillow. Sometimes he slept in his car or a hotel.

This was no nine-to-five operation. Longy chose his own hours which, to the frustration of some of his clients, could change without notice. Genevieve, who Longy came to know as 'The Boss' because of her role as unofficial personal assistant, was well versed in making apologies. Longy wasn't unreliable — just unpredictable. But this didn't stop the aches and pains coming through either the clinic's roller door or the more distinguished front entrance.

Longy resumed his link with Manly at the beginning of the 1997 season. In the following months he again worked on both sides of State of Origin's great divide, and spent the now inevitable late-night sessions with Terry Hill. Going to games was the highlight of his week. He sat on the sidelines, rolling with every tackle and line break, occasionally shouting out his own opinions and advice, or yelling insults at the referee. As with his life in general, he was rarely short of a word. But even he was left almost speechless the day he was invited to help prepare Troy Waters for a World Boxing Council fight against Puerto Rican welterweight Félix Trinidad.

'No worries,' he said. 'Where is it?'

'New York.'

'Shit!'

New York, the Big Apple, the city that never sleeps. Home of the Empire State Building, the Statue of Liberty, Central Park, ritzy Fifth Avenue, Wall Street, dog walkers, rollerbladers, Frisbee throwers, bagel sellers ... Longy had seen it all on television. It had never seemed real, though, more like part of the set for 'NYPD Blue'. Now he was to discover that it was very real, yet it was also part of a dream, one that began on a rickety boat sixteen years ago when a fearless teenager yearned for a life in America.

Longy was like a wide-eyed child when he sat in the cab from the airport. It was late afternoon. Staggered by his first glimpse of the glistening Manhattan skyline, he had an overwhelming wish to share this moment with his mother. He stared through the windscreen at the canyons between the skyscrapers. There was an unexpected likeness to Saigon's alleys and laneways. Both cities intimidated, yet enticed.

The footpaths were crowded with people bustling from store to store. Cars swept by, driven by an impatience that considered orange lights just another shade of green. Wherever Longy looked there was something to catch his attention: billboards, beggars, fire escapes, sirens, car horns, delis, stage doors, rappers, hansom cabs. This was a gigantic city of little space, lots of pace.

The Waters camp was based at a Broadway hotel. Longy could see the Hudson River from his room, but he soon had little time to admire the sights after Waters fractured his rib in a sparring session. It was only a matter of weeks before the fight, and this was an injury Longy couldn't magically fix. He could only ease the pain and try to reduce the swelling. He went to Chinatown and bought some herbal creams that he mixed with some scotch whisky, making his own special concoction. He worked it carefully into the area several times a day. His touch needed to be precise — a mere brush of the wrong spot would make Waters pull back in pain. The boxer was desperate to keep the injury a secret. If news reached the authorities the fight would be cancelled, destroying Waters's hopes of earning a lucrative world title shot.

This was, however, by no means his biggest worry. In Sydney, his brother Dean was on trial for murder. It was the latest drama in a sorry saga of incidents that had seen the Waters name pop in and out of the headlines for years. Under such harrowing stress, it was a wonder that Troy was able to concentrate on his fight at all.

Troy, a devout Christian, had his prayers answered two weeks before the bout when Dean was found not guilty. After this news, there was a fresh energy in the camp and the relatively simple matter of a fractured rib seemed easy to overcome. Yet in the final days before the bout, Longy was at his busiest. His main priority had shifted from treating the injury to hiding any hint of swelling or bruising for the medical examination. He did this by drying out the skin with his own special creams. It worked: the doctor glanced over the spot without a second's pause. Nor did officials raise any concerns at the weigh-in, where Waters, stripped to his underpants, was subject to close scrutiny.

His job done, Longy could afford to relax. That evening he went for a walk, passing overdressed crowds milling outside theatres and underdressed crews standing at stage doors. Within a few blocks he turned a corner to see a beggar in a tracksuit sitting on the footpath, leaning against a wall. He was in his forties, a slight man with short greying hair and lacklustre eyes. His appearance was a sad contrast to the photo at his side showing a beaming young soldier, chest out, shoulders back, in full uniform. Longy reached into his pocket and dropped whatever notes he had.

'Thank you, sir, God bless you.'

'You serve in Vietnam?'

'Yes, sir.'

'Where?'

'Pleiku.'

'No! Bullshit!'

Coincidence or fate? Either way, Longy felt immediate compassion for the man. They spoke for some minutes about the war, and their lives since. The beggar had three bullet wounds in one of his legs, his marriage had broken down, he was now an alcoholic living on the street. He'd gone to Vietnam without a strong knowledge of what the conflict was about. He returned without a clearer picture. Sure, it was about stopping communism, but why? It wasn't worth a limp, loneliness and a cheap bottle of drunkenness. He had every reason to be bitter. Longy felt embarrassed about his own good luck. He shook the beggar's hand and left, wondering about all the American victims beyond the 60 000 who were killed. At least one, he now knew, found it harder battling in the canyons of Manhattan than in the jungles of Pleiku.

The beggar wasn't there the next night Longy passed by, this time in a limousine with the Waters team heading to Madison Square Garden, the sentimental granddaddy of American fight venues. Mobs of Puerto Ricans jeered when they arrived. After passing stringent security checks they were taken into a dressing room in the bowels of the old building, where Longy helped Waters prepare. When the knock on the door came from officials, Longy joined the entourage for the walk into the cauldron. As the others advanced into the glare of lights to be met by the deep-throated theatrics of the ring announcer and the boos of the pro-Trinidad crowd, Longy turned back to the dressing rooms to watch on television. Number restrictions prevented him from being ringside, but he didn't mind. Just one step into Madison Square Garden was enough to have completed the journey.

The fight was over in the first round: a technical knockout. Waters copped a barrage of punches that sent him to the canvas, and on a plane to Sydney contemplating a life beyond boxing. It was different for Longy, who spent the trip imagining his life before he practised healing. What would have happened to him if he'd resettled in the United States instead of Australia? Would he have had the same opportunities? It was a question he couldn't answer, but he did know one thing — he was glad to be going home.

After the first bout of jet lag of his life, Longy slotted back into his regular routine of irregular appointments. As the script demanded, he again raced the clock to mend Terry Hill for a grand final appearance. This time it was a hip injury. Longy won, Hill played, Manly lost.

Among his new clients was a man who needed no introduction. Longy first met him after receiving an early morning phone call from his fitness trainer: 'Longy, Matt Garry here.'

'Hi, Matt, how you going?'

'Good, listen, I need your help.'

By mid-morning Longy had arrived at 2 Holt Street, Surry Hills, in Sydney's inner city. He parked in a no standing zone at the front of the office building, where Garry was waiting to carry in the massage table. They set up in the gymnasium, Longy listening to the trainer's brief: 'I pushed him a bit hard this morning and his back's pulled up a bit sore. It's good you could come and have a look at him.'

'I'm doing it for you, Matt, not because of who he is.'

An hour later Longy walked out again, Matt at his side carrying the table.

'Thanks for doing that. We'll see you again tomorrow.'

'No worries, but he has to come to the clinic.'

As he drove away, Longy glanced back at the grey stone, glass-fronted building: the home of News Limited in Australia. Had he really just worked on one of the world's most powerful media men? It hadn't really been different from any other house call. Rupert Murdoch was just another person with a body that needed help. Longy was more delighted he hadn't received a parking ticket.

The next day a limousine squeezed through Paddington's back streets until it stopped outside a particular roller door. Its passenger would make other visits during the week and further seek Longy's help on future visits to Australia.

At the time, two other high-profile individuals had joined Longy's client list. The first was a fit, bespectacled soccer player; the second had such a commanding presence that he once captained the English cricket team on film. Yet neither man had built his name through sport. Steven Lowy was the son of one of Australia's richest and most successful businessmen, Westfield magnate Frank Lowy; Hugo Weaving was one of the country's most distinguished actors, whose skills had swept him far beyond his role as Douglas Jardine in the *Bodyline* TV miniseries of the early 1980s. Both were to have an overwhelming influence on Longy's future.

Weaving played the first role. Longy considered him a 'no-bullshit bloke' whom he liked from the first time they met. He treated the actor for a hip problem, visiting the star's comfortable home, which had a backyard swimming pool, huge jacaranda tree and three-legged pet cat. 'It's funny the things you most remember about people!' Longy says now.

Weaving had just started shooting the much-publicised science fiction thriller *The Matrix* at Sydney's Fox Studios.

The film had already attracted widespread attention because it wasn't following the standard Hollywood production path. As it soon eventuated, the new route wouldn't just take in location shoots in Sydney's CBD, but also a common garage that was as far removed from a movie star's caravan as Beverly Hills was from Paddington.

Laurence Fishburne was the first of the American entourage to visit the clinic, announcing, 'Hugo recommended you to me' as he arrived.

'Shit! I'm doing a superstar!'

'No, I'm just an actor.'

Longy was struck by the common-man approach. Fishburne was more interested in hearing stories about Vietnam than shining in his own spotlight.

A few days later Longy received a phone call from a representative of *The Matrix*. It seemed Fishburne had spread the word on set.

'Hello, Longy, I'm speaking on behalf of Keanu Reeves. He's heard good things about you. He has a neck problem that you might be able to help him with.'

Keanu Reeves! Who would turn down that offer? In a rare moment of self-doubt, Longy thought he would. What would happen if he wrecked the neck, and the movie, and Reeves's whole career? The 'master of pressure points' was now putting pressure on himself. However, it was just a flash of uncertainty. The next morning he arrived eagerly at the Quay West apartments in the city. With the concierge carrying his table, he strode to the front desk.

'I'm here to see Keanu Reeves.'

'I'm sorry, sir, he's not staying here.'

'Yes, he is. I have an appointment to see him.'

'I'm sorry, sir.'

'But . . .'

The brewing conflict was halted by a smartly dressed man who introduced himself as Reeves's personal assistant. A bodyguard was with him. Longy was quietly told it was usual procedure that stars didn't book in under their own names. He was then escorted to Reeves's room, where introductions were made before Longy and Neo, the hero of *The Matrix*, were left alone. Longy's first impressions were of a 'quiet, small, skinny guy who had a thing for black': black shoes, black jeans, black belt, black T-shirt, black beanie.

They sat down and talked over a cup of coffee. Longy was surprised by Reeves's depth of knowledge about Eastern medicines and healing. This gave them a common ground to work from. Reeves revealed he'd had vertebrae fused together in an operation after he'd injured his neck in a motorcycle accident; he was worried he wouldn't have enough mobility to handle all his shoot commitments. After inspecting the area, Longy believed he could help, but agreed with his slightly apprehensive client there would be no manipulation. He treated the spot for two hours, gently using his knuckles to encourage circulation. Reeves lay quietly throughout. Afterwards, they had another coffee and a cigarette together. Despite literally rubbing shoulders with one of Hollywood's most famous pin-up boys, Longy wasn't overwhelmed.

The same couldn't be said when the fourth star of *The Matrix* arrived at the clinic.

'Keanu spoke about you. He said you're really good. Should I take all my clothes off?'

Carrie-Ann Moss — wow! The striking, leggy brunette was well used to taking people's breath away. Stripped to her underwear, she cheerfully chatted away while Longy went to work, a job for which he had no trouble finding motivation. When she left, Longy had already thought of the line to tell his friends: 'I've just polished my first Ferrari!'

Within a few days the prestige vehicle needed a service when she injured a rhomboid muscle. Longy was called onto the set at Fox Studios. From that moment on, he was there nearly every day from morning to night for eight months, a willing prisoner of *The Matrix*, moving continually from one star's caravan to the next. He smoked cigarettes with Keanu, ate lunch with Laurence, had dinner with Hugo, and listened to Carrie-Ann sing along to songs on the radio like a teenager. Much of his life revolved around Neo, Morpheus, Agent Smith, Trinity and the rest of the cast. He also developed a strong rapport with Larry and Andy Wachowski, the movie's directors and writers. Since his time as a boy peering through the projectionist's window at his mother's Pleiku cinema, Longy had had a love for the silver screen. Now, he had his very own role. For a man whose personality and ego lent itself more to Hollywood than home video, this was surely a fantasy. Lights, camera, action — Longy.

Despite the hectic schedule, Longy was still able to fulfil his other commitments, most prominently his league duties, which included travelling to Auckland to prepare the Australian team for a test match against New Zealand. By now his client base had grown to include — high-profile media commentator Alan Jones, tennis player Pat Rafter, bon vivant Leo Schofield, and international sprinters Darren Campbell and Frankie Fredericks. The discoloured white walls of his clinic had become unusual testimonies to his success, with autographs and messages scribbled in black felt pen: *Longie [sic] the best. JA Cassidy, 1998; To Longy, the best. Many thanks. Rupert Murdoch; Longy, you are the man who fixes the man. Anthony Mundine; To Longy, forever in your corner, Johnny Lewis*, amongst many others.

In these halcyon days of 1998, Longy lived in a whirlwind. He barely even stopped long enough to marry Ann in a quiet ceremony at a park in Wollongong, an hour's drive south of Sydney. The no-fuss occasion again reflected his wish to keep his private life very private.

It was a view he shared with the other client who was to have a significant bearing on his future. While Hugo Weaving had guided Longy into the glossy world of public lives, Steven Lowy opened a door into a family that shied from the spotlight. First treated by Longy for an Achilles tendon injury, Steven had returned on numerous occasions to be treated for other niggles. What began with an appreciation of Longy's skills soon sprouted into a friendship which eventually led to a phone call that wasn't altogether unexpected: 'Could you come and have a look at Dad, please? His back is no good.'

At the time Longy was sitting on the Manly team bus travelling to Canberra for a play-off game. The day after folding his table away in a smelly, sweat-drenched dressing room he was setting it up in the sparkling clean gymnasium of a multistorey, multimillion-dollar Sydney harbourside home. He'd only just finished preparations when his distinguished client walked in with a slightly uneasy step, trying to minimise the pain in his back. They shook hands, then after a brief discussion about the injury, Frank Lowy, one of the richest, shrewdest and most admired businessmen in Australia, lay face down and waited to discover if his son's high praise of this Vietnamese fellow was warranted.

It was.

In the following weeks Longy was a frequent visitor to the exclusive residence. Even after Lowy had no more pain, the phone calls kept coming: 'Longy, are you free this afternoon? ... Is tomorrow morning at six o'clock OK for you? ... Can you be on hand for tennis on Wednesday night?'

By the end of the year, the two had developed a close relationship which, from a distant observer's point of view, could have seemed absurdly incompatible. They were worlds apart, yet there were significant similarities. When only a boy in Czechoslovakia, Frank saw his family fragmented after his Hungarian Jewish father was taken away to the horrific Auschwitz concentration camp during World War II. He would never see him again. After fighting in the Israeli War of Independence (1948), Frank arrived in Australia to battle the familiar resettlement problems faced by any immigrant confronting a new culture and a new way of life. With unyielding self-belief and determination, he ventured into business as the part-owner of a small delicatessen in Sydney's western suburbs. It is now part of Australian legend that this was the birthplace of the multinational retail phenomenon Westfield, one of the country's most remarkable success stories. When their backgrounds were considered, František Lowy and Duy Long Nguyen were not so absurdly incompatible at all.

Longy needed just one word to show how deep his respect for Lowy had become: 'Uncle'. Just as a Saigon barber and a master healer in Cholon had strongly influenced his life, a billionaire businessman was now doing the same.

Despite his increasing commitments with 'Uncle Frank', he still found time for more work, which included treating another Ferrari whose scribble on the clinic wall became a popular conversation topic for future clients: *Longie, Where have you been all my life? You are the best and most special person. Love ♡ Elle XX*

The Ferrari, of course, was Elle Macpherson, 'The Body', Australia's international supermodel. Her visit to Longy's clinic prompted a piece in 'Page 13', the star-spotting gossip column of the *Daily Telegraph*. By this time, Longy had his own mini-celebrity profile. Only weeks earlier he'd appeared in the same paper in a photo with Keanu Reeves after the premiere of *The Matrix* in Sydney. He'd strolled the red carpet with aplomb, relishing the teenage screams, the twinkling of camera flashes, and the notepads and pens thrust in search of autographs. He sat through the movie, waiting for one particular moment. It came after the end, wedged in green type on black between Physical Trainers and Medical Advisors. It was just one of hundreds of names, but surely none deserved the scrolling second in the spotlight more than Sports Masseur: Longy Nguyin. The misspelling didn't worry him. He was still a star for the briefest of moments.

Longy also attended the film's premiere in Tokyo. As he walked through the neon-lit streets, he marvelled at his journey. Was it really eighteen years ago that he'd treated sumos, wrestled a jackhammer, and complained about going to Australia to live? Time had passed as quickly as *The Matrix* credit roll.

The next year, 1999, was no different, borne on the same swift feet that had swept Longy through 1998. In addition to his regular commitments, he travelled to Mexico City with the Australian Maccabi Masters soccer team, of which Steven Lowy was a member. However, he resisted the frequent requests to travel overseas with Frank — he was too busy at the clinic to leave for extended periods.

His life continued at a frenetic pace in 2000, the most important date in Australian sports history: the year of the Sydney Olympics. It wasn't surprising that Longy's services were highly sought after, but in an unexpected detour from the green and gold, he donned the Union Jack after accepting an invitation to help prepare British sprinter Darren Campbell ... whose coach was none other than Linford Christie.

Unfortunately Longy didn't have accreditation because he wasn't an officially sanctioned member of the British team. However, in a stroke of wonderful timing and good fortune, one of his clients was called away on business only days into the Games. He gave Longy his multi-access pass on this strict proviso: 'You can keep it as a memento, but don't try getting into any events.'

Considering officials boasted that security was the tightest ever at an Olympics, Longy should have met brick walls if he'd tried. But he thought he'd give it a go anyway. So on his very first opportunity he boldly hung the pass around the front of his Great Britain tracksuit, provided by Christie, and walked to the security gates of the Athletes' Village. He slotted the pass into the turnstile that read the barcode. *Click.*

No problems. Through he went. He did this every day for the rest of the Games. In a scene befitting a Monty Python movie, he bounced around the village, ate in the dining area, played games in the recreation rooms and, most importantly, gave Campbell intensive rubs. The 200-metre runner went on to win silver. But perhaps Longy had already claimed his own slice of gold: not one question was ever asked when he attended events. No-one even looked sideways at the cheerful Asian with a pass containing a photo and the name of one of the most identifiable people on the planet — Rupert Murdoch.

Longy's attentions then shifted back to Keanu and company for the shooting of the two remaining films in *The Matrix* trilogy. When added to his almost daily commitments with Frank Lowy, he realised the only possible way he could satisfy all his clients was to resume the identity of his childhood and again become 'the boy who never sleeps'. The lack of hours had defeated him. In a gradual streamlining of his work, he began to see more of a movie star's caravan, less of a rugby league dressing room, more of a Point Piper mansion, less of a Paddington garage. Yet he was still being beaten by time, which had become increasingly precious to him since the birth of his daughter, Denica. Something had to give.

With only two months to go on *The Matrix Revolutions*, the final film of the three, he received a call in his clinic while he was working on Keanu Reeves. It was Steven Lowy — his father needed treatment as soon as possible. By the time Longy hung up the phone, he'd agreed to go ... all the way to The Netherlands.

The next day he flew business class to Amsterdam. Although he would soon return to Sydney, Longy never looked back. He'd decided Frank was his priority. It wasn't full-time employment, more so 'any time' employment; no matter what hour of the day, Longy would put 'Uncle' first. This inevitably led to the reduction in number of his other clientele and the closure of the clinic in late 2002. To this day the walls remain the same, covered in autographs overlooking a tiny space that welcomed the world.

The world now welcomes Longy through the portholes of Frank Lowy's luxury jet and ocean cruiser. He spends as much as two months away at a time, hopping from one city to the next — Los Angeles, New York, London, Amsterdam, Tel Aviv — a journey begun in the jungle-thick highlands of central Vietnam.

In recent years his fingers have been turnstiles through which all walks of life have come and gone, including the proverbial who's who: Murdoch, Lowy, Reeves, Weaving, Fishburne, Moss, Macpherson, Christie, Campbell, Rafter, Hill, Jones, Fittler, Daley, Garlick, Johns, Cassidy, Davis, Seton, Maurice Greene, Ian Healy, Scott Miller, Kevin Schwantz, Megan Gale, Jimmy Barnes... Too many names to remember, but if challenged he can recall most of their injuries and the peculiarities of their bodies.

Longy continues to lead a hectic lifestyle, happily mixing with people from all classes. He keeps in touch with all his friends, although it may be several months between each phone call. That is the way Longy has always lived — darting from one place to the next, one event to the next, one person to the next.

Perhaps this stage of his life, which is still very much a work in progress, is best summed up by a trip he took in a stretch limousine in April 1999. He'd just arrived at Los Angeles airport after an executive-class flight from Sydney. He'd been flown over to treat the back of Larry Wachowski, one of the masterminds behind *The Matrix*. As he settled back comfortably into the leather seats, Longy was asked by the driver if he'd like to listen to the radio.

'Yes, please.'

The unforgettable raspy voice of Louis Armstrong meandered through the speakers: 'What a Wonderful World.'

THIRTY

Memories

'When a tiger dies he leaves behind his skin. When a man dies he leaves behind his reputation.'
VIETNAMESE PROVERB

April 25, 2003: Anzac Day. While thousands of ex-servicemen and women march through cities and towns across Australia, Vietnam Airlines flight 782 lifts off from Sydney's international airport in gentle rain. Reports of the new and potentially fatal SARS virus in Asia are striking hard at tourism. In seat 31B, Longy settles back comfortably and jokes to me: 'No SARS get me, brother. I escape plenty more dangerous shit than that! It's time to kick arse.'

We are flying to Vietnam to research this book. The subject and the author. After a nine-hour trip, the Boeing 767–300 lands at Ho Chi Minh City Airport at 3.50 p.m. local time. For Duy Long Nguyen, back in his former home for the first time in nearly two years, this city will always be known as Saigon. The immigration lines creep slowly past the inspection booths in which stern officers in olive green uniforms and face masks reek of antiseptic. Some wash their hands between examining each passport. Barely a word is spoken by the hundred or so waiting people. That is, until Longy reaches a booth. He immediately begins chatting, his grin quickly winning over the officer, whose mask stretches at the corners, the only possible indication of a smile underneath. Longy walks away after giving the officer his phone number. A new friend has been made.

Outside the terminal Longy, with suitcase in tow, strolls through the mass of taxi drivers haggling for business. Although back among his own people, he is so noticeably different. He is taller and broader, with clothes worth more than a life's wages for some of the people around him: a black designer shirt bought in Sydney's fashionable Oxford Street just the day before; black T-shirt; blue jeans; black R.M. Williams boots. He wears a thick gold necklace hung with dangling miniature boxing gloves that jab into his chest on every stride. His Raymond Weill watch with roman numerals is still on Australian time.

Thao spots him through a gap. She hurries. Longy turns towards her. Another grin. He hugs her, smacks his little sister on the bottom, and laughs.

Thao's brother-in-law, Hoai, drives everyone home in the family's Toyota van. The trip is full of animated gestures and banter. It is the Vietnamese way. When people are together, noise is rarely given a moment to catch breath. Longy shows his sister his latest toy, a palm-sized camera that not only takes photos but records snippets of video. Clicking through its memory, he stops at a picture of his daughter, Denica.

'Beautiful, eh?' he remarks. 'Good kid this one. Smart. Very smart!'

They arrive at Longy's lodgings, a thin three-storey house in a back street of District One. Only weeks earlier a family on the opposite side of the road was robbed of its gold and a young girl was shot in the stomach. She is back in front of her parents' business selling packets of Omo washing powder and Colgate toothpaste when Longy steps out of the car.

'Tough kid, eh?'

Thao's husband, Tam, and their two boys are waiting inside. Longy shakes Tam's hand, slaps him on the shoulder, then hugs his nephews. Six-year-old Balu with a bowl haircut and a smile that stretches into next week bounces from person to person with a Mr Potato Head toy in his hands. His brother, Tin Tin, seven years older and wearing glasses, sits quietly.

'Both good boys. Very smart. Top of their classes.'

Longy accepts a cigarette from Tam. He draws back slowly, and threads words through the smoke.

'You wouldn't see this at home, brother. You watch — I smoke while I'm here, but when I get back to Australia, no more. I give it up just like that.'

He is soon on the move again. Winding through alleys just wide enough for Hoai to negotiate in the van. Eventually he is forced to walk. Ten steps ahead, then a right, another few steps, another right, then a knock on a door. Truong answers. The two friends slap each other on their backs, trade jokes and insults, then giggle as though they are back in the laneways of their childhood.

They move on. A few minutes later they are in the Thanh family barber shop.

'We were just wondering when "Billy the Kid" would return,' says the wife of one of Uncle Ba's sons. Longy gives her a hug and a bottle of Johnnie Walker Black Label, then sits back in the barber's chair for a shave, facial and the curiously popular indulgence of having the ears cleaned with long wooden skewers topped with cotton wool.

It's now dark. If the Saigonese were to throw their memories back thirty years, the streets would be quiet, closing down for curfew. But now they are alive with people talking, laughing, arguing, chewing and watching their way through the remainder of the day. There are quacking scooter horns, the spits of boiling soup from food stalls, and bars pumping with 1980s Western music — Lionel Richie's 'Hello' and George Michael's 'Careless Whisper' are among the most popular tunes.

With face and head considerably fresher, Longy launches into the night on a new and much more suitable mode of transport in this bustling city — he sits with hands on knees on the back of Hoai's Yamaha Nuovo scooter. Truong follows, often struggling to keep up on his eleven-year-old Honda Dream II. They cruise the streets, Longy's open shirt billowing in the sultry air. After dinner they close out the night at a karaoke bar. Hoai is the undoubted star. He can barely speak a word of English in conversation, but with microphone in hand, he doesn't miss a syllable: 'Welcome to the Hotel Californ-ia'; 'It's nine o'clock on a Saturday'; and no performance is complete without 'Hello, I've just got to say hello'.

The next morning Longy takes a leisurely stroll in a park that during the war was a cemetery for South Vietnam's high-ranking officers and a former president.

'The Viet Cong dug up the bodies after the fall. I don't know where they were buried again.'

The park is now dotted with garbage bins in the shape of penguins, an incongruous sight in a land where temperatures climb above 100 degrees.

There is already a thick layer of sweat on Longy's forehead by the time he returns to his lodgings to find Hoai and Truong waiting, cigarettes in hand. It's only eight o'clock. By mid-morning they're sitting in a coffee shop that is full of Western influence. At nearby tables, teenage youths with sunglasses, hipster jeans and Britney Spears T-shirts smoke 555s, Marlboros and Dunhills. Their heads and feet move in time with the thumping music, and when pausing in conversation their mouths outline the words, 'Relax, don't do it, when you want to come'; 'Get down, get down, and boogie all around'; 'Billy Jean, bless my soul'.

On the move again, Longy stops opposite the Presidential Palace and looks in pity at a coconut seller, head bowed, crouching against a wall.

'It makes me very sad. Look at him. Four coconuts to his name and no-one is buying them. One day I will help people like him. My plan is to come back here and set up a massage and martial arts academy. I will teach blind people how to massage. They have the best touch because they must see through their hands. And I will teach poor children tae kwon do and karate. I will give something back. It is one of my dreams.'

Later on he rides with Hoai and Truong through the dusty streets of District Eight. They stop in front of a large yellow concrete building with a red tiled roof. It is partly hidden from the road by a 2-metre concrete fence, a wire gate and a guard's post, in which a single officer in green uniform is reading a newspaper.

Longy points to a road leading down behind the building.

'Our prison was down there. This is new — it has changed a lot.' He pauses, and turns away from the building, shaking his head. 'Two weeks of my life in there. I do not like it here. Let's go.'

That night, after performing acupuncture on a lingering neck problem of Thao's, Longy heads out for a meal with Hoai and Truong. It is midnight, yet the streets are still vibrant. The sunglasses-wearing, tight jeans-clad youth are wanting to be seen in the hippest of restaurants and bars. They leave their bikes on the footpaths, where teenage boys mark each seat with chalk before lining up the bikes side by side in long stretches. In the same frame there are cleaners in bright orange overalls and yellow hard hats sweeping the road with straw brooms, elderly women pushing carts of bananas and mangoes, and men of all ages slowly pedalling their pushbikes while shaking sticks with tin rattles.

'They do massages,' says Longy. 'They will work your whole body for an hour for about half a dollar. Hard work, brother. It could have been me.'

Longy and his mates sit near the road on plastic chairs that surround a rickety wooden table. A tiny man in his early forties takes the orders. No bigger than a schoolboy, he has lines — whole verses that today's students will never understand — written across his face. He and Longy smile at each other, then shake hands warmly. They talk as though they are neighbours. After some minutes the man walks away to a group of three women.

'They're his sisters. His name is Phung. We used to play soccer together. The sisters are all he has left. His parents are dead — his mother was killed in a bike accident — and his brother tried to escape on foot to Thailand. He was never seen again. They must work about twenty-one hours a day. But they never complain. Look at them — such peaceful people. A very sad story.'

After enjoying a dish of chicken *pho*, Longy gives Phung a tip. It's more money than the family will earn in at least the next month — unless Longy returns over the coming days. He then straddles the back of Hoai's bike, cigarette stiff in his mouth — 'Can you believe this is my eleventh today?' — and rides into the darkness: 'Tomorrow's a big day, brother.'

The new day begins with a laugh when Longy, dressed in singlet and underpants, unkempt hair and cigarette gravel still in his voice, reads out an early morning SMS sent from a friend in Australia.

'Saddam Hussein has been captured hiding in a field. The Americans sprayed it with Viagra, and the prick stood up.' A short, crackling chuckle follows.

By mid-morning the hair is in place, the pyjamas have made way for a crisp white Ralph Lauren shirt and blue jeans, and the voice is firm. Longy is standing in the dappled shade of a frangipani tree outside Saigon's central courthouse, a tired mustard-yellow brick and concrete building with cancer creeping from the outer edges. Inside, an old man sits in blue and white striped regulation prison uniform. Nam Cam is arguably the biggest crime figure ever to face trial in Vietnam. He is staring at almost certain execution. His charges are read out, echoing outside the court through a speaker wired to a jacaranda tree in full bloom. Underneath, hundreds of people listen intently.

'Illegal gambling on World Cup soccer matches ... The management of prostitutes and illegal brothels ... Cock fighting ... Murder ... Black-market dealings ...'

The charge list takes half an hour to read, after which the court rises for lunch. Longy leaves.

'If I'd stayed in Vietnam, you never know, that could have been me. Prison is no good. You are better off looking up at the lid of a coffin than being in prison.'

Back in the van, Longy is driven to his old school, the scene of his expulsion. Razor wire curls atop the brick wall outside the main building. Behind it, boys in blue and white uniforms with red kerchiefs play volleyball near the bland concrete quadrangle in which Longy flattened the obsequious prefect.

'It's still the same. Only the tree has grown.'

The tree, a sturdy jacaranda, was only a sapling when Longy was a student. What would Ho Chi Minh think about the development of both?

Over the following days, Longy passes sights that bring more memories: the trees he climbed for fruit after curfew; the laneways where he held cock fights; the streets where he rode tandem with Lan. He tastes the past too, when a swig of Coke reminds him of his release from prison. And sounds sweep him back to his days in Pleiku when, over a dinner, he listens to two war veterans singing South Vietnamese army songs. One of the ex-soldiers, whose well-worn tambourine skin shines as brightly as his bald head, leans on a crutch. His left leg is amputated below the knee. His partner, who strums a forty-year-old guitar that is held together by cellotape, is completely blind. Both suffered their injuries in battle. Between each song Longy jumps to his feet and offers the men a sip of his coconut shake. At the end he gives each a cigarette and a fistful of dong.

A woman who has been sitting nearby with an armful of books smells a sale; she approaches. Longy looks at the titles, feigning interest, then plucks out a cookbook. He pays the woman, waves away the change, and gives his purchase to Truong. He is a generous man, especially at night when those most needy seem to multiply by the kerbsides. An elderly woman selling lottery tickets and a young man hobbling on an awfully ill-fitting artificial leg can also vouch for his kindness.

Five days after his arrival, Longy is still to perform his most important duty.

'It doesn't matter when I do it. He and I don't need to talk — we just know. We understand each other. There is just a link between us. We don't need to be in touch all the time.'

Finally it happens. It is April 30th, twenty-eight years to the day since the fall of Saigon. Bespectacled 72-year-old Hien Duy Nguyen, a slight, short man still dressed in his pyjamas, is sitting on a chair in his bedroom when his son arrives. They meet with a hug and smiles; little other emotion is shown. This is the way it's always been: a general and his soldier. They sit down and talk in the lounge room, the same room in which Teresa was murdered. When a photo of father and son is suggested, father shuffles into his bedroom and returns immaculately dressed in a fresh cream shirt buttoned to the neck and pressed grey trousers with a white belt. The son, in black trousers and a black shirt unbuttoned to reveal a grey T-shirt, props on a back corner of his father's chair. They have similar smiles and similar facial structures. They both take pride in their appearance, posing proudly for the camera.

Click.
'And another.'
Click.
'And again.'
Click.
'Just Dad this time.'

They resume talking, then, on Longy's prompting, Hien shuffles back into his bedroom and makes a phone call. He comes back nodding. Yes, the general is in and would enjoy a visit.

The brigadier general: Le Trung Tuong. The former commander of the 23rd Division in Corps II. Injured five times in battle. Shot down twice in a helicopter. And one of the ARVN's few high-ranking officers who refused to desert Saigon in the lead-up to the North's victory. Afterwards, he spent thirteen years in re-education camps, including a few months in the bed next to Longy's father. Now he lives frugally in a tiny house in a back alley. None of his neighbours know of his past. Despite his hardships, he has an endearing charm. He welcomes his visitors with two-handed handshakes, a Vietnamese sign of respect.

'Excuse me if my English is not very good — I have had no need to use it for nearly thirty years. I have not seen a white person for that long.'

For the next hour, the three men discuss the war. Photos are taken. When it comes time to leave, Longy deftly places some money in Le Trung's shirt pocket.

'It is out of respect. You are one of my heroes.'

After returning home, Longy joins his family for lunch. They say grace and pray before the meal of fish, rice, prawns and lotus salad.

In the afternoon Longy and Truong walk through the alleys they terrorised as boys. They pose for a photo outside Truong's old house with a gate that no longer shows the dents of slingshots past. Within a few more metres they pass a man in his twenties with a bare chest and blackened fingers. He looks up from repairing the chain on his scooter. He pauses, then speaks with some uncertainty.

'Long?'

'Yes.'

The motorcycle repairer was no more than a boy, just six or seven, when Longy roamed the neighbourhood.

'You were the king,' he says.

Longy smiles, pleased that his reputation still flourishes in the neighbourhood's memory. He and Truong walk on, passing the narrow laneway where Longy had his first barehanded fight. Just a fortnight earlier, two gang youths were stabbed to death nearby.

'Imagine these lanes at night, brother. You have to be ready for anything. And you have to know your way around to survive.'

As if needing to prove his statement, Longy turns his shoulder into what appears to be just a crack in a wall, but upon entry it opens into a thin, ill-lit path.

'This leads to a lane that connects with the main street. I'll show you.'

Truong can't remember it, but follows as Longy edges sideways, first through a patch of darkness, then into bold sunlight. They are back in a lane. Two right turns later they are walking along the main street, just 150 metres away from the Nguyen family home.

'See, I told you,' says Longy. 'Longy's the king of the laneways. I'll never forget.'

As Longy walks towards home, he is recognised and stopped by five people. They all shake his hands, and are eager to hear of his life in Australia.

'We are proud of you,' says one.

'Please have a beer with us,' says another.

That night, Longy leans back and blows a steady stream of smoke from a chain of 555s as he sits and enjoys the coolest concert in town at a club across the road from the American embassy. Elvis Phoung has been singing for forty-two years.

During the war he performed for the GIs at the Honeypot Club. After the fall, many of his songs were banned by the government, but these days he is allowed a wide repertoire in Vietnamese, English and French. He is an institution, one of his country's most famous products. In the middle of his two-hour set, he stops, and although spotlight blindness prevents him from seeing many in the crowd, he knows a special friend is there.

'This song is for my brother, Long. He is very dear to me. I met him in Sydney. I haven't seen him for eight long years.'

Longy can't hide his pride. 'Not bad for a kid who used to dance with the mountain people.'

At 7.23 the next morning he eases into the back seat of the van for the journey to the town that is forever in his thoughts. The dragon hasn't been back to Pleiku for thirty years.

'A lot would have changed. I don't know what to expect. I'm a bit nervous.'

Tam drives. Hoai sits with Thao and her boys in the next two rows. It's a family affair, a rare excursion out of Saigon. They must take their identity permits with them. Within half an hour, they pass an accident. Two people lie dead by the roadside, their pushbikes tangled messes. Soon afterwards the van flashes past a shirtless, long-haired teenager with jeans rolled up to his knees. His eyes are filled with anger as he runs, waving a machete above his head at another youth who stands his ground without a visible weapon. The van turns a corner; the result of the fight will never be known.

The urban fringes make way for rural villages, settlements with houses built from thin wooden planks that are painted a vivid red by the dust. In another month's time, it will be the mud of the wet season. No matter how remote each house seems to be, it has one distinguishable feature: a television aerial. Some are perched at the top of strips of bamboo that lean with the breeze.

The road is hectic, populated by motorbikes, buses, pedestrians and many peasants on pushbikes. If not for their straining legs, it would be almost impossible to tell if they are moving under the conical leaf hats that dwarf their sinewy frames.

The further north the family travels, the more the war's skeletons are exposed. Lorries once used for transporting men now carry loads of fruit. Other military remnants are in hundreds of pieces, scattered between workshops whose mechanics build hybrid vehicles: a gearbox from a Jeep, doors from a lorry, metal for the body from machine-gun turrets.

They stop for lunch in a village with one roadside restaurant. Its walls are washed-out blue. The smell of garlic crowds the air. There is only one other table of customers — a group of four men, probably locals. Longy chats to the owner, a woman in her fifties with a plain ankle-length cotton dress that matches the colour of the walls. She has a tattoo on her left forearm: 'Left Home, Miss Mum'. She fought for the Viet Cong. Longy tips her handsomely.

The afternoon hurries along. Past purple bougainvillea on iron roofs, school children walking in single file by the road, groups of men playing chequers, rice farmers slapping water buffaloes, and, as sunset comes, the flickering colour of television sets in dark rooms.

At 7.08 p.m., almost twelve hours after leaving Saigon, Thao and Longy lean forward excitedly in their seats and peer through the windows. They have reached Pleiku.

Now sitting in the front, Longy directs Hoai through the centre of town: 'Down here should be a cinema ... yes, yes ... I told you. And there, that's where I went to market for Mum. It's very different now. Big buildings. There only used to be wooden huts. Right here — see the church? At the top of the hill. It's new. They pulled ours down.'

As they approach the church, they turn left into a wide road that rolls down a long slope. There is little activity, apart from a few women squatting and chatting on a footpath. Longy is on the edge of his seat, hands waving out the window.

'Here, here.'

He is out before the engine stops.

'The house — it's still here. It's still here. But my mango tree! They've cut down my mango tree. I can't believe they've cut down my fuckin' mango tree!'

The concrete frontage with a single door and shutter is closed up. Longy steps closer; without breaking stride he bends over, picks up a handful of dirt and kisses it.

'This is where the driveway used to be. The gates were there, and a garden. A beautiful garden. And this is where my mango tree was. I can't believe they've cut down my fuckin' mango tree. I'm glad the house is still here. My dignity is still here. So many memories, brother.'

Memories that over the following day are shown not to have faded with time. Longy's mind is sharp, photographic. The next morning when he visits Le Quy Don, a school that in a former life was St Paul's, he gives the impression that part of him yearns to be a boy in black shoes again. This time, however, he is a grown man sharing a cigarette and tea with the headmaster and deputy in their office. One cigarette becomes two, then three, fired by lighters with pictures of Vietnamese women sporting ballgowns and bikinis. It's a world away from the mass-manufactured 'authentic' GI Zippos that are sold in shops nearby.

Longy returns to his former classroom and poses for a photo next to the same blackboard that he took notes from. It shines with over-use.

'Nothing has changed, brother.'

Behind the school, the same order of nuns that ran St Paul's now operates a facility for orphans and the children of leprosy sufferers, most of whom come from the mountain tribes. The head sister escorts Longy on a tour through the sleeping quarters, the kitchen and classrooms.

She tells him that there are 68 000 'minority' people in the region. It is the duty of the nuns to help as many as possible. Midwifery has become a critical component of the support. In some tribes husbands still force their wives to stand up when giving birth because they believe gravity will help the delivery.

Longy meets another nun, Sister Nhi, who remembers the small boy who sang at the school concert so many years before.

'I remember it because there were army vehicles everywhere. More army men than children,' she says.

Longy is pleased. He poses for another photo, then leaves, vowing to return.

'Maybe this is where I set up my academy — to help the mountain people. They taught me so much when I was here. It is time to give something back.'

From the school it's fitting that he heads to his favourite playground, the home of the mountain people about 3 kilometres away. Over the final stages he is forced to get out of the van and walk when the tar roads make way for narrow paths of red dirt. The jungle canopy has gone, so too the thick undergrowth. Tin and wooden huts are now sprinkled near the tracks; a boy stares through the grills of a window; two women in leaf hats hunch over sheets of drying rice; a toy pushbike is parked next to a scooter; barbed wire crawls along fences — but the mountain people have gone, pushed away by progress. Longy walks into a clearing covered with rice fields.

'This is where they used to be. Their bamboo huts, the streams I swam in. I used to dance with them. Listen to their music. It's all changed. I'm shattered. They've all gone. Now look at it.'

It's mid-afternoon by the time the family begins the drive back to Saigon. They stop for the night in Ban Me Thout, an agricultural market town. A storm breaks, water overflows in the gutters and, as he moves under cover to light a cigarette, Longy again drifts back to his childhood.

'The rain reminds me of the soldiers. They used to protect themselves with their body bags. Everyone carried body bags. It would rain for days. Imagine being out in the bush in this.'

It's intriguing to hear him use the word 'bush' — his time in Australia has left its mark.

The family reaches the outskirts of Saigon the next afternoon. Early monsoonal clouds are gathering and the light is fading quickly. At 3.58 Longy stops to buy a bunch of yellow carnations and several packets of incense.

'It is time to visit the spirit.'

At 4.06 he is standing in front of his mother's grave. The family pays its respects one at a time, bowing silently, placing the burning incense sticks into a planter box in front of the carnations. Longy is last. There is one solitary roll of thunder.

'She is here, brother.'

Tam takes the cigarette he is smoking and prods an incense stick into the butt. He and Longy put it in a planter box away from the others.

'It's not a *Cam le* but she'll have it.'

One at a time the family leaves, clasping hands together and bowing again in front of the grave. As they drive away, it begins to rain.

For the remainder of the trip Longy is silent, but sparks up again that night when, after revisiting the Thanh barber shop for another shave and ear clean, he is approached by a man of similar age.

'I remember the fight you had with Victory Nguyen,' the man says. 'I helped clear the tables. You were the king!'

Only one significant trip into the past remains — a journey to the Mekong delta, scene of so many escape attempts. Longy and Hoai wait until Truong has a day off school, then they head south in the van. It takes just an hour to reach My Tho, the starting point for Longy's first failed escape. Longy hires a power boat, a luxury that Truong has never enjoyed before. They lean back on the padded seats.

They smoke, laugh and pose for photos. Longy delights in the happiness he sees in Truong's face.

'It's a small thing for me, but this is a big day for Truong. Look at him — a school teacher. He can't afford to do this. It makes me happy he can do it with me.'

Around them, peasants on skinny vessels laden with fruit push their way along the muddy brown water with bamboo poles. Fishing boats chug past, prompting various reactions from Longy.

'That bigger than the one we escaped on ...' 'That one is smaller ...' 'Very good cabin on that one, plenty of room ...' 'We had forty-eight on something half the size of that!'

The remaining days of his stay in Vietnam are spent with his family and friends, woven with dinners, karaoke and barbers visits. On one night he pays a taxi boat man to take him for a ride along the Saigon River. It is 11.30 p.m., a cloudless evening. The driver, wearing a short-brimmed cotton hat covered in grease, pays little regard to safety — he continually smokes while sitting next to an open bottle of fuel.

He is, perhaps, no more daring than the electricity workers called to Longy's lodgings on another night when there is no power. The two men in orange overalls and yellow hard hats arrive on a scooter. The supervisor carries a black vinyl bag, but as he looks at the wire connections above his head, he realises he is lacking one vital piece of equipment — it's hard to carry a ladder on a motorbike. He makes do by standing on a swivel chair on the top of a desk that Hoai and Truong have carried onto the street. He tampers with a collection of wires clumped together like a bird's nest. Longy watches, cigarette in hand.

'Imagine them doing this in Australia, brother. Occupational health and safety, what's that?'

Power is restored within minutes. Cigarettes are offered. The job is done.

'Different country, this one. There's only one Vietnam.'

* * *

May 10, 2003, 5 p.m. Thao meticulously packs her brother's suitcase. Longy has already said goodbye to his father — 'No big farewells needed. We've never had them.'

He gives Thao his new camera; Tam receives sunglasses and shoes; Hoai and Truong are quietly slipped cash.

The van heads to the airport; Hoai drives. Thao and Longy talk softly.

Truong trails on his Honda Dream II. Tam, with Tin Tin clinging to his waist, is further back on another scooter. Balu has stayed behind, as departures can be painful for the young.

At the airport they all share a meal, fill an ashtray, then acknowledge it's time. There are many hugs. Hugs that no longer need to be hidden behind closed doors or accompanied by whispers. Longy and Thao hold each other for several seconds.

'I love you,' he says.

She nods and smiles, then turns away, reaching into her pocket for a handkerchief to wipe her eyes.

Truong, stony-faced, comes forward for his third hug.

'There are no tears. But I am crying on the inside.' With those words, Longy looks briefly into the distance — in another time, another place, such a look would have been the 'thousand-yard stare'. He picks up his suitcase, grins at his family, walks through the passenger gate and glances at his watch. It is still on Australian time.

At 8.43 p.m. local time, Vietnam Airlines flight 783 lifts off from Ho Chi Minh City Airport. It's a packed flight. In seat 28C, Duy Long Nguyen sits back comfortably.

'A good trip, brother. We got a lot for the book. But I can't believe they cut down my fuckin' mango tree!'

ACKNOWLEDGMENTS
JAMES KNIGHT

Researching and writing this book was an enriching experience because of the remarkable person Longy is. Brother, we're mates for life: 'Pick and stick'. I am indebted to you for your patience, understanding and encouragement throughout the entire project (but less of the ordinary jokes and 3 a.m. wake-up calls next time!). I am also extremely grateful to Longy's family, both in Australia and Vietnam. A special thank you to Thao and Tam for your kindness when Longy and I visited Saigon in April/May 2003.

Were it not for all the people who contributed stories about, and insights into Longy, this book wouldn't have been possible. Thank you to each and every one of you. A special mention to Dr Diane Barnes of the University of New South Wales, who contributed invaluable information about Indo-Chinese immigration and integration. I'm also indebted to Kim, who was there to help me from the very first day of this project.

To all the staff at Harper Collins, again I say thank you, particularly to Shona Martyn and Alison Urquhart for your continued support, and to my senior editor, and close friend, Vanessa Radnidge, the biggest of big hugs. Thank you also to editor Sophie Hamley, Nicola O'Shea, Graeme Jones of Kirby Jones, Helen Beard, Rodney Stuart, Louise McGeachie, Judi Rowe, Frances Paterson, Tracey Gibson, Mel Cain, Christine

Farmer, Louise Cornegé and Karen-Maree Griffiths. Writing, publishing and marketing a book is an enormous team effort. Thank you one and all.

Also, none of this would have been possible without the support and wonderful friendship of my agent Jane Burridge, who has always lent an open ear and offered cheerful words.

Thank you to all my friends, in particular those who had to put up with my single-mindedness during this project: Tombsy and Carissa, Pete and Jess, Ando and Lyn, Phil, Dibbsy, Mel and Amy. You're all part of this.

Finally, a huge hug and kiss to the most influential writer in my life — Old Mother Knight. Mum, I couldn't have done it without you.

ACKNOWLEDGMENTS
LONGY NGUYEN

I've been lucky to have met hundreds and hundreds of people during my life. To thank every one of you here would be impossible, so if I forget to mention you, please give me a hard time when I see you next.

First, I must thank all my family, both here and in Saigon. It has been an incredible journey for all of us. You all inspire me, and I love you all very much. In addition to my relatives, I have adopted some very important 'uncles' in my life. I wouldn't be where I am today if it wasn't for the guidance of Uncles Ba and Nam, and more recently, Uncles Rupert and Frank. Thank you to all members of both the Murdoch and Lowy families. I love and respect you all; you mean the world to me. I also extend a very big thank you to John Hartigan for all his support and friendship. Allan Sloper is another great man who needs special mention.

A line about my close friend Truong needs to stand by itself. Truong, you have always been a brother to me. I both laugh and cry when I think of all we went through together. I will never forget.

My life is like a jigsaw puzzle. There are so many pieces of all shapes and sizes. To all those I'm about to mention, thank you for helping me become the person I am: The Mountain People of Pleiku; the soldiers of the ARVN base; the GI's of the Hoang Lan; the Nuns of St Paul's; Cardinal

Nguyen van Thuan; Fathers Anh and Chinh; my lieutenants and Thien Ly boys; my martial arts instructors; Achay; Nha and Tuan; Nam; the taxi-men; the captain and crew of the Sanko Oil tanker; the residents of the Laemsing refugee camp; the sumo wrestlers of Tokyo; all my schoolteachers in Sydney; Mr and Mrs John Smiley; Browny, Brad and Mark 'Big Bird'; Dr Haddad, and Nick and George the 'chemist men'; Cam Sieu from Hong Kong; the kick-boxing boys and the 'fat man' of Bangkok; Jimmy — my right-hand man and the eyes at the back of my head; Ian and 'his boys'; Terry 'pick and stick' Hill; Sean Garlick, Adrian Lam, Mark Coyne, 'Blocker', Bob Fulton, Paul Dunn and all my football brothers; Alan Jones (radio); Johnny Lewis; Troy Waters; Shannon Taylor; Linford Christie and his athletics team; Jimmy Cassidy; Elle Macpherson; Megan Gale; Hugo Weaving, Keanu Reeves, the Wachowski brothers and all *The Matrix* crew; David Bloom (QC), and every other single person I've been lucky enough to be respected and loved by.

Because of you all I am the luckiest person in the world.

Thank you. May every day be full of laughter, happiness, good health, and much, much love.

For more information on the book
you can visit
www.thedragonsjourney.com

BIBLIOGRAPHY

Asia Pacific Journal of Social Work, Dept of Social Work and Psychology, National University of Singapore, Vol 2 No 2, July 1992.

Austcare News, April 1980; February–March 1981, March 1983.

Barker, Anthony, *What Happened When: A Chronology of Australia from 1788*, Allen & Unwin, Sydney, 2000.

Concise Oxford Dictionary of Australian History, The, Oxford University Press, Melbourne, 2001.

Great Events in Australia's History: From Discovery to the Present, Child & Associates Publishing, Frenchs Forest, 1988.

Coleman, JD, *Pleiku, The Dawn of Helicopter Warfare in Vietnam*, St Martin's Press.

Colet, John, *Vietnam Handbook*, Footprint, England, 2002.

Collins, Jock, & Castillo, Antonio, *Cosmopolitan Sydney: Explore the World in One City*, Pluto Press, Leichhardt, 1998.

Daily Telegraph, The (various editions).

Dirks, Jo, *Sydney Downtown*, Kangaroo Press, Kenthurst, 1993.

Duong Van Mai Elliott, *The Sacred Willow: Four Generations in the Life of a Vietnamese Family*, Oxford University Press, New York, 1999.

Fenton, James, *All the Wrong Places: Adrift in the Politics of the Pacific Rim*, Little Brown, New York, 1988.

Furlonger, Brian (comp.), *Vietnam: A Reporter's War*, ABC Books, Sydney, 1975.

Grant, Bruce, *The Boat People: An Age Investigation*, Penguin, Melbourne, 1979.

Kolko, Gabriel, *Vietnam: Anatomy of a War, 1940–1975*, Allen & Unwin, London; Sydney, 1986.

Langley, Greg, *A Decade of Dissent: Vietnam and the Conflict on the Australian homefront*, Allen & Unwin, Sydney, 1992.

Lewins, Frank & Ly, Judith, *The First Wave: The Settlement of Australia's First Vietnamese Refugees*, Allen & Unwin, Sydney, 1985.

Lonely Planet, Vietnam, Lonely Planet Publications, Melbourne, 2003.

Margo, Jill, *Frank Lowy: Pushing the Limits*, HarperCollins*Publishers*, Sydney, 2001.

Moise, Edwin E, *Historical Dictionary of the Vietnam War*, Scarecrow Press, USA, 2001.

New Yorker, The, 15 April 1972.

New York Times, The, 2 May 1972.

Newsweek, 22 February 1965.

Oxford Companion to Australian History, The, Oxford University Press, Melbourne, 1988 or 2001.

Oxford Dictionary of Quotations, The, Oxford University Press

Page, Tim, and Pimlott, John, *Name: The Vietnam Experience 1965–75*, Hamlyn, New York, 1990.

Parrish, Robert D, *Combat Recon — My Year with the ARVN*, St Martin's Press, USA, 1991.

Pemberton, Gregory (ed), *Vietnam Remembered*, New Holland, Sydney, 2002.

People of Australia: Key Events in Population, Society, the Environment, Macquarie Library, North Ryde, 1998.

Sheehan, Neil, *A Bright Shining Lie: John Paul Vann and America in Vietnam*, Random House, New York, 1988.

Sydney Morning Herald, The (various editions).

Tucker, Spencer C, *Encyclopaedia of the Vietnam War*, Oxford University Press, USA, 2001.
Understanding Vietnamese Refugees in Australia, School of Community Studies, Phillip Institute of Technology.
US and World Report News, 12 May 1975.
Viviani, Nancy, *Australian Government Policies on the Entry of Vietnamese*, Griffith University, Australia, 1976–78.
Webster's Dictionary of the Vietnam War, Webster's New World
Wexler, Sanford, *The Vietnam War: An Eyewitness History*, Facts on File Inc., New York, 1992.
Womersley, Judith & Richmond, Mark, *Aussie Data: A Concise, User-Friendly Reference to People, Places, Events and Dates in Australian Life from Prehistory to the Present*, Wakefield Press, Adelaide, 2001.
Zulfacar, Diane, *Surviving Without Parents: Indo-Chinese Refugee Minors in NSW*, University of New South Wales Press, Sydney, 1984.
Zulfacar, Diane, *Policies, Programs and Outcomes for Unaccompanied Vietnamese Refugee Minors in Australia*, Universitiy of New South Wales Press, Sydney, 1988.

INDEX

A
Achay (friend in Saigon) 148
Afghanistan 228
Amanhang (machine parts coating) 177
American War
  in 1964 7–8
  ARVN *see* ARVN
  Easter Offensive 58–59
  effect on education 24
  heroin use in 159
  Jarai people 53
  protest rallies 19, 38, 45
  Tet Offensive 16–19
  Viet Cong *see* Viet Cong
  Vietnam War 10
  Vietnamese losses 19, 59
  'Vietnamisation' policy 27, 38, 75, 82
Anh, Father 61, 64
Anzac Day (2003) 381
April 30ers 109–110, 112, 114
Army Catholic Church (Pleiku) 1–2, 16, 35, 36, 46, 61
Arthur Phillips High School (Parramatta) 299
ARVN (Army of the Republic of Vietnam)
  'black flights' 101–106
  Cambodia 38
  corruption 13–14, 28, 92
  Easter Offensive 58–59
  fall of Saigon 100–106
  hunting expeditions 73–75
  losses 19, 59
  in Pleiku 2, 8, 27–28, 39–40, 99
  sent to re-education camps *see* re-education camps
  Tet Offensive 16–19
  Viet Cong 27, 384
Auschwitz (Germany) 376
Australia
  accepts Nguyen family 274–275, 281
  acohol consumption 308–309
  migrant hostels 291–292
  refugee intake 266, 289–290, 298
  Vietnam War 10, 19, 38, 75, 91
  Vietnamese in 288
Australia–Fiji test match 360
Australian Rugby League 355–357

B

Balu and Tin Tin (nephews) 383, 397
Ban Me Thout (Vietnam) 99, 394
Bangkok (Thailand) 266
Bankstown (Sydney) 328–329
Barnes, Jimmy 380
BBC World Service 100, 119, 127, 132, 259
Bell, Virginia 350–351
Belmore (Sydney) 315
Beuman, Mr 303, 307
Bien Ho (Vietnam) 14
Binh (friend from Pleiku) 67–71
black market 120–121, 174–176, 229–230 *see also* gold currency
Blacktown (Sydney) 306, 323
Bloom, David 367
boat people 132, 157, 184–185, 233, 242–249, 259, 288, 303 *see also* people smuggling; refugees
Botany Bay Gift 366
Brown, Craig ('Browny') 303, 305, 308, 310, 350–351
Buddhism 60, 251–252
Bui Tin, Colonel 106, 108

C

Cabramatta (Sydney) 306–307, 311, 322, 327–329, 331, 341, 343, 353
Café da (iced coffee) 205
Cam Sieu (reflexologist) 330
Cambodia 8, 9, 27, 38, 45, 153, 185, 334
Cambodian New Year 189
Camp Holloway (Pleiku) 8–9, 11, 25
Campbell, Darren 375, 378–379
Campbelltown (Sydney) 318
Can Tho (Vietnam) 227, 228, 232, 236, 239
Canada 266
Canberra Raiders 357
Cassidy, Jimmy 367, 375, 380
Casula High School (Sydney) 294–295
Catholicism in Vietnam 3, 5, 60–61
Chau Doc (Vietnam) 192, 227
Chi Hoa prison (Saigon) 197, 202, 209, 332
China 76, 81
Chinatown (Sydney) 314–315, 323
Chinese in Australia 331
Chinese in Vietnam 156, 184, 190
Chinh, Father (Pleiku) 61–71
Chinh, Father (Saigon) 260
Cholon (Saigon) 126, 156, 177, 339
Chon Buri (Thailand) 258
Christie, Linford 366, 378, 380
cock fighting 138–140, 147–152, 167–169
communism in Vietnam 7–9, 109–110, 117, 131–132, 170
Confucianism 60
Coyne, Mark 357
cricket fighting 50–51
crime networks in Australia 315
currency conversion 122 *see also* gold currency

D

Daley, Laurie 359, 380
Danang (Vietnam) 100
David (Maria's husband) 141, 235, 245, 248, 254, 261, 298, 318
Davis, Rodger 367, 380
Denica (daughter) 379, 382
Dien Bien Phu (Vietnam) 4, 6
Dieu (Teresa's brother) 100–101, 131
Dinh, David 347
Doi Basao re-education camp 216 see also re-education camps
Doi Ven (introduction of communism in schools) 117
drug trafficking in Australia 315, 341, 344–345
Dunn, Paul 362
Duong Van Minh, President General 98, 101, 106, 108
Duy Long ('Longy') Nguyen
  at 3 years old 19
  at 6 years old 37, 43
  at 7 years old 2–3, 44
  at 8 years old 70
  at 9 years old 77
  at 12 years old 132–133, 142
  at 18 years old 307
  Americans 38–39, 57–58, 101–102, 258
  animals 79–80, 167–168 see also dogs
  ARVN base 31, 43, 44, 46–47, 57, 67–68
  attitude to communism in Vietnam 121, 122–124, 178–181
  Australian citizenship 323
  birth and childhood 7, 9, 11–12
  Cambodian New Year 189
  cars 297, 306, 313
  character 30–31, 57, 76, 83–84, 93–95, 125, 219, 333
  clinic 358–359, 366–367, 372, 373, 375, 379–380
  cock fighting 138–140, 147–152, 167–169, 173–174, 213
  debt collecting 192–194, 314
  Diploma of Massage Therapy 347
  documentation 158, 164–165, 216
  dogs 56, 79–80, 84, 322, 330 see also animals
  driver's licence 307–308, 309–310
  Eastern medicine 324, 329–330, 333
  education 20–24, 43, 47, 87–88, 117, 122–125, 171–172, 180–181, 302–304, 311, 387
  escape attempts 158–166, 181–184, 187, 189–190
  ESL 294–295, 299, 302
  fighting 124–125, 171–172, 179
  girlfriends: Ann 342–343, 365, 375
  girlfriends: Jolanta 296–297
  girlfriends: Lan 187, 190, 226–227, 231, 237–238, 264, 339

Duy Long ('Longy') Nguyen
continued
  gold currency 178
  hobbies 279–280
  in Hong Kong 330
  hustling 37, 134–135, 141–144, 166–167, 174–176
  Internal Affairs 348–351 *see also* NSW police
  in Japan 272–273, 275–276
  Jarai people 52–55
  judo 27, 47
  karate 133, 170, 281–282, 285, 305, 385
  in Lieng Sing camp (Thailand) 260–265
  Long Thien Ly Boys (gang) 144–146, 147, 177, 179, 189, 339
  mango tree in Pleiku 2, 13, 28–30, 393, 397
  marijuana 309
  martial arts displays 304, 312
  martial arts teaching 311, 312, 314, 324, 342
  massage 55, 73, 126–127, 149, 205–206, 283–286, 386 *see also* masseur
  massage and martial arts academy plan 385
  masseur 312, 325–327, 341, 355–356 *see also* clinic
  media attention 363, 377
  names for 3, 10, 42, 45, 73, 90, 136, 144, 189, 339
  in New York 368–371
  NSW police 300–301, 328–329, 342 *see also* Internal Affairs
  physique 15, 132–133, 273, 338
  prison in Saigon 195–214, 385
  private investigator 343–344, 367
  'protection' work 311, 314–317, 323, 331
  religion 35, 61–72
  returns to Saigon 381–397
  security work 341–343, 351, 354, 358, 367
  smoking tobacco 40–41, 76–77
  smuggling 174–177
  sports 91, 135–137, 169–170, 304–305, 325–326
  street life 134
  sumotori (sumo wrestlers) 284–287
  swimming 56, 86–87, 91, 137, 304
  tae kwon do 12, 27, 48–50, 55, 72–73, 88, 91, 95–97, 124, 126, 133, 170, 275–276, 282, 285, 340, 385
  tai chi 148
  tattoos 77
  team tracksuits 359–360, 365, 378
  Tet Offensive 16–19, 25–26, 35
  in Thailand 325–327, 329
  Viet Cong 35–36
  visits Hien in camp 216–225
  weapons 2, 43–45, 56, 73–75, 113, 146, 238, 244, 247, 255, 293, 315, 316

E

East Hills (Sydney) 291–292
Eastern medicine 324, 329–330
Elvis Phoung 390–391

F

Fairfield (Sydney) 306
Filipinos in Vietnam 75
Fishburne, Laurence 373, 375, 380
Fittler, Brad 359, 360, 380
5T gang 197, 332, 341, 343–345, 352
Ford, Gerald 91, 100
Fox Studios (Sydney) 372, 374
France 3–4, 266
  Paris Peace Accords 75–76
Fraser Liberal government 290
Fredericks, Frankie 375
Fulton, Bob 362, 364–365

G

Gale, Megan 380
gambling 312, 315–316, 327
gangs
  in Bankstown 328–329
  in Cabramatta 327–329, 331
  5T 197, 332, 341, 343–345, 352
  K14 315
  Long Thien Ly Boys 144–146, 147, 177, 179, 189, 339
  in Saigon 124, 390
  in Sydney 197, 299, 312
  Tri Minh Tran 312, 331–332, 345, 352
Garlick, Sean 354–357, 367, 380
Garry, Matt 371–372
Geneva Accords 4
Gibbs, Nathan 363, 364
ginseng 128, 161
gold currency 13, 82, 121, 132, 153, 178, 189, 193–194, 199, 204 *see also* black market
Granville (Sydney) 305
Great Escape (movie) 271
Greene, Maurice 380
Gumbainggir people (NSW) 310

H

Haddad, Wadie 329, 343
Hai Hong (ship) 184
healing practices *see* Eastern medicine
Healy, Ian 380
Hien Duy Nguyen
  April 30ers 110
  ARVN 2–3, 10–11, 13–14, 27, 30, 39–40, 46, 58–59, 75, 101, 104–105, 115–116
  early life 4–5
  fall of Saigon 101, 111–112
  Long Binh college 82
  Longy 21, 30–31, 46, 73, 76–77, 114, 208, 222–225, 335–336, 388–389, 397
  prisoners-of-war exchange program 76, 115
  re-education camp 112–114, 118–119, 128–129, 178, 186–187, 222–225, 318
  religion 60–61
  Tet Offensive 16–19
  Viet Minh camp 6
  weapons 43
Hieu (naval officer) 235, 243, 246–247

Highway 19 (Vietnam) 99
Hill, Terry 360–365, 368, 371, 380
Hines, Deni 367
Ho Chi Minh 3, 13, 28, 110, 117, 123, 179, 219
Ho Chi Minh City (formerly Saigon) 110, 381 *see also* Saigon
Ho Chi Minh trail 9, 27, 45–46, 53, 193
Ho Van Tinh ('Uncle Ovaltine') 58, 235, 243
Hoai (relative) 383–386, 391, 392, 397
Hoang (friend in Saigon) 190–191
Hoang Lan café (Pleiku) 39–40
Hoi An (Vietnam) 5, 7
Hong Kong 330
Hong (Van's husband) 201, 239, 242, 261, 271–272, 298
Hue (Vietnam) 3, 4, 7, 100, 131
Hung ('Uncle Nam') *see* 'Uncle Nam'
hunting dogs (informers) 110–111, 114, 143
Hutton, Deborah 367

I
Independent Commission Against Corruption (NSW) 349–350
Iro, Tony 356

J
Japan 265, 268–269, 275–276, 378

Jarai people (Vietnam) 52–55, 57, 310, 394
Jen-shen (ginseng) 128, 161
Jimmy (protector) 315–317, 331, 336–337, 345
JJ Giltinan Shield 365
Johns brothers 357, 380
Johnson, Lyndon 9
Jones, Alan 367, 375, 380

K
Kampuchea *see* Cambodia
Kennerley, Kerri-Anne 367
K14 gang 315
Khmer Rouge 153, 185
kick boxing 325–326, 329
Kings Cross (Sydney) 293, 294
kneecapping 315
Koreans in Vietnam 12, 15, 27, 39, 48, 75

L
Lakemba (Sydney) 298
Lam, Adrian 356, 359
Laos 8, 9, 45, 58
Lap (friend in Sydney) 307–308
Le Bao Tinh school (Saigon) 87–88
Le Quy Don school (Pleiku) 393
Le Trung Tuong 119, 389
Lee, Bruce 72, 189
Lenin, Vladimir 109
Lewis, Johnny 375
Lieng Sing camp (Thailand) 260–265
loan sharks 327
Long Binh college (Saigon) 82
'Longy' Nguyen *see* Duy Long ('Longy') Nguyen

INDEX

Lowy, Frank 372, 376–377, 379–380
Lowy, Steven 372, 376, 378, 379
Luong (prisoner in Saigon) 199, 205–206, 209
Luu Luyen Club (Saigon) 169

M
Maccabi Masters soccer team 378
Macpherson, Elle 377, 380
Madame Noi's coffee shop (Lieng Sing, Thailand) 263
Madison Square Garden (NYC) 370–371
Madonna (5T gang member) 352
Malaysia 181, 184
Mang (orphan boy) 292–293, 296
Manly Sea Eagles 361–365, 367–368, 371, 376
Marx, Karl 109
Matrix (film) 372–375, 377–378, 380
Matrix Revolution (film) 379
Menzies, Robert 10
Mexico City (Mexico) 378
Middle Eastern boys in Casula 295
Miller, Scott 380
Minh, President General *see* Duong Van Minh
Moss, Carrie-Ann 374–375, 380
Mundine, Anthony 375
Muong Man (Vietnam) 216
Murdoch, Rupert 372, 375, 379, 380
My Tho (Vietnam) 158, 162, 181–182, 395
My ('Uncle Ba') *see* 'Uncle Ba'

N
Nam Binh (Vietnam) 217
Nam Cam 387
Nam Ha (Vietnam) 218–219
Nam (relative) 232, 235, 242–243
Netherlands 379
New York (USA) 368–371
New Zealand 75, 375
Newcastle Steelers 357
Newman, John 332–333, 345–346, 352
News Limited 372
Ngo Dinh Diem 60
Nguyen Chien Thang ('Victory') 171–172, 179, 395
Nguyen family
  emigrate to Australia 290
  Hien *see* Hien Duy Nguyen
  Longy *see* Duy Long ('Longy') Nguyen
  move to Nha Trang (Vietnam) 58–59
  move to Saigon 78–79
  in Pleiku *see* Pleiku (Vietnam)
Nguyen, James
  in Australia 274, 290, 298, 318
  childhood and education 7, 12, 36, 40–41, 79, 87
  escape attempts 181–184, 192
  Hien 113
  Longy 26, 47, 158, 292, 301
  MBA 342

Nguyen, James *continued*
  organises escape with Lam
    192, 207, 227–228,
    240–241, 245
  tanker 254
  Teresa 321
  in Thailand 261
  Tranthi Dao 263
  Viet Cong 132, 154–155, 186
Nguyen, Lam
  in Australia 334
  childhood and education 7,
    12, 26, 36, 43, 87, 155
  in hiding 186
  IT industry 342
  Longy 160
  organises escape with James
    192, 227–228, 232, 240,
    243, 245
  tanker 254
  Teresa 320–321
  Tet Offensive 18
  in Thailand 261
Nguyen, Linh
  in Australia 290, 319
  childhood and education
    40–41, 60, 87, 155
  escape 231, 235
  Hien 186
  Longy 160
  studies 342
  in Thailand 261
Nguyen, Maria
  childhood and education 6,
    12, 26, 40–41, 87, 141
  escape 235, 254
  Hien 186
  Lieng Sing camp (Thailand)
    261

  Longy 142, 158, 282
  in Sydney 298, 318, 342
  Teresa 321
Nguyen, Teresa *see also*
    Nguyen, Teresa and Longy
  Cam le leaves 6, 40, 42, 57,
    188–189, 395
  charity 88
  cinema in Pleiku 13, 35, 392
  early life 4–6
  gold currency 13, 82, 153
  Hien 3, 115–116, 130–131,
    186–187, 213, 228, 319
  killed in Saigon 319–321
  Longy visits grave 395
  pig farm in Pleiku 11, 13, 15
  religion 60–61, 64
  rheumatism 55, 127, 137,
    149, 159, 228
  Thien Ly coffee shop in
    Saigon 80–81, 119–120,
    136, 144, 263
Nguyen, Teresa and Longy
  cock fighting 147, 152
  eating as a family 136
  farewells 236–237
  favouritism 79
  fears for his future 133
  Hien 213–214
  his escape attempts 157,
    160–161, 181–184,
    189–190
  his reaction to Teresa's death
    320–323, 337–338
  hustling 142
  independence 26
  Jarai people 54–55
  letters 273, 281, 298
  mango tree 28–30

at school 21, 125
smoking tobacco 76–77
tae kwon do 47–48
'Teresa's boy' 42
Nguyen, Thao
  childhood and education 11, 60, 87–88, 115, 155
  Hien 186, 213
  Longy 54, 136, 142, 160, 164, 211–212, 236, 335–336, 382, 385, 397
  in Pleiku 391
  Teresa 231, 319–320, 323
  wedding 340
Nguyen, Thu (James' wife) 154, 246, 261, 298
Nguyen, Van
  childhood and education 7, 26, 87, 155
  escape 231, 235
  Hien 186
  Hong 242
  Longy 160, 211–212
  in Sydney 298, 319, 342
  in Thailand 261
Nguyen Van Thieu (President Thieu) 13–14, 27–28, 60, 82, 91–92, 98–101
Nha (friend in Saigon prison) 202–205, 208–210, 212
Nha Trang (Vietnam) 58–59, 235
Nixon, Richard 19, 27, 91
NLF (National Liberation Front) 8
Noell (Maria's daughter) 235, 254, 261, 298, 318
NSW police
  in Cabramatta 346
  corruption in 348–349
  Internal Affairs 348–351
  Longy 300–301, 305, 328–329, 342

O
organised crime 315
'orphan boys' at East Hills hostel 292–293, 296, 327

P
Paddington (Sydney) 358
PAVN (People's Army of Vietnam) 8, 17–19, 27, 38, 58–59, 98–99
people smuggling 162–166, 177, 184–185, 189–190, 233 *see also* boat people; refugees
Phung (friend in Saigon) 386
Phuoc Long (Vietnam) 98–99, 164
Phuoc (orphan boy) 293
Phuong Ngo 347
PLAF (People's Liberation Armed Forces) 8–9 *see also* Viet Cong
Pleiku (Vietnam) 1–3, 8, 13, 20, 39, 41–42, 58, 76, 99, 370, 392–394
poker machines 327
Pol Pot 185

Q
Qang Binh (Vietnam) 4
Quang Dao 347

R
racism 295
Rafter, Pat 375, 380

re-education camps 112–114,
    118–119, 128–129,
    186–187, 216, 389
Reeves, Keanu 373–374, 377,
    379, 380
reflexology 330
refugees
    boat people *see* boat people
    Indochinese 266, 290
    people smuggling *see* people
        smuggling
    by plane 288
    South China Sea 184, 249
    status 256
    treatment and placement
        259
Roosters (Sydney City)
    355–357, 360–361

S

Saigon River (Vietnam)
    Longy swims 86–87, 91, 137,
        338
    'river boys' 174–176, 187
Saigon (Vietnam)
    in 1970s and 80s 78–79,
        91–92
    Cabramatta (Sydney) 344
    communism 121, 156–157
    fall of 98–100, 100–106,
        111–112, 266, 288
    Longy visits 381–397
    prison 195–214
    renamed Ho Chi Minh City
        110, 381
    Viet Cong 108–109
St George Dragons 357,
    361–365
St Helen's Park (Sydney) 330

St Paul's School (Pleiku) 20–24,
    36, 393
Sanko Steamship Company
    tanker 257
SARS virus 381
Schofield, Leo 375
Schwantz, Kevin 380
Sen (Nguyens' senior
    housekeeper) 20, 24
Seton, Glenn 367, 380
Seven Hills High School
    (Sydney) 303–304, 311
Seven Hills (Sydney) 298, 318
Singapore 175
Smiley, Mr and Mrs John 309
smuggling in prison 206
Son (friend in Saigon) 170
Son My massacre 38
South China Sea 184, 249
Soviet Union 76, 81, 228
State of Origin series 359, 368
sumotori (sumo wrestlers)
    284–287
Sydney (NSW) 290 *see also*
    Cabramatta (Sydney)
Sydney Olympics (2000) 378

T

TAB agencies 327
Tam (Thao's husband) 383,
    391, 397
Taoism 60
Taylor, Shannon 366
Tet Offensive 16–17
Thailand
    kick boxing 325–326, 329
    pirates 249–252
    smuggling 167
    Vietnam War 75

Thanh family (Saigon) 383, 395
Thien Ly coffee shop (Saigon) 80–81, 119–120, 136, 144
Thieu, President *see* Nguyen Van Thieu (President Thieu)
Tho (Teresa's nephew) 101, 131
tigers in Vietnam 74–75
Tra Vinh (Vietnam) 192
Trang, Lady ('madam hustler') 174–176, 187
Tranthi Dao 254–255, 261–262
Tri Minh Tran 312, 331–332, 345, 352
Trinidad, Felix 368–371
Truong (friend in Saigon) 84–87, 108, 125, 135, 137, 142, 148, 157, 158, 167–168, 172, 178, 190, 212, 229–230, 237, 264, 274, 333
  Longy returns 336, 384–385, 389–390, 396–397
Tuan (friend in Saigon prison) 202–205, 206, 208–210, 212

U

'Uncle Ba' (My) 89–90, 125–126, 158, 178, 188–189, 212, 230, 282–283, 333–334, 339, 383
'Uncle Nam' (Hung) 126–128, 149, 158, 161, 170, 177, 230, 339
'Uncle Ovaltine' (Ho Van Tinh) 58, 235, 243
United Kingdom 266
United Nations 184, 256, 264

United States in Vietnam
  American deaths 19, 334, 370
  'black flights' 101–106
  defeat 108, 117
  Geneva Accords 4
  Hanoi 98–99
  Moscow Olympics 228
  refugee intake 266
  Tet Offensive 19
  Vietnam War 10 *see also* American War
USSR 76, 81, 228

V

Van Duc school (Pleiku) 36–37, 43, 50, 67
Van Tien Dung 98
Viet Cong (Vietnamese Communists)
  ARVN 27, 384
  fall of Saigon 106 *see also under* Saigon
  Highway 19 99
  Ho Chi Minh trail 27, 38
  James Nguyen 132, 154–155, 186
  Longy 35–36
  losses 106
  PLAF (People's Liberation Armed Forces) 8–9
  refugees 279
  in Saigon 108–109
  Tet Offensive 16–19
  weapons 11, 92
  woman in 392
Viet Minh (League for the Independence of Vietnam) 3, 6, 8

Vietnam *see also* Saigon
  communism in 7–9, 110, 117, 131–132, 170
  counting in Vietnamese 90
  drug trafficking from 341, 344–345
  economy 82–83, 91–92, 131, 153, 227, 334
  people smuggling 162–166
  separation and reunification 4, 132
  trains 216–217
  Vietnam War *see* American War
Vietnam, Democratic Republic of 28, 58, 98–99, 106
Vietnam War *see* American War
'Vietnamatta' (Sydney) 327 *see also* Cabramatta (Sydney)

W
Wachowski, Larry and Andy 375, 380
Walters, Steve 357
Wang, Lucy 346
Water Board, NSW 314
Watergate scandal 91
Waters, Dean 369
Waters, Troy 366, 368–371
Weaving, Hugo 372, 375, 380
Westfield 377
White Australia policy 290
Whitlam Labor government 289–290
Wollongong (NSW) 375
Wood, Justice James 349
Wood Royal Commission 349–351
Woodland Road Primary School (Sydney) 314

X
Xoi, Lady 88, 152
Xuan (police officer in Saigon) 193–194, 200, 204

JAMES KNIGHT was raised in the New South Wales country town of Gunnedah. After beginning his media career as a cadet journalist in Dubbo, he moved to Sydney, where he has spent more than a decade working in the various streams of television, radio and publishing. Nowadays he runs his own company, Knightwriter Productions. When not working, he is an intrepid traveller and keen marathon runner. He lives in Sydney. *The Dragon's Journey* is his third book

www.knightwriter.com.au